BARRIERS TO REENTRY?

BARRIERS TO REENTRY?

The Labor Market for Released Prisoners in Post-industrial America

SHAWN BUSHWAY, MICHAEL A. STOLL,
AND DAVID F. WEIMAN
EDITORS

Russell Sage Foundation · New York

The Russell Sage Foundation

Library of Congress Cataloging-in-Publication Data
Barriers to reentry? : the labor market for released prisoners in post-industrial America / edited by Shawn Bushway, Michael A. Stoll, David F. Weiman.
    p. cm.
    "This volume grows out of the joint Russell Sage and Rockefeller Foundations research program on the Future of Work"—P.
    Includes bibliographical references and index.
    ISBN 978-0-87154-087-4
    1. Ex-convicts—Employment—United States.   2. Criminals—Rehabilitation—United States.   3. Labor market—United States.   4. Social integration—United States.   I. Bushway, Shawn.   II. Stoll, Michael A.
III. Weiman, David F.   IV. Title: Labor market for released prisoners in post-industrial America.
    HV9304.B357   2007
    331.5'10973—dc22   2006102837

Text design by Suzanne Nichols.

RUSSELL SAGE FOUNDATION
112 East 64th Street, New York, New York 10021
10 9 8 7 6 5 4 3 2 1

Table of Contents

v

About the Authors

Shawn Bushway is associate professor of criminal justice at the University at Albany (SUNY).

David F. Weiman is Alena Wels Hirschorn '58 Professor of Economics at Barnard College, Columbia University.

Michael A. Stoll is professor of public policy at the University of California, Los Angeles.

Shauna Briggs is program assistant for the Center for Effective Public Policy.

Harry J. Holzer is professor of public policy at Georgetown University and visiting fellow at the Urban Institute.

Vera Kachnowski is a law student at Benjamin Cardozo School of Law, New York.

Jeffrey R. Kling is senior fellow and deputy director of economic studies at The Brookings Institution.

Christopher J. Lyons is assistant professor of sociology at the University of New Mexico.

Devah Pager is assistant professor of sociology and faculty associate of the Office of Population Research at Princeton University.

Becky Pettit is assistant professor of sociology at the University of Washington, Seattle.

Steven Raphael is professor of public policy at the University of California, Berkeley.

William J. Sabol is the chief of the Corrections Statistics Unit at the Bureau of Justice Statistics.

Faye Taxman is professor in the Wilder School of Government and Public Affairs at Virginia Commonwealth University.

Meridith Thanner is research associate at the Bureau of Government Research at the University of Maryland.

John H. Tyler is associate professor in the Department of Education at Brown University.

Mischelle Van Brakle is a doctoral student in the Department of Criminology and Criminal Justice at the University of Maryland.

Christy A. Visher is principal research associate in the Justice Policy Center at the Urban Institute, Washington, D.C.

Bruce Western is professor of sociology and faculty associate of the Office of Population Research at Princeton University.

═══ Preface ═══

DAVID F. WEIMAN

This volume originally grew out of the joint Russell Sage Foundation and Rockefeller Foundation research program on the Future of Work. Since 1994 the program has mobilized scholars from various social science disciplines to analyze the profound changes in U.S. labor markets since the 1970s, as evidenced by the steady erosion in the real hourly earnings of less-educated workers and the widening earnings gap between more- and less-educated workers (see, for example, Card and Blank 2000; Bernhardt et al. 2001; Applebaum, Bernhardt, and Murnane 2003). In addition to explaining the underlying causes of these large cumulative shifts in the levels and distribution of earnings, the research probed their social impacts on less-educated workers and explored the policy responses that would cushion economic impacts on these workers and bolster their labor-market prospects.

These concerns may seem to be unrelated to the issues discussed in this volume, but in fact the large cumulative shifts in less-skilled labor markets and mass incarceration are closely linked. After a lengthy debate sparked by David Cantor and Kenneth C. Land (1985), recent research has shown a direct causal link between the declining real wages and higher unemployment levels of less-educated workers and their criminal activity, especially "economic" crimes such as burglary and drug trafficking (see also Weiman, Stoll, and Bushway, chapter 2, this volume). Moreover, research in political economy and sociology strongly suggests that the politicization of street crime and the ultimate adoption of "get tough" criminal justice policies was a policy response, albeit symbolic, to the economic turbulence and labor-market dislocations between the mid-1970s and the mid-1990s (see, for example, Garland 2001 and the discussion in Western, chapter 11, this volume).

Together, these findings showed the relevance of "crime and punishment" matters to the Future of Work research agenda. Moreover, a review of the extant literature clearly justified strategic intervention to address the complementary issue of how a prison experience affects the labor-market prospects of those on the socioeconomic margins. At the time, few had studied this problem despite the rapid increase in U.S. incarceration rates since the late 1970s. And these researchers had reached divergent conclusions. According to one strand of research, a prison record and experience significantly diminished employment levels and earnings of ex-offenders, and so increased their likelihood of recidivism and a return to prison. A second set of studies, however, found that prison had no long-term effect on ex-convicts' labor-market outcomes.

After a preliminary meeting of scholars in fall 1999, the Russell Sage Foundation formed a working group on mass incarceration, which I coordinated. We framed our mandate in terms of a simple question: Does the increasing use of incarceration, especially for economic crimes by relatively marginal offenders, reinforce or just ratify their already poor labor-market prospects? The composition of the working group and the scope of the research agenda naturally co-evolved over time; the group included several members of the Future of Work Advisory Committee and the Russell Sage Foundation board of directors. My job as coordinator was to remind participants of two constraints on their research projects. Consistent with the Future of Work program agenda, they had to focus their research at least initially on the labor-market impacts of a prison record. Second, time and resource constraints meant that they should exploit as much as possible extant data sources.

Since the formation of the working group, the Foundation has funded over a dozen research projects in this area and has also supported the activities of several visiting scholars with related research interests. The contributions to this volume as well as several in its predecessor, *Imprisoning America: The Social Effects of Mass Incarceration*, on the social effects of mass incarceration, are based on the first round of research grants (Pattillo, Weiman, and Western 2004). The initial research proposals revolved around a core research design to track prisoners' post-release labor-market outcomes and recidivism rates. Because of the intrinsic difficulties and hence significant cost of following released prisoners over time, working-group members decided on a pragmatic course. They strategically selected states that accounted for a large share of the prison population but that varied in their criminal justice policies. They then assembled comprehensive longitudinal data sets based on the administrative records of their corrections departments and, if possible, linked them to records from law enforcement and employment agencies. A second group of researchers used existing survey data from the Multi-City Study of Urban Inequality and the

Fragile Families Study to analyze the labor market for released prisoners and their employment-earnings outcomes.[1]

More recently funded research projects have significantly expanded the initiative's domain. They have studied the long-term effects of a prison experience on men who were incarcerated as juveniles in the 1940s (Laub and Sampson 2003); the impact of incarceration on disadvantaged women in the Chicago area during the transformation of "welfare as we know it" (Cho and LaLonde 2005); the reentry process, including pre-release and post-release transitional programming (see the contribution by Visher and Kachnowski in chapter 3); and the quality of criminal background information supplied by the rapidly expanding private sector, itself a byproduct of mass incarceration (see Bushway et al., chapter 6, this volume). More recently, a new research group met at the headquarters of the Russell Sage Foundation to plan a comprehensive evaluation of "mass incarceration"—the actual public safety benefits and total fiscal and social costs of this vast social experiment, which currently places over seven million people under some form of correctional supervision.

As coordinator of the Foundation's working group on mass incarceration, I am grateful to the numerous scholars whose keen intellectual efforts transformed our initial thoughts into a vibrant research program. Some of them are the authors of chapters in this volume or the other Russell Sage publications on mass incarceration; some are the recipients of awards given by the Russell Sage Foundation Future of Work program.[2] Others faithfully and actively participated in working-group meetings, where they helped us to hone research proposals and preliminary research results, including: Kristen Butcher, Todd Clear, Kathryn Edin, Gerald Gaes, Jeffrey Grogger, Steven Levitt, Ann Chih Lin, Jeffrey Manza, Daniel Nagin, Anne Piehl, Dina Rose, and Christopher Uggen. Working-group members are also grateful to Eric Wanner, members of the of Future of Work Advisory Committee, and the Russell Sage Foundation board of directors—Anne Carter, Thomas Cook, Sheldon Danziger, Richard Freeman, Eugene Smolensky, Robert Solow, and Marta Tienda—for their commitment to the initiative and for their support in helping us to attain the high standards of social science research for which the Foundation is known. Finally, all of the authors and I especially greatly appreciate the work of Suzanne Nichols and her staff for their care, thoroughness, and patience.

Notes

1. A description of the Multi-City Study Survey and the original data can be found at the Inter-University Consortium for Political and Social Research (www.icpsr.umich.edu). For information on the Fragile Families and Child

Wellbeing Study and access to the data, see the project website at www
.fragilefamilies.princeton.edu.
2. See www.russellsage.org/programs/main/futureofwork/program_grants_
view for additional information.

References

Appelbaum, Eileen, Annette Bernhardt, and Richard J. Murnane, eds. 2003.
Low-Wage America: How Employers Are Reshaping Opportunity in the Workplace.
New York: Russell Sage Foundation.
Bernhardt, Annette D., Martina Morris, Mark S. Handcock, and Marc A. Scott.
2001. *Divergent Paths: Economic Mobility in the New American Labor Market.*
New York: Russell Sage Foundation.
Cantor, David, and Kenneth C. Land. 1985. "Unemployment and Crime Rates
in the Post–World War II United States: A Theoretical and Empirical Analy-
sis." *American Sociological Review* 50(3): 317–22.
Card, David E., and Rebecca M. Blank, eds. 2000. *Finding Jobs: Work and Welfare
Reform.* New York: Russell Sage Foundation.
Cho, Rosa, and Robert LaLonde. 2005. "The Impact of Incarceration in State
Prison on the Employment Prospects of Women." Unpublished paper. Uni-
versity of Chicago.
Garland, David. 2001. *The Culture of Control: Crime and Social Order in Contempo-
rary Society.* Chicago: University of Chicago Press.
Laub, John H., and Robert J. Sampson. 2003. *Shared Beginnings, Divergent Lives:
Delinquent Boys to Age 70.* Cambridge, Mass.: Harvard University Press.
Pattillo, Mary, David F. Weiman, and Bruce Western, eds. 2004. *Imprisoning
America: the Social Effects of Mass Incarceration.* New York: Russell Sage Foun-
dation.

Chapter 1

Introduction

SHAWN BUSHWAY, MICHAEL A. STOLL,
AND DAVID F. WEIMAN

The research reported in this volume analyzes the nexus between criminal-justice policies and labor markets, from the perspective of released prisoners. Like other formative social institutions, the labor market is integral to the successful reentry and reintegration of released prisoners into their families and communities. Their path away from crime and future prison spells, what criminologists call desistance, depends critically on employment, specifically finding and holding a good job (Sampson and Laub 1993; Hagan 1993; Uggen 2000; Bushway and Reuter 2002). By contrast, the probability of recidivism—cycling out of prison and back in—varies inversely with an individual's labor-market opportunities, measured by both employment and real wage rates.

Using varied data sources and empirical methodologies, the chapters in this book examine how released prisoners fare in the labor market, with a focus on how their prison experience affects their labor-market opportunities. Where appropriate, the contributors specify and test the hypothesis that a criminal-justice record in general and a prison spell in particular reinforce the steepening barriers to employment for those on the socioeconomic margins. Although the results may not be definitive (for reasons discussed presently), they suggest that the greater use of incarceration may confine less-educated individuals to the "secondary" labor market, characterized by erratic employment and low earnings. Given the link between employment and crime, the evidence further implies that ex-offenders face significant risks of recidivism and hence future prison spells, notably when they are released into relatively weak labor markets. In other words, poor labor-market prospects make ex-prisoners more likely to fall into a vicious cycle, a revolving door of prison release, crime, and reincarceration.

This labor-market perspective does not discount the public safety benefits of a vast prison system, but instead warrants a fuller accounting of its costs and net returns. Standard benefit-cost analyses focus on the benefits side of the equation—the reductions in crime rates because of the incapacitation and deterrent effects of tougher criminal sanctions (Levitt 1996, 2004; Nagin 1998; Spelman 2000). They measure the costs simply in terms of the fiscal expenditures on building and operating more prisons as opposed to other public goods. If mass incarceration causes significant unintended individual and social costs, then this standard accounting is biased in favor of imprisonment and against alternative sanctions.

To elaborate our point, we consider the most relevant counterfactual example, in which a nonviolent drug offender is sentenced to prison rather than a nonincarcerative sanction such as a drug court.[1] If the individual faces a greater likelihood of recidivism because of his prison experience, then the total social costs of the "get tough" policy should include the additional harm from his post-release criminal activity and the administrative costs related to his subsequent arrest, prosecution, and imprisonment. A growing scholarly literature on mass incarceration has identified a number of other potential unintended social costs, ranging from the disruptions to and burdens on families, especially children, the erosion of neighborhood social capital and consequent weaker informal social control mechanisms, and political alienation and distrust of public authority (Pattillo, Weiman, and Western 2004; Hagan and Dinovitzer 1999; Rose and Clear 1998; Clear, Rose, and Ryder 2001; Mauer and Chesney-Lind 2002; Huo and Tyler 2002; and Travis and Waul 2004).

Labor-Market Barriers to Reentry

Before reviewing the individual chapters, we first specify and elaborate the central hypothesis explored by each and then discuss limitations in their scope and methodology. The more narrow version of the hypothesis considers whether a felony conviction and prison term further diminish the prospects of more marginal offenders in formal, legal labor markets. That is, when compared to comparable individuals without a felony conviction and prison term, will ex-offenders realize lower employment and hourly earning rates?

A criminal-justice record can influence an individual's future labor-market experiences through distinct causal mechanisms whose cumulative impact will likely depend on the stage in an individual's life course when he first has a conviction.[2] A felony conviction with or without a prison term tarnishes marginal offenders with a social stigma, likened by Daniel S. Nagin (1998) to a scarlet letter. The stigma effect is clearest when it is inscribed by formal regulations and legal precedents (Holzer, Raphael, and Stoll 2004). State laws prohibit the employment of convicted felons in occupations ranging from child- and dependent-care service providers to barbers and hairdressers. Some states also cut off their access to public employment, which has been an important source of work for inner-city minorities. Even in the absence of explicit legislation, many employers are wary of employing convicted felons because of the mounting case law delineating their liability risks for "negligent hiring."[3]

The stigma effect can also be more subtle, triggering serious doubts if not fears on the part of those making the hiring decision. Employers may not trust convicted felons to handle valuable merchandise and cash, and may doubt whether they possess the requisite "soft" skills to interact effectively with customers (Holzer 1996; Moss and Tilly 2001). They may also worry about ex-felons' future entanglements with other employees, as well as with criminal-justice authorities that can disrupt the work environment and work routines. Survey evidence suggests that of several stigmatized groups—including welfare recipients, GED earners, and those with spotty work histories—managers are most reluctant to hire ex-offenders (Holzer, Raphael, and Stoll 2004). Also, as shown by Devah Pager (2003; see also chapter 5, this volume), the stigma of a criminal record is powerfully mediated and compounded by racial stereotypes.

Not only can a prison record tarnish a person's image, but a prison experience itself can also seriously erode an individual's human and social capital. If an inmate's human capital depreciates in prison, then upon release they will be a less productive and hence valuable worker. At the very least a prison spell will create a lengthy gap in a person's employment record and so raise questions about his reliability, an especially important job characteristic in more lean manufacturing and distribution systems. Regardless of formal training, valuable work skills are often learned, honed, and maintained through on the job experience. While in prison, individuals not only will experience the loss of their accumulated skills but also will fail to keep pace with peers who stayed straight and worked continuously during this time.

Prison life, especially in the era of mass incarceration, is unlikely to remedy the problem—if anything, it may compound it. Prison education and vocational programs, although at best an imperfect substitute, have in any case been significantly scaled back because of skepticism over their value and also because of budget constraints in the face of rapidly expanding prison populations.[4] At the same time prison is the quintessential "school of hard knocks," where survival demands the acquisition of skills and behaviors not well suited to the workplace. They are also breeding grounds for serious infectious diseases (notably

HIV/AIDs, tuberculosis, and hepatitis B and C) and psychological disorders such as drug addictions and depression (Petersilia 2003, 48–51; Hammett, Roberts, and Kennedy 2001).

Robert J. Sampson and John H. Laub (1993; 2005) have persuasively argued that the impacts of a criminal conviction and incarceration depend critically on an individual's stage in his life course. They can be especially noxious at the critical life-course transition from late adolescence through early adulthood. During this formative period most individuals are completing their educational training and beginning a period of experimentation and learning in the labor market. While searching for work and on the job, they acquire valuable, often intangible, general, and firm-specific skills. What's more, they forge social contacts, often the weak ties, that prove critical to future job mobility (Granovetter 1973). This perspective implies that by their late twenties most individuals will have acquired the complement of human and social capital to land an "adult" job and realize large, positive earnings from continued work experience.

A criminal and prison record during this pivotal moment will certainly delay if not completely derail this maturation process. Thus, instead of eventually settling down into a "good" job, released prisoners may find that they lack the requisite connections to get a foot in the door and, even if they do get a job, the skills to hold down such a position. Confined to the "spot" secondary market, they will tend to churn in and out of a series of dead-end jobs. Although in the short run these positions may yield higher earnings than a "regular" job, they afford limited opportunities for steady long-term employment, human-capital accumulation, and career advancement, and benefits.[5] With this employment track record, they may also find it more difficult to form other enduring attachments such as marriage, which has been shown to be another essential ingredient in desistance from crime (Laub, Nagin, and Sampson 1998; Sampson, Laub, and Wimer 2006).

Our arguments so far have focused on individual-level effects and so ignore a critical feature of mass incarceration, its disproportionate social and spatial incidence among less-educated minority men. The flip side of their exodus to prison is their eventual return, most often to their original or sending communities (Petersilia 2003, 22; Travis 2005, 31–34). Because of this "iron law" of imprisonment—that "they all come back"—we must be cautious in drawing any simple conclusion about the direct impacts of mass incarceration on local labor markets. The removal of large numbers of individuals to prisons may reduce local labor supplies and so benefit those who remain behind. These effects, however, are likely to be transitory, quickly offset by the return flow of released prisoners.

A more systematic approach must also consider the cumulative impact of "coercive mobility," measured as the stock of all individuals who have ever directly experienced prison (Rose and Clear 1998; Clear, Rose, and Ryder 2001). According to estimates by Becky Pettit and Bruce Western (2004), among others, nearly one-third of less-educated African American men have been imprisoned by their mid-thirties. Given this extraordinary social-spatial concentration, we must heed the lessons of urban geography and consider the possible neighborhood effects of mass incarceration on inner-city communities. Although intrinsically difficult to identify and measure empirically, these externalities may nonetheless exert powerful influences, reinforcing, weakening, or even transcending the individual-level ones.

Elaborating his basic metaphor of stigma, the scarlet letter, Nagin (1998) illustrates one unintended consequence of mass incarceration. He observes that a prison record only derives its potency as a social stigma and so deterrent when it is the exception and so brands the bearer as an outlier in the community. Over time, as the prevalence of a prison record steadily rises, it may eventually cross a critical threshold whereby the scarlet letter becomes more the norm and perhaps even a status symbol. Even more perverse, the evidence suggests, the policies of mass incarceration have strengthened, rather than weakened, the size and sway of criminal gangs both within and outside prison walls.[6]

The cumulative toll of incarceration may in turn disrupt the local low-skilled labor market as a whole, not just for released prisoners. Thus, Nagin's metaphor of the scarlet letter, while illuminating, is ultimately misleading. After all, with some exceptions, released prisoners do not bear a visible sign of their status. Without relatively inexpensive and reliable information on criminal-justice records, an employer must form a judgment about the applicant and will typically depend on external cues to do so—superficial characteristics that they associate with ex-convicts. In the context of mass incarceration, this form of statistical discrimination may result in de facto racial profiling, in which employers simply assume that less-educated African American and Hispanic men have a prison record. They will tend to treat all individuals in these demographic groups the same, regardless of their actual criminal-prison background (Holzer, Raphael and Stoll 2006; see also Pager 2003 and chapter 5, this volume).

This perspective has one clear implication about employers who draw on the low-skilled labor market in areas with concentrated populations of released prisoners. All other things being equal, they will more likely conduct criminal background checks, especially in the current era of new low-cost Internet search companies (Holzer, Raphael, and Stoll 2004; Holzer, Raphael, and Stoll, chapter 4, this volume; Bushway et al., chapter 6, this volume). This perspective identifies a potential and possibly significant recruitment cost facing these employers, especially if they are wary of or prohibited from hiring released prisoners and concerned about the quality of the background information. Thus, inner-city employers may actually face diminished labor supplies and a less hospitable business climate, factors that can reinforce a decision to relocate to suburban or rural areas and so diminish the total quantity and quality of jobs available in these neighborhoods.

Scope and Method

Although the authors address general issues about the prison and post-release experiences of ex-offenders, the decision was made that their empirical analyses should focus on men; thus, they ignore the most rapidly growing segment of the prison population, women. This decision was made on strictly pragmatic grounds. Despite the increasing number of women in the prison population, over 90 percent of all inmates are men, and so the vast majority of the annual flows into and out of prisons are men. This restriction yielded samples large enough to be finely parsed by demographic, socioeconomic, and spatial-temporal conditions and so best served our primary goal of sharpening the empirical estimates of prison effects.[7]

A second related research objective illustrates the qualitative importance of these differences in numbers. In chapter 2 we document the disproportionate arrest and incarceration rates of young African American men and women for drug crimes, especially more marginal nonviolent offenders. For black men, these levels have reached a point where prison has become a modal experience with potentially dire social consequences for the entire population, not just those who are arrested, convicted, and incarcerated.[8] By focusing on men these studies also shed empirical light on these elusive agglomeration, or neighborhood, effects, which have become a distinguishing feature of this new era of mass incarceration.

Methodologically, the concentration of incarceration among young, less-educated, inner-city minority men seriously confounds the empirical problem of identifying and measuring the effect of prison, as opposed to other causal factors, on ex-offenders' employment and earnings. Because of their low levels of human and social capital to start with, these individuals face dimmer labor-market prospects in the "new economy" anyway and so are at greater risk for criminal behavior and a prison spell. We cannot readily infer a prison effect from their spotty post-release work history, which may simply mirror their pre-prison labor-market experiences and so reflect underlying personal characteristics that led them into prison to begin with. In other words, the correlation between a prison spell and poor labor-market outcomes may be spurious.

Agglomeration effects from mass incarceration compound these selection biases. An obvious example of the former is racial profiling, whereby employers impute to all cohort members, not just ex-offenders, the same social stigma and so treat them the same. Consequently, even if there is a strong negative prison effect, researchers will observe negligible differences in the labor-market outcomes of those who do and do not experience a prison spell and incorrectly reject the prison-effect hypothesis.

To minimize these potential biases, the statistical analyses reported in Part III rely on rich longitudinal data sets based on state administrative records and careful research designs. The data sets include individual-level variables that can be used to control for the observed and unobserved personal characteristics that independently influence post-release employment outcomes such as educational attainment, marital status, and psychological propensities and individuals' prior labor-market experiences. To control for turning-point trajectories, they also include individuals incarcerated at the very end of the period, whose earlier labor-market outcomes are presumed to be untarnished by a prison record.[9] The data sets also exploit independent or exogenous conditions, such as local unemployment conditions, that differentially influence the labor-market experiences of ex-offenders and so help to identify the impact of a prison spell.

Needless to say, these solutions are not ideal, and cannot be expected to yield definitive results. Indeed, as explained in the methodological appendix to this chapter, the statistical analyses reported in Part III understate the full force of the prison effect. Because their sampling frame is limited to individuals who were incarcerated at some point during the 1990s, their analyses address how, not whether, a prison experience influences labor-market outcomes. Still, we believe that they furnish the most comprehensive and reliable statistical evidence to date on this critical aspect of the policy question. Our confidence is bolstered by the preponderance of indicators pointing in the same direction, but derived from different kinds of data sources—administrative records from diverse states, individual-level surveys, and audit studies—and empirical methods ranging from panel regression analysis to more narrative accounts. At the same time, we recognize that the findings published in this volume represent not the last word but an important first step on the topic and hope that our efforts will inspire replication and elaboration in a systematic attempt to determine the full costs as well as benefits of mass incarceration.

Plan of Book

The book is divided into three parts. The contributions to Part I set the stage conceptually and concretely for the subsequent statistical analyses of labor-market conditions facing ex-offenders and their labor-market outcomes. Part II focuses on the demand side of the market and specifies concretely the additional barriers confronting released prisoners, compared to other marginal workers, in their search for employment. The chapters in Part III all use administrative data to analyze individual-level outcomes—employment, earnings, and future imprisonment of ex-offenders in the wake of their release. The final chapter synthesizes the contributions to this volume from the perspective of evolving labor-market institutions in post-industrial America.

The recent run-up in incarceration rates is often conceived as a "social experiment," one combining more aggressive policing and prosecutions, the greater use of mandatory prison sentences and of stiffer prison sentences, and harsher prison and parole conditions.[10] In addition to documenting these policy shifts and their immediate impacts, chapter 2 draws out the implications of this "social experiment" metaphor. We present a variety of quantitative evidence to justify our views stated above, that mass incarceration is a novel policy regime and that it evolved in response to shifting labor-market conditions. Our analysis further points to the pivotal role of the crack cocaine epidemic and the War on Drugs, dating from the mid-1980s, which was seen to justify tougher penal sanctions against a wider range of drug crimes, not just more serious (that is, violent) drug offenders, than the previous practice. We then specify conceptually the critical question addressed by subsequent chapters: What are the labor-market impacts of incarcerating more marginal offenders.

In chapter 3, Christy A. Visher and Vera Kachnowski present data gathered from interviews with a representative sample of recently released male prisoners in Chicago about their employment experiences before, during, and after prison. The results reported here are part the larger study of men being released from state correctional institutions, launched by the Urban Institute in 2000.[11] The research here examines pre-prison, in-prison, and after-prison employment histories and the ways these vary with individual, family, and other important factors. One novel feature of this research is that the men are interviewed about their employment histories within the three-month period after their release from prison and again four to eight months after being on the outside.

Their results show that the employment rates of these men remained relatively low in the shorter and longer periods after prison, though these rates did rise somewhat between the first and second interviews.

The employment rates remained low despite the fact that ex-prisoners felt that employment was a key to their successful reintegration, were motivated to find work, and thought that once they got a job they would manage to keep it. A variety of factors seem to be correlated with whether ex-offenders find work after prison, including employment before prison, participation in a job training program during prison, strong family support, and avoidance of drugs after release.

The chapters in Part II consider the impacts of a criminal record on the employability of ex-offenders from the perspective of potential employers—the demand side of the labor market. Because most ex-offenders have limited formal education and job experience, Part II focuses on the lower end of the market, entry-level jobs requiring at most a high school degree or its equivalent. Employing distinct empirical methodologies, Harry Holzer, Steven Raphael, and Michael Stoll and Pager (chapters 4 and 5, respectively) examine employers' responses to a similar kind of question. Holzer, Raphael, and Stoll surveyed human resources managers in the Los Angeles labor market, asking them whether the firm would be willing to hire an individual with a criminal record. In Pager's more experimental audit study, managers in the Milwaukee area were confronted with the decision of whether to hire an individual with a criminal record or an otherwise equivalent job applicant and so had to decide the matter in context. The concluding chapter in Part II, by Shawn Bushway, Shauna Briggs, Mischelle Van Brakle, Faye Taxman, and Meridith Thanner, examines an increasingly important ingredient in firms' hiring decisions: the supply and quality of information about job applicants' criminal backgrounds.

A key variable in these analyses is what it means to have a criminal record. A criminal background search could lead to an entry if an applicant has been arrested but acquitted. Likewise, an offender with a criminal conviction need not have served time in prison and so will have no prison record. The nature of the record matters not only because of our concern over the unintended consequences of mass incarceration but also because it bears on the causal questions of how a criminal record affects an individual's labor-market opportunities, in this case, the perceptions and behaviors of employers. A felony conviction alone or even frequent arrests without prosecution and conviction may be sufficient to trigger a negative signal. A prison spell would reinforce the stigma, but also add the negative impacts on the applicant's human and social capital, such as his "soft" skills and personal references.

Holzer, Raphael, and Stoll's study considers the more general impacts of a criminal record, rather than of a prison spell per se. Based on a representative sample of employers, they delineate firms' preferences for hiring ex-offenders, as measured by managers' responses to the counterfactual question. Their focus on firms' more stated rather than actual demand for labor is an obvious limitation of the survey methodology. To test the consistency and hence reliability of these variables, the authors included additional relevant questions, for example, about firms' actual hiring of ex-offenders over the previous year and the frequency with which they conduct criminal background checks. With these and additional survey data, the authors carefully depict the types of firms—by sector, size, job characteristics, and so forth—that are more and less likely to employ ex-offenders and use associated screening practices. Given the timing of the data collection, the authors also shed some light on the impact of the "high-pressure economy" of the late 1990s and post-9/11 security concerns on the demands for these disadvantaged workers.

Pager's more experimental research design enables her to draw more causal inferences about the impacts of a drug conviction and prison spell, albeit over a more restricted set of firms and questions. The nature of her study limits the outcomes to a dichotomous variable— whether after submitting the job application the tester receives a callback. By contrasting the experiences of white and black pairs of testers and of testers who did and did not speak to the personnel manager at this initial stage, she adds the dimensions of race and personal contact to see how they individually and jointly influenced the demand for the released prisoners. The study is also confined to firms that were currently advertising for workers and in public sources. Because of deteriorating macroeconomic conditions, fewer firms were likely to have vacancies and so to search actively for new hires. Still, she reasons, firms that advertised in public venues would be less likely to discriminate, whether on the basis of race or criminal record. Consequently, finding lower callback rates among testers with a criminal record would be powerful evidence in support of the existence of an incarceration effect.

Both chapters show employers' reluctance to hire individuals with a criminal record. At the same time, they also identify a number of mediating factors that can reinforce or moderate this negative criminal background effect. Most striking, but not too surprising, is the powerful influence of race on potential employers, who seem to assume that black applicants are "guilty until proven innocent." Additionally, both studies point out some flexibility in managers' judgments, evidenced by their differential treatment of what we term the "marginal" versus the more hardened offender.[12]

In both instances, information about an individual's criminal background may be decisive in allowing him to get a foot in a company's door. Interestingly, despite reaching similar conclusions about the force of racial profiling or stereotyping, Holzer, Raphael, and Stoll and Pager express divergent views on the policy question of making criminal-justice records more or less accessible. Before resolving this important policy issue, Shawn Bushway and his colleagues, in chapter 6, insist that we must first assess the sources and quality of the information disseminated. Their contribution is especially timely, as they clearly depict a "revolution" in criminal-record reporting driven by both legal and technological innovations. On the legal side are court rulings on the question of access and also the increasing prevalence of public and private sanctions against hiring ex-offenders. At the same time the IT revolution has greatly accelerated the public-sector goal of creating centralized, comprehensive criminal-justice databases, while it has also reduced the entry cost for competitive private vendors.

Chapter 6 describes these two trends and then addresses the question of the quality, not simply the quantity, of the information supplied. Through qualitative analysis, Bushway and his colleagues consider the various public and private measures to produce more comprehensive, reliable reporting on criminal backgrounds, such as the FBI's National Crime Information Center, and the various measures of self- and public regulation of private-sector firms. Their account underscores the inherent problems in achieving this goal because of the highly decentralized U.S. criminal-justice system with its multiple and often incompatible information systems. They also question the effectiveness of government regulation in this case, as compared to the credit-history reporting industry, because of the proliferation of smaller firms, which are more difficult to monitor. They underscore these concerns through a simple empirical exercise comparing the information contained in the FBI database and provided by a larger private vendor for a sample of parolees in northern Virginia.

The study by Bushway and his colleagues raises some disturbing questions about the consequences of sketchy criminal-justice information, especially on young, less-educated black males, who are most vulnerable to profiling or stereotyping. And, they ask, are there any incentives for suppliers or demanders of this information to remedy the problems? For example, do employers purchase this information, regardless of its quality, merely to shield themselves from negligent-hiring lawsuits? Do county and state officials have the incentives and resources to digitize their records in compatible formats for integration into a national database? Answers to these questions, while important, still will not resolve the more pressing policy issue raised by Holzer, Raphael, and Stoll and Pager on how to deploy this information effectively, not only to bolster public safety but also to protect the rights of ex-offenders from the "collateral consequences" of their transgressions— possibly more enduring than incarceration's direct consequences.

Part III focuses on the life outcomes of ex-offenders upon their release from prison. The research in these chapters is unique in its use of large administrative data sets from departments of corrections in four states: California, Florida, Ohio, and Washington. With the exception of the California study, the authors have also collected administrative data on employment from the states' unemployment-insurance (UI) agencies, which they have linked to the corrections data.[13] Given the rarity of this type of administrative-data analysis, the simple state-by-state comparison of descriptive statistics is itself of considerable interest.

With this goal in mind the authors have derived comparable measures that they use to directly compare the sample populations to a single reference point, the Washington case.[14] Some of the baseline differences are striking. For example, African Americans make up 27 percent of the prison population in Washington, 46 percent in Florida, and 56 percent in Ohio. Employment outcomes prior to admission also differ greatly. In the year prior to admission prisoners in the Washington sample had a 50 percent chance of working, while those in the Florida and Ohio samples only had a 32 percent and 35 percent likelihood, respectively.

These chapters all analyze whether the incarceration experience can harm prisoners' post-release employment outcomes. They also consider how their employment prospects and recidivism rates are mediated by participation in prison programs and by post-release labor-market conditions. There is a substantial literature (see also chapters 4 and 5 in this volume) that clearly demonstrates that many employers are unwilling to hire ex-offenders. Becky Pettit and Christopher Lyons (chapter 7) are particularly concerned with the possibility that the incarceration experience will lead to declines in employment outcomes. They find a sizable positive (30 percent) increase in employment rates in the immediate post-release period relative to the year prior to incarceration, yet this spike in employment turns out to be transitory. It disappears entirely after one and a half years and actually becomes negative after three years. This unexpected result is partially corroborated by John H. Tyler and Jeffrey R. Kling (chapter 8) for Florida and William J. Sabol (chapter 9) for Ohio. Sabol's analysis implies the exact same time line and trajectory of employment rates: an immediate post-release spike that diminishes after 1.5 years. Analyzing earnings, not employment, Tyler and Kling show a sharp post-release increase in average levels that is most likely due to higher employment rather than to higher wage rates. They do not, however, find comparable evidence of a rapid decline in employment.

Pettit and Lyons and Sabol conjecture, reasonably, that the increase in employment is due to post-release supervision—the pressure parole officers exert on ex-prisoners to find and keep a job. In the Florida case, however, Tyler and Kling do not find a significant supervision effect.

We hope that future work can be directed at better understanding the cause of the post-release employment increase and at investigating whether there are ways to leverage this possibly short-term surge in employment for better long-term outcomes.

Pettit and Lyons also investigate the impact of incarceration on the wages of released prisoners. For about four years after their release, they earn slightly lower wages than they did in the pre-incarceration period. So although employment rates increase, wages do not. Their relatively flat wage trajectories are especially troubling when viewed in light of the more typical positive age-earnings profile of individuals in these formative years. An important question, which these data unfortunately cannot answer, is whether the declining employment outcomes of released prisoners are directly linked to their low wages and poor long-term labor-market prospects or to their criminal justice record.

Finally, Pettit and Lyons and the other authors show that there is no common incarceration effect on individuals. The negative impact of incarceration on wages, they predict, will be particularly large for inmates who had relatively better job opportunities prior to prison, a group that includes whites, high-status offenders, and less serious offenders. Their analysis largely confirms this prediction, and also shows a larger post-release employment spike for higher-risk than for more marginal offenders. These results do not have any clear policy implications, but do place the evidence of a modest race effect on the sentencing decisions, which is harsher for blacks, in a new context. Perhaps judges are aware that some groups experience greater extralegal sanctions from the community, and therefore need to be treated less harshly by the system itself.

Chapter 8 focuses on the impact of prison programming, specifically GED (general equivalency diploma) training and certification, on ex-inmates' employment outcomes. The analysis has a particularly strong quasi-experimental research design that relies on the panel structure of the data to control for selection bias, based on unobserved differences between individuals. As a purely methodological point, they show that the results of these models are not substantively different from those of models with extensive controls, including prior criminal history, education levels, and employment. As a guide to research, the result suggests that rich cross-sectional data sets may be just as effective as panel data sets in addressing selection problems.

Tyler and Kling report no significant overall effect of a GED on post-release earnings. Minority males, however, constitute an important exception, although the benefits of a GED on their wages, as on employment, appear to be transitory. They also test whether the benefit of a GED is merely a certification effect or due to learning while in prison.

Because of their careful research design and rich administrative data, their study represents the strongest evidence to date on the topic and yields similar results to a comparable study of Project Prep by William G. Saylor and Gerald G. Gaes (1999). William J. Sabol, in chapter 9, also looks at whether receiving a GED in prison improves employment outcomes and finds no effect for any group. This result is especially surprising, because Sabol's data set has a more limited set of controls and so cannot fully adjust for the expected positive bias in comparing self-selected participants to nonparticipants.

Sabol's main focus is the effect of local unemployment rates on employment and recidivism. Research in labor economics implies that local unemployment rates are correlated with an individual's chances of finding a job, especially for those such as released prisoners who are at the tail end of the job queue (Neumark 2002; Offner and Holzer 2002). Sabol finds a rather large labor-market effect, which is consistent with Holzer, Raphael, and Stoll's (2004) results that released prisoners are the last hired and the first fired, even in tight labor markets. The labor-market effect found by Sabol is nearly twice as large as results derived by Paul Offner and Holzer (2002) for less-educated black men.

Raphael and Weiman also examine the local labor-market–recidivism link, but in a context where parole revocations were common, accounting for 70 percent of new prison admissions. Although the average effect of the unemployment rate on the likelihood of recidivism is small, it increases with time. This result suggests that employment conditions are more important for lower-risk, less criminally prone offenders, who are more likely to survive the first few months of release without returning to prison. Raphael and Weiman test this hypothesis by contrasting the unemployment-recidivism connection for more and less serious offenders, where degree is measured by the number of prior prison spells. Since the local labor-market effect is the product of (1) the impact of local unemployment rates on the probability that a parolee finds a job and (2) the effect of having a job on the likelihood of violating parole, the authors use Sabol's estimate of (1) to derive an estimate of (2). For more marginal offenders, they show that this latter effect can be significant, a finding that has important policy implications.

Taken together, the results in this section present an intriguing picture of the employment prospects of ex-inmates. All four chapters show that pre-prison employment, prior criminal history, and pre-prison education levels are extremely important predictors of post-prison employment and recidivism rates. These differences dwarf even the most optimistic expectations about the potential impact of prison employment programs. Despite this sobering reality check, it is also true that the authors of all the chapters find large increases in immediate post-release employment rates, even for inmates with very low levels of pre-prison employment. These outcomes may partly depend on the local unemployment rates in the areas to which the inmates return. Local conditions, Sabol and Raphael and Weiman find, can significantly affect the prospects of released prisoners' finding a job and going straight.

This research does paint a rather dim picture of the prospects for more serious offenders with low levels of education and prior employment. All of the chapters suggest that this group will have very poor post-release employment outcomes, even if they participate in prison programs. Still, according to Tyler and Kling, prison programming may yield some benefit, albeit transitory, to minorities and so help the most disadvantaged group of inmates. Although supporters of GED programs might be discouraged by the relatively weak evidence for their efficacy in this volume, even weak evidence in favor of an effect is somewhat surprising, given the extremely poor employment prospects and criminal involvement of this group of ex-inmates.

In the final chapter, Bruce Western considers the contributions to this volume in terms of an emerging "institutional" perspective on mass incarceration. By this he means more than the mere fact that prisons are institutions with their distinct organizational charts, cultures, and norms. In the era of mass incarceration, he argues, prison has become institutionalized—the norm—in the lives of disadvantaged individuals, especially young, less-educated minority men living in inner cities. Harsh criminal-justice policies mean that they are more likely than other groups to wind up in prison and to bear its scars, which in the labor-market context can skew their employment opportunities and risk of recidivism.

In elaborating this perspective, Western highlights the volume's main themes. First, the policies of mass incarceration must be seen in the context of the political economy of inequality in the United States, especially inequality that occurs along racial-ethnic lines. Second, they can reinforce these inequalities by confining released prisoners to the erratic low-paying jobs of the secondary labor market, thereby increasing these young men's risk of recidivism. And finally, carefully designed programs, informed and honed by ongoing research, can weaken the revolving-door effect, but current investments in training and reentry programs are too limited in scale and scope to have much impact.

The contributions to this volume focus on the impacts of policy but do not venture any explicit policy prescriptions to deal with the connection between socioeconomic disadvantage and crime and the dim employment prospects of released prisoners. Their analyses do, however, bear on vital policy issues that come up at virtually every stage in the criminal-justice system and every level of government. Chapters 2, and

9 through 11 deliver the clear message that macroeconomic and employment policies can have a significant impact in preventing crime and incarceration to begin with and in improving the employment prospects of those marginal offenders reentering their communities. The analyses in Part 3 raise familiar doubts about the effectiveness of rehabilitation programs such as GED preparation, although they do note the potential benefits of employment experience, whether obtained prior to or during the prison spell. And finally the contributions to part II identify the potential benefits but also the pitfalls of recent policy innovations centralizing and disseminating criminal-justice records.

Chapters 2 and 11 deviate from this course and explicitly broach the issue of the policy alternatives to mass incarceration. Chapter 2, focusing on the War on Drugs, concludes with an assessment of drug courts, an alternative to incarceration, especially for more marginal offenders. Consistent with our perspective, we ask whether drug courts constitute an effective option to reduce recidivism and so enhance public safety, at a lower actual cost to governments and social cost to offenders and their communities. Western, in chapter 11, goes even further, maintaining that comprehensive investments in training and reentry programs, while symbolically important, are not likely to make more than a marginal difference in the lives of released prisoners because of these men's myriad deficits and the harsh environment that they face. In the end, he restates the viewpoint that motivated the research in this volume, that a more effective and humane policy would strive to reverse the isolation and alienation of those on the socioeconomic margins and in this way reduce their likelihood of winding up in prison in the first place.

Appendix: Defining and Estimating Prison Effects

Analyzing the impacts of mass incarceration on individual labor-market outcomes poses a number of thorny conceptual and methodological problems. At the most fundamental level, the notion of a "prison effect" has several connotations, corresponding to the range of policy innovations that have contributed to the dramatic run-up in incarceration rates since the late 1970s. We can assess the impacts of the following on individuals who have committed a felony offense:

1. More aggressive policing, which increases the likelihood of an arrest

2. Mandatory minimum sentencing policies, which increase the subsequent risk of a prison commitment

3. Steeper minimum sentences and truth-in-sentencing policies, which increase the length of a prison stay

(See, for example, Grogger 1995; Western 2002; and Kling 2006.)

We consider Western (2002) and Kling (2006), because they narrowly focus on the prison dimension of mass incarceration. Put simply, Western asks *whether*, while Kling asks *how*, a prison spell affects an individual's post-release earnings and employment trajectories. In turn, they analyze different data sets with different sampling frames. From the National Longitudinal Survey of Youth (NLSY) 1979, Western (2002) selects a subsample of individuals who either experienced an incarceration (prison or jail) spell by 1998 or reported other contact with criminal-justice authorities (ranging from police stops to a conviction and probation) in a 1980 supplement. Because he assumes that latter group were "at risk" for but eluded incarceration, he can interpret the difference between their labor-market trajectories as evidence of a prison effect—the stigma of an arrest, conviction, and a prison sentence plus any negative consequences of the prison experience itself. Because the NLSY 1979 survey data contain no detailed information on life behind bars for those who experienced prison, Western's analysis cannot resolve the prison effect into its constituent elements—that is, test the distinct causal theories discussed in the main text.

Kling (2006), as in the research reported in Part III of this volume, fills this empirical gap by estimating the labor-market effects of different prison experiences, in this case shorter versus longer prison spells.[15] It therefore draws on an alternative data source, the comprehensive records of the Florida Corrections Department, which document the prison spells of all individuals incarcerated during the sample period. Kling (2006) can only assesses whether more or less prison time, not imprisonment per se, adversely affected the post-release outcomes of ex-offenders, as well as any offsetting impacts from participation in and completion of rehabilitation or training programs available only to those serving longer terms.

We illustrate the basic hypothesis of a prison effect and the methodological problems in estimating it through a simple diagram based on Western (2006). The graphs in figure 1A.1 delineate the age-employment or age-earnings profiles of those with and without a prison record during their formative years, from late adolescence to early adulthood.

Their profiles are initially flat, reflecting the churning into and out of jobs, characteristic of new entrants.[16] Over time, individuals without a prison record are expected to accumulate labor-market and on-the-job experience and find a suitable job match. Once they land a "good" job, their employment rates and earnings will steadily increase (as shown by the curve labeled "True Comparison Group"). An incarcera-

Figure 1A.1   Hypothetical Employment-Earnings Profiles of "At-Risk" Young Men With and Without a Prison Record

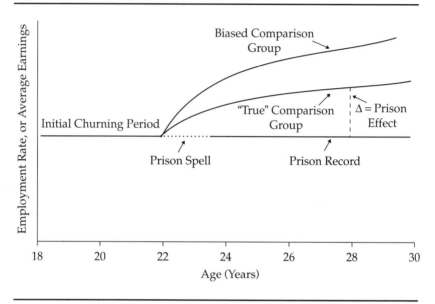

Source: Authors' compilation.

tion spell (noted by the dotted line) interrupts this vital life-course transition, and confines released prisoners to the secondary labor market. We depict their diminished labor-market prospects by a flat age-employment profile, at levels comparable to their pre-prison experience (as shown by the line marked "Prison Record").[17]

Conceptually, we gauge the prison effect by the widening gap between the employment-earnings profiles of the two groups as they age (denoted by Δ for age twenty-eight years), that is by quantitative difference in their slopes. Methodologically, an accurate or consistent estimate of this parameter depends critically on whether the two groups are truly comparable and so experience divergent labor-market outcomes only because of cumulative impact of an arrest, conviction, and prison commitment. If not, other factors may systematically influence their criminal and labor-market outcomes and so potentially skew or bias the parameter estimate. For example, instead of by mere chance, some in the comparison group may have avoided a prison spell because of personal characteristics or locational advantages that also made them more employable. The failure to incorporate this factor into the empirical model would overstate the influence of a prison record on the labor-market trajectories of the comparison group.

Graphically, we depict this problem of selection bias by adding a second, steeper, employment-earnings profile to figure 1A.1 (labeled "Biased Comparison Group"). In this case the comparison group is too broad. It includes individuals who systematically differ from released prisoners along a number of dimensions that significantly bolster their labor-market prospects but also lower their incarceration risks. Failure to identify and control for these factors, then, will result in a spurious negative correlation between labor-market outcomes and a prison record—in other words, an overestimation of the prison effect.

Avoiding these methodological pitfalls hinges critically on the proper specification of the empirical model and ultimately on the quality of the data set. It must include sufficient background information to control for the influence of confounding factors that affect both labor-market and incarceration outcomes. With the rich information in the NLSY 1979 survey data, Western can account for individual differences along a number of relevant dimensions such as human capital, psychological dispositions, and social attachments. Moreover, the data set tracks individuals' prior labor-market histories, which can serve as a benchmark to gauge the influence of relevant unobserved factors that do not vary over time (that is, "fixed effects"). Still, these data and methods are not ideal and so cannot detect all of the relevant factors that specify the comparison group, especially if they cumulate over time. One example is the prevalence of incarceration itself, which may systematically affect the likelihood of an arrest leading to prison and of a contact leading to a good job.[18]

The empirical analysis in Kling (2006) and in Part III of this volume must resolve similar methodological pitfalls. As in the previous example, a strong positive correlation between the length of a prison term and the prison effect on post-release outcomes may be spurious. In states with mandatory guidelines and truth-in-sentencing laws, for example, more serious offenders committing more serious crimes will serve longer terms. Thus, their criminal record, rather than the length of the prison spell per se, may directly limit their post-release labor-market prospects.[19] Moreover, the evidence of such crimes and longer sentences may be symptomatic of underlying personal characteristics that would likewise disqualify individuals for good jobs (such as impulsivity or a drug addiction).

To minimize these selection biases, Kling (2006) constructs a rich data set that links prison, arrest, and employment administrative records. Consequently, the empirical model can control for direct evidence on inmates' criminal history, including the most recent offense, but also unobserved factors that are reflected in their pre-incarceration employment history. Although Kling finds no significant long-term impacts of lengthier prison spells, we must still be cautious in interpreting this result for several reasons. The data sources, for example, may not contain pertinent information about the ex-felons' pre-prison labor-market experiences such as employment and earnings off of the books or the influence of an even earlier prison spell. Moreover, the very question under investigation may be relevant to only select prison populations, whose greater incarceration rates depended more on increasing the length of the prison term as opposed to increasing the rate of arrest or of a prison commitment following an arrest (Blumstein and Beck 1999, 34–36; Western 2006, 45).

Notes

1. We elaborate and concretize this example in the conclusion to chapter 2, where we present actual estimates of the net social benefits from assigning drug offenders to drug courts rather than confining them to jail or prison. These net benefits are just the flip side of the net social costs of "business as usual," the prison option. Throughout we use the pronouns "him" or "his," because the research in this volume focuses on male prisoners.
2. This discussion draws on and elaborates the theoretical analysis of prison effects and methodological issues in estimating them found in Bruce Western, Jeffrey R. Kling, and David F. Weiman (2001).
3. Under the principle of negligent hiring, employers can be held liable for an employee's criminal actions if they "know, or should have known" of the employee's past criminal behavior (Bushway 1996; Glynn 1988). Employers have lost 72 percent of negligent-hiring cases and have had to pay an average settlement cost of more than $1.6 million per case for "punitive damages as well as [plaintiffs'] . . . loss, pain, and suffering" (Bushway 1996; Connerley, Arvey, and Bernardy 2001). The high probability of losing coupled with hefty settlement awards suggest that fear of litigation may substantially deter employers from hiring applicants with criminal-history records. We have found no data on the number of negligent-hiring suits, but anecdotal evidence indicates that they are on the rise.
4. Indeed, the most recent Bureau of Justice Statistics evidence shows that state and federal prisons are operating near or above their optimal capacity (Harrison and Beck 2005, 7). According to Caroline Wolf Harlow (2003, 4), participation rates of state prisoners in all educational programs except vocational training declined between 1991 and 1997. Tyler and Kling and William Sabol (chapters 8 and 9, respectively, this volume) evaluate the post-release employment benefits of prison GED programs.
5. See Nagin and Waldfogel (1998); and Western (2002). Figure 1A.1 in the appendix graphically illustrates this more dynamic version of the "prison-effect" hypothesis and the methodological conundrums in accurately estimating its magnitude.
6. See John Hagedorn and Perry Macon (1988, 84–86, 158–62) and Hagedorn (1998, 399–400); and Sudhir Alladi Venkatesh and Steven D. Levitt (2000). Prisons are ideal venues for recruiting new gang members and for gang leaders to meet to coordinate their geographically dispersed operations. In

the Chicago case studied by Venkatesh and Levitt, the authors imply that a prison experience was a necessary credential for upward mobility in the gang hierarchy, much like a college degree for middle-class youths.

7. Paige M. Harrison and Allen J. Beck (2005, 4–5, 8) provide 2004 estimates of the prison population and incarceration rates by demographic group. By way of illustration we contrast the annual flows of women entering and exiting prisons in California and Washington, the sample states with the largest and smallest prison populations. In 1998 there were approximately 13,000 female and 120,000 male prisoners in California, and in Washington there were 800 women and 5,500 men (see the Bureau of Justice Statistics data at www.ojp.usdoj.gov/bjs/dtdata. htm#corrections). An empirical study of female prisoners with a comparable level of detail, therefore, must consolidate release cohorts over several years (see, for example, Cho and Lalonde 2005).

8. By 2004 the incarceration rate for black men had reached 3.2 percent of the total population, as opposed to only .2 percent of black women. Consequently, nearly one-third of black men would likely experience imprisonment in their lifetimes, as compared to only 5.6 percent of black women, approximately the same rate as for white men (Bonczar 2003, 1).

9. Individuals incarcerated at the end of the sample period constitute a kind of control group, whose earlier labor-market experiences may illustrate the "counterfactual" case: the age-earnings profiles of released prisoners in their late twenties who had not been incarcerated in their mid-twenties. Of course, the individuals in the comparison group may have experienced an earlier prison spell, before the data set was constructed, which would skew their 1990s labor-market record.

10. The sentencing component of this mix is itself a bundle of reforms, including the abolition of discretionary parole release; determinate sentencing commissions and guidelines; mandatory minimum sentences, including, in the extreme, "three-strikes" sentences for repeat offenders; and "truth-in-sentencing" policies. In chapter 2 we describe each policy type and specify when and where the most notable examples were enacted.

11. For an overview of the Urban Institute research, see "Understanding the Challenges of Prisoner Reentry," at www.urban.org/url.cfm?ID=411289.

12. The notion of a marginal offender is defined in economic and criminological terms in the third section of chapter 2.

13. The UI data in Florida and Ohio only provide information on individuals' quarterly earnings from covered jobs, whereas the Washington data also include reported hours from which average wages can be derived (equal to quarterly earnings divided by quarterly hours). The UI records serve as a rough indicator of employment opportunities, but only in the formal sector. Missing is any evidence of employment and earnings from informal work such as day labor and of course any illegal activity, which may be found in self-reported survey data (see for example Uggen 2000; Western 2002; and Kornfeld and Bloom 1999).

14. In terms of criminal-justice policies, Washington state falls on the more lenient end of the spectrum. Its overall prison incarceration rate in 2005 was only 263 inmates per 100,000 people, as compared to the national aver-

age of 488 and a rate of 392 in Ohio, 456 in California, and 492 in Florida (Harrison and Beck 2005). Furthermore, in Washington, maximum prison sentences and time served are shorter on average than in the other states, even though the inmates serve a greater fraction of the maximum sentence (Ditton and Wilson 1999).

15. The chapter by Tyler and Kling analyzes a similar question, whether prisoners who participated in and completed a GED training program had different post-release outcomes. Chapters by Pettit and Lyons, Sabol, and Raphael and Weiman, by contrast, assess the impact of a comparable prison experience on ex-offenders who differ by race, education, or destination upon release.

16. Our analysis in figure 1A.1 depicts the aggregate, or average, trajectory of individuals in this cohort, that is, it "averages" over the more volatile experiences of individuals.

17. Although they examine a different issue, all of the studies in Part III show a sharp but transitory increase in post-release employment rates and total earnings. Our case, therefore, illustrates the long-term trajectories, after employment rates fall back to their pre-prison levels.

18. If quantitatively important, this factor would add another component to the estimated prison effect, the agglomeration effect (also call the concentration, or neighborhood, effect) of mass incarceration taken as a complex of policies.

19. As shown by Holzer, Raphael, and Stoll and Pager (chapters 4 and 5, respectively), employers' likelihood of hiring an ex-offender is contingent on the offense that landed them in prison in the first place. They may be more likely to overlook a first-time nonviolent drug offense than an assault.

References

Bernhardt, Annette D., Martina Morris, Mark S. Handcock, and Marc A. Scott. 2001. *Divergent Paths: Economic Mobility in the New American Labor Market*. New York: Russell Sage Foundation.

Blumstein, Alfred, and Allen J. Beck. 1999. "Population Growth in U.S. Prisons, 1980–1996." *Crime and Justice: Prisons* 26: 17–61.

Bonczar, Thomas P. 2003. "Prevalence of Imprisonment in the U.S. Population, 1974–2001." Special report, no. NCJ 197976. Washington: U.S. Department of Justice, Bureau of Justices Statistics, available at http://www.ojp.usdoj.gov/bjs/pub/pdf/piusp01.pdf.

Bushway, Shawn D. 1996. "Labor Market Effects of Permitting Employer Access to Criminal History Records." Unpublished manuscript. University of Maryland.

Bushway, Shawn, and Peter Reuter. 2002. "Labor Markets and Crime." In *Crime: Public Policies for Crime Control*, edited by James Q. Wilson and Joan Petersilia. Oakland, Calif.: Institute for Contemporary Studies.

Cho, Rosa, and Robert Lalonde. 2005. "The Impact of Incarceration in State Prison on the Employment Prospects of Women." Unpublished paper. University of Chicago.

Clear, Todd R., Dina R. Rose, and Judith A. Ryder. 2001. "Incarceration and the

Community: The Problem of Removing and Returning Offenders." *Crime and Delinquency* 47(3): 335–51.

Connerley, Mary L., Richard D. Arvey, Charles J. Bernardy. 2001. "Criminal Background Checks for Prospective and Current Employees: Current Practices Among Municipal Agencies." *Public Personnel Management* 20(2): 173–83.

Ditton, Paula M., and Doris James Wilson. 1999. "Truth in Sentencing in State Prisons." Special report, NCJ no. 170032. Washington: U.S. Department of Justice, Bureau of Justice Statistics, available at http://www.ojp.usdoj.gov/bjs/pub/pdf/tssp.pdf.

Glynn, Timothy P. 1988. "The Limited Viability of Negligent Supervision, Retention, Hiring, and Infliction of Emotional Distress Claims in Employment Discrimination Cases in Minnesota." *William Mitchell Law Review* 24(2): 581–633.

Granovetter, Mark. 1973. "The Strength of Weak Ties." *American Journal of Sociology* 78(6): 1360–80.

Grogger, Jeffrey. 1995. "The Effect of Arrests on the Employment and Earnings of Young Men." *Quarterly Journal of Economics* 110(1): 51–71.

Hagan, John. 1993. "The Social Embeddedness of Crime and Unemployment." *Criminology* 31(4): 465–91.

Hagan, John, and Ronit Dinovitzer. 1999. "Collateral Consequences of Imprisonment for Children, Communities, and Prisoners." *Crime and Justice: Prisons* 26: 121–62.

Hagedorn, John. 1998. "Gang Violence in the Postindustrial Era." *Crime and Justice* 24: 365–419.

Hagedorn, John, and Perry Macon. 1988. *People and Folks: Gangs, Crime, and the Underclass in a Rust-Belt City.* Chicago: Lake View Press.

Hammett, Theodore M., Cheryl Roberts, and Sofia Kennedy. 2001. "Health-Related Issues in Prisoner Reentry." *Crime and Delinquency* 47(3): 390–409.

Harlow, Caroline Wolf. 2003. "Education and Correctional Populations." Special report, no. NCJ 195670. Washington: U.S. Department of Justice, Bureau of Justice Statistics.

Harrison, Paige M., and Allen J. Beck. 2005. "Prison and Jail Inmates at Midyear 2004." Bulletin, no. NCJ 208801. Washington: U.S. Department of Justice, Bureau of Justice Statistics, available at http://www.ojp.usdoj.gov/bjs/pub/pdf/pjim04.pdf.

Holzer, Harry J. 1996. *What Employers Want: Job Prospects for Less-Educated Workers.* New York: Russell Sage Foundation.

Holzer, Harry J., Steven Raphael, and Michael A. Stoll. 2004. "Will Employers Hire Former Offenders? Employer Preferences, Background Checks, and Their Determinants." In *Imprisoning America: The Social Effects of Mass Incarceration*, edited by Mary Pattillo, David F. Weiman, and Bruce Western. New York: Russell Sage Foundation.

———. 2006. "Perceived Criminality, Background Checks, and the Racial Hiring Practices of Employers?" *Journal of Law and Economics* 49(2): 451–80.

Huo, Yuen J., and Tom R. Tyler 2002. *Trust in the Law: Encouraging Public Cooperation with the Police and Courts.* New York: Russell Sage Foundation.

Kling, Jeffrey R. 2006. "Incarceration Length, Employment, and Earnings." *American Economic Review* 96(3): 863–76.

Kornfeld, Robert, and Howard S. Bloom 1999. "Measuring Program Impacts on Earnings and Employment: Do Unemployment Insurance Wage Reports from Employers Agree with Surveys of Individuals?" *Journal of Labor Economics* 17(1): 168–97.

Laub, John H., Daniel S. Nagin, and Robert J. Sampson. 1998. "Trajectories of Change in Criminal Offending: Good Marriages and the Desistance Process." *American Sociological Review* 63(2): 225–38.

Levitt, Steven D. 1996. "The Effect of Prison Population Size on Crime Rates: Evidence from Prison Overcrowding Litigation." *Quarterly Journal of Economics* 111(2): 319–51.

———. 2004. "Understanding Why Crime Fell in the 1990s: Four Factors That Explain the Decline and Six That Do Not." *Journal of Economic Perspectives* 18(1): 163–90.

Mauer, Marc, and Meda Chesney-Lind. 2002. *Invisible Punishment: The Collateral Consequences of Mass Imprisonment*. New York: New Press.

Moss, Philip I., and Chris Tilly. 2001. *Stories Employers Tell: Race, Skill, and Hiring in America*. New York: Russell Sage Foundation.

Nagin, Daniel S. 1998. "Criminal Deterrence Research at the Outset of the Twenty-First Century." *Crime and Justice* 23: 1–42.

Nagin, Daniel, and Joel Waldfogel. 1998. "The Effect of Conviction on Income Through the Life Cycle." *International Review of Law and Economics* 18(1): 25–40.

Neumark, David. 2002. "Youth Labor Markets in the United States: Shopping Around vs. Staying Put." *Review of Economics and Statistics* 84(3): 462–82.

Offner, Paul, and Harry Holzer. 2002. "Left Behind in the Labor Market: Recent Employment Trends Among Young Black Men." Washington, D.C.: Brookings Institution.

Pager, Devah. 2003. "The Mark of a Criminal Record." *American Journal of Sociology* 108(5): 937–75.

Pattillo, Mary E., David F. Weiman, and Bruce Western, eds. 2004. *Imprisoning America: The Social Effects of Mass Incarceration*. New York: Russell Sage Foundation.

Petersilia, Joan. 2003. *When Prisoners Come Home: Parole and Prisoner Reentry*. Oxford and New York: Oxford University Press.

Pettit, Becky, and Bruce Western. 2004. "Mass Imprisonment and the Life Course: Race and Class Inequality in U.S. Incarceration." *American Sociological Review* 69(2): 151–69.

Rose, Dina R., and Todd R. Clear 1998. "Incarceration, Social Capital, and Crime: Implications for Social Disorganization Theory." *Criminology* 36(3): 441–79.

Sampson, Robert J., and John H. Laub 1993. *Crime in the Making: Pathways and Turning Points Through Life*. Cambridge, Mass.: Harvard University Press.

———. 2005. "A Life–Course View of the Development of Crime." *Annals of the American Academy of Political and Social Science* 602(1): 12–45.

Sampson, Robert J., John H. Laub, and Christopher Wimer. 2006. "Does Marriage Reduce Crime? A Counterfactual Approach to Within-Individual Causal Effects." *Criminology* 44(3): 465–507.

Saylor, William G., and Gerald G. Gaes. 1999. "The Differential Effect of Industries and Vocational Training on Post Release Outcome for Ethnic and Racial Groups." Research note. Washington: Federal Bureau of Prisons, Office of Research and Evaluation, Available at http://www.bop.gov/news/research_projects/published_reports/recidivism/oreprprep_s1.pdf.

Spelman, William. 2000. "What Recent Studies Do (and Don't) Tell Us About Imprisonment and Crime." *Crime and Justice: Prisons* 27: 418–93.

Travis, Jeremy. 2005. *But They All Come Back: Facing the Challenges of Prisoner Reentry*. Washington D.C.: Urban Institute Press.

Travis, Jeremy, and Michelle Waul, eds. 2004. *Prisoners Once Removed: The Impact of Incarceration and Reentry on Children, Families, and Communities*. Washington, D.C.: Urban Institute Press.

Uggen, Christopher. 2000. "Work as a Turning Point in the Life Course of Criminals: A Duration Model of Age, Employment, and Recidivism." *American Sociological Review* 65(4): 529–46.

Venkatesh, Sudhir Alladi, and Steven D. Levitt. 2000. "'Are We a Family or a Business?' History and Disjuncture in the Urban American Street Gang." *Theory and Society* 29(4): 427–62.

Western, Bruce. 2002. "The Impact of Incarceration on Wage Mobility and Inequality." *American Sociological Review* 67(4): 526–46.

———. 2006. *Punishment and Inequality in America*. New York: Russell Sage Foundation.

Western, Bruce, Jeffrey R. Kling, and David F. Weiman. 2001. "The Labor Market Consequences of Incarceration." *Crime and Delinquency* 47(3): 410–27.

═ Part I ═

Macro and Micro Contexts of Prisoner Reentry

═ Chapter 2 ═

The Regime of Mass Incarceration: A Labor-Market Perspective

DAVID F. WEIMAN, MICHAEL A. STOLL, AND SHAWN BUSHWAY

In this chapter we set the stage empirically and conceptually for the subsequent contributions that analyze the labor-market conditions for and experiences of the increasing numbers of released prisoners in the United States. Empirically, we situate the problem of prisoner reentry into the labor market within the context of the harsher political economic realities facing those on the socioeconomic margin since the mid-1970s, especially young, less-educated, inner-city minority males.

First we present evidence for a new criminal justice policy regime which we term mass incarceration; in the chapter's second section we analyze the new economy of diminished labor-market opportunities and expectations for less-skilled and -educated workers. Together, we show, these profound political economic shocks contributed to the rising rates of crime and incarceration, especially in inner-city minority communities.

In the third section we relate these political and economic shocks through an analysis of the War on Drugs during the 1980s and early 1990s. Contrary to the perceptions of policy analysts and policymakers at the time (and even among some today), we regard this moment as the product of specific political economic conditions that spurred a sharp but transitory surge in violent drug crimes among otherwise marginal offenders. We see the harsh criminal-justice policy response in terms of a fundamental shift in the policies "governing social marginality," one from social inclusion to exclusion. This perspective takes in the broader sweep of conservative policies, from the attack on social welfare spending and unions to the War on Drugs and their cumulative impact on crime and incarceration rates.

In the conclusion we consider a central question of this volume: Have these "get tough" criminal justice policies reinforced the already steep barriers to legitimate employment for those on the socioeconomic margin and thus risked institutionalizing these individuals' socioeconomic isolation? Focusing on the criminal-justice side, we formulate this thesis in terms of a "revolving door" of prison release, recidivism, and incarceration, where the labor market mediates the prison-release–recidivism link. We find evidence of higher reincarceration rates for more recent cohorts of released prisoners because of technical parole violations rather than the more conventionally measured recidivism route of a new arrest or felony conviction.

Combined, the tougher "front-end" and "back-end" criminal-justice policies of mass incarceration have sustained the current high levels of imprisonment, despite the sharp drop-off in crime rates. The former have increased the number of those imprisoned on a new conviction and commitment, while the latter "net-widening" parole policies have increased their likelihood of a quick return trip upon release. To break this cycle, we explore a policy alternative that preempts a prison spell in the first place: drug courts. Novel policy experiments such as this one represent a step toward a more "rehabilitative" than punitive model of criminal-justice policies and show promising signs of curbing drug use and recidivism.

Mass Incarceration

From the vantage point of the early 1970s, Alfred Blumstein and Jacqueline Cohen (1973; Blumstein, Cohen, and Nagin 1976) advanced a provocative theory on the "stability of punishment." By punishment, they meant the application of formal social control by criminal-justice authorities, most evident in the imprisonment of those who deviate from accepted societal rules. Weighing the benefits of public safety and social order against the fiscal and political costs of incarceration, they argued that a society such as that of the United States would adjust the boundary between acceptable and deviant behavior to limit the scope of officially sanctioned punishment and thus, the extent of incarceration. These "adjustments," they reasoned, would most likely occur on the margins and so apply to nonviolent, victimless crimes and less serious first-time offenders.

As evidence of the stability of punishment, Blumstein and Cohen documented the "striking" constancy in the prison incarceration rate since the mid-1920s (Blumstein and Beck 1999, 17). Over a nearly fifty-year period marked by profound economic, political, and social turbu-

Figure 2.1   **Prison and Total Incarceration Rates, 1925 to 2004**

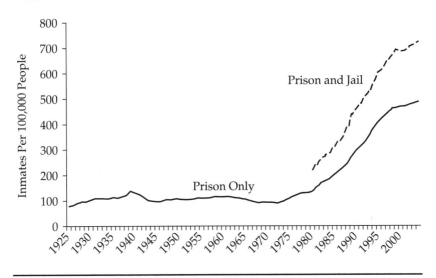

Source: Pastore and McGuire (2006, tables 6.28.2004 and 6.13.2005).

lence, the average prison incarceration rate hovered narrowly around 107 inmates per 100,000 people (see figure 2.1).[1] More to their point, the prison incarceration rate actually declined by nearly 18 percent between 1961 and 1967 and remained relatively stable until the mid-1970s, despite sharp increases in arrest and crime rates, including violent crimes.[2]

Consistent with their hypothesis, Blumstein and Cohen (1973, 206) interpreted these divergent trends in terms of the "liberalized adaptation" of criminal-justice sanctions to changing patterns of offending behavior, notably in the realm of drug violations. In response to the rapid growth of drug arrests (and presumably crimes) over the 1960s, Congress in 1970 repealed mandatory minimum sentences, which was netting an increasing number of young white offenders, "not hardened criminals … [or] even hardened drug addicts."[3] And drug arrests actually declined by 4 percent per year between 1974 and 1979, despite evidence of rising drug use (Boggess and Bound 1997, 733; Tonry 1995, 83–92).

Over two decades later, Blumstein revisited the trends in the U.S. prison population, but now to document and explain the "dramatic change in [the] use of incarceration" (Blumstein and Beck 1999, 17). Between the late 1970s and 1997, the prison incarceration rate had multiplied more than four-fold, from the historic average of 107 per 100,000 population to 445 (see figure 2.1). More comprehensive data since 1980 clearly show the full scope of this aggregate trend. Despite persistent regional differences in the "use of incarceration"—with the highest rates in the South and lowest in the Northeast—the relative expansion of the prison population was comparable across all regions of the country. (The correlation coefficient between regions varies from .957 for Northeastern versus Southern states to .997 for Midwestern versus Western states.) Moreover, the change embraced all facets of correctional supervision. Between 1980 and 2004 the total population behind bars, including jails, jumped from .5 million to 2.1 million, corresponding to a total incarceration rate of 724 per 100,000 (see figure 2.1). The total population under some form of correctional supervision, including those on parole and probation, totaled nearly 7 million people in 2004, or 9 percent of the prime-age male population, the population most "at risk" of punishment.[4]

We interpret the recent dramatic acceleration in the incarceration rate as evidence of a *new* policy regime, of *mass* incarceration. By a new regime, we mean a decisive break in criminal-justice policies, and not simply in quantitative trends, since the late 1970s.[5] The prior system has been characterized by the complementary ideals of indeterminate sentencing and rehabilitation.[6] At least in principle, it reserved prison for more serious crimes and criminal offenders, and judges and correctional administrators were given wide discretion in meting out sentences and actual prison terms to further the goal of rehabilitation.

The current system, by contrast, is premised on the principles of "just deserts," or retribution, and a "get tough" utilitarianism. These standards imply that sentences should be structured to fit the crime as well as to reduce crime by incapacitating actual offenders and deterring potential offenders.[7] Their clearest expression is seen in the dramatic shift toward stiffer determinant sentencing policies: higher mandatory minimum sentences and sentencing guidelines to limit judicial discretion, "truth in sentencing" laws to ensure that offenders serve out most of their term, and "three strikes" laws to punish repeat offenders (see table 2.1). The changes are in fact broader in scope, covering all aspects of the criminal-justice system, from more aggressive policing and prosecution—resulting in more arrests, criminal prosecutions, convictions, and prison commitments—to a harsher penal environment aimed at "warehousing" offenders.

Following David Garland (2001a), the term "mass" connotes not simply the vast scale of the American prison system but also the "social concentration" of incarceration. The greater incidence of incarceration among poor, disadvantaged urban males is certainly not novel; indeed, crime and imprisonment have historically been greatest on the margins of society (Sampson and Laub 1993b; Greenberg 1999; Western, Kleykamp, and Rosenfeld 2004; Western and Pettit 2002). Still, we maintain that the recent dramatic growth in incarceration rates has in dialectical

Table 2.1   **From Indeterminate to Determinate Sentencing: Basic Reforms Since the Mid-1970s**

Policy	Discussion
Mandatory minimum sentencing laws	Legislation, instead of the presiding judge, determines how much time offenders must serve in prison before they become eligible for parole or early release. Nearly three-quarters of all states and the federal government have enacted mandatory minimum sentences for possession or trafficking of illegal drugs (U.S. Department of Justice, Bureau of Justice Administration 1998, 8–9). Two notable examples: • The 1973 New York Rockefeller Drug Law, which initiated the recent trend of stiffer mandatory penalties for drug convictions and imposed the "harshest" penalties, for example fifteen to twenty-five years for the sale of one ounce or possession of two ounces of a narcotic like heroin. (Joint Committee on New York Drug Law Evaluation 1977, 159–56) • The federal Anti-Drug Abuse Act of 1986, which imposed a minimum sentence of five years for possession of either five grams of crack or five hundred grams of powder cocaine (Musto 1999, 273–78).
Abolition of discretionary parole release	These policies eliminate or curb the power of administrative parole boards to release prisoners to parole, where under supervision they complete the term of their sentence. • Maine was the first state to eliminate discretionary parole release in 1976. By 2002 sixteen states had entirely abolished discretionary parole release, and five more eliminated parole for violent and other felony offenses. (Petersilia 2003, 65–68) • Between 1980 and 1999 the share of prisoners released on discretionary parole by a parole board declined, from 55 to 24 percent, and the share released under statutorily mandated parole more than doubled, from 18 to 41 percent (Hughes, Wilson, and Beck 2001, 4).
Determinate sentencing and sentencing guidelines	Determinate sentencing laws remove discretion from judges in determining prison sentences and terms. They specify simple rules or a grid that set prison sentences according to the seriousness of the crime and the offender's criminal history; the actual time served may be reduced by earned time credits (Tonry 1996, especially chapters 2 and 3). Guidelines have the same goal, but are weaker. Judges can deviate from presumptive guidelines, but must justify their decision, and they must take voluntary guidelines into consideration when they determine their sentences. • In 1978 Minnesota and Pennsylvania established commissions to develop sentencing guidelines. The 1984 Sentencing Reform Act set up the U.S. Sentencing Commission with the mandate of establishing a rigid set of presumptive guidelines.

Table 2.1   *Continued*

Policy	Discussion
	• According to recent surveys, twenty-four states have some form of determinate sentencing, including sentencing commissions and guidelines (Stanford Law School, Stanford Criminal Justice Center 2006; Sabol et al. 2002; U.S. Department of Justice, Bureau of Justice Administration 1998).
Truth-in-sentencing (TIS)	These laws limit parole release by requiring offenders to complete a "substantial portion" of their sentences, at least 85 percent of the term (Ditton and Wilson 1999; Sabol et al. 2002). • Washington State enacted the first TIS law in 1984, but the most significant reform occurred in 1994 with the passage of the federal Crime Act. In return for grants to build new or expand existing correctional facilities, the law required states to adopt the 85 percent standard for offenders convicted of serious violent crimes. • By the end of the decade twenty-nine states had met the federal standard and fourteen others had enacted weaker TIS laws (Sabol et al. 2002, 8–12).
Three- (or two-) strikes laws	A form of mandatory minimum sentences, these laws impose harsh mandatory prison terms on repeat serious offenders. • First enacted in Washington State in 1993, three-strikes laws had been adopted by nearly one-half of all states and the federal government by the end of the nineties. • The California law is deemed to be the most onerous and effective. For two strikes, offenders must serve twice the term of the second offense; and for three strikes, they are given a sentence of twenty-five years to life. After a decade of operation, over 40,000 offenders had been sentenced under the California law, as compared to only 10,600 in all other three-strikes states (Schiraldi, Colburn, and Lotke 2004).

Source: Authors' compilation.

fashion fundamentally altered the place of prison among the most affected groups and neighborhoods. For less-educated young minority males, a prison spell has become a modal, or predictable, not an exceptional, part of life. Consequently, the impacts of incarceration may no longer be limited to the individual offender and his (and increasingly her) family, but may extend to their communities and even to the larger political economy.

Crime and Punishment

To corroborate our view of a new policy regime of mass incarceration, we first present empirical evidence showing a decisive shift since the mid-1970s in the relationship between crime and punishment. We frame this hypothesis in terms of the Blumstein and Cohen (1973) thesis. The rapid growth in incarceration rates would be consistent with the "stability of punishment," if this trend were fueled by increasing rates of violent crimes committed by more hardened offenders. For these cases, Blumstein and Cohen note, a society would have little other recourse but to expand the prison system. By contrast, a strong empirical link between incarceration rates and less serious property and drug crimes or "exogenous" shifts in sentencing policies and the political climate would constitute contradictory evidence, indicating changes in the social norms and the institutional mechanisms that had previously regulated the use of prison (Garland 1993; Zimring and Hawkins 1991, chapter 1).

Critics of the "race to incarcerate" have clearly framed these related empirical hypotheses. They question the link between violent crime and incarceration rates and instead implicate changes in policing and sentencing policies, especially the War on Drugs (see Tonry 1995; Mauer 1999, 2001). Blumstein and Allen J. Beck (1999) empirically elaborate their central claims. Focusing on six major crimes accounting for the vast majority of prison inmates, Blumstein and Beck partition the growth in crime-specific incarceration rates into four variables corresponding to the steps leading from a criminal offense to a completed prison term: changes in crime, arrest, and prison commitment rates and the average prison term.[8]

It is striking that for all crimes except drug offenses (including the most serious victim crimes of murder, robbery, and assault), nearly 90 percent of the growth in the incarceration rate is "explained" by the last two variables—more prison commitments per arrest and longer prison terms—and not the first two, more crimes and arrests.[9] As Blumstein and Beck conclude, the growth in the prison population, at least for these crimes, has occurred mainly at the "sanctioning phase" of the process, where juries and judges have handed out new, harsher, punishments. In other words, it derives from changes in policy variables, not in crime rates. Employing similar analyses, Scott Boggess and John Bound (1997) and Bruce Western (2006, 43–45) reach the same conclusion, and a comparative study by James P. Lynch (2002; see also Young and Brown 1993) explains higher U.S. incarceration rates relative to those of other OECD (Organization for Economic Cooperation and Development) countries such as Austria, France, Germany, and Sweden by harsher punishments—the greater use of imprisonment and longer terms—for less serious property and drug crimes.

The very nature of drug crimes complicates the analysis of the drug incarceration rate.[10] Because these victimless crimes are not reported to criminal-justice authorities, they can only be gauged indirectly and partially, for example, by surveys of drug use and evidence of serious

Figure 2.2   Distribution of State Prisoners, by Most Serious Offense, 1980 to 2002

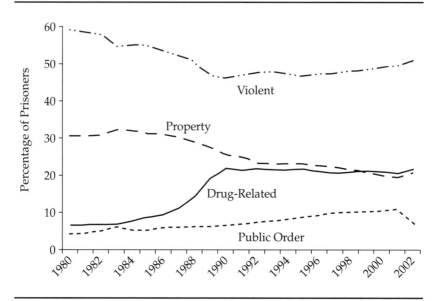

Source: Harrison and Beck (2005).

addiction (Boggess and Bound 1997, 734–76; Fryer et al. 2005). The accounting exercise, therefore, must start at the arrest, not crime, stage and so conflates the impact of the two variables. This limitation is especially problematic for drug crimes, because variations in drug arrests over time (and across space) largely reflect changes in discretionary policing policy, not criminal behavior (Beckett 2004; Fagan 2004). In other words, the analysis can only diagnose the growth in the drug incarceration rate in terms of variables that bear a strong policy influence, either directly or indirectly.

These results clearly support the War on Drugs hypothesis—that the War on Drugs and related policies have fueled the growth in the prison population. The incarceration rate for drug offenses grew by nearly 13.7 percent per year over the entire period, almost twice the aggregate rate. The most dramatic expansion occurred between 1983 and 1990, when the drug incarceration rate increased by 25 percent each year, and the share of inmates imprisoned for drug crimes jumped from 6.8 to 21.8 percent (see figure 2.2).[11] The decomposition analysis, moreover, identifies the dramatic impact of more aggressive policing and punitive sentencing policies. Together, the rapid growth between 1983 and 1990 in drug arrest rates by 4.8 percent and in prison commitment rates by 8.8

percent account for virtually all of the growth in the drug incarceration rate during that period. Blumstein and Beck find no trend in average prison-term length, which declined modestly until 1987, but then increased by a full year, from 1.3 to 2.3 years, by 1996. They suggest, however that the initial decline may be an artifact of rapid growth, which netted less serious offenders, who served shorter terms.[12]

Statistical analyses furnish more causal evidence in support of our view, and delineate key features of the new policy regime and its underlying political currents. To discern these complex relationships, these analyses explain variations in incarceration rates across states over time in terms of changes in crime rates, sentencing policies, the political environment, and demographic and socioeconomic conditions [13] All studies show a statistically significant but quantitatively modest connection between incarceration and violent-crime rates. Over the 1980s, for example, violent crime rates increased by only 22.3 percent but incarceration rates more than doubled. Applying the pooled regression estimates of David F. Greenberg and Valerie West's model three (2001, table 2), the increase in violent-crime rates accounts for only 7.2 percent of the increase in incarceration rates, whereas the implied impact of more drug-crime arrests is almost three times as large.[14] In support of our thesis of a policy regime shift, these regression analyses find stronger associations between incarceration rates and state policy choices and ultimately politics as well as demographic and socioeconomic conditions. Incarceration rates are negatively correlated with social welfare spending and more liberal Democratic political power. Additionally, states with higher incarceration rates tend to have higher poverty and unemployment rates and larger black and immigrant populations. Although these factors are highly correlated with crime, the regression analysis controls for variations in crime rates and so identifies their independent influence.

Race and Space

Our notion of mass incarceration also implies the increasing prevalence of imprisonment, notably among less-educated young minority men and in inner-city communities. The extent of and concerns over racial-ethnic disproportionality in the criminal-justice system predate the era of mass incarceration (Blumstein 1982, 1993; Sampson and Lauritsen 1997). The graph in figure 2.3, which compares incarceration rates between African American and white males from 1980 to 2004, illustrates the point.[15] Although the black-to-white ratio steadily increased to a peak of nearly 7.7 to 1 (or by 20 percent) between the mid-1980s and early 2000, that is, over the course of the War on Drugs, it had started from a relatively high base of 6.4 to 1.[16]

Figure 2.3   Incarceration Rates for African American and White Men

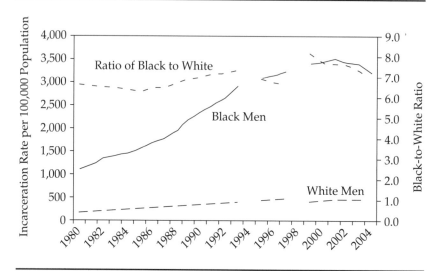

Source: Harrison and Beck (2005), Bureau of Justice Statistics bulletins on "Prisoners in 2004, 2003, 2002, 2001, 1999, 1998, 1997, 1996," and Snell (1995).

When cumulated over time, these disparate and high rates of incarceration imply the greater incidence of imprisonment among black as opposed to white men. For each date, the prevalence rate measures the share of current and former prisoners in the population at a particular point in time and so for men at a given stage in their life course (Bonczar 2003). With inmate survey data from 1974 to 2001, the Bureau of Justice Statistics (BJS) estimates of prevalence have been updated six times and show the rapid diffusion of a prison experience among black men during the era of mass incarceration, especially between 1986 and 1997 (see figure 2.4). The prevalence of incarceration was relatively stable in the latter half of the 1970s, just prior to the onset of this social experiment. It then increased sharply over the next two decades, from 8.9 to 15.0 percent for blacks and from 1.5 to 2.3 percent for whites. Although the rate of increase was actually greater for white men, we are more concerned with the extraordinary level for blacks, which increased to 16.6 percent by 2001. In other words, by the onset of the new millennium, nearly one in six black men (versus only one in thirty-eight white men) had directly experienced prison in their lives.

A more comprehensive but also conjectural measure, the cumulative risk of incarceration, takes a prospective view and gauges the fraction of men in each new cohort who will serve time at some point in their lives (Bonczar and Beck 1997; Bonczar 2003). The results, graphed in

Figure 2.4   Prevalence of Incarceration Among Adult Males, 1974 to 2001

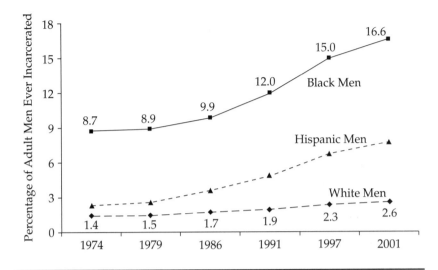

Source: Bonczar (2003).

figure 2.5, show an escalating risk of incarceration for all men after 1980. For blacks the likelihood of imprisonment more than doubled between 1979 and 1991, from 13.4 to 29.4 percent, and then inched up to nearly 33 percent by 2001. The trend increase for white men was greater in magnitude, but more continuous over the two-decade period. Taking past demographic patterns as a guide to future ones, these estimates imply that black males born in 2001 faced a one-in-three risk of ultimately being incarcerated as compared to an only one-in-seventeen risk for white males. This large persistent racial gap certainly squares with the notion that a prison experience has become so commonplace in black communities that the vast majority of individuals either directly experience prison or have direct personal contact with someone who has (Pattillo-McCoy 1999; Rose and Clear 2004).

More refined analyses reveal the mediating impact of social class and context on the incarceration-race nexus (Sampson and Lauritsen 1997; Pettit and Western 2004; Western 2006). Within the limitations of existing data sets, the class dimension is typically measured by educational level. Yet, as we argue in the next section, in the "new" economy, educational attainment beyond the traditional high school diploma has become an increasingly critical determinant of an individual's labor-market prospects and so of their risk of criminal offending and incarceration.

Steven Raphael (2006) uses decennial census data to track trends in

Figure 2.5   Cumulative Risk of Incarceration for Adult Men, 1974 to 2001

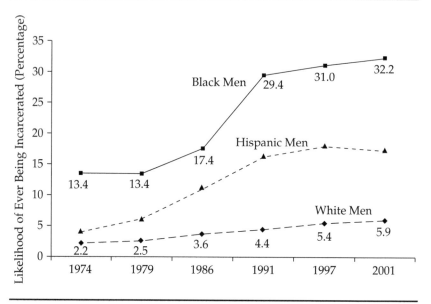

Source: Bonczar (1997), Bonczar and Beck (2003).

incarceration rates by race and educational attainment between 1970 and 2000.[17] Not surprisingly, the employment and incarceration rates of college-educated African American men were comparable to those of their white peers. For less-educated black men, by contrast, incarceration rates increased at least four-fold over the period, from 4 to 19 percent for high school dropouts and from 2 to 8 percent for those with at most a high school diploma. For comparable white men, incarceration rates only doubled, to much lower levels of 4 and 2 percent, respectively. Through a case study of California, Raphael affirms the greater prevalence of incarceration among young less-educated men, but also large racial gaps. Among young black male high school dropouts, for example, a prison experience is "practically a certainty," that is, around 100 percent, as compared to only 30 percent for their white peers.

Using a variety of survey data, Becky Pettit and Western (2004) estimate the cumulative risk of incarceration by age thirty to thirty-four years for men born between 1945 and 1949 and between 1965 and 1969. Those in the earlier cohort reached their early thirties by the end of the 1970s, whereas those in the later one matured during the period of mass incarceration. Their results show a much greater cumulative risk of incarceration for all noncollege educated men, black and white, in the 1965–1969 cohort group. For black men, the likelihood of imprisonment by age thirty to thirty-four increased from 12 to 30 percent over the period. The risk for white men also grew by 150 percent, but from only 2.1 to 5.3 percent. Strikingly, for black men with some college education, the estimated cumulative risk fell slightly, to 5 percent, the same rate as that for the younger cohort of less-educated white men.

Analyzing a succession of cohorts over time, Pettit and Western find an increasing risk of incarceration for men born after 1960, but especially for those without a college degree. Moreover, the prison experiences of the latter group were comparable, regardless of whether they dropped out of or graduated from high school or even attended some college.[18] For the earlier cohorts, by contrast, high school and college graduates more closely resembled each other at least along this dimension. In other words, their results (like the research on recent earnings inequality discussed in the next section) imply that for men coming of age after the mid-1970s, a high school diploma was no longer a sure route to a good job, but could relegate them to the socioeconomic margins where they would be at greater risk for criminal activity and imprisonment.

The social concentration of incarceration by race and socioeconomic class translates directly into the spatial concentration of the prison population by sending community. The connection between the two distributions is not surprising, as it reflects the persistent residential segregation of disadvantaged minorities in urban America (Jargowsky 1997; Bobo, O'Connor, and Tilly 2001; Massey and Denton 1993). In states with the largest prison populations, the vast majority of inmates come from the largest urban counties: Los Angeles in California, Houston and Dallas in Texas, and Miami-Dade in Florida (Lawrence and Travis 2004). Within these urban regions, the extent and rates of incarceration are greatest in a handful of poor, minority neighborhoods. For example, in Maryland, between 1987 and 1994, 60 percent of annual prison admissions came from only 45 (or 17 percent of) Baltimore neighborhoods (Lynch and Sabol 2004, 144–47). In New York City, in the mid-1980s, seven community board districts accounted for nearly three-quarters of all state prisoners (Fagan et al. 2003, 1568–69; see also Cadora, Swartz, and Gordon 2004).[19] In addition to the racial-ethnic composition of their populations, these source communities are characterized by high levels of economic disadvantage and social disorder as measured by high rates of poverty, dropping out of high school, and residential vacancy and turnover.

Structural Changes in Low-Skilled Labor Markets and Crime

The changes in the levels and composition of the incarcerated population over the late 1970s and 1980s occurred during a period of profound flux in the U.S. economy and in the labor market for less-educated male workers in particular. Prior to this period, from the early 1900s through the 1960s, the real earnings of less-educated male workers grew markedly.[20] Increased productivity gains, relative shortages of less-skilled workers as well as expanding unionization and federal government minimum-wage legislation underwrote increases in the economic fortunes of less-educated male workers decade by decade.

A marked shift in this trend occurred in the 1970s and 1980s. Over these decades and especially after the oil embargo–induced recession of 1973, the real wages paid to less-skilled male workers declined steadily in absolute terms, as well as relative to the earnings of more-educated workers, those with at least a college degree. These declines accelerated during the 1980s, especially for young males with a high school degree or less (Blackburn, Bloom, and Freeman 1990, 1993).

These trends were especially pronounced for young black men. Their real earnings and employment levels declined generally over the late 1970s and 1980s, but they also fell relative to those of comparable white men (Bound and Freeman 1992). This pattern reversed trends dating from about the 1940s, when decade by decade the black-white earnings gap gradually narrowed (Jaynes and Williams 1989).

To explain the dramatic reversal in the economic fortunes of less educated men over this period, scholars have cited a number of factors. They fall largely into two categories. The first embraces changes in the technology and organization of production that increased the skill requirements of jobs and hence weakened employer demands for less-educated workers. The second emphasizes significant institutional and policy innovations, notably falling unionization rates and the declining real value of the minimum wage (Blackburn, Bloom, and Freeman 1990).

While these factors help to account for the deterioration in young black men's earnings and employment, other conditions disproportionately affected their labor-market experiences. Weakened enforcement of antidiscrimination polices as well as narrowing coverage of affirmative action programs are likely to have influenced their outcomes (Jaynes and Williams 1989). In addition, changes in the industrial structure as well as declines in the economic vitality of central cities played a role (Bound and Freeman 1992).

Over this period American cities were being transformed from centers of goods production to centers of the new service economy. In 1950, about one in three metropolitan residents worked in manufacturing, mostly in central-city plants. By 1990, only about one in five worked in this sector, mostly employed by plants in more suburban locations (Farley, Danziger, and Holzer 2000). In their place emerged service-sector jobs that required on average more skills and educational credentials (Kasarda 1995).

In his landmark study of the sources of concentrated poverty and its social and economic consequences in inner-city black communities, William Julius Wilson (1987) emphasized these structural spatial-economic changes. The decline in manufacturing employment in central cities, he argued, marginalized economically and socially less-skilled black men. His proposition is supported by more recent studies suggesting that changes in industrial structure, in particular the disappearance of manufacturing work, has played a significant role in lowering black men's employment and earnings over the 1980s.[21]

During this period cities were losing not only manufacturing jobs but also other low skilled jobs. The cumulative result of these trends was a widening spatial mismatch between poor, heavily black inner-city communities and more suburban (and rural) areas with expanding labor-market opportunities for less-skilled workers. As Michael A. Stoll, Harry J. Holzer, and Keith R. Ihlandfeldt (2000) and Steven Raphael (1998) show, this factor contributed significantly to the declining employment and earnings of young black men.

These spatial-economic transformations reinforced the social disadvantages and turmoil in inner-city black communities. Between 1970 and 1990 the number of poor people living in high-poverty areas nearly doubled. Much of this growth occurred in predominantly black neighborhoods, with a vast majority located in central cities. Moreover, much of the increase in impoverished neighborhoods occurred because poverty spread to more and more neighborhoods, not because poor people increasingly moved to poor neighborhoods (Jargowsky 1997). Thus, the declining fortunes of less-educated workers coupled with changes in the economic structure of cities influenced the growing concentration and social isolation of the poor.

Wilson (1987) warned of the dire consequences of deepening economic decline in and isolation of poor but especially black central-city communities. They increased the out-migration of more stable middle-class households, which served as positive role models, and weakened strong pro-social institutions such as active churches and functional schools. This spiral of cumulative disadvantage created negative "concentration effects." In the absence of these vital mechanisms of informal social control, crime became more prevalent and, Wilson argued, a community norm that was increasingly expected and accepted (see, for example, Sampson and Raudenbush 1999; see also Sampson and Wilson 1995; Krivo and Peterson 2004; and Krivo, Peterson, and Payne 2006).

Combined, the economic, social, and institutional transformations over the 1980s contributed to rising rates of criminal activity nationally and in poor black neighborhoods in particular. To be sure, the extent of criminal behavior has manifold causes and correlates, including demographic conditions like the age-gender distribution, patterns of family and household formation, and the incidence of biomedical and psychological stresses, as well as crime control strategies (Wilson and Petersilia 1995). Still, local labor-market opportunities matter, especially for those on the socioeconomic margin who commit economic crimes such as robbery, theft, and drug dealing (Fagan and Freeman 1999; Piehl 1998; Freeman 1995, 1996). Their decisions will hinge on the expected pecuniary returns from, say, selling drugs (adjusted for the risk of arrest and incarceration or of injury and possibly death) relative to their earnings from legitimate work. Participation in criminal activity does not, however, imply a complete withdrawal from the legitimate labor market. More often, individuals will simply devote more of their time and effort to illegal activities at the expense of their participation in legal ones.[22]

The local labor-market–crime nexus finds strong empirical support in several recent studies based on varying data sources and empirical methodologies.[23] They all show statistically significant correlations between crime rates and local labor-market conditions—negative for real wages and positive for unemployment rates. Moreover, as expected, these correlations are stronger for property crimes than for violent crimes, and so imply the greater relevance of the economic model to the former than to the latter.

An obvious question is whether these results reflect a truly causal relationship between crime and local labor-market conditions or are merely spurious, evidence of other underlying factors. After all, individuals with very low skills and motivation are likely to be less employable and more prone to criminal activity. Moreover, high concentrations of crime and criminals in inner cities could prompt employers to move from or avoid these places and thereby cause lower employment and wages of individuals there. With appropriate instrumental variables for local economic conditions, these analyses can control for these reciprocal links and still detect a strong economic effect on criminal activity.[24]

Having settled the matter of statistical significance, we turn to the second vital question of economic importance, whether these empirical models can account for the actual quantitative changes in crime rates during the 1980s and 1990s. As shown in figure 2.6, property and violent crime rates increased from the early 1980s until the early 1990s and then declined over the rest of the decade.[25] Arrest rates for drug offenders followed a similar course initially, but after a sharp drop in the early 1990s they quickly rebounded by 1997 and then declined gradually until 2002.

Applying Jeff Grogger's (1998) estimate of a unitary real wage-property crime elasticity, the decline in real wages over the 1980s more

Figure 2.6   Property-Crime, Violent-Crime, and Drug Arrest Rates,
               1970 to 2005

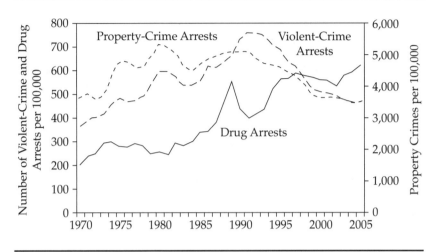

Source: U.S. Federal Bureau of Investigation, Uniform Crime Reporting Program, Crime in the United States (at http://www.fbi.gov/ucr/oscius/index.html), U.S. Census Bureau, Statistical Abstract, table H-23 (at http://www.census.gov/statab/hist), and U.S. Department of Justice, Bureau of Justice Statistics, Drug and Crime Facts (at http://ojp .usdoj.gov/bjs/dcf/tables/arrtot.htm).

than explains the actual property crime increase over the period. Focusing on counties in metropolitan regions, Eric D. Gould, Bruce A. Weinberg, and David B. Mustard (2002, 54) find a similar result, that declining real wages rather than rising unemployment rates spurred the increase in property crimes in the late 1980s. As further support for their economic model, they turn to the "high pressure" labor market of the late "roaring nineties" (Hines, Hoynes, and Krueger 2001; Freeman 2001). In this case they show that the "rising tide" in the form of falling unemployment rates for less-educated workers accounted for virtually all of the drop in property crime rates (appropriately adjusted for demographic shifts).[26] Likewise, Raphael and Rudolf Winter-Ember (2001) attribute 40 percent of the drop in property crimes to the economic boom.

Explaining the trends in violent-crime and drug arrests rates is more complicated. The incidence of property crime and violent crimes are highly correlated, at least until the period associated with the War on Drugs.[27] This result is not too surprising. Robbery and aggravated assault are the largest components of the total violent-crime index, and are directly motivated by or are often a means to pecuniary ends. As corroborating evidence, regression estimates of the economic model for these violent crimes, but not others such as murder or rape, are "quite similar to those for property crimes" (Gould, Weinberg, and Mustard 2002, 54–55; Raphael and Winter-Ember 2001, 275–76).

Participation in the illicit drug trade no doubt depended on the same risk-reward calculus as did property crimes. Still, it is difficult to square this simple economic logic with the divergent trends in drug arrest rates, which increased more sharply over the 1980s, by 84 percent as compared to only 14 percent for property-crime rates, and then barely fell in the late 1990s, despite the rapid economic expansion. More striking but also more relevant to our analysis in the next section, during the War on Drugs period (from the mid-1980s to the mid-1990s), drug arrest rates were more strongly correlated with violent crimes, in particular homicide, than with property-crime rates.[28]

We explain these empirical anomalies by "exogenous" increases in the market for illegal drugs and hence drug violations, but also by adoption of tougher drug enforcement policies leading to more arrests per actual number of drug offenses. Although changes in social norms increased the acceptability of illegal drug use and hence demand, the timing of the surge in drug arrests points to an innovation in the drug trade, the spread of crack cocaine beginning in the early 1980s (see, for example, Golub and Johnson 1994; Grogger and Willis 2000; and Fryer et al. 2005). It spurred the growth of drug use and trafficking in inner-city minority neighborhoods, which in turn became the frequent targets of aggressive police sweeps that netted increasing numbers of users and dealers (for the New York City case see Bowling 1999; Fagan and Davies 2000). A critical mediating factor was the rash of lethal handgun violence by drug gangs that plied this lucrative market.

According to Richard B. Freeman (1996), less-skilled young men will increase their criminal activity even in the face of the greater certainty and severity of punishment, if they are responsive to the economic returns to crime and if these returns are rising. Though there is limited evidence on their labor- supply elasticity in the drug trade, a variety of data strongly suggest that the benefits from drug dealing increased sharply over the 1980s and early 1990s (Hagedorn 1998a, 1998b; Reuter, MacCoun, and Murphy 1990; Levitt and Venkatesh 2000). These factors imply a "zero incapacitation effect, since each criminal locked up is replaced by another" (Freeman 1996, 36; Blumstein 1998, 130–31). In other words, if the rewards from participation in the drug economy are rising relative to those in the legitimate economy, more and more young men will likely be pulled into this industry despite rising incarceration or risk of arrest.

The real puzzle for the economic model is the late 1990s boom, when the crack market matured and then waned, at least among younger cohorts. In this case the evidence points to declining legitimate employ-

Figure 2.7   Percentage of Blacks Arrested for Major Crimes in U.S. Cities, 1980 to 2000

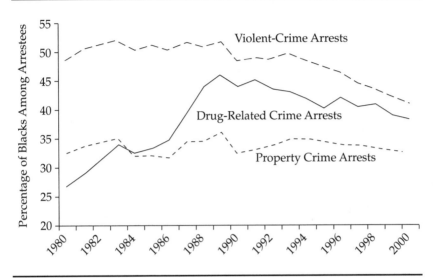

Source: Pastore and Maguire (2006) and earlier editions of the *Sourcebook of Criminal Justice Statistics* (at http://www.albany.edu/sourcebook/archive.html), section 4 (Arrests, Seizures).

ment opportunities for less-skilled young black males, not the increasing rewards to drug dealing. Although the boom modestly increased the wages of those who were in the labor market, it did not stem the secular decline in their employment and labor-force participation rates.[29] These downward trends, however, were not observed for comparable white or Hispanic men. Given this evidence of uneven expansion, it is likely that young black men's participation in the drug economy continued over the 1990s despite more robust national economic conditions.

The growth in drug arrest rates also depended on discretionary drug enforcement policies, not only rising drug-crime rates. As evidence, we point to the divergent trends in the share of African Americans among those arrested for property, violent, and drug crimes during the 1980s and 1990s (see figure 2.7). By this measure, blacks were no more likely to participate in property- and violent-crime offenses than whites. They accounted for a stable share of the arrests for property crimes over the period, and a declining share of violent-crime arrests in the 1990s. By contrast, the share of blacks in drug arrests jumped from 27 to around 45 percent in the 1980s. According to survey evidence, African Americans were no more likely to use cocaine (or heroin) than whites, but tended to buy drugs through local dealer networks in outdoor markets where they were more vulnerable to police sweeps.[30]

These trends in drug arrests were reinforced by racial disproportionality in the subsequent stages of the criminal-justice system, which together account for the increasing prevalence of incarceration among black men during the War on Drugs period. In the early 1990s black men accounted for 35 percent of drug-related arrests, but 55 percent of drug-related convictions and 74 percent of prison sentences for drug-related crimes. Put another way, the rise in the number of convictions, sentences, and prison commitments for drug offenses over the late 1980s and early 1990s accounted for 42 percent of total growth in the number of black inmates, but only 26 percent of the growth in white inmates (Mauer and Huling 1996; Sampson and Laub 1993a).

Institutionalizing Marginality: The War on Drugs as a Case Study

To illustrate and elaborate our view on mass incarceration, we consider the policies that constituted the War on Drugs. This case is particularly apt for several reasons. First, trafficking in illegal drugs is a classic economic crime, and it attracted increasing numbers of young minority men in disadvantaged and disordered inner-city communities during the 1980s and early 1990s. Second, these policies were quantitatively important in explaining the growth of prison admissions and prison inmates over this period and in particular, the increasing incarceration rates of less-educated inner-city minority men.

Viewed in light of the Blumstein-Cohen thesis—that society would adjust drug law and enforcement policies to limit the scope of officially sanctioned punishment and thus, the extent of incarceration—the War on Drug policies also represent a clear anomaly. They intensified the use of coercive control against what had been deemed to be more marginal offenders and offenses and amplified rather than offset the trend of increasing incarceration rates. Contemporary policymakers and analysts advocating these "get tough" measures took a different view, and advanced at least three distinct arguments in favor of these policy innovations and their selective application. The most extreme explained the rash of violent drug-related crime by the breakdown of values or conventional social norms in disadvantaged communities, evidenced by the spread of families headed by young single women dependent on welfare. This environment, it was argued, bred new cohorts of "superpredators," violent sociopaths for whom incapacitation through a lengthy prison spell was the only alternative (see, for example, DiIulio 1996a, 1996b; Wilson 1975).

A second related view, referred to as the "broken windows" thesis, questioned the very notion of a marginal offender and offense (Wilson and Kelling 1982). Even minor infractions, it was argued, would reinforce disorder and antisocial norms in already disadvantaged neighborhoods and eventually cause more serious crime. The final view, popular among policymakers, proclaimed the dire epidemiological and pharmacological properties of "crack" versus powder cocaine and reinforced the concerns about "broken windows" and "superpredators" (Murakawa 2005, 19–20; Harrison 2001). Crack was considered to be "instantly addictive" and inherently criminogenic, inciting users to violence, and so defied the very notion of a "casual" user. And addicted young mothers, it was assumed, readily transmitted the drug to their newborn children and so spread its noxious properties intergenerationally.

Despite their initial popularity, none of these arguments have fared well under close scholarly scrutiny. Strikingly, at the time of the congressional debates that singled out crack-related violations for harsher punishment, there was scant research to justify the assertions of its harmful effects. And, as reported in the U.S. Sentencing Commission's (1995) special report on crack, subsequent research has found no evidence to support any of the claims about crack, especially in comparison to powder cocaine and other legal drugs such as alcohol. Likewise, systematic studies of inner-city communities see a spurious causal connection between "broken windows" and serious crime, both of which stem from neighborhood social disorder and disadvantage (Sampson and Raudenbush 1999; Taylor 2000; Fagan and Davies 2000).

Last but not least, the notion of a cohort of "superpredators" is inconsistent with the trends in drug-related lethal violence from the mid-1980s to early 1990s. As seen in figure 2.8, these ideas gained wide circulation because of the "unprecedented epidemic" of homicides committed by male adolescent and young adults.[31] Yet in 1985, at the onset of the crack epidemic, these cohorts "experienced a far lower homicide rate (of both commission and victimization)" than they did in the early 1990s, near the epidemic's peak. Moreover, their homicide (victimization) rates in 1985 were among the lowest of any cohort since the early 1960s.[32] In other words, in 1985—when they were ten to fourteen and fifteen to nineteen years old—these adolescents displayed none of the moral lapses later attributed to them, and in fact were less likely to be involved in lethal violent crime than any cohort in the preceding two decades.

The sharp rise and equally precipitous decline in homicide commission rates is more consistent with an epidemic—tied to a particular time period rather than a particular cohort. This alternative hypothesis focuses on pivotal innovations in the drug trade, the spread of crack cocaine, and the social organization of crack distribution networks. A composite "crack index," based on arrests, police self-reports, hospital

Figure 2.8   Male Homicide Offending Rates, by Race and Age, 1976 to 2005

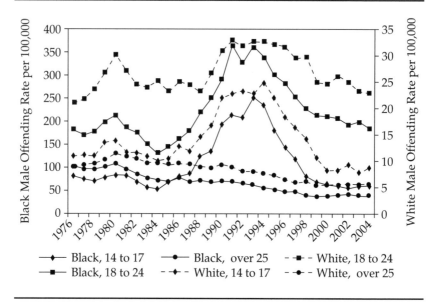

Source: Fox and Zawitz (2006).

admissions for overdoses, death records, and newspaper reports, is strongly correlated with the rash of lethal handgun violence (Fryer et al. 2005). Moreover, the onset of the homicide epidemic tended to follow by about one to two years the spread of crack into cities first on the northern East Coast and the West Coast and then into interior regions (Cohen et al. 1998; Cork 1999).

Crack cocaine, unlike the purer powder form, tapped a large potential demand in the prevailing conditions of economic decline and social disorder in inner-city minority neighborhoods (Reuter, MacCoun, and Murphy 1990; Hagedorn 1998b; Levitt and Venkatesh 2000). Diluted through processing, it is a less volatile but still potent drug, which can be smoked to yield an immediate intense high even in small inexpensive doses. The vaster more open market for crack, in turn, sparked the transformation of inner-city gangs from social peer groups into economic organizations for mass distribution. Paralleling the shift in the gang's ethos from a "family" to a "business," its membership policies took on a more decidedly "corporate" flavor and opened recruitment to the able-bodied, not necessarily the like-minded. Because of their dim prospects in legal labor markets, adolescent boys flocked to these fledgling enterprises to queue up for entry-level positions as touts, lookouts, and runners in the drug trade and persisted in the gangs for extended spells.[33] Moreover, they were routinely equipped with hand-guns and wielded these weapons in the social-economic regulation of the drug trade, especially in the early phases of market expansion, when disputes over territory and lines of market and organizational authority were more frequent.

In retrospect, then, we can see the War on Drugs as an overreaction to this transitory episode, what has been likened to a "moral panic."[34] This perspective raises the obvious question of why policymakers advocated and the public embraced this decisive shift in criminal-justice policies, especially as the "get tough" rhetoric followed so quickly on the heels of the early 1970s initiatives to liberalize drug laws. Synthesizing the research on the criminology and politics of the period, we suggest two ways to explain both the direction of this policy innovation and the greater openness to it.

To understand the policy change, we must reconsider the notion of a marginal offender, so central to the Blumstein-Cohen thesis and the earlier policy debates. To criminologists, the term "marginal offender" connotes one pole on a spectrum of the propensity to commit crimes over say the course of a year, which they call lambda (Blumstein 1983; Spelman 2000b, 111). Marginal offenders are seen to have lower individual crime rates (lambdas), but also commit less serious (nonviolent, victimless) crimes. Economists, by contrast, see marginal offenders in terms of a tradeoff, an allocation of time by a person between legal and illicit work, depending on the relative rewards and risks of each. On the margin between legal and illicit work, their criminal participation is economically contingent, and increases to offset their poor prospects in formal labor markets such as lower real wages and declining or more erratic work hours.

Most offenders are marginal in both senses. They commit crimes for economic reasons, but limit the scope of their criminal activity to be able to maintain their legal employment and contact with their families (Hagedorn 1998b; Piehl 1998; Fagan and Freeman 1999; Edin et al. 2004). One exception to this generalization, and possibly the most significant one, was the low-level gang members who trafficked in the crack cocaine trade during the mid-1980s to early 1990s. Economically motivated, they also contributed significantly to the lethal handgun violence (see figure 2.8). According to estimates based on the 1997 survey of state prison inmates, approximately 20 to 25 percent of "marginal" drug offenders, who were apprehended with small drug amounts or played a "minor role" in drug dealing, reported having a violent-crime or gun record (Sevigny and Caulkins 2004, 414–15; Lynch and Sabol 2000, 11). And about one-half more had a prior nondrug conviction. Thus, it was critically significant that at this historical juncture, proponents of the War on Drugs had ample exemplars to convince a public increasingly wary of street crime, especially in its more lethal forms, of the need for harsher sanctions against more marginal offenders and offenses.

What must still be explained is the scope of the policy reform and its uneven incidence. Even though Eric L. Sevigny and Jonathan P. Caulkins (2004, 422) reject the common criticism that drug laws have filled prisons with "low-level" nonviolent drug sellers with no prior record, they still conclude that "most incarcerated drug offenders gave no evidence of being violent and [of] . . . having played a sophisticated organizational role" in drug gangs. Indeed, they estimate that the modal offender (40 percent of the total) was a "juggler" who committed drug or other nonviolent crimes to support a habit. Moreover, the evidence suggests, casting the indiscriminate net of "get tough" policies led to the disproportionate arrest, conviction, and incarceration of male drug offenders in inner-city minority communities, not just those in the "underclass" (Lynch and Sabol 2000, 10–12).

We conceptualize this dimension of the problem in terms of an "inclusion-exclusion" scale to describe policies "governing social marginality."[35] More inclusive policies seek to incorporate disadvantaged individuals into the socioeconomic mainstream or at the very least to provide them with a modicum of material support. Inclusive policies comprise social welfare and antipoverty redistributive programs but also civil rights laws and enforcement efforts and employment-labor relations policies. Indeed, the last two are credited with significantly narrowing the racial employment-earnings gap from the late 1940s until the early 1970s (see, for example, Heckman and Payner 1989; Zeitlin and Weyher 2001).

By contrast, the policies of mass incarceration are "situated far toward the exclusion pole" (Greenberg and West 2001, 623). This characterization is perhaps surprising, given the conventional placement of social welfare and civil rights agencies and the criminal-justice system into distinct policy domains. Yet, it is entirely consistent with the "get tough on crime" rhetoric dating from the late 1950s and culminating in the War on Drug policies of the 1980s. As initially formulated by conservative southern Democrats and Republicans, it was directed against civil rights legislation and protests and regarded the promise of racial equality and integration as criminogenic forces (Beckett 1997, 30–35; Murakawa 2005, 89–91). Fueled by race riots and surging crime rates in inner cities in the late 1960s and early 1970s as well as the macroeconomic turbulence of the latter decade, it evolved into a sustained critique of Great Society reforms that were seen as the cause, not the cure, of poverty, social disorder, and crime as well as of economic stagnation (see Guetzkow 2006b; Garland 2001b).

Statistical analyses discussed in the first section of this chapter corroborate the qualitative accounts drawn from congressional debates and hearings, party platforms, and the speeches of high-level officials. They show a robust inverse correlation between state-level incarceration rates (or spending on prisons) and welfare expenditures, which locate state governments on the social inclusion-exclusion scale. Likewise, they find that a political realignment from more liberal Democratic to more conservative Republican control is positively correlated with a shift in spending priorities from social inclusion to social exclusion policies and in turn to an increase in incarceration rates. According to the results of Greenberg and West (2001, 633), additional state welfare spending of thirty dollars per person would reduce state incarceration rates by 19 percent. Likewise, the analysis by Katherine Beckett and Western (2001, 47) implies that the gap in state welfare spending between Texas and New York can account for roughly one-third of the difference in their incarceration rates.

Significantly, the implied trade-off between social inclusion and social exclusion policies steepened during the 1980s and early 1990s, precisely when inner-city minority communities suffered from both cyclical and structural economic shocks. This evidence corroborates our labor-market thesis on mass incarceration, but also underscores our emphasis on the political over the more narrowly conceived economic causes. While acknowledging the impacts of skill-biased technological and organizational change, recent research on the declining fortunes of less-skilled workers and their communities in the 1980s assigns a significant causal role to more "episodic" policy-institutional changes, notably the erosion of the real value of the minimum wage and of union bargaining strength.[36]

The case of the minimum wage vividly illustrates the conservative backlash against the policies of social inclusion (see figure 2.9). The failure to adjust the nominal level to keep pace with inflation over the decade 1979 to 1989 depressed the minimum wage's real value by 30 percent, from $7.41 to $5.22 per hour. Relative to the average wages of all private nonsupervisory workers, the minimum wage measures the increasing earnings gap facing young, less-educated workers in formal labor markets and the lower opportunity cost of allocating their labor from legal to illegal work. Thus, the political realignments and policy shifts from the late 1970s through the 1980s not only resulted in harsher criminal sanctions against all drug offenders, but contributed significantly to the social economic disorder in inner-city minority communities that spawned the violent drug epidemics.

A Revolving Door?

In conclusion we shift our focus from prison admissions to releases. As Jeremy Travis (2005, xxii–xxvi) reminds us, this alternative perspective follows inexorably from the "iron law" of imprisonment. Because "they

Figure 2.9   Real and Relative Value of the Minimum Wage, 1970 to 2005

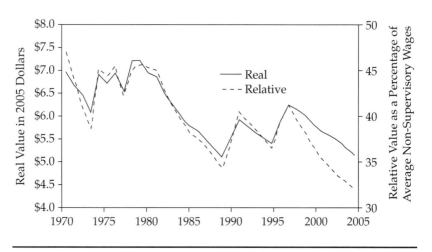

Source: Mishel, Bernstein, and Allegretto (2006).

all come back [from prison]," mass incarceration necessarily leads to the mass exodus of released prisoners. Over 93 percent of all state prisoners will eventually leave prison; they will either complete their sentences in prison or be released under parole supervision (Petersilia 2003, 22). Indeed, estimates derived from a 1997 survey imply that nearly one-half of state inmates will be released within one year, and three-quarters will be released within five years (U.S. Government Accountability Office 2001, 13).

The graphs in figure 2.10 vividly illustrate Travis's iron law. They trace out the annual flow of men into and out of state prisons from 1977 to 1998, that is, from the onset of the regime of mass incarceration through the War on Drugs.[37] Over these two decades the number of men entering prison annually soared from 153,600 to 553,200, or by 260 percent, which virtually matches the run-up in incarceration rates. Annual prison releases moved in parallel fashion, as evidenced by the simple correlation coefficient of .996 between the two series. According to the most recent BJS estimates, 697,100 and 672,200 individuals, respectively, entered and exited state prisons in 2004 (Harrison and Beck 2005, 6).

Travis's study focuses on the manifold "challenges" facing released prisoners as they reenter life on the outside. These challenges emanate from distinct political-economic sources. Travis (2005) emphasizes the more political, which range from the "extended reach of supervision" to the "expanded universe of invisible punishment." The former refers

Figure 2.10   Men Admitted to and Released from Prison, 1977 to 1998

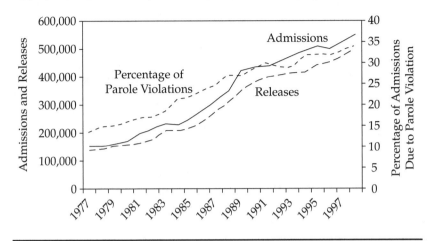

Source: U.S. Department of Justice, Bureau of Justice Statistics (2006).

to growth in the proportion of prisoners under conditional release, who are subject to close monitoring by parole officers.[38] The latter refers to state and federal legislation that denies "rights and privileges" (such as voting rights) to many ex-felons and so extends the official length of their sentences, in some cases indefinitely.[39] For example, individuals convicted of a drug felony offense lose their eligibility for federal welfare benefits, subsidized housing, and higher education tuition and loan programs (U.S. Government Accountability Office 2005).

These barriers to prisoner reentry also operate at an informal, more "environmental," level. The vast majority of prisoners return to their home communities and so face the same gloomy socioeconomic conditions as when they left, although the cumulative toll of mass incarceration may cause further socioeconomic disadvantage and disorganization. What's more, these individuals return with a prison experience, which can weaken if not dissolve attachments to families, social networks, and the formal labor market.

These combined challenges do not prevent released prisoners from "going straight," but they do diminish their odds. In other words, they increase the likelihood that released prisoners will commit a technical parole violation, misdemeanor, or more serious felony offense, and so wind up back in prison. A more extended prison spell or additional prison spells can in turn transform the marginal offender into a more serious one, who has accumulated a lengthier rap sheet but also has become more deeply enmeshed in illegal rather than legal social networks. Thus, the regime of mass incarceration threatens to confine those on the socioeconomic margin to a revolving door of crime–prison–release–crime and so to stamp them more indelibly as outcasts.

The subsequent chapters in this volume test this revolving-door hypothesis at the individual, or micro, level. Working on the premise that there is a connection between employment, crime, and imprisonment, they assess how a prison record affects an individual's employment prospects (see also the analyses in chapters 7, 8, and 9) and how local labor-market conditions affect the likelihood of recidivism and a return trip to prison (see chapters 9 and 10). To set the stage for their more in-depth causal analyses, we present more aggregate evidence of this revolving door in operation.

The third graph in figure 2.10 (see the broken line) shows a disturbing trend, a steady increase in the share of new prison admissions that are due to parole revocations. These unsuccessful parole stints accounted for only 13 percent of new prison admissions in 1977, 36 percent in 1998, and 34 percent in 2004. Put another way, 39 percent of those exiting from parole were reincarcerated either for a technical parole violation or an arrest and conviction for a new felony offense (Glaze and Palla 2005, 9). Technical violations are by far the more common cause. Even if a parolee has been arrested for a new felony offense, criminal-justice authorities often opt for pursuing the parole violation, because it is an easier pathway back to prison than a new crime, trial, and judgment.[40]

One would expect parole revocations on technical grounds to tend to be greater in states where parole budgets have not kept pace with the swelling parole population (Petersilia 1999, 499–506). Burdened with increasing caseloads, parole agents are unable to monitor their charges closely, and being risk-averse, they tend to use technical violations preemptively as an indicator of future more serious offending. California is the prime example. The percentage of male parolees who were returned to prison within a year of their release soared from 11 percent in 1975 to 88 percent in 1989, although the figure has declined steadily to 61 percent in 2004. Over the same period, the share of parole reincarceration for technical violations increased from one-half to just over three-quarters.[41]

Trends in recidivism rates offer an alternative, stricter test of the revolving-door hypothesis. The BJS gauges recidivism along two dimensions, the point of contact with the criminal-justice system (a new arrest by the police versus a new conviction and prison sentence by the courts) and time since release. The most recent systematic evidence is based on a fifteen-state sample of inmates released in 1994 (see figure 2.11). After six months, 30 percent of the sample population had been arrested on a new felony charge, but only 5 percent had been returned

Figure 2.11   Recidivism Rates of State Prisoners Released in 1994

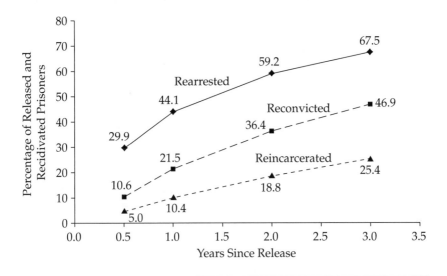

Source: Langan and Levin (2002).

to prison to serve a new sentence. After three years, these figures increased to around 68 percent of the sample that had been arrested on a new felony charge and 25 percent who returned to prison to serve a new sentence—and another quarter of the sample population was back in prison on parole revocations (Langan and Levin 2002, 7).

The experience of the 1994 cohort justifies concerns about high recidivism rates, but not necessarily a more rapidly revolving door. When they compared cohorts of prisoners released from the same eleven states in 1983 and 1994, Patrick A. Langan and David J. Levin (2002) found only a slight but statistically significant increase in rearrest rates, from 62.5 percent to 67.5 percent (see column 1 of table 2.2).[42] There is, however, one significant exception to this generalization. Over the decade rearrest rates for released drug offenders jumped by nearly a third, from 50.4 percent to 66.7 percent. While this aggregate evidence suggests that changes in the drug trade and drug enforcement policy may have snared drug offenders within the same revolving door as the one that snared other prisoners, it may also reflect changes in the composition of this growing prison population to include those more likely to recidivate.

Although not strictly comparable, reincarceration rates, including those for parole revocations, increased sharply between 1983 and 1994, from 41.4 percent to 51.8 percent for all released prisoners and from

30.3 percent to 49.2 percent (or by 60 percent) for drug offenders (see the last column in table 2.2).[43] Significantly, the recent rash of technical parole violations accounted for around half of all returning prisoners among the 1994 cohort. The frequent preemptive use of technical violations to return parolees to prison, moreover, implies that conventional measures will likely understate recidivism rates in 1994 as compared to 1983.[44]

The evidence from both cohorts also contrasts the recidivism rates of more marginal and serious offenders, in the criminological sense. The analysis gauges marginality by the number of prior arrests, where those with only one prior arrest were released from their first prison spell. As shown in figure 2.12, more serious offenders with more prior arrests experienced higher rearrest rates one and three years after their release from prison (on their most recent commitment). For the 1994 cohort, marginal offenders with one prior arrest had one-year rearrest rates averaging 20.6 percent, and the most hardened types with sixteen arrests or more had 61 percent rearrest rates. The same overall pattern holds for three-year arrest rates, although over this longer period more marginal offenders face nearly double the recidivism risk.

The graphs in figure 2.12 also display the same cross-sectional relationships for the 1983 cohort. Viewed together, the graphs suggest that despite the sharp increase in incarceration rates, especially for drug crimes, over the decade, marginal offenders did not face a greater recidivism risk, at least measured along this dimension. Still, because of the mounting reincarceration risk over the period, the pattern implies a new pathway of increasing recidivism. Whether he returns to prison on a new conviction and commitment or a technical violation, a marginal offender will likely face a greater rearrest risk upon his subsequent release, in part because he may receive closer scrutiny from his parole officer and the local police and less lenient treatment upon rearrest.

The increasing flux of prison admissions for technical parole violations, rather than new commitments, reinforces our central message that policy matters. In this case we are referring to the phenomenon of "back-end" sentencing through the parole system rather than "front-end" sentencing by the courts. As the careful research of Travis and his colleagues has convincingly shown, shifts in parole policy, whether conscious or inadvertent, not in criminal offending by parolees, explain the dramatic fluctuations in technical parole revocations (Travis 2005, 49–50). And as the extreme case of California clearly demonstrates, the combination of a harsh regime of punishment on both the "front" and "back" ends has resulted in persistent, high incarceration rates, despite the recent abundant evidence of sharp declines in criminal offending.

These divergent trends—in prison admissions and populations on the one hand and crime rates on the other—raise the concern that un-

Table 2.2   Recidivism Rates, by Offense Type and Year of Release

Most Serious Offense	Prisoners Released		Rearrested Within Three Years		Reconvicted Within Three Years		Returned to Prison Within Three Years[a]		
	1983	1994	1983	1994	1983	1994	1983, New[b]	1994, New[b]	All[c]
All released prisoners	100.0%	100.0%	62.5%	67.5%	46.8%	46.9%	41.4%	25.4%	51.8%
Violent	34.6	22.5	59.6	61.7	41.9	39.9	36.5	20.4	48.8
Property	48.3	33.5	68.1	73.8	53.0	53.4	47.7	30.5	56.4
Drug	9.5	32.6	50.4	66.7	35.3	47.0	30.3	25.2	49.2
Public-order	6.4	9.7	54.6	62.2	41.5	42.0	34.7	21.6	48.0
Other	1.1	1.7	76.8	64.7	62.9	42.1	59.2	20.7	66.9
Released prisoners	108,580	272,111							

Source: Langan and Levin (2002, 11).

[a] The first six columns are based on samples of released prisoners from the same eleven states. In the last column the 1994 data are based on samples of prisoners from fifteen states, including the original eleven.

[b] "New" stands for the released prisoners returned to prison on a new felony sentence.

[c] "All" includes prisoners returned on a technical parole violation as well.

Figure 2.12   One-Year and Three-Year Rearrest Rates, by Prior Arrests, for 1983 and 1994 Cohorts of Released Prisoners

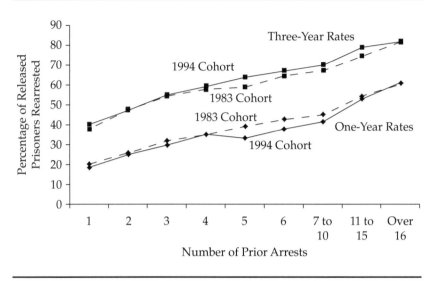

Source: Langan and Levin (2002).

der the new regime of mass incarceration the United States is locked into a new stable equilibrium of punishment, albeit at levels vastly greater than Blumstein and his colleagues originally conceived in the early 1970s. Before we hazard such a prediction, however, it is worth repeating the obvious but central lesson from any such extrapolation based on historical data. The past is prologue, Blumstein and Cohen (1973, 200) note, only if we assume "a given society in a relatively stable period." Writing in the early 1970s they hardly could have foreseen the impending seismic shifts that would transform the U.S. political economy and its criminal-justice system over the next two decades. They were certainly cognizant, however, of the considerable ferment over the increasing levels of street crime and criminal justice policies, but they selectively focused on, for example, the more "liberal" rather "coercive" provisions of the 1970 Drug Abuse Prevention and Control Act (Peterson 1985; see also Tonry 1996, 6–130).

Likewise, any projection of recent trends in incarceration rates must focus on only one side of the current debate over criminal justice policies, and ignore novel policy experiments offering alternatives to prison. Because our analysis centered on the impact of the War on Drugs on marginal drug offenders, we consider the case of drug courts, which have proliferated across all fifty states since the mid-1990s. Drug courts represent a combination of criminal justice and medical models, that is, coercive sanctions and rehabilitative programming. Evidence from a randomized experiment in Baltimore suggests that the benefits of drug courts depend on sustained effective substance abuse and related treatments, and that sanctions are a necessary component to enlist otherwise reluctant candidates into these program and to ensure completion (Banks and Gottfredson 2003; see also Belenko 2001; Rempel et al. 2003; National Institute of Justice 2006).

The increasing popularity and investments in drug courts have made them subject to increasingly systematic and sophisticated evaluations, including comprehensive benefit-cost calculations. For the cases where researchers have sufficient data based on experimental (or quasi-experimental) designs, they find that drug courts satisfy three criteria of effectiveness. At the minimal level, their threat of sanctions for non-compliance with treatment programs results in higher completion rates than for control populations. According to Banks and Gottfredson (2003, 405–7), it is of critical importance that courts ensure that participants receive a minimum threshold of treatment necessary to influence outcomes. As for the outcomes, in the majority of cases extended participation in, if not completion of, drug court treatment significantly lowers recidivism rates, by 12 percentage points in the Clarke County, Georgia, experiment and 15 to 16 percentage points in the Baltimore case (U.S. National Institute of Justice 2006; Gottfredson et al. 2006; Belenko 2001). More-limited evidence also suggests that these effects are enduring beyond the treatment period.

Finally, a comprehensive benefit-cost calculation also favors drug courts over "business as usual." In terms of direct expenditures, their greater treatment costs are more than offset by economies in the use of jail and probation. Furthermore, lower recidivism rates translate into substantial notional savings to potential victims and criminal-justice authorities for the additional offenses not committed by longer-term participants and graduates. These public safety and fiscal benefits tend to be greater for low- to midlevel drug offenders, who commit crimes to feed their drug habits. In other words, "jugglers" identified by Sevigny and Caulkins are the most appropriate candidates for the drug court alternative. Because they make up at least 40 percent of all prisoners incarcerated for drug crimes and thus almost 10 percent of all inmates, the potential impact of institutionalizing this reform is by no means marginal.

David Weiman would like to acknowledge research support from Barnard College and the able research assistance of Rachel Barza, Nayirie Kuyumjian, and Jessica Swithenbank.

Notes

1. The prison incarceration rate is defined as the total number of offenders in federal and state prisons per 100,000 of the population. The series is based on the extant, comprehensive data on the U.S. prison population in Ann L. Pastore and Kathleen McGuire (2006, tables 6.28.2004 and 6.13.2005). Blumstein, Cohen, and Daniel S. Nagin (1976, 318–19) present similar evidence for Norway and Canada, although their incarceration rates were only one-half of the U.S. level. One measure of stability is the coefficient of variation, the ratio of the standard deviation to the mean, which was only 11.2 percent.

2. The total-crime and violent-crime rates (per 100,000 people) more than doubled over the 1960s. The longer series on arrest rates shows a steady increase since 1951 (Carter et al. 1997, series H952 and 953).

3. The quotation is Senator Christopher Dodd's contribution to the 1969 congressional debate, quoted in Ruth D. Peterson (1985, 255; see also Murakawa 2005, 14–15).

4. Prison and jail inmates made up 31 percent of the total; the rest were either on parole (10 percent) or probation (59 percent). See www.ojp.usdoj.gov/bjs/glance/tables/corr2tab.htm.

5. The exact timing of the trend break is unclear. Incarceration rates increased sharply between 1973 and 1978, but so did factors associated with greater crime such as rising unemployment rates and declining real wages. More striking, especially in relation to earlier cyclical patterns, is the continued increase in incarceration rates during the economic recovery of the late 1970s and the mid-1980s.

6. David J. Rothman (1980/2002, see especially chapter 2) and the American Bar Association, Justice Kennedy Commission (2004, 11) refer to the "rehabilitative or 'medical' model," while Michael H. Tonry (1996, 4) and Jeremy Travis (2005, chapter 1) emphasize the "system" or "ideal" of indeterminate sentencing. In practice, of course, the prior regime did not always live up to its lofty principles. Analyzing U.S. incarceration trends since the mid-nineteenth century, Margaret Cahalan (1979, 37–38) observes only a slight drift toward the use of prison for more serious violent crimes. The vast majority of inmates, she concludes, were imprisoned for economic or property crimes, which often inflicted only modest economic losses (though, in the case of robbery, a threat of violence). Likewise, advocates of sentencing reform in the 1970s documented procedural lapses and racial-class biases of judges and parole boards in determining prison sentences and terms, and questioned the effectiveness of prison programming in the face of high crime and recidivism rates (see Frankel 1972; for a more recent take, see Tonry 1996, 7–10; Travis 2005, 17–20; and Hofer et al. 2004).

7. Conversely, the benefits of an expanded prison system are measured by incapacitation and deterrent effects, the quantitative impact on crime rates of imprisoning additional offenders. Needless to say, these concepts are easier to define than to estimate empirically (Levitt 1996; Nagin 1998; and Spelman 2000a, 2000b).

8. The six categories—murder, robbery, assault, burglary, drugs, and sexual

assault—accounted for 77 percent of all state prison inmates in 1996. The analysis uses a simple accounting identity: incarceration rate = (crime rate) (arrests/crime)(prison commitments/arrest)(average prison term). Like the incarceration rate, the crime rate is measured per 100,000 people. The average prison term is estimated by the number of prisoners per new commitments and so includes the additional time for parole violations.

9. The one exception is aggravated assault, where crime rates increased sharply over the period and accounted for nearly 40 percent of the growth in the incarceration rate. Still, criminologists question whether these data are measuring more crimes or more reporting of crimes, especially for sexual abuse and domestic violence (Blumstein and Beck 1999, 30; Boggess and Bound 1997, 726–30).

10. By drug crimes and drug incarceration rate, we are referring to arrests and imprisonment for drug possession and drug trafficking.

11. The distribution of prison admissions by crime type may more accurately measure the quantitative impact of the War on Drugs, because the prison population more heavily weights serious crimes, which carry longer prison sentences and terms. Between 1980 and 1990 the number of new court commitments to state prisons per 1,000 drug arrests increased from 19 to 103, and by 2001 drug crimes accounted for nearly one-third of prison admissions (see Ditton and Wilson 1999, 4; and the BJS spreadsheets on "The Most Serious Offense of State Prisoners," at http://www.ojp.usdoj.gov/ bjs/prisons.htm#selected).

12. On the basis of the actual time served by cohorts of released prisoners, Western (2006, 45) estimates that average prison terms for drug offenders increased from 14.3 to 24.3, or by 10 months, between 1980 and 2000. According to Timothy A. Hughes, Doris James Wilson, and Beck (2001, 5), the average sentence for drug offenses remained virtually constant over the 1990s, but the mean time served increased by seven months, or about one-third. In other words, drug offenders served 42.8 percent of their sentence in 1999, as compared to only 32.9 percent in 1990.

13. See Beckett and Western (2001); Greenberg and West (2001); Western (2006); and Joshua Guetzkow (2006a). Typical independent variables include violent-crime, property-crime, and drug arrest rates; the adoption of determinate sentencing policies; a Republican governor (or Democratic legislature), welfare expenditures, and popular political attitudes; and the racial-ethnic composition of the population and urbanization, unemployment, and poverty rates.

14. Greenberg and West (2001, 637) downplay the War on Drugs, because, as they correctly observe and our calculations confirm, changes in crime and drug arrest rates account for less than one-half of the increase in incarceration rates in the 1980s. Their assessment of the War on Drugs, however, ignores the drug–violent-crime nexus during this period. This link may help to explain their regression estimates (2001, table 3). They show a strong positive correlation between changes in incarceration rates and the lagged level of the violent-crime rate, which in our view precipitated the "moral panic" over the crack–violent-crime epidemic (Sampson and Lauritsen 1997, 36).

15. We focus only on African American and white populations because of limitations in the data. Patrick A. Langan (1985, 1991) estimates the racial composition of new prison admissions over a longer horizon, from 1926 to 1986, and shows a doubling of the black share from 21 to 44 percent. The sharpest increase occurred in the immediate post–World War II period. See also Pamela E. Oliver and James E. Yocom (2004).

16. The gaps in figure 2.3 arise because the BJS significantly revised its methodology for estimating the racial-ethnic composition of the prison population in 1997 (Dillard and Beck 1998, 9–10). Because of the changes, earlier and later population estimates, especially of white inmates, may not be consistent. (For example, according to BJS estimates, the white prison population fell by one-quarter between 1997 and 1999.) Despite the gaps, the evidence suggests a linear increase in the black-to-white ratio from 7.3 to 1 in 1993 to 7.7 to 1 in 2000, which yields our 20 percent growth rate over the War on Drugs.

17. The census survey does not explicitly enumerate the prison population, but it does note whether individuals were institutionalized during the survey period. By interpreting this variable as an indicator of incarceration, Raphael derives national estimates of the prison population that roughly accord with official counts. He compares the fraction of black males incarcerated (that is institutionalized) by age and educational level.

18. In grouping together those with at most some college education, Pettit and Western control for selection bias stemming from the increasing rates of high school graduation over the period.

19. Lynch and William J. Sabol (2000) document similar patterns showing the disproportionate share of the Ohio state prison population from Cleveland neighborhoods, as do Todd R. Clear, Dina Rose, and Judith A. Ryder (2001) for the Florida prison population from Tallahassee neighborhoods.

20. See Lawrence R. Mishel, Jared Bernstein, and Sylvia Allegretto (2006, especially chapter 3). The real hourly wage of production and nonsupervisory workers grew from $9.00 in 1947 to $15.76 in 1973 (2.3 percent per year), but then fell over the next two decades to $14.81 in 1995, or by −.4 percent per year. The decline in the wages of entry-level male workers with a high school degree was even sharper, from $13.39 in 1973 to $10.15 in 1995, an annual decline rate of −1.32 percent.

21. See John Bound and Richard B. Freeman (1992) and Lincoln Quillian (2003). In a recent article Louis Uchitelle ("Labor's Lost; for Blacks, a Dream in Decline," New York Times, October 23, 2005, section 4, 1) emphasizes the interaction between the decline in key industrial sectors and industrial unions, because blacks were disproportionately represented in and benefited from unions (see also Ashenfelter 1972; Freeman and Medoff 1984, 48–52; Zeitlin and Weyher 2001).

22. See Peter Reuter, Robert MacCoun, and Peter Murphy (1990); Samuel L. Myers (1992); and Hagedorn (1998a, 9–10). Caroline Wolf Harlow (2003) presents some corroborating evidence based on the 1997 survey of state prison inmates. Over 60 percent of prisoners, even those without a high school degree, reported full- or part-time legitimate work and hence legal

sources of income during the month prior to their arrest. At the same time, 16 percent of jail inmates had to drop out of high school because of their illegal activities.

23. See Gould, Weinberg, and Mustard (2002); Raphael and Rudolf Winter-Ember (2001); Freeman and William M. Rodgers III (2000); and Grogger (1998). Earlier analyses of the labor-market–crime nexus detected a small positive relationship between unemployment and property crimes (Cook and Zarkin 1985; Chiricos 1987). David Cantor and Kenneth C. Land (1985) attributed this result to the offsetting impact of diminished crime opportunities during a cyclical downturn. Later studies questioned the empirical relevance of this effect (Devine, Sheley, and Smith 1988; Greenberg 2001; Britt 1997), but also the value of aggregate data in resolving the empirical issue (Levitt 2001). We therefore focus on more recent studies, which exploit finer variations across states or local areas like metropolitan counties.

24. Eric D. Gould, Bruce A. Weinberg, and David B. Mustard (2002, 52–53); and Raphael and Winter-Ebmer (2001, 274–76). Keith R. Ihlandfeldt (2007) also shows a strong correlation between neighborhood unemployment and crime rates, especially in black communities. Lance Lochner and Enrico Moretti (2004) offer an alternative perspective, finding a strong negative correlation between criminal activity and educational attainment, which affects individuals' labor-market opportunities. They do not, however, specify the precise causal mechanism through which schooling influences individual decisions to engage in criminal activity.

25. The chart tracks rates of property crimes (burglary, larceny, motor vehicle theft, fraud, possession and selling of stolen property, destruction of property, trespassing, vandalism, and other offenses), violent crimes (murder, manslaughter, rape, sexual assault, robbery, assault, extortion, and other offenses), and drug-related arrests for possession, manufacturing, trafficking, and other offenses. The recent data come from U.S. Federal Bureau of Investigation (FBI), Uniform Crime Reporting Program, Crime in the United States 2005 (at http://www.fbi.gov/ucr/05cius/index.html); historical data have been compiled by the U.S. Census Bureau, Statistical Abstract, Table H-23 on crime rates (http://www.census.gov/statab/hist) and the U.S. Bureau of Justice Statistics for drug arrests (http://www.ojp.usdoj.gov/bjs/dcf/enforce.htm).

26. Citing the same studies, Steven D. Levitt (2004, 170–71) downplays the direct effects of the economic boom in lowering crime rates. Levitt, however, only focuses on the unemployment-crime relationship, whereas Gould, Weinberg, and Mustard (2002) and, earlier, Grogger (1998) emphasize the impact of wages as well.

27. The simple correlation coefficient between property-crime and violent-crime rates is .983 for the period 1960 to 1986 but only .477 for the period 1983 to 1995.

28. Between 1983 and 1995 the simple correlation between drug arrest and violent-crime rates is .605, as compared to .275 for property-crime rates.

29. See Freeman and Rodgers (2000); and Holzer, Paul Offner, and Elaine Sorensen (2005). Although the economic boom reversed the hemorrhaging of

jobs in downtown business districts, the evidence suggests that jobs continued to leave black neighborhoods in the late 1990s (Raphael and Stoll 2002;
Rosen, Kim, and Patel 2003).

30. On the greater use of illegal drugs by whites than by blacks, see Johnson,
et al. (1996); Jonathan P. Caulkins and Sara Chandler (2006); Tonry (1995,
chapter 3); and Marc Mauer (1999, chapter 9). The evidence on drug dealing is sketchier but points in the same direction (Riley 1997; Hagedorn
1998a; Fairlie 2002). Robert W. Fairlie, for example, finds that among those
interviewed in the 1980 wave of the NLSY 1979 sample, whites were more
likely to engage in drug dealing than blacks. Benjamin Bowling (1999), Fagan and Davies (2000), Darnell F. Hawkins and Cedric Herring (2000), and
Beckett (2004) discuss racial profiling in the policing of drug markets.

31. See Philip J. Cook and John H. Laub (1998); Blumstein and Richard Rosenfeld (1998); and Jeffrey Fagan, Franklin E. Zimring, and June Kim (1998).
The data on homicide offending rates come from the Bureau of Justice Statistics webpage, "Homicide Trends in the U.S.," at http://www.ojp.usdoj
.gov/bjs/homicide/tables/oarstab.htm.

32. Because of data limitations, Cook and Laub (1998, 52–53) estimate involvement in lethal violence by homicide victimization, not offending, rates. As
their analysis shows, these measures are highly correlated because they
gauge the same phenomenon. See also Cook and Laub (2002) and Ted Joyce
(2004a, 2004b). The "superpredator" thesis also cannot explain the coinci-
dental sharp increase in homicide offending rates, albeit at much lower
levels, by white adolescents and young adults shown in figure 2.8. For a
more general critique of such cohort or "group-based" hypotheses of crime
trends, see Sampson and Laub (2005).

33. Researchers disagree on the returns to these jobs. Reuter, MacCoun, and
Murphy (1990) estimated that the average drug-trade foot soldier in Washington, D.C., earned thirty dollars per hour in 1989; see also Freeman (1996)
and John Hagedorn (1998a). The Chicago gang members studied by Levitt
and Sudhir Alladi Venkatesh (2000) barely made the minimum wage, but
could dramatically increase their earnings if they survived and advanced
up the gang hierarchy. Because of their dim prospects in formal legal labor
markets, founding members did not "mature out" of gangs until they were
older and formed the upper echelons of a more-organized but not necessarily bureaucratic venture (Hagedorn and Macon 1988; Fagan and Chin 1990;
Hagedorn 1998b; Venkatesh and Levitt 2000; Levitt and Venkatesh 2000).

34. See David F. Musto (1999); Sampson and Janet L. Lauritsen (1997, 361);
Hagedorn (1998b, 376); and Garland (2001b). The scant research evaluating
the War on Drug policies only reinforces our skepticism. Systematic research in this area is confounded by the profound difficulties in collecting
reliable data (see MacCoun and Reuter 2001; Manski, Pepper, and Petrie
2001). Weak evidence suggests that these policies marginally reduced drug
consumption (Chaloupka, Grossman, and Tauras 1999; Farrelly et al. 2001),
although Ilyana Kuziemko and Steven D. Levitt (2004) do find that drug
incarcerations lowered the incidence of more serious property and violent
crimes, most likely those involving drug dealers (Fagan and Chin 1990;
Johnson, Golub, Fagan 1995). Still, even Kuziemko and Levitt (2004, 2063)

conclude that "most generous estimates of the crime reduction attributable to prison suggest that current levels of incarceration are excessive." In other words, "It is not easy to justify drug imprisonment based on" these more utilitarian public safety grounds.

35. See Greenberg and West (2001, 623); Beckett and Western (2001); Guetzkow (2006a); and Greenberg (1999). The alternative formulation sees these policies as polar forms of social control over the poor, from the more accommodative-supportive to the more coercive.

36. See, for example, Nicole M. Fortin and Thomas Lemieux (1997); John Di-Nardo and Lemieux (1997); David Card and DiNardo (2002). The data on the real value of the minimum wage comes from Economic Policy Institute (2006, see http://www.epi.org/content. cfm/issueguides_minwage_minwage). This perspective helps to explain why the real earnings of less-educated workers fell more sharply and earnings inequality increased more sharply in the United States (and the U.K.) relative to other OECD countries (Gottschalk 1997; Gottschalk and Smeeding 1997; Blau and Kahn 1996).

37. We limit our analysis to these dates because the BJS stopped reporting disaggregated data on prison admissions and releases in 2000 (for the years through 1998). More current aggregate data are published in its annual bulletin, "Prison and Jail Inmates at Midyear" (Harrison and Beck 2005; personal communication from Dr. Allen Beck with the author, August 8, 2005).

38. As explicitly stated in the California Parolee Handbook, Conditions of Parole Explained: "You, your residence, and property can be searched at any time of the day or night, with or without a search warrant and with or without cause. The search can be done by a parole agent or any law enforcement agency." See http://www.corr.ca.gov/ParoleDiv/Handbook/Conditions_ex.asp.

39. According to the research of Christopher Uggen and Jeff Manza (2002), fourteen states currently disenfranchise some ex-felons, not just prisoners and parolees; see their 2004 map of Felon Disenfranchisement Restrictions at http://www.soc.umn.edu/%7Euggen/Map1_DisenfranRestrict.pdf.

40. In the case of Colorado, for example, arrest on a new felony offense or conviction for misdemeanor are technical violations subject to parole revocation. Moreover, the mast majority of parole violators sampled in 1997 named a new arrest or conviction as the reason for their return to prison on a technical violation (Hughes, Wilson, and Beck 2001, 14).

41. California Department of Corrections (2005). California, as an outlier in terms of the size of parole population and low success rate, skews the national averages. Removing California from national totals significantly raises the aggregate success rate in 1999 from 42 to 53 percent (Hughes, Wilson, and Beck 2001, 12).

42. A comparison of reconviction rates leads one to similar conclusions. Rearrest rates are regarded as the most reliable measure of recidivism, even if some individuals are wrongly charged. This source of error, it is argued, is more than offset by the number of released prisoners who are arrested but not prosecuted, or if prosecuted and convicted, are not returned to prison on a new sentence (Beck and Shipley 1989, 2).

43. We use the dates as a shorthand to refer to the cohorts of prisoners released in that year. The comparison is not strictly valid, because the 1994 estimate is derived from a sample of released prisoners from fifteen states, four more than were included in the 1983 sample. The BJS study downplays the difference in reincarceration rates because of the disproportionate share of technical parole revocations in California (Langan and Levin 2002, 8). Their summary omission simply begs the question of whether the California experience is truly an anomaly or just reflects one end of the spectrum of parole policies.

44. There are two sources of potential underestimation. First, parolees who commit new crimes may be returned to prison on a technical violation instead of a new conviction and prison commitment. Second, even before a parolee is arrested or commits a new crime, he or she may be returned to prison on a technical violation by a wary parole officer. Joan Petersilia (2003, 73) identifies another mechanism involving parole boards that will have a similar effect.

References

American Bar Association, Justice Kennedy Commission. 2004. "Reports with Recommendations to the ABA House of Delegates." Chicago: American Bar Association.

Ashenfelter, Orley. 1972. "Racial Discrimination and Trade Unionism." *Journal of Political Economy* 80(3): 435–64.

Banks, Duren, and Denise C. Gottfredson. 2003. "The Effects of Drug Treatment and Supervision on Time to Rearrest Among Drug Treatment Court Participants." *Journal of Drug Issues* 33(2): 385–412.

Beck, Allen J., and Bernard D. Shipley. 1989. "Recidivism of Prisoners Released in 1983." Bulletin. Washington: U.S. Department of Justice, Bureau of Justice Statistics.

Beckett, Katherine. 1997. *Making Crime Pay: Law and Order in Contemporary American Politics*. New York: Oxford University Press.

———. 2004. "Race and Drug Law Enforcement in Seattle." University of Washington, Seattle.

Beckett, Katherine, and Bruce Western. 2001. "Governing Social Marginality: Welfare, Incarceration, and the Transformation of State Policy." In *Mass Imprisonment: Social Causes and Consequences*, edited by David Garland. London: Sage Publications.

Belenko, Steven. 2001. "Research on Drug Courts: A Critical Review 2001 Update." Unpublished paper. Columbia University, National Center on Addiction and Substance Abuse.

Blackburn, McKinley, David E. Bloom, and Richard B. Freeman. 1990. "The Declining Economic Position of Less Skilled American Men." In *A Future of Lousy Jobs? The Changing Structure of U.S. Wages*, edited by Gary Burtless. Washington, D.C.: Brookings Institution.

———. 1993. "Changes in Earnings Differentials in the 1980s: Concordance, Convergence, Causes and Consequences." In *Poverty and Prosperity in the*

USA in the Late Twentieth Century, edited by Dmitri B. Papadimitriou and Edward N. Wolff. New York: Macmillan.

Blau, Francine D., and Lawrence M. Kahn. 1996. "International Differences in Male Wage Inequality: Institutions Versus Market Forces." *Journal of Political Economy* 104(4): 791–836.

Blumstein, Alfred. 1982. "On the Racial Disproportionality of the United States' Prison Population." *Journal of Criminal Law and Criminology*, 73(3): 1259–81.

———. 1983. "Selective Incapacitation as a Means of Crime Control." *American Behavioral Scientist* 27(1): 87–108.

———. 1993. "Racial Disproportionality of the U.S. Prison Population Revisited." *University of Colorado Law Review* 64(3): 743–60.

———. 1995. "Youth Violence, Guns, and Illicit-Drug Industry." *Journal of Criminal Law and Criminology* 86: 10–36.

———. 1998. "U.S. Criminal Justice Conundrum: Rising Prison Populations and Stable Crime Rates." *Crime and Delinquency*, 44(1): 127–35.

Blumstein, Alfred, and Allen J. Beck. 1999. "Population Growth in U.S. Prisons, 1980–1996." *Crime and Justice: Prisons* 26: 17–61.

Blumstein, Alfred, and Jacqueline Cohen. 1973. "A Theory of the Stability of Punishment." *Journal of Criminal Law and Criminology* 64(2): 198–207.

Blumstein, Alfred, Jacqueline Cohen, and Daniel S. Nagin. 1976. "The Dynamics of a Homeostatic Punishment Process." *Journal of Criminal Law and Criminology* 67(3): 317–34.

Blumstein, Alfred, and Richard Rosenfeld. 1998. "Explaining Recent Trends in U.S. Homicide Rates." *Journal of Criminal Law and Criminology* 88(4): 1175–1216.

Bobo, Lawrence, Alice O'Connor, and Chris Tilly, eds. 2001. *Urban Inequality in the United States: Evidence from Four Cities*. New York: Russell Sage Foundation.

Boggess, Scott, and John Bound. 1997. "Did Criminal Activity Increase During the 1980s? Comparisons Across Data Sources." *Social Science Quarterly* 78(3): 725–39.

Bonczar, Thomas P. 2003. "Prevalence of Imprisonment in the U.S. Population, 1974–2001." Special report, no. NCJ 197976. Washington: U.S. Department of Justice, Bureau of Justice Statistics, available at http://www.ojp.usdoj.gov/bjs/pub/pdf/piusp01.pdf.

Bonczar, Thomas P., and Allen J. Beck. 1997. "Lifetime Likelihood of Going to State or Federal Prison." Special report no. NCJ-160092. Washington: U.S. Department of Justice, Bureau of Justice Statistics.

Bound, John, and Richard B. Freeman. 1992."What Went Wrong? The Erosion of the Relative Earnings and Employment Among Young Black Men in the 1980s." *Quarterly Journal of Economics* 107(1): 201–32.

Bowling, Benjamin. 1999. "The Rise and Fall of New York Murder: Zero Tolerance or Crack's Decline?" *British Journal of Criminology* 39(4): 531–54.

Britt, Chester L. 1997. "Reconsidering the Unemployment and Crime Relationship: Variation by Age Group and Historical Period." *Journal of Quantitative Criminology* 13(4): 405–17.

Cadora, Eric, Charles Swartz, and Mannix Gordon. 2004. "Criminal Justice and Health and Human Services: An Exploration of Overlapping Needs, Resources and Interests in Brooklyn Neighborhoods." In *Prisoners Once Removed: The Impact of Incarceration and Reentry on Children, Families, and Communities*, edited by Jeremy Travis and Michelle Waul. Washington, D.C.: Urban Institute Press.

Cahalan, Margaret. 1979. "Trends in Incarceration in the United States Since 1888: A Summary of Reported Rates and the Distribution of Offenses." *Crime and Delinquency* 25(1): 9–41.

California Department of Corrections. 2005. *Parole Handbook*. www.corr.ca.gov/offenders/conditions_ex.html.

Cantor, David, and Kenneth C. Land. 1985. "Unemployment and Crime Rates in the Post–World War II United States: A Theoretical and Empirical Analysis." *American Sociological Review* 50(3): 317–22.

Card, David, and John E. DiNardo, 2002. "Skill-Biased Technological Change and Rising Wage Inequality: Some Problems and Puzzles." *Journal of Labor Economics* 20(4): 733–83.

Carter, Susan, Scott Gartner, Michael R. Haines, Alan Olmstead, Richard Sutch, and Gavin Wright, eds. 1997. *Historical Statistics of the United States on CD-ROM: Colonial Times to 1970—Bicentennial Edition.* New York: Cambridge University Press.

Caulkins, Jonathan P., and Sara Chandler. 2006. "Long-Run Trends in Incarceration of Drug Offenders in the United States." *Crime and Delinquency* 52(4): 619–41.

Chaloupka, Frank J., Michael Grossman, and John A. Tauras. 1999. "The Demand for Cocaine and Marijuana by Youth." In *The Economic Analysis of Substance Use and Abuse*, edited by Frank J. Chaloupka, Michael Grossman, Warren K. Bickel, and Henry Saffer. Chicago: University of Chicago Press.

Chiricos, Theodore G. 1987. "Rates of Crime and Unemployment: An Analysis of Aggregate Research and Evidence." *Sociological Problems* 14(2): 187–211.

Clear, Todd R., Dina R. Rose, and Judith A. Ryder. 2001. "Incarceration and the Community: The Problem of Removing and Returning Offenders." *Crime and Delinquency* 47(3): 335–51.

Cohen, Jacqueline, Daniel Cork, John Engberg, and George Tita. 1998. "The Role of Drug Markets and Gangs in Local Homicide Rates." *Homicide Studies* 2(3): 241–62.

Cook, Philip J., and John H. Laub. 1998. "The Unprecedented Epidemic in Youth Violence." *Crime and Justice* 24: 27–64.

———. 2002. "After the Epidemic: Recent Trends in Youth Violence in the United States." *Crime and Justice* 29: 1–37.

Cook, Philip J., and Gary A. Zarkin. 1985. "Crime and the Business Cycle." *Journal of Legal Studies* 14(1): 115–28.

Cork, Daniel. 1999. "Examining Space-Time Interaction in City-Level Homicide Data: Crack Markets and the Diffusion of Guns Among Youth." *Journal of Quantitative Criminology* 15(4): 379–406.

Devine, Joel A., Joseph F. Sheley, and M. Dwayne Smith. 1988. "Macroeconomic and Social-Control Policy Influence on Crime-Rate Changes, 1948–1985." *American Sociological Review* 53(3): 407–20.

Dillard, Darrell K., and Allen J. Beck. 1998. "Prison and Jail Inmates at Midyear

1997." Bulletin, NCJ no. 167247. Washington: U.S. Department of Justice, Bureau of Justice Statistics.

DiNardo, John, and Thomas Lemieux. 1997. "Diverging Male Wage Inequality in the United States and Canada, 1981–1988: Do Institutions Explain the Difference?" *Industrial and Labor Relations Review* 50(4): 629–51.

Ditton, Paula M., and Doris James Wilson. 1999. "Truth in Sentencing in State Prisons." Special report, NCJ no. 170032. Washington: U.S. Department of Justice, Bureau of Justice Statistics, available at http://www.ojp.usdoj.gov/bjs/pub/pdf/tssp.pdf.

DiIulio, John J., Jr. 1996a. "Help Wanted: Economists, Crime and Public Policy." *Journal of Economic Perspectives* 10(1): 3–24.

———. 1996b. "Fill Churches, Not Jails: Youth Crime and 'Superpredators.'" Testimony before Senate Judiciary Committee, Subcommittee on Youth Violence, February 28, available at www.brook.edu/views/testimony/ diiulio/ 19960228.htm.

Economic Policy Institute. 2006. *EPI Issue Guide—Minimum Wage.* Washington, D.C.: EPI, available at http://www.epi.org/ issueguides_minwage.

Edin, Kathryn, Timothy J. Nelson, and Rechelle Paranal. 2004. "Fatherhood and Incarceration as Potential Turning Points in the Criminal Careers of Unskilled Men." In *Imprisoning America: The Social Consequences of Mass Incarceration,* edited by Mary Pattillo, Bruce Western, and David F. Weiman. New York: Russell Sage Foundation.

Fagan, Jeffrey. 2004. "Crime, Law, and the Community: Dynamics of Incarceration in New York City." In *The Future of Imprisonment,* edited by Michael Tonry. New York: Oxford University Press.

Fagan, Jeffrey, and Ko-lin Chin. 1990. "Violence as Regulation and Social Control in the Distribution of Crack." In *Drugs and Violence,* edited by Mario De La Rosa, Elizabeth Lambert, and Bernard Gropper. Rockville, Md.: National Institute on Drug Abuse.

Fagan, Jeffrey, and Garth Davies. 2000. "Street Stops and Broken Windows: Terry, Race and Disorder in New York City." *Fordham Urban Law Journal* 28(2): 457–504.

Fagan, Jeff, and Richard B. Freeman. 1999. "Crime and Work," *Crime and Justice* 25: 225–90.

Fagan, Jeffrey, Valerie West, and Jan Holland. 2003. "Reciprocal Effects of Crime and Incarceration in New York City Neighborhoods." *Fordham Urban Law Journal* 30(5): 1551–602.

Fagan, Jeffrey, Franklin E. Zimring, and June Kim. 1998. "Declining Homicide in New York City: A Tale of Two Trends." *Journal of Criminal Law and Criminology* 88(4): 1277–1324.

Fairlie, Robert W. 2002. "Drug Dealing and Legitimate Self-Employment." *Journal of Labor Economics* 20(3): 538–67.

Farley, Reynolds, Sheldon Danziger, and Harry J. Holzer. 2000. *Detroit Divided.* New York: Russell Sage Foundation.

Farrelly, Matthew C., Jeremy W. Bray, Gary A. Zarkin, and Brett W. Wendling. 2001. "The Joint Demand for Cigarettes and Marijuana: Evidence from the National Household Surveys on Drug Abuse." *Journal of Health Economics* 20(1): 51–68.

Fortin, Nicole M., and Thomas Lemieux. 1997. "Institutional Changes and Rising Wage Inequality: Is There a Linkage?" *Journal of Economic Perspectives* 11(2): 75–96.

Fox, James Alan, and Marianne W. Zawitz. 2006. "Homicide Trends in the United States." Washington: U.S. Department of Justice, Bureau of Justice Statistics, available at http:// www.ojp.usdof.gov/bjs/homicide/homtrnd.htm.

Frankel, Marvin. 1972. *Criminal Sentences: Law Without Order.* New York: Hill & Wang.

Freeman, Richard B. 1995. "Crime and the Labor Market." In *Crime*, edited by James Q. Wilson and Joan Petersilia. San Francisco: ICS Press.

———. 1996. "Why Do So Many Young American Men Commit Crimes and What Might We Do About It?" *Journal of Economic Perspectives* 10(1): 25–42.

———. 2001. "The Rising Tide Lifts . . . ?" NBER working paper no. 8155. Cambridge, Mass.: National Bureau of Economic Research.

Freeman, Richard B., and James L. Medoff. 1984. *What Do Unions Do?* New York: Basic Books.

Freeman, Richard B., and William M. Rodgers III. 2000. "Area Economic Conditions and the Labor Market Outcomes of Young Men in the 1990s Expansion." In *Prosperity for All? The Economic Boom and African Americans*, edited by Robert Cherry and William M. Rodgers III. New York: Russell Sage Foundation.

Fryer, Roland G., Paul S. Heaton, Steven D. Levitt, and Kevin M. Murphy. 2005. "Measuring the Impact of Crack Cocaine." NBER working paper no. 11318. Cambridge, Mass.: National Bureau of Education Statistics.

Garland, David. 1993. *Punishment and Modern Society: A Study in Social Theory.* Chicago: University of Chicago Press.

———. 2001a. "The Meaning of Mass Imprisonment." Introduction. *Mass Imprisonment: Social Causes and Consequences.* London: Sage Publications.

———. 2001b. *The Culture of Control: Crime and Social Order in Contemporary Society.* Chicago: University of Chicago Press.

Glaze, Lauren E., and Seri Palla. 2005. "Probation and Parole in the United States, 2004." Bulletin, no. NCJ 210676. Washington: U.S. Department of Justice, Bureau of Justices Statistics.

Golub, Andrew, and Bruce D. Johnson. 1994. "A Recent Decline in Cocaine Use Among Youthful Arrestees in Manhattan, 1987 Through 1993." *American Journal of Public Health* 84(8): 1250–54.

Gottfredson, Denise C., Stacy S. Najaka, Brook W. Kearley, and Carlos M. Rocha. 2006. "Long-term Effects of Participation in the Baltimore City Drug Treatment Court: Results from an Experimental Study." *Journal of Experimental Criminology* 2(1): 67–98.

Gottschalk, Peter. 1997. "Inequality, Income Growth, and Mobility: The Basic Facts." *Journal of Economic Perspectives* 11(2): 21–40.

Gottschalk, Peter, and Timothy M. Smeeding. 1998. "Cross–National Comparisons of Earnings and Income Inequality." *Journal of Economic Literature* 35(2): 633–87.

Gould, Eric D., Bruce A. Weinberg, and David B. Mustard. 2002. "Crime Rates and Local Labor Market Opportunities in the United States: 1979–1997." *Review of Economics and Statistics* 84(1): 45–61.

Greenberg, David F. 1999. "Punishment, Division of Labor, and Social Solidarity." In *The Criminology of Criminal Law*, edited by William S. Laufer and Freda Adler. New Brunswick, N.J.: Transactions Publishers.

———. 2001. "Time Series Analysis of Crime Rates." *Journal of Quantitative Criminology* 17(4): 291–327.

Greenberg, David F., and Valerie West. 2001. "State Prison Populations and Their Growth, 1971–1991." *Criminology* 39(3): 615–53.

Grogger, Jeff. 1998. "Market Wages and Youth Crime." *Journal of Labor Economics* 16(4): 756–91.

Grogger, Jeff, and Michael Willis. 2000. "The Emergence of Crack Cocaine and the Rise in Urban Crime Rates." *Review of Economics and Statistics* 82(4): 519–29.

Guetzkow, Joshua. 2006a. "Bars Versus Butter: The Prison-Welfare Tradeoff and Its Political Underpinnings." Unpublished paper. University of California, Berkeley.

———. 2006b. "Common Cause? A Cultural Analysis of the Links Between Welfare and Criminal Justice Policies, 1960–1996." Unpublished paper. University of California, Berkeley.

Hagedorn, John. 1998a. "The Business of Drug Dealing in Milwaukee." *Wisconsin Policy Research Institute Report* 11(5).

———. 1998b. "Gang Violence in the Postindustrial Era." *Crime and Justice* 24: 365–419.

Hagedorn, John, and Perry Macon. 1988. *People and Folks: Gangs, Crime, and the Underclass in a Rust-Belt City*. Chicago: Lake View Press.

Harlow, Caroline Wolf. 2003. "Education and Corrections Population." Special report, no. NCJ 195670. Washington: U.S. Department of Justice, Bureau of Justice Statistics.

Harrison, Lana D. 2001. "The Revolving Prison Door for Drug-Involved Offenders: Challenges and Opportunities." *Crime and Delinquency* 47(3): 462–85.

Harrison, Paige M., and Allen J. Beck. 2004. "Prisoners in 2003." Report, no. NCJ 205335. Washington: U.S. Department of Justice, Bureau of Justice Statistics.

———. 2005. "Prison and Jail Inmates at Midyear 2004." Bulletin, no. NCJ 208801. Washington: U.S. Department of Justice, Bureau of Justice Statistics.

Hawkins, Darnell F., and Cedric Herring. 2000. "Race, Crime, and Punishment: Old Controversies and New Challenges." In *New Directions: African Americans in a Diversifying Nation*, edited by James S. Jackson. Washington, D.C.: National Policy Association.

Heckman, James J., and Brook S. Payner. 1989. "Determining the Impact of Federal Antidiscrimination Policy on the Economic Status of Blacks: A Study of South Carolina." *American Economic Review* 79(1): 138–77.

Hines, John R., Jr., Hilary W. Hoynes, and Alan B. Krueger. 2001. "Another Look at Whether a Rising Tide Lifts All Boats." In *The Roaring Nineties: Can Full Employment Be Sustained?* edited by Alan B. Krueger and Robert M. Solow. New York: Russell Sage Foundation.

Hofer, Paul J., Charles Loeffler, Kevin Blackwell, and Patricia Valentino. 2004. "Fifteen Years of Guidelines Sentencing: An Assessment of How Well the Federal Criminal Justice System Is Achieving the Goals of Sentencing Reform." Washington: U.S. Sentencing Commission.

Holzer, Harry J., Paul Offner, and Elaine Sorensen. 2005. "Declining Employment Among Young Black Less-Educated Men: The Role of Incarceration and Child Support." *Journal of Policy Analysis and Management* 24(2): 329–50.

Hughes, Timothy A., Doris James Wilson, and Allen J. Beck. 2001. "Trends in State Parole, 1990–2000." Special report, no. NCJ 184735. Washington: U.S. Department of Justice, Bureau of Justice Statistics.

Ihlanfeldt, Keith R. 2007. "Neighborhood Drug Crime and Young Males' Job Accessibility." *Review of Economics and Statistics* 89(1): 151—64.

Jargowsky, Paul. 1997, *Poverty and Place: Ghettos, Barrios, and the American City.* New York: Russell Sage Foundation.

Jaynes, Gerald D., and Robin M. Williams Jr., eds. 1989. *A Common Destiny: Blacks and American Society.* Washington, D.C.: National Academy Press.

Johnson, Bruce D., Andrew Golub, and Jeffrey Fagan. 1995. "Careers in Crack, Drug Use, Drug Distribution, and Nondrug Criminality." *Crime and Delinquency* 41(3): 275–95.

Johnson, Robert A., Dean R. Gerstein, Rashna Ghadialy, Wai Choy, and Joseph Gfoerer. 1996. "Trends in the Incidence of Drug Use in the United States, 1919–1992." Rockville, Md.: U.S. Department of Health and Human Services, Substance Abuse and Mental Health Services Administration, Office of Applied Studies.

Joint Committee on New York Drug Law Evaluation. 1977. *The Nation's Toughest Drug Law: Evaluating the New York Experience—Final Report of the Joint Committee on New York Drug Law Evaluation.* New York: Association of the Bar of the City of New York.

Joyce, Ted. 2004a. "Did Legalized Abortion Lower Crime?" *Journal of Human Resources* 39(1): 1–28.

————. 2004b. "Further Tests of Abortion and Crime." NBER working paper no. 10564. Cambridge, Mass.: National Bureau of Education Statistics.

Kasarda, John D. 1995. "Industrial Restructuring and the Changing Location of Jobs." In *State of the Union: America in the 1990s*, edited by Reynolds Farley. New York: Russell Sage Foundation.

Krivo, Lauren J., and Ruth D. Peterson. 2004. "Labor Market Conditions and Violent Crime Among Youth and Adults." *Sociological Perspectives* 47(4): 485–505.

Krivo, Lauren J., Ruth D. Peterson, and Danielle C. Payne. 2006. "Segregation, Racial Structure, and Neighborhood Crime." Unpublished paper. Ohio State University.

Kuziemko, Ilyana, and Steven D. Levitt. 2004. "An Empirical Analysis of Imprisoning Drug Offenders." *Journal of Public Economics* 88(9–10): 2043–66.

Langan, Patrick A. 1985. "Racism on Trial: New Evidence to Explain the Racial Composition of Prisons in the United States." *Journal of Criminal Law and Criminology* 76(3): 666–83.

————. 1991. "Race of Prisoners Admitted to State and Federal Institutions, 1926–86." Special report, no. 125618. Washington: U.S. Department of Justice, Bureau of Justice Statistics.

Langan, Patrick A., and David J. Levin. 2002. "Recidivism of Prisoners Released in 1994." Special report, no. 193427. Washington: U.S. Department of Justice, Bureau of Justice Statistics.

Lawrence, Sarah, and Jeremy Travis. 2004. "The New Landscape of Imprisonment: Mapping America's Prison Expansion." Research report. Washington, D.C.: Urban Institute, Justice Policy Center.

Levitt, Steven D. 1996. "The Effect of Prison Population Size on Crime Rates: Evidence from Prison Overcrowding Litigation." *Quarterly Journal of Economics*, 111(2): 319–51.

———. 2001. "Alternative Strategies for Identifying the Link Between Unemployment and Crime." *Journal of Quantitative Criminology* 17(4): 377–90.

———. 2004. "Understanding Why Crime Fell in the 1990s: Four Factors That Explain the Decline and Six That Do Not." *Journal of Economic Perspectives*, 18(1): 163–90.

Levitt, Steven D., and Sudhir Alladi Venkatesh. 2000. "An Economic Analysis of a Drug–Selling Gang's Finances." *Quarterly Journal of Economics* 115(3): 755–89.

Lochner, Lance, and Enrico Moretti. 2004. "The Effect of Education on Crime: Evidence from Prison Inmates, Arrests, and Self–Reports." *American Economic Review* 94(1): 155–89.

Lynch, James P. 2002. "Crime in International Perspective." In *Crime: Public Policies for Crime Control*, edited by James Q. Wilson and Joan Petersilia. Oakland, Calif.: Institute for Contemporary Studies.

Lynch, James P., and William J. Sabol. 2000. "Prison Use and Social Control." *Criminal Justice* 3: 7–44.

———. 2001. "Prisoner Reentry in Perspective." Crime Policy Report no. 3. Washington, D.C.: Urban Institute, Justice Policy Center.

———. 2004. "Effects of Incarceration on Informal Social Control." In *Imprisoning America: The Social Consequences of Mass Incarceration*, edited by Mary Pattillo, Bruce Western, and David F. Weiman. New York: Russell Sage Foundation.

MacCoun, Robert, and Peter Reuter. 2001. *Drug War Heresies: Learning from Other Vices, Times and Places.* New York: Cambridge University Press.

Manski, Charles F., John V. Pepper, and Carol V. Petrie, eds. 2001. *Informing America's Policy on Illegal Drugs: What We Don't Know Keeps Hurting Us.* Washington, D.C.: National Academy Press and National Research Council, Committee on Data and Research for Policy on Illegal Drugs.

Massey, Douglas S., and Nancy A. Denton. 1993. *American Apartheid: Segregation and the Making of the Underclass.* Cambridge, Mass.: Harvard University Press.

Mauer, Marc. 1999. *Race to Incarcerate.* New York: New Press/Sentencing Project.

———. 2001. "The Causes and Consequences of Prison Growth in the United States." In *Mass Imprisonment: Social Causes and Consequences*, edited by David Garland. London: Sage Publications.

Mauer, Marc, and Tracy Huling. 1996. "Young Black Men and the Criminal Justice System: A Growing National Problem." Report. Washington, D.C.: Sentencing Project.

Mishel, Lawrence R., Jared Bernstein, and Sylvia Allegretto. 2006. *The State of Working America 2006/2007.* Ithaca, N.Y.: ILR Press.

Murakawa, Naomi. 2005. "Punitive Race-to-the-Top: Elections, Race, and the Mandatory Minimum Electoral Staircase." University of Washington: Seattle.

Musto, David F. 1999. *The American Disease: Origins of Narcotic Control.* 3rd ed. New York: Oxford University Press.

Myers, Samuel L., Jr. 1992. "Crime, Entrepreneurship, and Labor Force Withdrawal." *Contemporary Policy Issues* 10(2): 84–97.

Nagin, Daniel S. 1998. "Criminal Deterrence Research at the Outset of the Twenty-First Century." *Crime and Justice* 23: 1–42.

Oliver, Pamela E., and James E. Yocom. 2004. "Explaining State Black Imprisonment Rates, 1983–1999." Unpublished paper. University of Wisconsin, Madison.

Pastore, Ann L., and Kathleen Maguire, eds. 2006. *Sourcebook of Criminal Justice Statistics.* Online reference work. Available at http://www.albany.edu/sourcebook/.

Pattillo-McCoy, Mary. 1999. *Black Picket Fences: Privilege and Peril Among the Black Middle Class.* Chicago: University of Chicago Press.

Petersilia, Joan. 1999. "Parole and Prisoner Reentry in the United States." *Crime and Justice: Prisons* 26: 479–529.

———. 2003. *When Prisoners Come Home: Parole and Prisoner Reentry.* Oxford; New York: Oxford University Press.

Peterson, Ruth D. 1985. "Discriminatory Decision Making at the Legislative Level: An Analysis of the Comprehensive Drug Abuse Prevention and Control Act of 1970." *Law and Human Behavior* 9(3): 243–69.

Pettit, Becky, and Bruce Western. 2004. "Mass Imprisonment and the Life Course: Race and Class Inequality in U.S. Incarceration." *American Sociological Review* 69(2): 151–69.

Piehl, Anne Morrison. 1998. "Economic Conditions, Work, and Crime." In *The Handbook of Crime and Punishment,* edited by Michael Tonry. New York: Oxford University Press.

Quillian, Lincoln. 2003. "The Decline of Male Employment in Low-Income Black Neighborhoods, 1950–1990." *Social Science Research* 32(2): 220–50.

Raphael, Steven. 1998. "The Spatial Mismatch Hypothesis of Black Youth Unemployment: Evidence from the San Francisco Bay Area." *Journal of Urban Economics* 43(1): 79–111.

———. 2006. "The Socioeconomic Status of Black Males: The Increasing Importance of Incarceration." In *Public Policy and the Income Distribution,* edited by Alan J. Auerbach, David Card, and John M. Quigley. New York: Russell Sage Foundation.

Raphael, Steven, and Michael A. Stoll. 2002. "Modest Progress: The Narrowing Spatial Mismatch between Blacks and Jobs in the 1990s." Washington, D.C.: Brookings Institution, Center on Urban and Metropolitan Policy.

Raphael, Steven, and Rudolf Winter-Ember. 2001. "Identifying the Effect of Unemployment on Crime." *Journal of Law and Economics* 44(1): 259–83.

Rempel, Michael, Dana Fox-Kralstein, Amanda Cissner, Robyn Cohen, Melissa Labriola, Donald Farole, Ann Bader, and Michael Magnani. 2003. "The New York State Adult Drug Court Evaluation." New York: Center for Court Innovation.

Reuter, Peter, Robert MacCoun, and Peter Murphy. 1990 "Money from Crime: A Study of the Economics of Drug Dealing in Washington, D.C." Santa Monica, Calif.: RAND Corporation.

Riley, K. Jack. 1997. "Crack, Powder Cocaine, and Heroin: Drug Purchase and Use Patterns in Six U.S. Cities." Research report. Washington: National Institute of Justice, Office of National Drug Control Policy.

Rose, Dina R., and Todd R. Clear. 2004. "Who Doesn't Know Someone in Jail? The Impact of Exposure to Prison on Attitudes Toward Formal and Informal Controls." *Prison Journal* 84(2): 228–47.

Rosen, Kenneth T., Grace J. Kim, and Avani A. Patel. 2003. "Shopping the City: Real Estate Finance and Urban Retail Development." Washington, D.C.: Brookings Institution, Center on Urban and Metropolitan Policy.

Rothman, David J. 1980/2002. *Conscience and Convenience: The Asylum and Its Alternatives in Progressive America.* New York: Aldine de Gruyter.

Sabol, William J., Katherine Rosich, Karmala Malik Kane, David P. Kirk, and Glenn Dubin. 2002. "The Influences of Truth-in-Sentencing Reforms on Changes in States' Sentencing Practices and Prison Populations." Research report. Washington, D.C.: Urban Institute, Justice Policy Center.

Sampson, Robert J., and John H. Laub. 1993a. "Structural Variations in Juvenile Court Processing: Inequality, the Underclass, and Social Control." *Law and Society Review* 27(2): 285–312.

———. 1993b. *Crime in the Making: Pathways and Turning Points Through Life.* Cambridge, Mass.: Harvard University Press.

———. 2005. "A Life-Course View of the Development of Crime." *Annals of the American Academy of Political and Social Science* 602(1): 12–45.

Sampson, Robert J., and Janet L. Lauritsen. 1997. "Racial and Ethnic Disparities in Crime and Criminal Justice in the United States." In *Ethnicity, Crime, and Immigration: Comparative and Cross-National Perspectives*, edited by Michael Tonry. Chicago: University of Chicago Press.

Sampson, Robert J., and Stephen W. Raudenbush. 1999. "Systematic Social Observation of Public Spaces: A New Look at Disorder in Urban Neighborhoods." *American Journal of Sociology* 105(3): 603–51.

Sampson, Robert J., and William Julius Wilson. 1995. "Towards a Theory of Race, Crime, and Urban Inequality." In *Crime and Inequality*, edited by John Hagan and Ruth D. Peterson. Palo Alto: Stanford University Press.

Schiraldi, Vincent, Jason Colburn, and Eric Lotke. 2004. "Three Strikes and You're Out: An Examination of 3 Strikes Laws 10 Years After Their Enactment." Policy brief. Washington, D.C.: Justice Policy Institute.

Sevigny, Eric L., and Jonathan P. Caulkins. 2004. "Kingpins or Mules: An Analysis of Drug Offenders Incarcerated in Federal and State Prisons." *Criminology and Public Policy* 3(3): 401–34.

Snell, Tracy L. 1995. "Correctional Populations in the United States, 1993." Report no. NCJ-156241. Washington: U.S. Department of Justice, Bureau of Justice Statistics.

Spelman, William. 2000a. "The Limited Importance of Prison Expansion." In *The Crime Drop in America*, edited by Alfred Blumstein and Joel Wallman. New York: Cambridge University Press.

———. 2000b. "What Recent Studies Do (and Don't) Tell Us About Imprisonment and Crime." *Crime and Justice: Prisons* 27: 418–93.

Stanford Law School, Stanford Criminal Justice Center. 2006. *State Sentencing*

Commissions. Available at http://www.lhc.ca.gov/lhcdir/sentencing/Dansky Aug06-sentencingcommissions.pdf.

Stoll, Michael A., Harry J. Holzer, and Keith R. Ihlanfeldt. 2000. "Within Cities and Suburbs: Racial Residential Concentration and the Distribution of Employment Opportunities Across Sub-Metropolitan Areas." *Journal of Policy Analysis and Management* 19(2): 207–31.

Taylor, Ralph B. 2000. *Breaking Away from Broken Windows: Baltimore Neighborhoods and the Nationwide Fight Against Crime, Grime, Fear, and Decline*. Boulder, Colo.: Westview Press.

Tonry, Michael H. 1995. *Malign Neglect: Race, Crime, and Punishment in America*. New York: Oxford University Press.

———. 1996. *Sentencing Matters*. New York: Oxford University Press.

Travis, Jeremy. 2005. *But They All Come Back: Facing the Challenges of Prisoner Reentry*. Washington, D.C.: Urban Institute Press.

Uggen, Christopher, and Jeff Manza. 2002. "Democratic Contraction? Political Consequences of Felon Disenfranchisement in the United States." *American Sociological Review* 67(6): 777–803.

U.S. Department of Justice, Bureau of Justice Administration. 1998. *1996 National Survey of State Sentencing Structures*. Monograph. Washington: U.S. Department of Justice, Bureau of Justice Administration.

U.S. Department of Justice, Bureau of Justice Statistics. 2006. "Corrections Spreadsheets." Available at http://www.ojp.usdoj.gov/bjs/dtdata.htm#corrections.

U.S. Government Accountability Office. 2001. "Prisoner Releases: Trends and Information on Reintegration Programs." Report to congressional committees, no. GAO-01–483 (June). Washington: GAO.

———. 2005. "Drug Offenders: Various Factors May Limit the Impacts of Federal Laws That Provide for the Denial of Selected Benefits." Report to congressional requesters, no. GAO-05–238 (September). Washington: GAO.

U.S. National Institute of Justice. 2006. "Drug Courts: The Second Decade." Special report, NIJ no. 211081. Washington: U.S. Department of Justice, Office of Justice Programs.

U.S. Sentencing Commission. 1995. "Cocaine and Federal Sentencing Policy." Special Report to the Congress. Available at http://www.ussc.gov/crack/exec.htm.

Venkatesh, Sudhir Alladi, and Steven D. Levitt. 2000. "Are We a Family or a Business?" History and Disjuncture in the Urban American Street Gang." *Theory and Society* 29(4): 427–62.

Western, Bruce, and Becky Pettit. 2002. "Beyond Crime and Punishment: Prisons and Inequality." *Contexts* 1(3): 37–43.

Western, Bruce, Meredith Kleykamp, and Jake Rosenfeld. 2004. "Crime, Punishment, and American Inequality." In *Social Inequality*, edited by Kathryn M. Neckerman. New York: Russell Sage Foundation.

Western, Bruce. 2006. *Punishment and Inequality in America*. New York: Russell Sage Foundation.

Wilson, James Q. 1975. *Thinking About Crime*. New York: Basic Books.

Wilson, James Q., and George L. Kelling. 1982. "Broken Windows." *Atlantic Monthly* 249(3): 29—38.

Wilson, James, and Joan Petersilia, eds. 1995. *Crime*. San Francisco: Institute for Contemporary Studies.

Wilson, William Julius. 1987. *The Truly Disadvantaged: The Inner City, the Underclass, and Public Policy*. Chicago: University of Chicago Press.

Young, Warren, and Mark Brown. 1993. "Cross-National Comparisons of Imprisonment." *Crime and Justice* 17: 1–49.

Zeitlin, Maurice, and L. Frank Weyher. 2001. "'Black and White, Unite and Fight': Interracial Working-Class Solidarity and Racial Employment Equality." *American Journal of Sociology* 107(2): 430–67.

Zimring, Franklin E., and Gordon Hawkins. 1991. *The Scale of Imprisonment*. Chicago: University of Chicago Press.

= Chapter 3 =

Finding Work on the Outside: Results from the "Returning Home" Project in Chicago

Christy A. Visher and Vera Kachnowski

Finding employment after release is one of the most important reintegration challenges facing ex-prisoners, and is one that can have a significant impact on their chances of remaining crime-free. Prior research shows that finding and maintaining a legitimate job after release can reduce the chances of reoffending following release from prison (Sampson and Laub 1993, 1997; Harer 1994), especially for older offenders (Uggen 2000). Research also indicates that the higher the wages ex-offenders receive, the less likely persons released from prison are to return to crime (Bernstein and Houston 2000; Grogger 1998). The importance of employment for a successful transition from prison to the community is acknowledged by prisoners themselves: most soon-to-be-released prisoners report that finding a job will be the single most important factor in staying out of trouble once they leave prison (Visher, La Vigne, and Farrell 2003; Visher et al. 2004).

Although two-thirds of former prisoners reported that they held a job just prior to their incarceration (Lynch and Sabol 2001), most prisoners experience great difficulties finding jobs after their release. During the time they spend in prison, individuals lose work skills, forfeit the opportunity to gain work experience, and sever interpersonal connections and social contacts that could lead to legal employment opportunities upon release (Western, Kling, and Weiman 2001; Sampson and Laub 1997; Hagan and Dinovitzer 1999). And, though the period of incarceration could be viewed as an opportunity to build skills and prepare for placement at a future job, the evaluation literature provides mixed support for the effectiveness of in-prison job-training programs

(Bushway and Reuter 2001; Gaes et al. 1999; Wilson et al. 1999). After release, the stigma of the ex-prisoner status makes the job search even more difficult: a recent survey of three thousand employers in four major metropolitan areas revealed that two-thirds of the employers would not knowingly hire an ex-prisoner (Holzer et al. 2004).

In addition to the effect jobs have on former prisoners' likelihood of recidivism, finding and maintaining stable employment is an important element of a positive post-release adjustment in its own right. Yet few studies have systematically examined the employment experiences of persons released from prison or identified characteristics of released prisoners who are successful in locating employment after release (but see Bushway and Reuter 2001; also, Uggen and Thompson 2003, for an analysis of the determinants of illegal earnings). William J. Sabol (chapter 9, this volume), using unemployment insurance records on released prisoners in Ohio, finds that pre-prison employment experience, but not education or in-prison training programs, affects the likelihood of finding employment.

In general, a relatively limited set of independent variables has been used to explain employment among former prisoners. Other research on the lives of former prisoners suggests that their post-release circumstances may be significant predictors of success or failure, including finding and keeping a job (Laub and Sampson 1993). For example, individuals' attitudes and health, their relationships with family and peers, and even the neighborhood in which former prisoners reside may affect the likelihood of employment. However, examining the impact of these ex-prisoner attributes on employment outcomes has not been common in existing research because such analyses require expensive data collection techniques to gather self-reported information.

In this chapter we use data gathered through the Urban Institute's Returning Home project in Illinois, which involves multiple interviews with prisoners and former prisoners who returned to Chicago. We present findings on pre- and in-prison experiences that might prepare prisoners for employment after release and on post-release employment outcomes at one to three months (first interview) and four to eight months (second interview) after release. In addition, we examine factors predicting current employment and number of months employed since release: demographic and other pre-prison characteristics, criminal history and in-prison experiences, and post-release circumstances.

The Returning Home Project

The purpose of the Returning Home project is to develop a deeper understanding of the reentry experiences of returning prisoners, their families, and communities. The project explores the phenomenon of prisoner reentry within five domains (Visher and Travis 2003):

1. The individual experience, as documented through interviews with prisoners before and after release from prison

2. The family experience, as documented through interviews with family members of returning prisoners

3. The peer-group experience, as documented through prisoner interviews both before and after their release

4. The community experience, as documented through interviews with key community stakeholders and through focus groups with residents

5. The broader policy environment at the state level, including information on relevant state policies regarding parole supervision, workforce development, drug treatment, and financial assistance.

Employment Data Gathered from Returning Home

The data collection instruments used in the Returning Home study include many questions about workforce participation, and gather information about employment history before prison, during prison, and after release. During a self-administered survey completed two to three months before release, prisoners are asked about their work experiences during the six months prior to the current prison term. They are asked how many jobs they worked, the total number of hours worked each week, the type of work they did, and how much they earned. In this survey, respondents are also asked about their work experiences while in prison—whether they hold an in-prison job, what kind of work they do, how many hours they work, how long they have had the job, and how much money they earn. Respondents are also asked about their expectations and plans for employment after their release, including how they plan to find employment, how much money they expect to earn, and how difficult they anticipate finding and keeping a job to be.

During one-on-one interviews conducted at one to three and four to eight months after release, respondents are asked more extensive questions about job experiences and job training received during prison. In particular, they are asked whether they were offered or participated in employment readiness or job training classes while in prison and whether they had a work-release job while in prison. The interview includes questions about their experiences looking for work since release—whether, how, and for how long they looked for a job, and how their criminal record may have affected their job search. They are asked whether, for how long, and in what capacity they are working, as well as how many hours per week they work and how much they earn. In addition they are asked how they found their current job (if employed), how far their place of work is from where they live, and how they get to their job. Finally, respondents are asked a series of questions regarding their satisfaction with their work.

Sampling Strategy and Methodology

Our sampling goal in Illinois was to recruit four hundred male prisoners who had been sentenced to at least one year by an Illinois court and were serving time in an Illinois state prison; were returning to the city of Chicago; were within thirty to ninety days of release; and were representative of all state releases for the year, in terms of release reason, offense type, time served, race, and age. In accordance with Institutional Review Board approval of the study, only prisoners who were eighteen years of age or older were eligible for recruitment.

Working with the Illinois Department of Corrections (IDOC), we chose five facilities that housed prisoners of a range of security levels, offered a variety of programming, and would enable us to reach our sampling goal of four hundred respondents within five months. Thus, we aimed to obtain a "temporal sample" of the population of prisoners being released from these facilities over the course of a five-month period. Participants in the Returning Home study were recruited from groups of prisoners who were participating in the IDOC's PreStart program.[1] Study participants were representative of all Chicago-bound males released from prison in 2001 with respect to race, sentence length, time served, and conviction offense. Prisoners in our sample were a little older, had somewhat more prior incarcerations, were less likely to have been incarcerated for a technical parole violation, and were more likely to be released to supervision, when compared to all Chicago-bound male releasees (see table 3.1).[2]

Of the four hundred male prisoners who elected to participate in this study, 83 percent were African American, 5 percent were white, and 12 percent were from other racial groups. Ten percent of the sample was Hispanic. The average age at the time of the pre-release interview was thirty-four. Less than half of the sample (49 percent) had a high school education or higher (high school diploma, GED, some college). The majority (58 percent) had never been married; 15 percent reported being divorced or separated; 10 percent were married; and 11 percent were never married but were living with their partner prior to

Table 3.1   Comparison of Study Participants and All Chicago-Bound
Prisoners Released in 2001

	Study Participants, N = 400	All Chicago-Bound Male Prisoners, N = 13,728
Demographics		
Average age at release*	34 Years Old	32 Years Old
African American	83%	84%
White	5%	6%
Other racial groups	12%	10%
Hispanic origin	10%	9%
Criminal History and Current Incarceration		
Average number of prior incarcerations*	1.9	1.2
Convicted of violent offense	21%	24%
Convicted of drug offense	47%	50%
Convicted of property offense	30%	24%
Average sentence length	54 Months	57 Months
Average time served	18 Months	16 Months
Currently incarcerated for a technical violation*	5%	27%
Released to supervision*	99%	83%

Source: Analysis of data provided by the Illinois Department of Correction to the authors.
*p = .05 (significant difference)

this prison term. Many of these prisoners left children behind: 61 percent had children under eighteen years old, and another 12 percent had grown children.

Overall, the prisoners included in our sample had fairly extensive criminal histories. Over three-quarters (78 percent) of respondents had first been arrested at the age of eighteen or younger and about one-third (34 percent) had served time in a juvenile facility. As adults, 87 percent had been convicted more than once; 75 percent had been in prison at least once before; and 61 percent had had their parole revoked in the past. Drug use was prevalent among this sample: in the six months prior to their current prison term, 66 percent reported drug use, including 22 percent who reported daily heroin use and 15 percent who reported daily cocaine use. Almost half (48 percent) reported excessive use of alcohol.

Regarding their current prison term, almost half of the sample (49 percent) had been convicted of drug offenses, and another 11 percent had been convicted of violent offenses. The average prison stay was about eighteen months, with approximately 60 percent of the respondents serving less than a year. The majority (90 percent) had spent most of their prison term in either a minimum- or a medium-security facility, and 11 percent reported having spent time in a maximum security facility.

After release, we conducted interviews with some of the original 400 sample members at two points in time. Between one and three months after release, we interviewed 264 respondents. When we compared those who were interviewed at one to three months (N = 264) to those who were not (N = 136), we found no significant differences between the two groups across any of the demographic and criminal history characteristics listed in table 3.1, except for race. The respondents who were interviewed at one to three months were somewhat more likely to be black and somewhat less likely to be Hispanic than those not interviewed.

We interviewed 205 respondents between four and eight months after release. Eighty-one percent of the respondents interviewed at this point had also been interviewed at one to three months after release; the balance were respondents from the original pre-release sample who were being interviewed for the first time post-release at four to eight months. When we compared respondents interviewed at four to eight months (N = 205) to those interviewed at one to three months (N = 264), we found no significant differences between the two groups across any of the demographic or criminal justice characteristics listed in table 3.1. (Appendix A provides a detailed discussion of the tracking strategies used to locate and conduct interviews with the released prisoners in the community.)

Prior research on employment among former prisoners has relied on administrative records of employment, principally state unemployment insurance records. These records permit analysis of individual employment records by employers who report such data to these state agencies. However, many legal employers may not report earnings of workers, especially smaller employers and those who recruit employees for a short period, for example, moving companies. The approach in this study is to gather self-reported data on employment experiences at multiple points in time. This method may more accurately capture all legal work experiences, whether reported by employers to state agencies or not. Interviews with former prisoners permit expanded collection of information about the former prisoner, his characteristics, attitudes and life circumstances that are unavailable in administrative records. Such data will enable a more thorough understanding of former prisoners' job experiences after release. Of course, self-reports have their own limitations, including the possibility that individuals may exaggerate or fail to document actual experiences. However, extensive research based on self-reports, including studies on sensitive topics such as substance use and criminal behavior, supports their validity and reliability.

In the remainder of this chapter we first describe pre-prison employment experiences of our sample and their in-prison work or program involvement. Then we describe employment experiences at one to three months after release and at four to eight months after release. Next we examine the factors that predict current employment at four to eight months and number of months worked since release based on data gathered during the in-prison and first post-release interview. Finally, we summarize our findings and discuss the implications for future research.

Results

This chapter presents three sets of analyses of the employment experiences of our interviewed respondents, which provide a longitudinal view of self-reported employment prior to incarceration and up to eight months after release: pre-prison employment experiences and in-prison work-related program involvement; employment experiences one to three months after release, and employment experiences four to eight months after release. We then estimate multivariate models to predict current employment and months worked reported at the second interview, using pre-prison and post-release (from the first interview) individual characteristics and circumstances.

Pre-Prison Employment Experiences

The majority of respondents in our sample had some employment experience before entering prison most recently, although it was often inconsistent and was supplemented by illegal income. During the six months before entering prison, 60 percent of the respondents in our sample were employed for at least some amount of time. Of those who were employed, one-third (33 percent) held one job, and two-thirds held two or more jobs simultaneously. The most common jobs included food service industry jobs, construction, and maintenance. About three-quarters (76 percent) of those who held jobs said their main job had a regular schedule, and two-thirds (66 percent) of those who were employed worked forty or more hours at their main job.[3] The average hourly pay ranged from $1.50 to $50, the median being $8.50.[4] Sixty percent of respondents reported that some or all of their income during the six months before they entered prison came from illegal activity (see figure 3.1). In terms of lifetime employment history, about one-third (34 percent) of respondents reported having been fired from a job at least once before. A little over half (53 percent) reported having held a job for at least two years.

Figure 3.1   Percentage of Releasees' Income Derived from Illegal Activity During the Six Months Before Prison (N = 388)

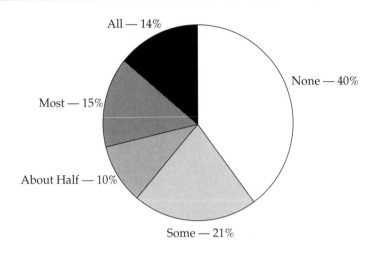

Source: Authors' compilation.

In-Prison Programming and Work Experience

During the time they spent in prison, some respondents participated in programs aimed at improving job skills and educational levels. In our sample, 9 percent of respondents participated in a GED (general equivalency diploma) program during their time in prison, with 4 percent completing and earning a GED. About 31 percent of respondents reported having participated in an employment readiness program while in prison, while much smaller shares of respondents participated in job-training programs (9 percent) or work-release jobs (9 percent). About one-quarter (24 percent) of respondents reported wanting to take a class but not being able to and the majority of these respondents indicated that they were not incarcerated long enough to be eligible to participate in a desired program.

At the time of the pre-release interview, 42 percent of respondents reported that they currently held a job in prison. The most common in-prison job types included dietary-kitchen and janitorial work. Of those who held in-prison jobs at the time of the interview, about half (49 percent) had held their job for one to six months and one-fifth (20 percent) worked forty hours per week.

The majority (86 percent) of respondents in our sample reported participating in a pre-release program while in prison, PreStart.[5] The PreStart program is a mandatory two-week pre-release program administered to prisoners who are scheduled to be released in the next one to twelve months and who will be supervised after release. Of the respondents who reported participating in a pre-release program, 79 percent said that job-search strategies were covered during the program. A smaller share (32 percent) reported that a job referral was provided during the program. About one-third (31 percent) of respondents were provided at least one referral to a community program; many of these were to the Safer Foundation, a Chicago-based organization that, among other services it offers, assists ex-prisoners in finding employment. Over two-thirds (70 percent) of respondents who had participated in a pre-release program "agreed" or "strongly agreed" that the program was helpful for their return to the community.

Most respondents were hoping to find jobs after release but also expected to experience some difficulty in doing so. At the time of the pre-release interview, nearly all respondents (96 percent) "agreed" or "strongly agreed" that it was very important to them to find a job after their release, and the majority (87 percent) thought that having a job would be important in helping them stay out of prison. At the same time, respondents generally expected finding a job to be "pretty hard" or "very hard" (59 percent). By contrast, most respondents (86 percent) expected keeping a job to be "pretty easy" or "very easy." Ninety-two percent of respondents said they wanted "some help" or "a lot of help" finding a job after release. In addition, 89 percent of respondents said they wanted "some help" or "a lot of help" getting job training after release.

Employment Experiences: One to Three Months After Release

About three-quarters (77 percent) of respondents who were not employed at the first interview one to three months after release indicated that they had spent some time looking for a job since their release. The number of hours respondents spent looking for work each week ranged from one to seventy-two hours, the average being fifteen hours. Respondents reported having contacted anywhere from one to over one hundred potential employers. Only one-quarter (26 percent) of the respondents who were interviewed at one to three months thought their neighborhood was a good place to find a job. Perhaps as a result, respondents reported that they would be willing to put in fairly long commutes to jobs: 46 percent of respondents said they would be willing to commute an hour each way, and another 32 percent reported that they would commute up to two hours each way to get to a job.

Despite their job-search efforts and willingness to commute, very few respondents worked for any period of time during the first months after release. Of the respondents interviewed one to three months after release, 20 percent indicated that they had worked for at least one week since release, while 14 percent were currently employed at the time of the interview. Just 10 percent were currently employed full-time (forty or more hours per week).

Almost two-thirds (60 percent) of respondents interviewed at one to three months after release reported that their criminal record had affected their job search to some degree. In response to an open-ended question, most who said their criminal record had affected their job search made comments such as "[Employers] do not want to hire people with records" or "I think [my record] is the reason I have never gotten a callback." However, the majority of respondents who were currently employed at one to three months reported that their current employer knew about their criminal history at the time they were hired.

Among those who were currently employed (full-time or otherwise), the vast majority (94 percent) worked at one job and the most common job types were construction, manual labor, and maintenance. Most respondents who were currently employed went to former employers, talked to friends, and talked to relatives to find their jobs. Only 36 percent of those employed said they were happy with the amount they were being paid. Hourly pay for currently employed respondents ranged from $4.50 to $40, with the median being $9. Respondents, especially those not currently employed, also reported receiving financial support from spouses, family, or friends. Over three-quarters of unemployed respondents relied on these personal connections for financial support. Roughly one-quarter of both employed and unemployed respondents relied on public assistance for financial support.

Employment After Release: Four to Eight Months After Release

As respondents spent more time in the community, an increasing number reported that they had worked for at least some time since release. Of the respondents who were interviewed four to eight months after release (at second interview), a little less than half (44 percent) said they had worked for at least one week since release, as compared to 20 percent at one to three months out. Less than a third (30 percent) of respondents were currently employed at the time of the interview, and just 24 percent of all respondents were currently employed full-time (forty or more hours per week). As at the earlier interview, 60 percent of respondents reported that their criminal record had affected their job search to some degree, although 79 percent of those employed at the second interview reported that their current employer knew about their criminal history at the time they were hired.

The majority (85 percent) of those currently employed were working at one job and the most common job types included construction (20 percent), maintenance (18 percent), and warehouse work and shipping (15 percent). The two most common methods currently employed respondents used to find their jobs involved personal connections: about one-third (30 percent) talked to relatives to find their job, and 18 percent talked to friends. Currently employed respondents' jobs were located anywhere from zero to fifty miles from their homes, the average being 10 miles. The largest share (59 percent) of currently employed respondents relied on public transportation to get to work, while smaller shares drove their own cars (16 percent), were driven by someone else (13 percent), or got to work by other means (12 percent).

Most employed respondents were satisfied with their jobs and "agreed" or "strongly agreed" with several indicators of work quality. The majority of currently employed respondents reported that they got along with their supervisors (97 percent), liked the work they were doing (90 percent), got along with their coworkers (88 percent), were treated fairly by their supervisors (85 percent), thought the job would give them better opportunities in the future (75 percent), and would be happy to have their current job in one year (73 percent). On the other hand, nearly two-thirds (65 percent) of respondents reported that they were not happy with the amount of pay they were receiving for their work. The average pay for those who were currently employed ranged from $3 to $31 per hour, a mean of $9 per hour.

Unemployed respondents continued to rely heavily on financial support from their spouses, families, or friends at four to eight months after release. In addition, about one-third of unemployed respondents relied on some form of public assistance for financial support, as did 18 percent of currently employed respondents. Reported monthly income from all sources for employed respondents ranged from $0 to $8,000, the median being $900—an increase of $180 from the earlier interview; for unemployed respondents, monthly income ranged from $0 to $5,200 (median: $200).

Although more respondents were able to find work as time progressed, they also reported that finding a job was much harder than they had expected—and their expectations at the pre-release interview were not high. Less than half (41 percent) of respondents expected that finding a job would be easy; after release, fewer than 15 percent of respondents at each interview reported that finding a job had been easy. With regard to keeping a job, respondents had higher expectations at the pre-release interview—86 percent expected keeping a job to be easy. When we asked those who had found a job whether it was easy to keep it, the vast majority agreed it was (over 90 percent at both interviews).

Figure 3.2   Percentage of Releasees Employed at One to Three and Four to Eight Months After Release (N = 165)

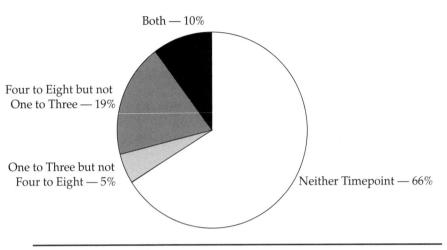

Source: Authors' compilation.

Finally, we examined the stability of employment among the 165 respondents who completed both post-release interviews. As shown in figure 3.2, the majority was not employed at the time of either interview (66 percent), and only 10 percent were currently employed at the time of the interview for both time periods. However, more respondents became employed during the eight-month period after release: 5 percent were initially employed, and employment increased to 19 percent by the second interview. We also examined the number of months worked for these respondents (see figure 3.3): 51 percent worked zero months; 22 percent worked one to two months; 16 percent worked three to four months; 11 percent worked five to six months and less than 1 percent worked seven to eight months, indicating that almost half had some work experience during the first eight months after their release.

Characteristics of Successful and Unsuccessful Job Seekers

We were interested in whether respondents who reported that they were currently employed when interviewed at four to eight months after release differed in any way from those who were not currently employed in terms of personal characteristics, pre- or in-prison experiences and post-release circumstances. Appendix B provides descriptive statistics on all variables used in these analyses, including details about

Figure 3.3   Percentage of Releasees, by Number of Months Worked Post-Release (N = 165)

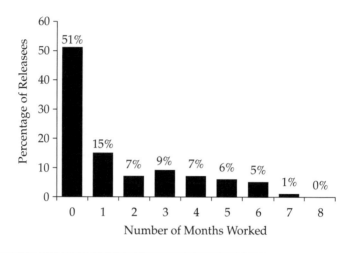

Source: Authors' compilation.

the construction of all scales. We began by examining the bivariate relationships between all proposed predictors (see appendix table 3B.1) and both current employment (yes or no) and the reported number of months worked at the time of the second interview. As this research is exploratory, we use a significance level of at least .10 to identify possible predictors of interest at the bivariate level, and then estimate multivariate models predicting current employment and number of months worked since release. Table 3.2 presents the results of the bivariate analysis.

Demographic and Pre-Prison Characteristics   Other research suggests that pre-prison employment experiences are important predictors of post-release employment outcomes, even more than local labor-market conditions (Sabol, chapter 9, this volume). The importance of pre-prison employment was evident in our sample as well: respondents who worked before prison were more likely to work after release and they reported working more months. There were no significant differences between employed and unemployed respondents in terms of age, education, number of prior convictions, length of time served, marital status, number of minor children, or negative family influences. Employed respondents and those working more months were more likely to have stronger family relationships before prison and to have lived in their own house or apartment. Those who used drugs weekly or more often

Table 3.2   Bivariate Analyses Predicting Employment Outcomes

	Outcome	
Independent Variable	Currently Employed at Four to Eight Months Out	Number of Months Worked at Four to Eight Months Out
Control variables		
Age	NS	NS
Race is nonwhite[a]	NS	Whites worked more months
Number of prior convictions	NS	NS
Length of time served	NS	NS
Pre-prison characteristics		
High school graduate	NS	NS
Married or living with someone as married	NS	NS
Number of minor children	NS	NS
Worked before prison	More likely to be currently employed	Worked more months
Illegal drug use weekly or more often	Less likely to be currently employed	NS
Negative family influences	NS	NS
Better family relationship quality	More likely to be currently employed	Worked more months
Lived in own house or apartment before prison	More likely to be currently employed	Worked more months
In-prison history		
Property-conviction offense	Less likely to be currently employed	Worked fewer months
Violent-conviction offense	More likely to be currently employed	NS
Participated in job training	More likely to be currently employed	NS
Held work-release job	NS	NS
Higher satisfaction with police	More likely to be currently employed	Worked more months
Spirituality	NS	NS

(Table continues on p. 94)

Table 3.2   *Continued*

Independent Variable	Currently Employed at Four to Eight Months Out	Number of Months Worked at Four to Eight Months Out
	Outcome	
Intended to commit crimes or use drugs	NS	NS
Used medication for health condition while in prison	Less likely to be currently employed	Worked fewer months
Any visits from family last six months of prison	More likely to be currently employed	NS
Greater need for help after release	Less likely to be currently employed	NS
Need for job, education, or financial help after release	Less likely to be currently employed	NS
Need for counseling or treatment help after release	Less likely to be currently employed	NS
Will be hard to get job	Less likely to be currently employed	Worked fewer months
No close family	NS	Worked fewer months
Doesn't know where will be living after release	NS	NS
Post-release circumstances at one to three months out		
Neighborhood is good place to find job	NS	NS
Neighborhood disorder	NS	NS
Any drug use or intoxication post-release	NS	NS
Reported fair or poor health	NS	Worked fewer months
Depressed	Less likely to be currently employed	NS
Family relationship quality	NS	NS
Living with spouse or partner	More likely to be currently employed	Worked more months

Table 3.2   *Continued*

	Outcome	
Independent Variable	Currently Employed at Four to Eight Months Out	Number of Months Worked at Four to Eight Months Out
Living with anyone who is often drunk or using drugs	NS	NS
Self-esteem	NS	NS
Tired of problems caused by own crimes	NS	NS
Wants to get life straightened out	NS	NS
Attitude toward parole officer	NS	NS
Owes debt	NS	NS

Source: Authors' compilation.
Note: NS = not significant
[a] Ninety-eight of the sample was nonwhite.

before prison were less likely to be currently employed at four to eight months after release.

In-Prison History, Attitudes, and Expectations   As shown in table 3.2, offense type, job training, participation in work release, health, relationships with family, and recognition of need for assistance after release showed significant bivariate relationships with post-release employment outcomes. These relationships are generally in the expected direction: those who participated in job training were more likely to be employed; those who had family visits in the last six months of their prison term were more likely to be employed; those with no close family worked fewer months; and those who reported more need for assistance after release were less likely to be employed. Health of respondents, as indicated by whether they were on medication while incarcerated, negatively affected post-release employment outcomes. Respondents convicted of violent offenses were more likely to be employed, while those convicted of property offenses were less likely. It is probable that other characteristics of violent and property offenders are responsible for these differences. Finally, respondents who reported greater satisfaction with the police—an indicator of attitudes toward the legal system—were more likely to be currently employed.

Post-Release Circumstances   We also compared respondents who were and were not currently working at the second interview with regard to their post-release circumstances, using several scales to assess the strength of respondents' relationships with their families, children, and intimate partners after release, and to gain some insight into possible effects of respondents' mental health status and attitudes after release. All of the scales included in this analysis are based on at least four survey items, most of which were in the form of statements with a four-point, Likert-type response set ("strongly agree," "agree," "disagree," or "strongly disagree"). All scales have reliabilities of at least .7. Each scale is coded such that a higher score indicates more of the attribute being measured. For example, a score of 4 indicates both highest levels of depression and highest levels of family relationship quality (see notes to table 3B.1 for more information).

When comparing those who were currently employed to those who were not, several significant differences in terms of post-release circumstances emerged. Specifically, measures of overall physical and mental health were correlated with current employment or number of months worked since release: those with poor health or rated as depressed were less likely to be employed. However, those who were living with a partner or spouse after release were more likely to be currently working and reported working more months. Other post-release circumstances—including reported drug use, neighborhood characteristics, and several personal attitudes, such as self-esteem and spirituality—were not related to employment or number of months worked.

Multivariate Analysis of Employment Outcomes

Having observed that a variety of personal and social characteristics of former prisoners are associated with post-release employment outcomes, we estimated separate multivariate models predicting current employment and number of months worked at four to eight months after release. These models were estimated in stages: first, including pre-prison characteristics only, second, adding in-prison history and attitudes, and third, adding measures of post-release circumstances at the initial interview (at one to three months). A final, reduced model includes independent variables that were significant in any prior stage. Four control variables—age, race, number of prior convictions, and length of time served—are included in all models. Results of these analyses are presented in tables 3.3 and 3.4. The results differ somewhat according to the choice of employment measure, either currently employed or number of months worked; substantively important differences are discussed where appropriate.

In tables 3.3 and 3.4, the results from model A that includes only pre-prison characteristics indicate that age and time served were not significant predictors of post-release employment. Contrary to Sabol's finding that individuals with prior incarcerations were employed fewer quarters after release (chapter 9, this volume), in our sample, respondents with more convictions were more likely to work more months. It is possible that these repeat offenders may be receiving more intensive supervision (recall that virtually all respondents in our sample were under supervision), which would support Sabol's results regarding the impact of supervision on employment. Although nonwhite respondents were more likely to report working fewer months, this finding may not be substantively important because of the low number of whites in the sample.

Looking at other pre-prison characteristics of respondents, as expected, pre-prison employment predicted current employment and number of months worked at four to eight months after release. In addition, higher levels of family relationship quality before prison led to better employment outcomes.

Looking at model B in tables 3.3 and 3.4, five indicators of in-prison history and attitudes emerged as predictors of either or both employment outcomes. Respondents who participated in job training while in prison were more likely to be currently employed at four to eight months, while those convicted of a property offense and those who used medications during their prison term were less likely to be employed. (Those on medication also reported working fewer months.) Perhaps motivated by necessity, respondents who expressed pre-release uncertainty about their post-prison living arrangements were also more likely to be employed when interviewed four to eight months after release. Those who expressed satisfaction with the police had worked more months.

Model C in tables 3.3 and 3.4 presents the results after adding indicators of early post-release circumstances (measured at the first interview). Three predictors emerged when examining current employment at four to eight months; however, no post-release circumstances predicted number of months worked. Those who exhibited signs of depression and those with low levels of self-esteem were less likely to have found work, while those who were living with a spouse or partner shortly after release were more likely to be employed at the second interview.

Model D, the final reduced equation, reveals somewhat different results, depending on the choice of employment measure. Significant predictors of current employment are: worked before prison, pre-prison family relationship quality, property conviction offense, participated in job training, unknown living arrangements after release, family relationship quality at initial interview, living with spouse or partner after release, and self-esteem. Fewer respondent characteristics predicted number of months employed: nonwhite, number of prior convictions,

Table 3.3 Multivariate Logistic Regression Models Predicting Current Employment at Four to Eight Months After Release[a]

Independent Variable	Model A: Pre-Prison Characteristics Only	Model B Pre-Prison Characteristics and In-Prison History	Model C: Pre-Prison Characteristics, In-Prison History, Post-Release Circumstances	Model D: Final Reduced Model
Control Variables				
Age	.988	.988	.978	.984
Race is nonwhite	.470	.404	.349	.413
Number of prior convictions	1.191	1.392*	1.261	1.219
Length of time served	1.008	1.007	1.011	1.007
Pre-prison characteristics				
High school graduate	.877	—	—	—
Married or living with someone as married	.951	—	—	—
Number of minor children	1.081	—	—	—
Worked before prison	2.678**	3.192**	3.699**	3.286**
Illegal drug use weekly or more often	.751	—	—	—
Family relationship quality	2.067**	1.596	2.022*	1.926*
Lived in own house or apartment before prison	1.290	—	—	—
In-prison history				
Property-conviction offense	—	.312*	.287*	.354*
Participated in job training	—	4.261**	3.527*	3.917**
Held work-release job	—	.940	—	—
Satisfaction with police	—	1.992*	1.558	1.443

Spirituality	—	.955	—	—
Used medication for health condition while in prison	—	.221**	.289*	.308*
Any visits from family during last six months of prison	—	1.999	—	—
Need for job, education, or financial help after release	—	.552	—	—
Doesn't know where will be living after release	—	2.494*	2.236	2.235*
No close family	—	.409	—	—
Post-release circumstances at one to three months out				
Neighborhood disorder	—	—	.611	—
Any drug use or intoxication post-release	—	—	1.432	—
Reported fair or poor health	—	—	.629	—
Depressed	—	—	.119**	.123**
Family relationship quality	—	—	1.479	—
Living with spouse or partner	—	—	5.666***	4.784***
Living with anyone who is often drunk or using drugs	—	—	1.669	—
Self-esteem	—	—	.220**	.425*
Tired of problems caused by own crimes	—	—	1.180	—
Wants to get life straightened out	—	—	2.012	—
Attitude toward parole officer	—	—	1.189	—
Owes money	—	—	1.667	—
Constant	.033*	.019*	.032	.295
Model R-square[b]	.099	.239	.287	.264
Percentage of missing data	12.1%	15.2%	15.2%	12.1%

Source: Authors' compilation.

[a] Odds ratios are reported. Ratios less than 1.0 are associated with a lower likelihood of current employment, and ratios above 1.0 are associated with a greater likelihood.

[b] Reported as Cox and Snell R-square for logistic regression.

*$p \le .10$, **$p \le .05$, ***$p \le .01$

Table 3.4 Multivariate Regression Models Predicting Number of Months Worked at Four to Eight Months After Release[a]

Independent Variable and Control Variables	Model A: Pre-Prison Characteristics Only	Model B: Pre-Prison Characteristics and In-Prison History	Model C: Pre-Prison Characteristics, In-Prison History, Post-Release Circumstances	Model D: Final Reduced Model
Age	-.019 (.02)	-.020 (.02)	-.021 (.02)	-.023 (.02)
Race is nonwhite	-1.684 (1.01)*	-1.601 (.96)*	-1.789 (1.03)*	-1.924 (.95)**
Number of prior convictions	.216 (.13)*	.301 (.12)***	.248 (.13)*	.264 (.12)**
Length of time served	.004 (.01)	.002 (.01)	.006 (.01)	.003 (.01)
Pre-prison characteristics				
High school graduate	.133 (.35)	—	—	—
Married or living with someone as married	.324 (.40)	—	—	—
Number of minor children	.040 (.12)	—	—	—
Worked before prison	.631 (.36)*	.945 (.34)***	.660 (.35)*	.669 (.33)**
Illegal drug use weekly or more often	-.072 (.35)	—	—	—
Family relationship quality	.573 (.24)**	.149 (.25)	.420 (.27)	.349 (.24)
Lived in own house or apartment before prison	.271 (.36)	—	—	—
In-prison history				
Property conviction offense	—	-.728 (.38)*	-.699 (.39)*	-.694 (.36)*
Participated in job training	—	.695 (.53)	—	—
Held work-release job	—	.011 (.55)	—	—
Satisfaction with police	—	.631 (.29)**	.598 (.32)*	.606 (.29)**

Spirituality	—	-.021 (.25)	—	-.832 (.39)**
Used medication for health condition while in prison	—	-.892 (.39)**	-.553 (.44)	—
Any visits from family during last six months of prison	—	.532 (.36)	—	—
Need for job, education, or financial help after release	—	-.154 (.31)	—	—
Doesn't know where will be living after release	—	.377 (.35)	—	—
No close family	—	-.918 (.74)	—	—
Post-release circumstances at one to three months out				
Neighborhood disorder	—	—	-.130 (.31)	—
Any drug use or intoxication post-release	—	—	.355 (.51)	—
Reported fair or poor health	—	—	-.727 (.54)	—
Depressed	—	—	-.394 (.54)	—
Family relationship quality	—	—	-.092 (.38)	—
Living with spouse or partner	—	—	.610 (.42)	—
Living with anyone who is often drunk or using drugs	—	—	-.131 (.55)	—
Self-esteem	—	—	-.194 (.40)	—
Tired of problems caused by own crimes	—	—	.178 (.18)	—
Wants to get life straightened out	—	—	.099 (.47)	—
Attitude toward parole officer	—	—	-.202 (.33)	—
Owes money	—	—	.271 (.46)	—
Constant	.699 (1.45)	.740 (1.58)	1.397 (2.32)	.965 (1.40)
Model R-square	.118	.264	.215	.172
Percent missing data	12.1%	15.2%	12.7%	9.1%

Source: Authors' compilation.

[a] Unstandardized beta values (with standard errors in parentheses) are reported. Positive beta values correlate with a higher number of months worked, and negative values correspond to a lower number of months worked.

*p ≤ .10, **p ≤ .05, ***p ≤ .01

worked before prison, property conviction offense, pre-prison satisfaction with police, and used medication for health condition while in
prison. None of the immediate post-release circumstances predicted reported number of months employed at the second interview.

Discussion and Future Directions

These findings shed some light on the preparation of soon-to-be-
released prisoners to reenter the workforce after release and their actual
employment experiences once back in the community. Most respondents in our sample entered prison with some employment experience,
typically at low-paying jobs that they did not keep for long periods of
time and often supplemented with illegal income. During the time they
spent in prison, small shares (less than a third) of respondents participated in programming aimed at improving education levels and job
skills. Even while they were still in prison, less than half of respondents
thought it would be easy to find a job after release and the vast majority
wanted help in locating employment and securing job training after
release.

Indeed, in the first few months after release, very few respondents
were employed for any period of time. Those who were employed held
low-skilled, low-paying jobs. Over time, more respondents found jobs
for at least some period of time, although the job types remained the
same. Nonetheless, those who were employed at each interview period
expressed satisfaction with their jobs in every area but pay. Employed
respondents supplemented their income with financial support from
family, friends, and spouses, and public assistance, and unemployed
respondents relied on these sources to an even higher degree. Other
studies have found an immediate but transitory increase in the employment of released prisoners, which may be related to post-release supervision (Pettit and Lyons, chapter 7, this volume). However, in our sample, nearly all respondents (99 percent) were released to supervision
and were on supervision throughout the follow-up period, so we cannot examine the impact of supervision status on employment.

The multivariate analysis examined simultaneously the impact of demographic characteristics, criminal and substance-use history, in-prison
experiences, and post-release circumstances on post-release employment. Results indicated that pre-prison and in-prison characteristics of
former prisoners seem to be more important influences on early employment outcomes (four to eight months after release) than post-
release circumstances. In particular, whether the respondent had been
working before incarceration is a strong predictor of post-release employment. Although the lack of impact of post-release circumstances

was somewhat unexpected, it may be that sufficient time had not elapsed for post-release circumstances to influence job prospects, especially as only 30 percent were currently employed at the second interview. Some differences existed between the model predicting current employment and the model predicting number of months worked. It is interesting to note that a few post-release circumstances (health, family relationships, and self-esteem) predicted current employment, but not number of months worked. However, with the modest sample size available for these analyses, it is difficult to interpret the substantive meaning of these differences and future analyses with larger samples may be needed to explore this issue in more detail.

An important methodological issue in the study of employment among former prisoners is whether self-reports of behavior and experiences produce the same results as studies based on administrative data. The chapters in this volume are primarily based on administrative data. Former prisoners' self-reports of their post-release employment experiences from the Illinois Returning Home project are consistent in some ways with these other studies, but some differences also emerged. Harry J. Holzer, Steven Raphael, and Michael Stoll (chapter 4, this volume) report that employers are more likely to hire ex-offenders if the jobs involve limited customer contact. Self-reports from respondents in the Returning Home study support this finding: most former prisoners find jobs in construction, custodial and maintenance work, or warehouse and shipping jobs.

However, chapters in this volume reach different conclusions about the effect of prisoner involvement in job training or readiness programs in prison on post-release employment. In contrast to the findings of a positive effect of job training on employment at four to eight months after release in this chapter, Sabol (chapter 9, this volume) found an unanticipated effect: participation in a vocational training program reduced post-release employment for a sample in Ohio. However, results from this chapter and John H. Tyler and Jeffrey Kling (chapter 8, this volume) both found no effect for a work-release program. With respect to the effects of other correctional programs, Tyler and Kling also found that participating in GED course work did not lead to higher wages after release for white ex-offenders, and for minority ex-offenders, the small benefit of the GED disappeared by the second year. Consistent with this finding, in analyses not shown in this chapter using the Illinois Returning Home data, earning a GED in prison had no effect on post-release employment. Although a recent meta-analysis of 30 studies concluded that work and education programs for the general-offender population reduced recidivism by 5 to 13 percent (Aos et al. 2006), many of the studies included in the meta-analysis are quite dated. More contemporary tests of the role of correctional programs on post-release outcomes using rigorous methods such as those used by Tyler and Kling (chapter 8, this volume) are sorely needed.

This examination of early post-release employment experiences among men released from Illinois prisons and returning to Chicago increases our understanding of the role of work in these men's lives. The majority worked for wages prior to their incarceration, most at low-skilled jobs not requiring a high school education. Nearly all respondents said that it was very important to find a job after release, but they expected that finding a job would be difficult and that they would need help. After release, those who found jobs relied on family, friends, and former employers—people who knew about their criminal record. Specific job training in prison was more useful to ex-prisoners than education or work-release programs. And those with strong family relationships were more likely to be employed. However, several difficult personal circumstances appear to impede employability among recently released prisoners: housing, health conditions requiring medication, depression, and low self-esteem. Thus, community service providers must be prepared to address these problems before full employment can be achieved.

This chapter is an early product of our larger study, Returning Home: Understanding the Challenges of Prisoner Reentry, which is examining prisoner reentry in four states—Maryland, Illinois, Ohio, and Texas. Additional analyses of data gathered from interviews with ex-prisoners in Chicago at twelve to sixteen months after their release are planned and will allow us to determine whether the initial increase and then decline in employment rates found by Sabol (chapter 9, this volume), Becky Pettit and Christopher Lyons (2002), and others is evident among the Chicago ex-prisoners in our sample as well. We also plan to combine data from Chicago with data collected from men returning to Cleveland and Houston, which will provide a larger sample and permit us to examine state-specific differences in employment experiences. With the expanded sample, we will also be able to address other research questions such as whether post-release supervision improves employment outcomes.

Our results illustrate the added value of interviews with prisoners both before and after release for understanding the individual, family, and community circumstances affecting reentry success and failure. Such interviews, combined with analyses of official records, help identify needs of former prisoners, such as housing, employment, and health care, and the specific types of assistance that are most beneficial to a successful post-release adjustment, such as family support. The longitudinal aspect of this study will help practitioners prioritize programs by focusing on some of these needs during incarceration so that individuals can be better prepared for employment opportunities after release.

Appendix A: Locating Respondents for the Illinois Returning Home Post-Release Interviews*

Tracking and locating respondents in the Illinois Returning Home study was an integral part of the field data collection effort and a key activity in securing good response rates. In order to gain cooperation from respondents, our locating strategy involved (re-) establishing contact with the former prisoners at each successive data collection wave.

The first important step in a successful locating strategy was to gather contact information from the inmates in the course of the pre-release interview. To this end, the Urban Institute prepared "locator" forms, which study participants were asked to fill out at this interview. The form asked the respondent to provide personal identifying information including full name, aliases, date of birth, Social Security number, and driver's license or state ID card number. He was also asked to provide address and telephone information for the place where he expected to live after release and the name of and his relationship to the primary resident at that address. Telephone and address information of a spouse or partner and up to three relatives or friends who usually know the respondent's whereabouts were also collected. Finally, the form asked the respondent if a message could be left for him at any of the telephone numbers provided, and what type of message he preferred the Metro Chicago Information Center (MCIC) to leave.

Table 3A.1 shows the number of pieces of information provided in the locator form and the completion rates for the first and second post-release interviews. As the table indicates, the fewer contacts provided, the lower the response rate in the follow-up interviews. Although it is possible that respondents who provided fewer relatives and friends' information for renewed contact really had no other information to provide, encouragement to provide more information might have led to greater success in locating the respondents in subsequent waves.

In addition to the twenty-one respondents who provided no home address at all, two specifically wrote in "homeless," nine indicated they would go to a shelter or halfway house but did not know which, and five listed a specific halfway house in Chicago, St. Leonard's.

All of the information on the locator form was keyed and printed on the face-sheet for each case. The face-sheet is the main case-assignment

---

*Alisú Schoua-Glusberg wrote the appendix.

Table 3A.1   Information Provided by Respondent on Locator Form Before Release

	Home address	Home telephone	Number of Re-Contacts Provided by Respondent Before Release					
			6	5	4	3	2	1
	379	294	6	8	28	72	116	132
First post-release completes			83%	87.5%	84.6%	79%	78.5%	69%
Second post-release completes			67%	75%	64.3%	75%	71.5%	62%

Source: Based on analysis of interviewer records.

document provided to interviewers for each case. It contains all of the locating information known for the inmate as well as his release date from prison and the institution where he was interviewed at pre-release, but does not show his Social Security number, since that information should not be "floating" around in the field. The respondent may see his face-sheet in the course of the interview and not appreciate seeing sensitive information such as the Social Security number visible in plain sight.

In each post-release interview wave, the face-sheet incorporated any new addresses or other locating information obtained in the prior interview. However, instead of listing only the most recent information, the face-sheets listed the "history of addresses," which included every prior address and phone number ever provided by the respondent or found through field locating. Interviewers have found that this mobile population often returns to prior addresses. Therefore, it is important to keep every piece of locating information available throughout the study. For instance, in the second post-release interview wave, of the 222 respondents interviewed outside of prison, 135 were at the original address they had provided while still incarcerated. Twelve percent of them had moved elsewhere in the intervening months.

Through the partnership established by the Urban Institute with both the Illinois Criminal Justice Information Authority and the Illinois Department of Corrections (IDOC), the IDOC gave MCIC access to the protocol system. This is the system used in Illinois to keep the parole system informed as to parolees' whereabouts. Inmates are instructed to call a toll-free number to provide any changes of address or telephone information. IDOC gave permission to MCIC to make email inquiries about batches of inmates on a regular basis over the course of the study.

Another time-consuming but effective locating strategy consisted of regular and periodic checking of the Illinois Department of Corrections Inmate Locator webpage to obtain information on reincarcerations and releases. Although the locating information from the protocol system was invaluable at times, checks were not frequent enough for interviewers to remain up to date on the prison comings and goings of the members of the sample. This meant that interviewers did not have information necessary for them to prioritize adequately about which of their cases to set aside and which ones to concentrate on because a sample member had been newly incarcerated. Similarly, timely information on the fact that a sample member had been released in the last week or two allowed them to try again to contact him while he would be most likely to have interest in the incentive payment. The IDOC website was searched sometimes as often as weekly, at other times every two or three weeks. Additionally, the website of the Cook County sheriff also allowed on-line checking of persons incarcerated in the Cook County jail system. Unfortunately, however, the sheriff's website does not use the prisoner ID number system of the IDOC, making it necessary to search by name and birth date, a process more prone to errors and misidentification.

Toward the end of the second post-release wave, interviews were attempted with respondents who were reincarcerated in the state prisons of the IDOC. Two teams of interviewers were dispatched throughout the state and visited approximately twenty institutions, where they completed forty-four interviews. A similar approach is being employed for the third post-release interviews.

A successful respondent-locating strategy rests to a great extent on the abilities of the field interviewers assigned to the study. For Returning Home–Illinois, MCIC selected only experienced field interviewers who had previously worked with populations similar in geographic distribution and socioeconomic status in the city of Chicago. These experienced interviewers did not need guidance on how to track and locate respondents, as that was already part of their skill set. The interviewers selected were known to be resourceful and persistent in their efforts to find respondents.

Because Returning Home–Illinois recruited participants prior to their release from prison and fielded cases for post-release interviews according to the date of the prior interview, fresh cases were made available to interviewers on a rolling basis. This provided each interviewer with a good mix of worked and new cases so that she or he was able to continue tracking efforts in the field while simultaneously completing newer, easier-to-find cases. This is important from the standpoint of interviewer morale.

There are two views as to the advisability of having the same interviewer conduct subsequent follow-up interviews with each respondent.

On the one hand, establishing rapport with a respondent can lead to a more open interview in which the respondent answers the questions with more interest and attention. Success in completing a follow-up interview is also higher when the same interviewer contacts the respondent again. However, some interviewer-effects research has shown underreporting of socially undesirable activities when the interviewer is known by the respondent from earlier interviews. Nonetheless, strictly from a locating perspective, assigning the case to the same interviewer who completed the case in an earlier wave is highly advisable. In Illinois, Returning Home interviewers were reassigned in each wave to the cases they had completed previously. The interviewers themselves attribute a good part of their success in locating respondents to the rapport they had previously established with the former prisoner's relatives, both through the post-release family interview and the locating calls in the prior wave. Mothers, sisters, and grandmothers have proved to be willing and helpful associates to the interviewer in locating the respondent. One grandmother who would not reveal the phone number of her released grandson set up a three-way call to put the interviewer in touch with the respondent. Many stories such as this one reveal equally resourceful and helpful relatives.

Contacting a respondent begins with telephone calls, if telephone numbers were provided by the respondent. After all telephone leads had been exhausted, the interviewer began field-locating efforts, going in person to the last known address for the respondent. Often, telephones had been disconnected (generally as a result of nonpayment of bills), yet the respondent was at the address the interviewer visited. The presence or absence of the respondent's last name in the mailbox for an apartment building has been found to be unrelated to his actual presence at that address. Interviewers visited addresses and spoke to residents and neighbors to establish whether the respondent could actually be found there. Persistence was instrumental in success: one interviewer visited an address to find out that the respondent had moved out and left no forwarding address. After chatting with a neighbor, the neighbor indicated that once in a while she ran into the respondent on the bus. The interviewer gave the neighbor her card and asked her to put it in her purse in case she ran into the respondent on the bus. When that happened next, the neighbor gave the respondent the card and he called the interviewer to set up the appointment.

Although keeping cases in the hands of interviewers who had successfully completed them in prior waves generally proved to be a successful approach, occasionally interviewers would be stumped in their efforts to locate a respondent. Contacts and neighbors may get tired of seeing them looking for the respondent and no longer react in a helpful manner. The interviewers themselves may become too discouraged to

Table 3B.1   Variables Used in Bivariate and Multivariate Analyses

	Minimum	Maximum	Mean	Std. Dev.
Dependent variables				
Currently employed	0	1	0.29	0.46
Number of months worked	0	7	1.48	1.97
Control variables				
Age	19	65	35.05	9.94
Race is nonwhite	0	1	0.98	0.15
Number of prior convictions	0	4	2.31	1.47
Length of time served (months)	1.48	200.99	20.93	32.91
Pre-prison characteristics				
High school graduate	0	1	0.44	0.50
Married or living with someone as married	0	1	0.24	0.43
Number of minor children	0	20	1.46	2.07
Worked before prison	0	1	0.64	0.48
Illegal drug use weekly or more often	0	1	0.60	0.49
Family relationship quality[a]	1	4	3.23	0.69
Lived in own house/ apartment before prison	0	1	0.43	0.50
In-prison history				
Property conviction offense	0	1	0.27	0.44
Participated in job training	0	1	0.13	0.33
Held work release job	0	1	0.10	0.31
Satisfaction with police[b]	1	4	2.20	0.60
Spirituality[c]	1	4	3.25	0.69
Used medication for health condition while in prison	0	1	0.22	0.41
Any visits from family last 6 months of prison	0	1	0.35	0.48
Need for job/ education/ financial help after release[d]	0	2	1.07	0.53
Doesn't know where will be living after release	0	1	0.31	0.47
No close family	0	1	0.08	0.26
Post-release circumstances at one to three months out				
Neighborhood disorder[e]	1	4	1.98	0.63
Any drug use or intoxication post-release	0	1	0.13	0.34
Reported fair/poor health	0	1	0.13	0.34
Depressed[f]	0	1	0.14	0.35

(Table continues on p. 110)

Table 3B.1   *Continued*

	Minimum	Maximum	Mean	Std. Dev.
Family relationship quality	1	4	3.58	0.55
Living with spouse/partner	0	1	0.19	0.40
Living with anyone who is drunk often or using drugs	0	1	0.11	0.31
Self-esteem[g]	1	4	3.39	0.55
Is tired of problems caused by own crimes[h]	1	4	2.99	0.96
Wants to get life straight-ened out[i]	1	4	3.76	0.43
Attitude towards parole officer[j]	1	4	3.16	0.58
Owes debt	0	1	0.16	0.37

Source: Authors' compilation.

[a] The family-relationship-quality scale consisted of eleven items indicating the degree to which respondents had someone in their family to talk to about their problems, to enjoy spending time with, and to love and make them feel wanted. The scale had a reliability of 0.95 and scores ranged from 1 to 4, with higher scores equaling greater (more positive) family relationship quality.

[b] Satisfaction with police was measured by six items indicating the degree to which respondents believed police did a good job dealing with neighborhood problems, were unbiased, and were able to maintain order. The scale had a reliability of 0.74 and scores ranged from 1 to 4, with higher scores equaling greater satisfaction with police.

[c] Spirituality was measured by six items indicating whether respondents believed in prayer, whether they found strength in religion and spirituality, and how much a part of their life was defined by their faith. The scale had a reliability of 0.86, and scores ranged from 1 to 4, with higher scores equaling greater spirituality.

[d] Need for job, education, or financial help was measured by seven items indicating how much help respondents believed they would need finding a job, getting more education or job training, and obtaining financial assistance. The scale had a reliability of 0.87 and scores ranged from 0 to 2, with higher scores equaling greater need for help.

[e] The neighborhood-disorder scale consisted of five items measuring the degree of trouble, safety, crime, and disorder in respondents' neighborhoods. The scale had a reliability of 0.72, and scores ranged from 1 to 4, with higher scores equaling more neighborhood disorder.

[f] Depression diagnosis was derived from respondents' answers to twenty items measuring their feelings of sadness and other symptoms of depression. The questionnaire utilized the Center for Epidemiologic Studies Depression (CES-D) Scale, which measures the frequency of these symptoms; scores of 16 and above indicate a high likelihood of depression (details available from author).

[g] Self-esteem was measured by six items (items 14, 41, 48, 61, 71, 79) taken from the Texas Christian University Client Evaluation of Self and Treatment, Intake Version (TCU CEST-Intake) (see website: http://www.ibr.tcu.edu/pubs/datacoll/Forms/cesi.pdf, accessed on January 15, 2007). The scale had a reliability of 0.81, and scores ranged from 1 to 4, with higher scores equaling greater self-esteem.

[h] Scores ranged from 1 to 4, with higher scores equaling greater agreement with the statement.

[i] Scores ranged from 1 to 4, with higher scores indicating greater agreement with the statement.

[j] Attitude toward parole officer was measured by seven items indicating the degree to which respondents felt their parole officer was helpful, respectful, and trustworthy. The scale had a reliability of 0.83, and scores ranged from 1 to 4, with higher scores equaling a more positive attitude.

be creative and resourceful. At this point, field management would switch cases around so that a fresh outlook on a case could be pursued by another interviewer.

Keeping the same interviewer assigned to a case in future waves also provides a check to make sure that the person purporting to be the respondent is really the person we are looking for. Asking participants to provide proof of identity is not conducive to creating good rapport with the interviewee. In addition, many released prisoners do not have proof of identity. In one case where the second post-release interviewer was different from the first post-release interviewer, a man reached at the respondent's telephone number set up the appointment and met the interviewer to complete the survey. However, that week's check of the Cook County sheriff webpage showed that the actual respondent was in jail and had been incarcerated on the date of the interview. A comparison of the respondent's signature on the incentive payment receipt with the inmate's signature at the pre-release and first post-release interviews revealed this was not the same person, and the second post-release interview was destroyed.

Interviewers had to become familiar with the shelters and halfway houses in Chicago. When they received a case that listed a respondent at such a location, they established contact with the facility manager, explained the reason for their need to contact the respondent, and gained facility cooperation, which not only led to finding the respondents as they moved in or out of the facility but also to securing a private space in the building where they could conduct the interview.

While locating released prisoners who are back in the community is, in many ways, no different than finding other populations of respondents of similar demographics in comparable neighborhoods, it requires learning and using some new skills and adding some extra steps, as we learned in the Illinois Returning Home study. The men in the study proved to be quite mobile, yet by and large remained connected to family even as they moved. Reincarceration and re-release happened fast for many, and it was important to stay informed of that for maximum efficiency in locating and interviewing them. Establishing and maintaining a good relationship with prisoners' female relatives was instrumental to success in making contact with the respondents. It also helped to have the same interviewer continue to work the case in subsequent waves.

The Russell Sage Foundation provided funding for a pilot study for the Returning Home project in Maryland which developed and tested the instruments and data collection methods for the overall project. Data collection for Returning Home in Illinois was supported by the John D. and

Catherine T. MacArthur Foundation, the Rockefeller Foundation, the Woods Fund of Chicago, the Annie E. Casey Foundation, and the Illinois Criminal Justice Information Authority. The Metro Chicago Information Center (MCIC) conducted the original data collection, under the expert direction of Alisú Schoua-Glusberg. We thank Jennifer Castro of the Urban Institute's Justice Policy Center for her assistance in conducting the sampling and attrition and multivariate analyses and Nancy La Vigne for her suggestions on an earlier draft.

Notes

1. The Illinois Department of Corrections (IDOC) requires the vast majority of prisoners to complete this two-week pre-release program, which gathers groups of ten to thirty prisoners in a classroom setting. We scheduled a time during regular PreStart program hours to explain the study and distribute a self-administered survey to those willing to participate. This strategy resulted in a participation rate of 76 percent.
2. The fact that prisoners in our sample were more likely to have been released to supervision may be explained by the fact that Illinois prisoners who are incarcerated for a technical parole violation are not eligible for the PreStart class (as presumably they had completed it during their initial term of confinement), and that prisoners released without supervision are more likely to have been incarcerated for a technical parole violation.
3. "Main job" is that for which the respondent worked the most hours, on average.
4. Ninety-seven percent of respondents who worked in the six months before they entered prison reported hourly wages between $1 and $50. Five respondents who earned more than $50 per hour were excluded from the analysis.
5. This statistic is based on a question that asks respondents whether they participated in a pre-release program but does not specify PreStart by name. Even though we know all respondents did participate, since we sampled through PreStart, it is likely that some respondents did not think of PreStart as a "pre-release program" and therefore answered no to this question.

References

Aos, Steve, Marna Miller, and Elizabeth Drake. 2006. *Evidence-Based Adult Corrections Programs: What Works and What Does Not*. Olympia, Wash.: Washington State Institute for Public Policy.
Bernstein, Jared, and Ellen Houston. 2000. *Crime and Work: What We Can Learn from the Low-wage Labor Market*. Washington, D.C.: Economic Policy Institute.
Bushway, Shawn, and Peter Reuter. 2001. "Labor Markets and Crime." In *Crime*, 2d, edited by James Q. Wilson and Joan Petersilia. Oakland, Calif.: ICS Press.
Gaes, Gerald G., Timothy J. Flanagan, Lawrence Motiuk, and Lynn Stewart. 1999. "Adult Correctional Treatment." *Prisons: Crime and Justice* 26: 361–426.
Grogger, Jeff. 1998. "Market Wages and Youth Crime." *Journal of Labor Economics* 16(4): 756–91.

Hagan, John, and Ronit Dinovitzer. 1999. "Collateral Consequences of Imprisonment for Children, Communities, and Prisoners." *Prisons: Crime and Justice*
26: 121–62.

Harer, Miles D. 1994. *Recidivism of Federal Prisoners Released in 1987.* Washington: Federal Bureau of Prisons, Office of Research and Evaluation.

Holzer, Harry J., Steven Raphael, and Michael Stoll. 2004. "Will Employers Hire
Former Offenders? Employer Preferences, Background Checks, and Their
Determinants." In *Imprisoning America: The Social Effects of Mass Incarceration*,
edited by Bruce Western, Mary Pattillo, and David Weiman. New York: Russell Sage Foundation.

Laub, John L., and Robert J. Sampson. 1993. "Turning Points in the Life Course:
Change Matters to the Study of Crime." *Criminology* 31: 301–25.

Lynch, James P., and William J. Sabol. 2001. *Prisoner Reentry in Perspective.*
Washington, D.C.: Urban Institute Press.

Pettit, Becky, and Christopher Lyons. 2002. "Community Corrections." In
Crime: Public Policies for Crime Control, edited by James Q. Wilson and Joan
Petersilia. Oakland, Calif.: Institute for Contemporary Studies Press.

Sampson, Robert J., and John L. Laub. 1993. *Crime in the Making: Pathways and
Turning Points Through Life.* Cambridge, Mass.: Harvard University Press.

———. 1997. "A Life-Course Theory of Cumulative Disadvantage and the Stability of Delinquency." *Advances in Criminological Theory* 7: 133–61.

Uggen, Christopher. 2000. "Work as a Turning Point in the Life Course of
Criminals: A Duration Model of Age, Employment, and Recidivism." *American Sociological Review* 65(4): 529–46.

Uggen, Christopher, and Melissa Thompson. 2003. "The Socioeconomic Determinants of Ill-Gotten Gains: Within-Person Changes in Drug Use and Illegal
Earnings." *American Journal of Sociology* 109(1): 146–85.

Visher, Christy, Vera Kachnowski, Nancy La Vigne, and Jeremy Travis. 2004.
Baltimore Prisoners' Experiences Returning Home. Washington, D.C.: Urban Institute Press.

Visher, Christy, Nancy La Vigne, and Jill Farrell. 2003. *Illinois Prisoners' Reflec-
tions on Returning Home.* Washington, D.C.: Urban Institute Press.

Visher, Christopher, and Jeremy Travis. 2003. "Transitions from Prison to Community: Understanding Individual Pathways." In *Annual Review of Sociology,*
vol. 29, edited by John Hagan and Karen Heimer. Palo Alto: Annual Reviews.

Western, Bruce, Jeffrey Kling, and David F. Weiman. 2001. "The Labor Market
Consequences of Incarceration." *Crime and Delinquency* 47(3): 410–427.

Wilson, David B., Catherine A. Gallagher, Doris L. MacKenzie, and Mark Coggeshall. 1999. "A Quantitative Review and Description of Corrections-Based
Education, Vocation, and Work Programs." *Corrections Management Quarterly*
3(4): 8–18.

= Part II =

The Demand Side of
the Labor Market

.

= Chapter 4 =

The Effect of an Applicant's Criminal History on Employer Hiring Decisions and Screening Practices: Evidence from Los Angeles

HARRY J. HOLZER, STEVEN RAPHAEL, AND MICHAEL A. STOLL

B etween 1988 and 2000, the nation's incarceration rate doubled, from about 250 to nearly 500 per 100,000 persons. The Bureau of Justice Statistics (BJS) estimates that approximately 9 percent of all men will serve some time in state or federal prisons, with considerably higher figures for blacks (about 30 percent) and Latinos (16 percent). These trends are especially pronounced for California and, within California, for Los Angeles. California houses a disproportionate share of the nation's recently released prisoners. In 2001, roughly 23 percent of the 600,000 prisoners released during the year resided in California, though the state accounted for only 11 percent of the national population. What's more, nearly one-third of the 140,000 California state prisoners released in 2001 returned to Los Angeles County.[1]

Reintegrating this growing population of ex-prison inmates into noninstitutionalized society is a top policy problem faced by state and local governments throughout the nation. Reintegration failures often result in additional crimes committed by ex-inmates (Raphael and Stoll 2004), further incarceration spells for released inmates, and, given the racial composition of ex-offenders, a greater degree of racial socioeconomic inequality (Holzer, Offner, and Sorenson 2005).

Gainful employment opportunities for ex-offenders are important for facilitating the successful reintegration of released inmates. However, suitable employment opportunities for ex-offenders are likely to be scarce, relative to the supply of ex-offenders, for a number of reasons.[2] To start, having served time is likely to diminish workers' value to potential employers, for the workers' human capital may depreciate while they are incarcerated, as they fail to accumulate additional work experience, and as incarceration may negatively affect the "soft skills" that employers value.

Beyond these supply-side effects, however, ex-offenders are also likely to encounter reluctance among potential employers to hire workers with criminal history records. Employers in businesses that entail frequent customer contact may avoid hiring ex-offenders in the belief that former inmates are likely to victimize customers, exposing the employer to potential legal liability. Moreover, some employers in certain industries and hiring into certain occupations are legally prohibited from hiring ex-offenders.

In earlier work on employer demand for ex-offenders, we demonstrate many of the demand-side barriers that ex-offenders face and the impact of employer sentiments on hiring outcomes. Specifically, using establishment surveys (establishments are businesses that hire workers) from the early 1990s we documented the strong reluctance of employers to hire ex-offenders, the types of employers that will and will not hire ex-offenders, as well as the interaction between employer aversion to ex-offenders and screening behavior. With respect to the latter topic, we document the extent to which employers formally screen the criminal history records of applicants or informally screen by statistically discriminating against applicants with demographic characteristics (such as race and gender) perceived to be correlated with the likelihood of having a criminal past (Holzer, Raphael, and Stoll 2004, 2006a, 2006b).[3] While instructive, these earlier research efforts relied on fairly crude measures of employer sentiment regarding ex-offenders and a very vaguely worded question regarding whether the employer checks criminal backgrounds.

In this chapter we analyze a more recent survey of employers in the Los Angeles metropolitan area that includes considerably more detailed information regarding employer sentiments about ex-offenders, actual hiring behavior with respect to ex-offenders, and the methods used to screen the criminal histories of applicants. With this new survey we present empirical evidence regarding a number of basic questions that could not be answered with existing employer data. For example, does employer willingness to hire ex-offenders vary with the nature of the offense committed? Does an employer's stated aversion to ex-offenders correlate with actual hiring behavior? How exactly do most employers check the criminal histories of applicants, and at what point in the hiring process?

We investigate these questions using a survey of employers in Los Angeles carried out during the year 2001. While many of the results confirm our earlier findings, we are able to paint a more nuanced portrait of how employers consider criminal history records in making hiring decisions. Our analysis reveals that, although a substantial fraction of employers indicate that they would probably not hire an ex-offender, a sizable number are willing to consider mitigating factors, such as the type of offense committed and when the offense occurred. This suggests that employer demand for ex-offenders, though low, may be more flexible than previously believed. In addition, we find that the use of criminal history checks has increased considerably over the past decade, with a substantial fraction of employers using private services to perform such checks. Finally, we investigate the correlates of the use of criminal background checks and the likelihood that employers have recently hired an ex-offender. In general, larger establishments with more formal human resource systems screen the criminal backgrounds of employees. Regarding hiring, firms that are legally prohibited from hiring ex-offenders, as well as employers hiring into jobs involving customer contact, the handling of cash, and interaction with children are considerably less likely to hire felons.

Description of the 2001 Establishment Survey

Our data come from a twenty-minute telephone survey of 619 establishments in Los Angeles, conducted between May 2001 and November 2001. Our survey focuses on Los Angeles employers for a variety of reasons. Los Angeles is a large and populous metropolitan area in a state with a large incarcerated population. Moreover, nearly a third of recently released prisoners return to Los Angeles County (the geographic boundaries of our sampling area).

At the time of the survey, the local unemployment rate stood at a thirty-year low. However, while the survey was in the field, the Los Angeles economy began to weaken, along with the national economy, with the manufacturing sector suffering the most pronounced slowdown. Moreover, the time frame of the survey brackets the September 11 terrorist attacks. These events are likely to have affected employer willingness to hire ex-offenders, perhaps negatively. We explore this possibility later in the chapter.

Our sampling strategy and survey instrument closely resembles those used in the earlier establishment survey, which we analyze in our prior research.[4] Employers were sampled from lists compiled by Survey Sampling Inc., primarily from telephone directories. This list was stratified ex-ante into four establishment-size categories, where size refers to the number of employees. We used a random-stratified sampling strategy to select employers whereby establishments were sampled across strata in proportion to the amount of regional employment accounted for by the establishment-size category. Within strata, we sampled establishments at random. Thus, the sample is representative of the distribution of the workforce in the Los Angeles region across establishment-size categories without any need for additional size weighting.

Telephone interviews were conducted with the person in the establishment responsible for entry-level hiring. Establishments were screened according to whether they had hired an employee into a position not requiring a college degree over the previous year—but this screen eliminated no firms from our sample. The overall survey response rate was about 65 percent, in the range of other similar recent firm surveys (Holzer and Stoll 2001).

The survey contains extensive information on the establishment's characteristics (for example, size, industry, presence of collective bargaining, minority ownership status, and the racial composition of its applicants) as well as on the characteristics of the most recently filled job that did not require a college degree. This includes the screening and hiring practices of employers used in filling the job and the task and skill requirements for the job, among other factors. Most important, the survey also contains a number of questions regarding employer demand for ex-offenders.

In this paper we focus principally on employers' stated willingness to hire ex-offenders, their actual hiring of ex-offenders, and the methods that employers use to screen the criminal history records of job applicants. Concerning willingness to hire, we asked all respondents whether they would accept an applicant with a criminal record for the last noncollege job filled. The possible responses included "Definitely will," "Probably will," "Depends on the crime," "Probably not," and "Absolutely not." We also asked about the acceptability of various types of applicants with criminal records, varying the type of felony. In addition, we asked employers the following question: "Suppose you were contacted by an employment agency that was trying to place young males with criminal records. Do you currently have any open positions that you might consider filling with this group of workers?" Here, the possible responses are simply "Yes" or "No." To gauge employers' actual hiring of ex-offenders we ask whether the employer knows of any instance over the past year where the business hired a male with a criminal background. Possible responses to this question include "Yes," "No," and "Don't know."

With regard to employer screening practices, we ask a number of detailed questions to ascertain whether, the extent to which, and the manner in which employers perform criminal background checks of prospective employees. First, we inquire about the frequency with which employers check the criminal backgrounds of applicants, with possible responses including "Always," "Sometimes," and "Never." We also include a series of questions concerning whether the employer checked for the last filled noncollege position, whether they were legally required to do so, from what source they gleaned information on the applicant's criminal background, and when in the hiring process they conducted the check.

To be sure, our measures of employer demand are not perfect; they have some obvious shortcomings that merit discussion. For example, our measures of employer willingness to hire ex-offenders rely on what employers say rather than their actual behavior. This measure of employer preferences and demand is relatively uncontaminated by inter-establishment variation in the supply of ex-offenders they face; but this subjective variable might understate or overstate actual employer demand for ex-offenders. With respect to our measure of actual hiring, whether a firm has hired an ex-offender in the last year will reflect a mix of demand-side as well as supply-side factors that might influence access of such workers to these firms. To the extent that ex-offenders are geographically clustered or rely on limited information networks in seeking employment, actual hiring may understate true demand. Nonetheless, a comparison of stated and actual demand for ex-offenders should be quite instructive. Moreover, given that both measures reveal a fairly strong reluctance to hire ex-offenders, such concerns do not compromise the results presented below.

In addition to the conceptual difficulties associated with trying to measure employer demand, there are several other concerns that deserve mention. The first concerns the exact definition of "criminal background." For the purposes of this study, a person has a criminal history record if he or she has been previously convicted of a felony, regardless of whether the person has served time in prison. The questions in the survey inquire about the prospective and actual hiring of those with criminal records. Thus, we cannot say with certainty whether our results accurately reflect employer sentiments with regard to released inmates. However, we are able to examine the extent to which employer responses depend on the nature of the applicant's offense and on whether the applicant has recently served time.

An additional issue involves whether employers know they have hired ex-offenders. If employers don't ask, employees have a clear incentive not to tell. Nonetheless, there are reasons to believe that most employers are likely to be aware of whether they have hired men with criminal records. As we document below, about half of the employers in this survey actually check for criminal backgrounds, and another 20 percent check sometimes. Moreover, previous work using similar employer surveys show that a large fraction of employers (about 30 percent) have contact with employment agencies that attempt to place disadvantaged workers, including ex-offenders, into jobs (Holzer and Stoll 2001). Finally, employers face a host of incentives to screen the backgrounds of their employees, including being able to claim the Work Opportunity Tax Credit (though we find that not many employers claim such credits) and limiting exposure to legal liability under the theory of negligent hiring.[5] Moreover, as we will document below, employers reveal a very strong aversion to hiring those with criminal records, and thus one would expect employers to act on this aversion.

Thus, a fair share of employers, but certainly not all of them, are likely to know whether they have hired an ex-offender. However, employer uncertainty might bias our estimates of actual hiring downward.[6] Moreover, we have little information regarding how this bias is likely to vary with employer characteristics.

Results

We present results in the following section on employer willingness to hire offenders and on their use of criminal background checks.

Employer Willingness to Hire and Actual Hiring of Ex-Offenders

Figure 4.1 presents the distribution of employer responses to the question about employer willingness to accept an applicant with a criminal record. Over 40 percent of employers indicate that they would "probably not" or "definitely not" be willing. Only 20 percent of employers indicate that they would definitely or probably consider an applicant with a criminal history. On the other hand, approximately 35 percent of employers indicate that their willingness depends on the crime of the applicant. This latter category is the modal response.

While these figures are not directly comparable to those from our earlier analysis of an establishment survey from the early 1990s, the general patterns do suggest that employer willingness to accept applicants with criminal histories did not increase significantly over the 1990s, a period corresponding with a sustained economic boom.[7] This apparent relative stability may reflect an effect of September 11 on employer willingness to hire offenders, or perhaps the beginning of the economic slowdown. Alternatively, this lack of an increase in demand for ex-offenders with a tightening labor market may reflect the continuing shrinking of those sectors (such as manufacturing) where such demand is relatively high. However, some of our earlier research compared employer responses from a survey done from 1992 to 1994, when

Figure 4.1   Employer Willingness to Accept Applicants with a Criminal Record into Last-Filled Noncollege Job, 2001

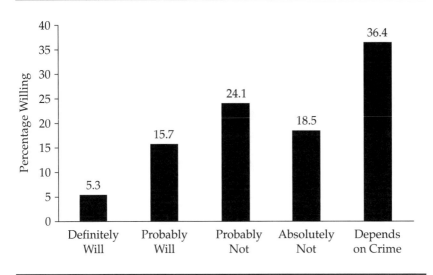

Source: Authors' computation of data from employer survey in Los Angeles, 2001.

the economy was weak, to those from one done for 1998 to 1999, when the economy was strong, and found little difference in employer willingness to hire those with criminal histories.[8] Thus, these results confirm our earlier findings that the demand for ex-offenders is low and does not exhibit a great deal of sensitivity to business cycles.

To put these employer responses in perspective, it is useful to compare the patterns in figure 4.1 to the results from similarly worded questions on employer willingness to accept applications from other groups of low-skilled and possibly stigmatized workers, such as welfare recipients, applicants with a GED but no high school diploma, applicants with spotty work histories, and applicants who have been unemployed for a year or more. Approximately 93 percent of employers indicate that they would definitely or probably hire former or current welfare recipients, 97 percent indicate that they would probably or definitely hire workers with a GED in lieu of a high school diploma, 66 percent indicate that they would hire workers with a spotty employment history, and 80 percent indicate that they are likely to consider an application from an individual who has been unemployed for a year or more. In contrast, only 20 percent of employers indicate that they definitely or probably would accept an application from an ex-offender. Even if we add the "depends on the crime" response to willing, the fraction of employers that would consider ex-offenders (55 percent) is

Figure 4.2   **Percentage of Employers Who Hired Ex-Offenders In Preceeding Year, by Willingness to Accept Applicants with Criminal Records, Measured in 2001**

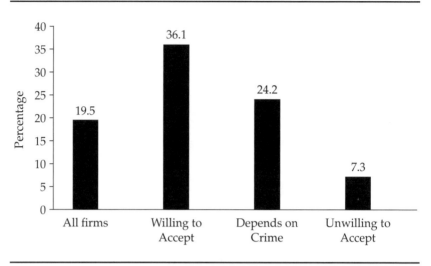

Source: Authors' computations.

still well below that for these other groups. Moreover, note that the one group for whom demand is particularly low, those with spotty work histories, is likely to overlap considerably with the population of former inmates.

These results confirm our analysis of several other establishment surveys, with the one difference being our ability to identify a large group of employers who are willing to consider the particularities of the applicant's criminal past. Nonetheless, these subjective responses to this question may not reflect actual hiring practices, and thus are subject to some uncertainty. To explore whether stated willingness is indicative of actual hiring practices, figure 4.2 presents the fraction of employers that have hired at least one ex-offender over the past year, conditional on their stated willingness to consider ex-offenders.[9]

About 20 percent of employers responded that they hired at least one ex-offender over the past year.[10] For purposes of comparison, roughly 30 percent of employers indicated that they had hired a former welfare recipient over the past year.[11] For employers who indicated that they would definitely or probably hire an ex-offender (grouped into the category "willing"), 36 percent hired an ex-offender in the previous year. For those who responded "Probably not" or "Definitely not" (here grouped into the "unwilling"), the comparable figure is only 7 percent.

For those responding that it depends on the crime, 24 percent hired an ex-offender over the past year. Thus, both measures of employer demand paint a fairly consistent picture of who will and who won't hire those with criminal histories; the two measures thus validate each other.

Our results are broadly consistent with evidence from Devah Pager (2002), who found limited employer demand for offenders in her audit study of employers in Milwaukee.[12] While the percentages of offender applicants who actually received callbacks or offers from employers in her study—especially for blacks—are lower than in ours, it is important to remember that her applicants were competing against others who were not part of the study, and this no doubt limited the numbers of callbacks or offers they received. Indeed, even among the white non-offender applicants in her study, only about a third got callbacks from employers. On the other hand, it is impossible for us to gauge the interaction between an applicant's race and his criminal history, since self-reported employer attitudes about race are notoriously unreliable in this kind of large-sample survey format.

Our results also differ somewhat from those reported by Pager and Lincoln Quillian (2005), who report little correlation between how employers answer survey questions on their willingness to hire offenders and their actual hiring behavior in audit studies. Our survey results indicate stronger correlations between reported willingness to hire and actual hiring, perhaps reflecting our much larger sample sizes and our broader measure of hiring activity.[13]

To explore how establishment and employer characteristics vary with employer willingness to hire ex-offenders and actual hiring practices, table 4.1 displays averages of establishment characteristics, stratified by the responses to our two principal demand measures. Establishment characteristics include industry, size, vacancy rates, the percentage of jobs that are unskilled, establishment location, whether the establishment checks criminal background, is union, or is nonprofit, and whether the establishment is minority-owned.[14]

There are several clear patterns shown in table 4.1. First, the distribution of industries among those most willing to accept ex-offenders is skewed toward manufacturing, construction, and transportation; these are precisely the industries that are likely to have fewer jobs requiring customer contact. Moreover, the distribution of establishments that actually hire ex-offenders is similarly skewed, which follows from the strong correlation between willingness to hire and actual hiring of ex-offenders in these industries. We also find that establishments willing to hire ex-offenders are disproportionately those with a large fraction of unskilled jobs (> .200). On the other hand, we find that the service-

Table 4.1   Means (Standard Deviations) of Firm-Level Characteristics, by Employer Willingness to Accept Applicants with Criminal Backgrounds and Actual Hiring of Ex-Offenders Last Year

Characteristics of Employer	All	Willing to Accept	Depends on Crime	Unwilling to Accept	Have Hired	Have Not Hired
Industry						
Manufacturing	0.171	0.230	0.142	0.162	0.242	0.154
Retail	0.186	0.213	0.194	0.166	0.233	0.174
Service	0.435	0.344	0.436	0.470	0.308	0.465
Construction	0.034	0.049	0.028	0.036	0.058	0.028
Transportation, communications, and utilities	0.053	0.057	0.085	0.028	0.067	0.051
Firm Size						
1 to 19	0.172	0.190	0.176	0.174	0.085	0.192
20 to 99	0.422	0.397	0.373	0.488	0.402	0.427
Over 100	0.406	0.413	0.451	0.339	0.513	0.380
Job vacancy rate	0.030	0.039	0.023	0.033	0.022	0.031
	(0.071)	(0.087)	(0.044)	(0.084)	(0.046)	(0.076)
0.000	0.560	0.545	0.542	0.577	0.547	0.563
0.001 to 0.040	0.235	0.231	0.276	0.195	0.291	0.222
Over 0.040	0.205	0.223	0.182	0.228	0.162	0.216
Percentage of jobs	0.337	0.389	0.330	0.307	0.426	0.315
for unskilled	(0.334)	(0.353)	(0.333)	(0.321)	(0.359)	(0.325)
0.000	0.460	0.402	0.460	0.494	0.350	0.487
0.001 to 0.200	0.189	0.189	0.227	0.170	0.200	0.186
Over 0.200	0.351	0.410	0.313	0.336	0.450	0.327
Central city	0.312	0.254	0.322	0.312	0.283	0.319
Always checks						
criminal background	0.444	0.287	0.531	0.433	0.442	0.445
Collective bargaining	0.240	0.200	0.232	0.263	0.291	0.228
Not-for-profit	0.213	0.131	0.213	0.263	0.158	0.226
Minority-owned	0.216	0.295	0.175	0.215	0.192	0.222

Source: Authors' computations of employer survey data from Los Angeles, 2001.

sector establishments are disproportionately represented more among those unwilling to accept and among those that have not hired ex-offenders.

Table 4.1 also reveals some firm characteristics whose association with the employer's stated willingness to accept ex-offenders differs from their association with actual hiring behavior. Most important, establishments that always check criminal backgrounds are disproportionately represented among those that say they are not willing to accept applicants with criminal records. This pattern is different for the actual hiring measure. Establishments that always check criminal backgrounds are equally represented among those firms that have hired ex-offenders and those that have not, suggesting that criminal background checking is not correlated with the actual hiring of ex-offenders at the firm.

There are a number of potential explanations for this latter pattern. For example, given that our measure of actual hiring is whether the firm has hired an offender at least once, the lack of a relationship between hiring and checking may reflect positive correlations between such hiring and establishment size (which we do find) or the numbers of ex-offender applicants across firms.

Alternatively, it may be that employers use criminal background checks not necessarily to exclude all ex-offenders from consideration (at least for jobs where ex-offenders are not legally barred from employment) but to select applicants that are least likely to steal, harm a customer, or expose the employer to the risk of a negligent-hiring lawsuit. This would imply that the characteristics of ex-offenders employed at firms that check should differ from the characteristics of those employed at firms that don't. This would also indicate that the likelihood of hiring may be augmented by the use of formal screening devices. We probe this latter hypothesis by examining the relationship between actual employer hiring outcomes and indicators of whether the employer uses private sources for checking criminal history records, whether their willingness to hire ex-offenders depends on the type of crime, and whether they display a propensity to seek additional information about the criminal backgrounds of applicants.

Potential support for the preceding explanation is provided in table 4.1. The data show that employers who indicated "Depends on the crime" are among those who disproportionately check the criminal backgrounds of their applicants. This suggests that their willingness to hire any individual from this group is conditional on specific information about the ex-offender. A formal criminal history review is likely to reveal a host of factors that help such employers assess the risks of hiring an ex-offender, such as how recently the offender was released from prison, the offense committed, the number of prior criminal convictions, as well as whether they have any work experience.

Figure 4.3 provides information on whether employer willingness to hire ex-offenders varies with offender characteristics. The responses depicted reflect those of employers who either are willing to hire or indicate that their willingness depends on the particulars of the applicant. The survey asks employers about their willingness to hire offenders who are recently released from prison and lack work experience, and their willingness to hire offenders by the offense committed (that

Figure 4.3   Percentage of Employers Willing to Hire Ex-Offenders, by Characteristics of Offenders, 2001

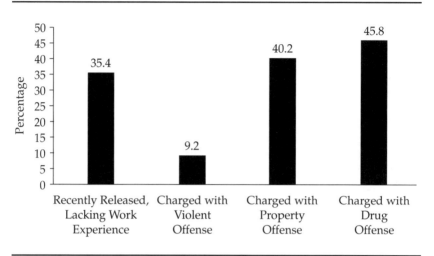

Source: Authors' computations.

is, a violent crime, a property crime, or a drug offense).[15] There are other factors that are likely to matter to employers but that were not part of our survey, including whether the offender has multiple offenses, is on probation, or is bonded.

The results show some predictable patterns. Employers are strongly averse to hiring ex-offenders charged with violent offenses. Employers also seem somewhat averse to those who are recently released from prison and without work experience, though we are unable to specify which of these is a more important factor driving this response. Employers seem less averse to those charged with property or drug-related crimes.

This variation by offender characteristic indicates that employer demand for nonviolent offenders may be somewhat more flexible than previously believed. Employers are clearly less averse to those charged with drug offenses. Over the 1990s, much (though not all) of the dramatic rise in the prison population was driven by increases in drug-related offenses, a disproportionate share of them charged to young black men. On the other hand, employers report being more averse to hiring ex-offenders charged with violent crime, but violent criminals make up a smaller and declining fraction of all offenders (Holzer, Raphael, and Stoll 2006a).

Thus, this variation in employer demand by category of offense could have important implications for the employment opportunities

Figure 4.4   Proportion of Recently Filled Jobs (and Applicants) into Which Black Men and Women Were Hired by Use of Criminal Background Checks, 2001

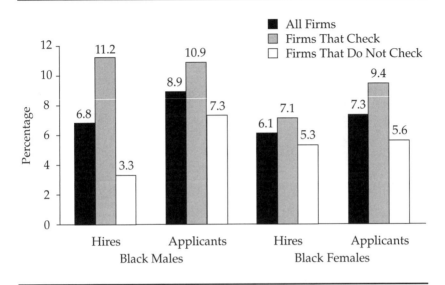

Source: Authors' computations.

of offenders. Specifically, it may create situations in which third-party intermediaries might provide more detailed information about offender backgrounds that convinces employers to hire applicants who otherwise might be turned away.

Employers' Use of Criminal Background Checks

The results thus far indicate that employer willingness to hire ex-offenders is limited, but this willingness is in part conditional on the characteristics of ex-offenders. How do employer screening practices reflect their aversion to applicants with criminal records? Some employers may use proxies of criminality, such as race, age, sex, and perhaps residential location (among others) in their hiring decisions to exclude ex-offenders from employment. Our previous research finds that this practice seems prevalent among employers who do not use criminal background checks (Holzer, Raphael, and Stoll 2006b), and significantly decrease the likelihood that African American applicants are hired. Using this more recent data for Los Angeles, figure 4.4 reproduces this result. The figure presents the proportion of recent hires as well as the proportion of the applicant pool that is black for firms that check criminal history records and firms that do not. Separate tabula-

**Figure 4.5   Frequency with Which Employers Check the Criminal
Backgrounds of Applicants, 1992 to 1994 and 2001**

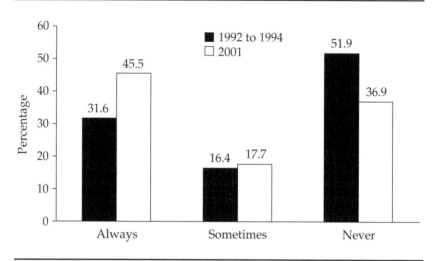

Source: Authors' computations of employer survey data, 1992–94 and 2001.

tions are provided for African American men and women. As can be
seen, checking is positively correlated with hiring black applicants, and
the difference between firms that check and those that don't is largest
for African American men. Moreover, the differences in hiring outcomes (for men) exceed the difference in their proportionate representation in the applicant pool.

Hence, this evidence strongly suggests that employers who do not
check for criminal backgrounds engage in a form of "statistical discrimination" against black men more broadly, based on their aversion to
hiring offenders as well as their very limited information about exactly
which individuals in their applicant pool have this characteristic.[16] This
pattern occurs despite the fact that black men are overrepresented
among those with ex-offender backgrounds. Given this fact, we should
have expected the hiring of black men to decline with employer's use
of criminal background checks. Apparently, the additional information
revealed by background checks of prior criminality among black male
applicants is lower than employers' subjective assessments.

Besides crude statistical discrimination, employers can act on their
aversion to those with criminal backgrounds by conducting criminal
background checks. Figure 4.5 presents the distribution of employer
responses to the question concerning the frequency with which employers check the criminal background of job applicants. In addition,
we present the distribution of these responses to the exact same ques-

tion asked in the earlier employer survey data collected in Los Angeles from 1992 to 1994. The earlier survey likely collected data on this question before the emergence of Internet services that provide low-cost criminal background checks.[17]

The results show that the use of criminal background checks among employers in Los Angeles rose substantially during the 1990s. For example, while 32 percent of employers always checked during the early 1990s, the comparable figure for 2001 is 45 percent. Moreover, the proportion of employers that never check declined from 52 percent to 37 percent.

As to what explains the increased use of this screening device, we can offer a few possible explanations. Prime among them would be the decline in costs and the ease with which criminal history records can be ordered from private services online. Moreover, this decrease in costs is likely to interact with employer fears about negligent hiring lawsuits. To protect themselves from these lawsuits, employers may be increasingly using criminal background checks. While we cannot evaluate these claims with the current survey, understanding this screening tool and its increased usage is clearly a fruitful area for future research.

An interesting question deriving from the results in figure 4.5 concerns whether the increased usage of criminal background checks over the 1990s occurred equally across different types of establishments. To explore this question, table 4.2 shows the percentage of firms that indicate that they always checked in the earlier and later surveys, after the samples were stratified by industry, establishment size, location, and by whether the establishment is unionized and whether it is nonprofit. The table also presents the difference in means within each category across the two surveys.

The results show that checking increased over this time period in most of these categories of establishments. However, we find variation across categories in the differences in checking over this time period. Checking increased rather dramatically in retail trade, manufacturing, in large firms (over one hundred employees), and in the suburbs. On the other hand, checking decreased in construction and wholesale trade industries, and increased nominally in small firms, who are also among the least likely to check, in 2001.

Given the increase in checking over the 1990s, one might wish to assess whether employers check because they think they are legally required to or because they find checking a valuable screening device. Many states, including California, require background checks for certain jobs and occupations from which ex-offenders are legally barred, a group that includes many that involve interaction with children or the elderly. There is also some evidence that the proportion of jobs from which ex-offenders are legally barred has increased (Legal Action Center 2004). This alone would drive an increase in employer checking.

Table 4.2   Percentage of Firms that Always Check Criminal Backgrounds of Applicants, 1992 to 1994 and 2001

Characteristics of Employer	Percentage of Firms that Always Check		Difference In Checking
	1992–1994	2001	
Industry			
Construction	36.1	28.6	−7.5
Manufacturing	14.6	33.0	18.4
Transportation, communications, and utilities	45.3	51.5	8.2
Wholesale trade	21.2	20.6	−0.6
Retail trade	26.6	46.1	19.5
FIRE	46.7	59.4	12.7
Service	39.9	50.9	11.0
Firm size			
1 to 19	19.6	21.2	1.5
20 to 99	31.6	41.8	10.2
Over 100	39.6	57.3	17.7
Location			
Central city	33.1	44.0	10.9
Suburbs	30.5	44.6	14.1
Collective bargaining	49.0	58.3	9.3
Not-for-profit	60.8	65.2	4.4

Source: Authors' computations of employer survey data, 1992 to 1994 and 2001.

Although we do not have information from the earlier survey regarding whether employers are legally required to screen out ex-offenders, we do have some information from the more recent survey. Thus, while we cannot speak to whether legal mandates are driving the changes observed in figure 4.5, we can at least assess how important such mandates are in determining employer use of these screens. Figure 4.6 displays the employer response to the question regarding whether employers check because they perceive that they are legally required to do so.[18] The question was asked of those who say they checked backgrounds in filling noncollege jobs.

Figure 4.6 shows that about half of employers indicate that they were legally required to conduct the criminal background check for the most recently filled noncollege position. We also display this information stratified by the distribution of employer responses to the question of how often employers check criminal backgrounds generally. We find that a little over 50 percent of employers that always check believe that

**Figure 4.6   Percentage of Employers Legally Required to Check
Criminal Backgrounds, 2001**

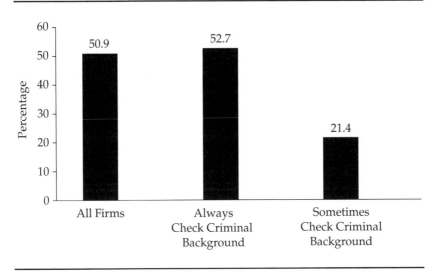

Source: Authors' computations.

they are legally required to do so, whereas the comparable figure for firms that sometimes check is about 20 percent. Thus, compared with firms that check sometimes, firms that always check seem much more likely to do so because of a perceived legal obligation.

Of course, we are unable to disentangle whether employers are actually required to check or whether they simply perceive they are required to check. We can, however, gain some insight into this question by examining the different methods employers use to perform background checks. In California, employers who were statutorily required to check backgrounds for certain jobs had to use the public repository to do so and were not allowed to use private sources. Though not shown here, the data indicate that 56 percent of employers who indicate that they were legally required to check used criminal justice methods (which is consistent with the use of public repositories), while 31 percent of these used private methods. This compares with 19 and 67 percent, respectively, for checking employers who indicate that they were not required to check. Thus, these results suggest that a majority of employers who indicated that they were required to check provided accurate answers.

What firm characteristics are associated with criminal background checking, and do these characteristics differ for firms where employers indicate they are legally required to check? In table 4.3, we examine

Table 4.3   Means (Standard Deviations) of Firm-Level Characteristics, by Whether Firm Checks Applicants' Criminal Background

	All	Always	Sometimes	Never	Legally Required
Industry					
Manufacturing	0.171	0.127	0.187	0.224	0.025
Retail	0.186	0.193	0.150	0.188	0.117
Service	0.435	0.498	0.477	0.341	0.742
Construction	0.034	0.022	0.037	0.045	0.008
Transportation, communications, and utilities	0.053	0.062	0.065	0.040	0.050
Firm size					
1 to 19	0.172	0.081	0.183	0.284	0.078
20 to 99	0.422	0.396	0.423	0.450	0.379
Over 100	0.406	0.522	0.394	0.266	0.543
Vacancy rate	0.030	0.037	0.035	0.019	0.049
	(0.071)	(0.086)	(0.071)	(0.049)	(0.110)
0.000	0.560	0.444	0.548	0.704	0.371
0.001–0.040	0.235	0.300	0.221	0.167	0.302
>0.040	0.205	0.256	0.231	0.130	0.328
Percentage of jobs for	0.337	0.301	0.333	0.387	0.248
unskilled workers	(0.334)	(0.314)	(0.324)	(0.359)	(0.279)
0.000	0.460	0.484	0.486	0.417	0.533
0.001 to 0.200	0.189	0.229	0.140	0.157	0.258
Over 0.200	0.351	0.287	0.374	0.426	0.208
Central city	0.263	0.309	0.336	0.309	0.308
Always checks criminal background	0.444	1.000	0.000	0.000	0.975
Collective bargaining	0.240	0.317	0.190	0.163	0.435
Not-for-profit	0.213	0.313	0.168	0.112	0.525
Minority-owned	0.216	0.160	0.308	0.247	0.167

Source: Author's computations of employer survey data from Los Angeles, 2001.

establishment characteristics, stratified by employer responses to the question concerning the frequency with which employers check criminal backgrounds generally and whether they are legally required to do so. The results indicate that establishments that are large, are in the service sector, are in the central city, or are not-for-profit, as well as those with collective bargaining agreements, are overrepresented among those firms that always check. On the other hand, manufacturing, smaller or minority-owned firms, or those with a larger percentage of unskilled jobs are overrepresented among those firms that never check.

These results are consistent with our earlier work and suggest that firms in industries with greater customer contact, with more formal human resource systems, and that are closer to ex-offender populations are more likely to run background checks (Holzer, Raphael, and Stoll 2004). These patterns are similar for firms in which employers indicate that they were legally required to check.

Taken together, these results suggest that the greater propensity of certain categories of firms to always check (for instance, large or service firms) is at least partly prompted by their perception of legal requirements. Given the very widespread legal barriers to employment in many occupations that occur in most states, it is perhaps not surprising that legal requirements drive a great deal of employer behavior in this regard. But these findings also suggest that the laws that prevent employers from hiring offenders might need to be reviewed, in light of the strong negative effects they appear to have on the ability of ex-offenders to gain employment, as we shall document later.

The substantial increase over the 1990s in the proportion of establishments that always check the criminal histories of applicants suggests that the growing availability of low-cost checking services in the private market may be in part driving this increase. Although we do not have data for the earlier survey on the method by which employers check backgrounds to fully explore these factors, our 2001 survey does ask this question. Figure 4.6 shows the method by which employers check criminal histories for those that perform background checks. The data show that nearly 50 percent of employers in Los Angeles in 2001 use a private source to check criminal backgrounds of applicants. Nearly 40 percent use criminal-justice agencies such as the attorney general's office and the police. Interestingly, only 6 percent of employers gather this information by asking the applicants themselves.

The data in figure 4.7 do suggest that the availability of low-cost criminal background checking services has played a part in the increase in checking over time, especially since there were few such services available during the early 1990s. Of course, the increasing availability of these services may have allowed the latent demand for these services by employers to be realized. Moreover, this demand may have increased over the 1990s as employer awareness of the growing presence of ex-offenders in the low-skill labor supply increased as well.

There has also been little evidence to date on when employers conduct criminal background checks. Figure 4.8 shows employers' responses to a question pertaining to when in the hiring process a criminal background check is conducted. The vast majority of employers who check criminal backgrounds do so before they fill the position. About 20 percent of employers check criminal backgrounds after they have filled the position, while a small fraction, about 5 percent, check

Figure 4.7   Method by Which Employers Check Applicants' Criminal Backgrounds, 2001

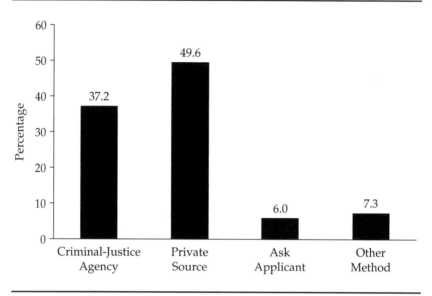

Source: Authors' computations.

at some other time. Though not shown here, our data also show that employers who check after they have filled the position mostly do so during the employees' probationary period.

Thus, employers check criminal records before most ex-offenders have had a chance to demonstrate their ability to successfully hold the jobs to which they are applying. The potential negative effect of such information on the employment prospects of offenders is thus reinforced.

Finally, and as noted earlier, our survey was conducted over the period of May 2001 to November 2001, during which time the events of September 11 took place. In fact, about 62 percent of our surveys were completed before September 11, leaving a substantial fraction that were completed thereafter. These events no doubt raised awareness about the backgrounds, in particular criminal backgrounds, of individuals, and perhaps increased employers' concerns about the risks associated with hiring ex-offenders. Figure 4.9 presents some data on employer responses pre– and post–September 11 to the questions on the hiring of ex-offenders and whether they perform criminal background checks. The data show that employers report no difference in hiring ex-offenders over the past year pre– and post–September 11, which is expected—since these events came well after much of this hiring had

Figure 4.8   Timing of Employers' Criminal Background Checks of Applicants, 2001

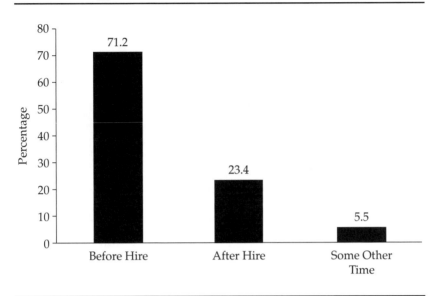

Source: Authors' computations.

taken place. However, when asked whether they would consider hiring ex-offenders currently, about 12 percent of employers surveyed before September 11 indicated that they would, while only 6 percent of employers surveyed afterward said they would. In addition, a slightly higher fraction of employers indicated that they always check criminal backgrounds of applicants after September 11.

Effects of Firm Characteristics and Employer Attitudes on the Use of Criminal Background Checks and Hiring of Ex-Offenders

Given the large number of employer attributes that appear to be correlated with whether firms conduct background checks and their actual hiring of ex-offenders, we investigate the independent partial correlations of these characteristics with our outcomes using multivariate analysis. Table 4.4 presents estimation results from logit regression equations in which the dependent variables are whether the firm checks the criminal background of applicants or whether the firm hired at least one ex-offender over the past year. We do not examine factors related to employers' willingness to hire ex-offenders, since these are highly correlated with their actual hiring (and since estimates using this alter-

Figure 4.9   Percentage of Employers Responding to Questions Concerning Hiring of Ex-Offenders and Use of Background Checks Before and After September 11, 2001

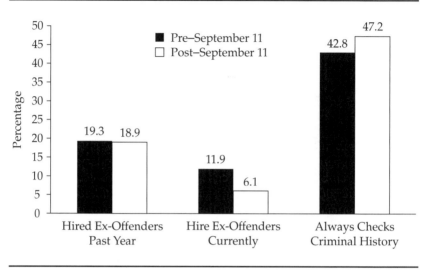

Source: Authors' computations.

native dependent variable that are not reported here yielded qualitatively similar results).

Most of the independent variables in the models are those listed in tables 4.1 and 4.3, already described. However, in the second specification of these regressions, we include variables that measure the tasks involved in the most recently filled job at the establishment. These tasks include customer contact, and the handling of children, cash, and expensive merchandise.[19] We include these to further investigate the extent to which certain tasks, or those that might engender greater employer concern about whether an ex-offender is hired into that job, are associated with checking backgrounds and hiring ex-offenders. One concern with adding these variables into the model is that, because they measure these tasks for the last-filled job rather than at the firm level (that is, average tasks at the firm), they may be flawed as measures of general firm screening and hiring practices. Thus, we include these in a separate model specification. Still, to the extent that the tasks of the last-filled job are highly correlated with measures of the average tasks at the firm, we should be able to detect their association with these factors.[20]

Many of the results in table 4.4 confirm findings from our earlier tables. Employers who are willing to hire ex-offenders are also those

Table 4.4   Regression Results for Whether Firm Checks Criminal Background of Applicants and Whether Firm Hired an Ex-Offender Over the Past Year

Characteristics of Employers	A. Checks Criminal Background		B. Hired Ex-Offender Over Past Year	
	1	2	1	2
Industry[a]				
Manufacturing	−1.102***	−1.186***	1.161*	1.163*
	(0.462)	(0.483)	(0.650)	(0.652)
Wholesale trade	−1.601***	−1.784***	0.657	0.555
	(0.593)	(0.614)	(0.776)	(0.799)
Retail trade	−0.665	−1.043**	0.791	0.931
	(0.449)	(0.471)	(0.671)	(0.690)
Service	−0.679	−0.918**	0.277	0.282
	(0.426)	(0.436)	(0.668)	(0.674)
Construction	−1.132*	−1.315**	1.521*	1.456*
	(0.664)	(0.680)	(0.838)	(0.841)
Transportation, communications, and utilities	−0.442	−0.666	1.110*	1.114*
	(0.571)	(0.594)	(0.678)	(0.680)
Firm size				
1 to 19	−1.640***	−1.679***	−0.966**	−0.938**
	(0.334)	(0.345)	(0.432)	(0.444)
20 to 99	−0.613***	−0.658***	−0.170	−0.159
	(0.210)	(0.215)	(0.258)	(0.260)
Vacancy rate				
0.000	−0.764***	−0.709***	0.251	0.225
	(0.248)	(0.253)	(0.326)	(0.330)
0.001 to 0.040	−0.331	−0.297	0.275	0.229
	(0.293)	(0.299)	(0.365)	(0.369)
Percentage of jobs unskilled				
0.000	0.310	0.393	−0.315	−0.323
	(0.247)	(0.253)	(0.307)	(0.311)
0.001 to 0.200	−0.265	−0.205	−0.616**	−0.634**
	(0.235)	(0.245)	(0.303)	(0.314)
Central city	−0.290	−0.241	0.017	−0.024
	(0.214)	(0.219)	(0.265)	(0.270)
Collective bargaining	0.277	0.193	0.223	0.262
	(0.238)	(0.245)	(0.280)	(0.289)
Not-for-profit	0.716***	0.627**	−0.155	−0.075
	(0.261)	(0.273)	(0.341)	(0.352)
Minority-owned	−0.016	−0.002	−0.161	−0.103
	(0.236)	(0.243)	(0.292)	(0.297)

(Table continues on p. 140)

Table 4.4   *Continued*

Characteristics of Employers	A. Checks Criminal Background		B. Hired Ex-Offender Over Past Year	
	1	2	1	2
Preference for ex-offenders				
Willing to hire	−0.613***	−0.549**	1.683***	1.705***
	(0.250)	(0.262)	(0.297)	(0.303)
Depends on crime	0.413**	0.442**	1.116***	1.093***
	(0.212)	(0.216)	(0.281)	(0.285)
Post–September 11	0.322*	0.321*	−0.272	−0.237
	(0.194)	(0.196)	(0.245)	(0.243)
Checks criminal background	—	—	0.177	0.183
			(0.252)	(0.256)
Tasks of job[b]				
Customer contact	—	0.591***	—	0.458*
		(0.239)		(0.282)
Handle cash	—	0.050	—	−0.573*
		(0.284)		(0.349)
Handle expensive merchandise	—	0.161	—	0.240
		(0.202)		(0.244)
Handle children	—	0.480*	—	0.594*
		(0.284)		(0.365)
Log Likelihood	−346.41	−337.31	−255.28	−246.88
N	587	587	587	587

Source: Authors' computations.
Note: Standard errors are in parentheses. Financial Services is the reference group for industry and unwilling to hire ex-offenders is the reference group for employer preferences.
[a]Coefficient results for agriculture and mining are suppressed.
[b]Coefficient results for phone tasks, reading and writing tasks, math tasks, and computer tasks are suppressed.
***statistically significant at the .01 percent level, **at the .05 percent level, and *at the .10 percent level.

who are less likely to check criminal backgrounds, while those who indicate that it depends on the crime (or those who may want more information about ex-offenders) are more likely to check. Also, checking is more likely to occur after September 11, even after other relevant factors are taken into account. Other results in table 4.4 are fairly consistent with those reported in table 4.3. That is, establishments in manufacturing, construction, and wholesale trade industries, and smaller establishments are less likely to do criminal background checks. Nonprofits, on the other hand, are more likely than for-profits to conduct checks. Thus, even after controlling for relevant factors, these results suggest that firms in industries with less customer contact and without more formal human resource systems (that is, larger firms) are much more likely to check criminal backgrounds.

The role of customer contact in influencing checking is more directly illustrated in the second specification, which adds the tasks variables to the model. Employers filling jobs involving customer contact and interaction with children are more likely to check criminal backgrounds. Including these variables does not appreciably affect the coefficients of the other variables in the model except those for industry. Here, employers in the retail trade and service industries are now less likely to check (than those in the financial services and real estate sector), once job tasks are taken into account. This suggests that employer concerns about ex-offenders harming customers, or legal requirements (as in the case of job tasks involving children), are likely driving such industries to conduct background checks.[21]

Panel B presents regression results where the dependent variable is an indicator of whether the employer hired an ex-offender over the past year. These results are largely consistent with the unadjusted results presented in table 4.1, as well as with the regression results for checking backgrounds. Firms in manufacturing, construction, and transportation industries (those industries where checking is relatively scarce) are more likely to have hired an ex-offender over the last year. Moreover, firms with a large share of unskilled jobs are also more likely to have hired. Interestingly, smaller firms are less likely to have hired an ex-offender, even though they are less likely to check criminal backgrounds. This result is consistent with our work on statistical discrimination on the basis of perceived criminality, since smaller firms are disproportionately represented among firms that don't check and are unwilling to hire ex-offenders (Holzer, Raphael, and Stoll 2006b). Finally, firms that are willing to hire ex-offenders and whose preferences for ex-offenders depend on the crime are more likely to have hired an ex-offender than unwilling employers, confirming our results presented in figure 4.2. As expected, we do not find a September 11 effect on hiring ex-offenders over the past year, since these events came well after much of this hiring had taken place. We do find such an effect on whether employers would hire ex-offenders currently, though we do not show results of these regressions here.

As in our comparison of means, performing a criminal background check is not associated with the hiring of ex-offenders over the past year. Again, there could be a number of reasons that account for this as we discuss above. Most prominently, firms that do not do back-

Table 4.5   Coefficient Estimates on Criminal Background Checking Variables for Full Sample and by Employer's Willingness to Hire Ex-Offenders (Dependent Variable = Hired Ex-Offender Over the Past Year)

	1 Full Sample	2 Willing to Hire	3 Depends on Crime	4 Unwilling to Hire
Checks criminal background	0.177	0.072	1.133**	−0.579
	(0.252)	(0.498)	(0.529)	(0.589)
Legally required to check				
Yes	−0.589*	−0.543	−0.314	−0.480
	(0.359)	(0.639)	(0.590)	(0.624)
No	0.681**	−0.718	1.260***	1.117
	(0.279)	(0.674)	(0.465)	(0.724)
Method of checking[a]				
Criminal-justice agency	−0.637	−1.417**	−0.597	−0.453
	(0.404)	(0.739)	(0.604)	(0.922)
Private sources	0.619**	0.698	0.823*	0.531
	(0.295)	(0.455)	(0.475)	(0.750)
N	587	118	198	217

Source: Authors' computations.
Note: All regressions include independent variables listed in table 4.4, specification 1. Reference variable in all equations is firm does not check backgrounds of applicants. Standard errors are in parentheses.
[a]Coefficient results for "Ask applicant" or "Other method of checking" are suppressed because of small sample sizes.
***indicates statistically significant at the .01 percent level, **at the .05 percent level, and * at the .10 percent level.

ground checks are less likely to know the criminal status of their workers. This factor is likely to lead to conservative estimates of its association with hiring ex-offenders, or, depending on the extent to which checking is actually negatively associated with hiring, will bias the coefficient toward being positive or zero.

The second specification adds the tasks variables to the model and shows some anticipated results. Employers filling jobs that are more likely to involve customer contact, handling cash, and interacting with children are much less likely to have hired ex-offenders over the past year. Moreover, the inclusion of these factors does not affect the other variable coefficients.

Finally, table 4.5 presents logit estimation results from different versions of the hiring models presented in table 4.4, where the dependent variable is whether the firm has hired an ex-offender in the past year and where use of criminal background checks is an independent variable that is specified in a variety of ways. Here, we only present the coefficients on the background check variables, since all other results are similar. We experiment with three separate specifications: (1) the model in table 4.4 that specifies only whether the firm checks; (2) an alternative where dummy variables for being legally required to check and not being legally required to check are substituted for checking (and where the reference category is those who do not check); and (3) a model where those who check are captured by a set of dummies indicating the method used to check criminal backgrounds. We present these additional estimates to further investigate a number of hypotheses discussed above about the relationship between checking, hiring ex-offenders, and employer behaviors. The estimates are also presented for the entire sample of employers, and then separately for those stating that they are willing to hire offenders, that they are unwilling to hire them, or that it depends on the crime.

The first row presents logit coefficient estimates when the basic criminal background checks variable is used. Column 1 presents the results for the full sample (reproduced from table 4.4), and again shows no statistical relationship between checking and hiring ex-offenders. Columns 2 through 4 show the estimates for the subsamples stratified by employer willingness to hire ex-offenders. These coefficients are presented to examine the hypothesis of whether some employers—namely, those who indicate that their willingness to hire ex-offenders depends on the crime—use background checks not necessarily to completely exclude ex-offenders from employment but to generate information about specific offender characteristics that can help guide their employment decisions.

The coefficient on doing background checks for those employers who say that their willingness to hire depends on the crime is positive and significant, offering some support for the above hypothesis. This result appears to be driven by those employers who indicate that they are not legally required to check and who use private sources. Note that these employers (those whose willingness to hire depends on the crime) are also those most likely to check backgrounds, as we document above. On the other hand, the association between checking and hiring ex-offenders is negative for those who indicate that they are legally required to check, as expected.

Finally, we investigate whether employers use background checks to protect themselves from negligent-hiring lawsuits. For employers motivated by this reason, use of such checks is likely not to completely exclude ex-offenders from employment. We investigate this question by examining the relationship between private checking and hiring ex-offenders. If employers use such checks as a kind of protection mechanism, they are more likely to use private sources of checking because they are cheap and quick. The results are consistent with this idea and show that use of private sources of checking is significantly and positively associated with hiring ex-offenders in the full sample and especially for those employers who indicate that their willingness to hire depends on the crime. We do not find this relationship for employers who use criminal justice agencies to do such checking. In fact, we find a significant, negative association between checking with such agencies and hiring of ex-offenders for willing employers as anticipated.

Conclusions

In this paper, we analyze employer demand for ex-offenders using a recent employer survey taken in Los Angeles in 2001. We analyze not only employer-stated preferences to hire offenders but also the extent to which they actually do so. In addition, we examine employer behavior and practices that might limit the employment prospects of ex-offenders, namely the extent to which employers check criminal backgrounds of job applicants they are considering. This examination also considers the extent to which such checking has increased over time, the methods that employers use to do such checking, and when they check during the hiring process. In most instances, we investigate the firm characteristics that correlate with these measures of employer demand. Finally, we also examine differences in employer behaviors and attitudes toward ex-offenders pre– and post–September 11.

We report several findings here. First, consistent with previous studies, employers' stated willingness to hire ex-offenders is still very limited, even relative to other groups of disadvantaged workers (such as welfare recipients). Despite the boom of the 1990s, employer demand for offenders does not seem to have risen much over time. Also, this willingness appears to have been negatively affected by the events of September 11.

Nonetheless, employer aversion to ex-offenders seems to vary with the characteristics of the offenders. Employers report being less averse to those charged with drug or property offenses, and more averse to those who have been charged with a violent crime or are recently released from prison and lack work experience.

Moreover, we find evidence that employers' stated willingness to hire ex-offenders correlates with their actual behavior, thus putting greater confidence in our demand measures for this group. Employer willingness to hire is highly correlated with establishment characteristics in predictable ways that are consistent with previous research, but our work here shows that such correlations appear to translate into their actual hiring of ex-offenders. For instance, employers' willingness to hire ex-offenders in establishments with a high percentage of unskilled jobs or in manufacturing, construction and transportation industries is correlated with their actual hiring of them.

The results further show that employer tendencies to check criminal backgrounds have increased over (and maybe since) the 1990s, perhaps in response to the events of September 11. Over the 1990s, this increase in checking occurred most dramatically in retail trade, manufacturing, suburban, and large firms. This increase in checking appears to be driven at least partly by legal requirements to do so. In fact, our results show that about half of firms that check criminal backgrounds indicate that they do so because this is legally required. A near majority of firms use private services when they conduct criminal background checks, and over half of employers check before they hire an applicant.

But there seem to be other factors at play as well. Our results suggest that checking may have increased because of employer fear of negligent-hiring lawsuits or perhaps from greater employer desire to know more about ex-offender backgrounds in making intelligent risk-assessed employment decisions about this group, especially given their growing presence in society over this time period. Consistent with these ideas, we find that employers who use private sources of checking (which are quick and cheap and can act as a protection mechanism against such lawsuits) are actually more likely to hire ex-offenders than employers that use criminal-justice agencies to check methods or who do not check at all. Moreover, we also find that employers who indicate a strong desire to know more about the backgrounds and characteristics of ex-offenders that they may consider for employment are more likely to check backgrounds than most other employers. They are also more likely to hire ex-offenders than other employers despite their use of background checks during employment screening.

These results not only are interesting in their own right but also raise a number of important questions. For instance, how accurate is the criminal history information that is provided by private services, many of whom are Internet-based?[22] Do such services provide information on arrest, conviction, or imprisonment? Are the apparent effects of September 11 on decreasing employers' willingness to hire ex-offenders and increasing the frequency with which they check backgrounds relatively short-lived or long-term trends?

Our findings also suggest a number of important implications for policy. For instance, some advocates seek to suppress the information to which employers have access regarding criminal records. But it is possible that the provision of more information to these firms will *increase* their general willingness to hire young black men, as we show here, and since we have previously found evidence that employers who do not have such information often engage in statistical discrimination against this demographic group (Holzer, Raphael, and Stoll 2006a, 2006b).

The provision of more information (assuming it is accurate) might even help men who have criminal records. Indeed, our data suggest that a large fraction of employers want more information about the characteristics of ex-offenders to help them make employment decisions with respect to this group. Labor-market intermediary organizations are one of a number of potential agencies or methods that can provide such information to employers about the nature of the offense committed by offenders, and about any productive work experience that they might have gained before or since release.[23] In fact, the relatively lesser aversion employers express to those ex-offenders with some recent work experience suggests some potential returns to the provision of such experience, in the form of publicly provided "transitional jobs," to those leaving prison.

Some public funding for organizations that provide this information to employers, as well as various services or work experience to the offenders, might therefore be appropriate. Furthermore, given that so many employers check backgrounds and often refuse to hire ex-offenders because they are legally required to do so, some review of these legal barriers—particularly the laws that prevent employers from hiring them into specific occupations and industries—might be in order as well.

This research was made possible by grants from the Charles Stuart Mott and Russell Sage foundations.

Notes

1. These data are reported from the Bureau of Justice Statistics (2001) and the U.S. Census Bureau (2002) for California.
2. Several studies have analyzed the labor-market consequences of involvement in the criminal justice system by testing for direct effects on future employment and earnings of being arrested (Grogger 1995) or of serving time (Freeman 1992; Kling 1999; Kling, Weiman, and Western 2000). These studies tend to show that arrests and imprisonment are both associated with lower employment and earnings, evidence consistent with an effect of incarceration on the general employability of former inmates.
3. A limited number of questions on willingness to hire ex-offenders have also been included in other employer surveys that we administered in the late 1990s. See, for instance, Harry J. Holzer and Michael Stoll (2001).
4. Holzer developed and administered this survey, called the Multi-City Telephone Employer Survey (MCTES). MCTES includes observations on 3,220

employers in four cities (approximately 800 per city): Atlanta, Boston, Detroit, and Los Angeles. The Los Angeles portion of this survey used the identical geographic sampling unit as that used in the survey we report on here. See Holzer (1996) for an extensive discussion of the survey methods and data.

5. In fact, our survey asked of those employers who had hired an ex-offender over the last year whether they claimed the Work Opportunity Tax Credit (WOTC) when hiring ex-offenders; and only 21 percent of employers indicated that they did.

6. While the category of "Don't know" should, at least in principle, fully capture any such uncertainty about ex-offender status of workers, it is still possible that many employers assume no criminal record when they are not aware of one.

7. Similarly worded questions are included in our earlier employer survey, 1992 to 1994, for Los Angeles. However, our current survey is slightly different, for it includes a "Depends on the crime" response, whereas our previous survey does not. Still, if we examine the extreme response categories to this question, we find that in Los Angeles, for both 1992 to 1994 and 2001, about 20 percent of employers indicate that they will absolutely not accept ex-offender applicants. Alternatively, 13 percent of employers in 1992 to 1994 indicate that they definitely will accept ex-offender applicants, whereas 5 percent of employers responded this way in 2001.

8. See Holzer, Raphael, and Stoll (2006a). Those data showed little increases in willingness to hire within the Detroit or Los Angeles metropolitan areas, but significantly more willingness to hire in Milwaukee than elsewhere. While some of the differences between Milwaukee and other areas might reflect the extreme tightness of the labor market that they experienced in the past decade, it is also possible that the cross-sectional differences reflect variation in attitudes, political climate, and other such factors.

9. Alternatively, we compare the current prospective overall demand for ex-offenders defined in figure 4.3 with actual overall demand for ex-offenders over the past year, arguably a more direct comparison. We find that the correlation is positive (.35) and statistically significant at the 1 percent level of confidence.

10. Of the employers that had hired at least one ex-offender over the past year, our survey shows that about 70 percent of these employers indicated that the ex-offenders they hired had work experience since being released from prison, and 21 percent of employers used the WOTC when hiring them, as noted earlier. The low level of use of the WOTC in hiring ex-offenders indicates that the efficacy of these tools will be limited without more outreach to firms or assistance from intermediaries in helping them obtain it.

11. Of course, these differences in actual hiring between ex-offenders and welfare recipients are determined by supply as well as demand. And surely, welfare reform as well as a strong economy pushed many welfare recipients into the labor market by the time our survey was administered. But if anything, there is more downward bias in the percentage reported for welfare recipients, as the previous recipient status of many who had been on welfare but left the rolls will be unknown to employers.

12. See also Pager and Bruce Western (2005) for similar results in an audit study of employers in New York City.
13. Pager and Quillian surveyed only employers in Milwaukee who had been audited by Pager in her earlier work; the sample of employers who actually responded to this survey is much smaller than ours in Los Angeles. Furthermore, our measure of actual employer hiring of offenders is based on any hiring over the previous year, and not just employer response to one matched pair of auditors.
14. Unskilled jobs refer to jobs that do not require any particular skills, education, previous training, or experience.
15. These questions are asked of employers who indicated that they are currently willing to hire ex-offenders; employers who indicated that they are currently not willing to hire ex-offenders are excluded. It is likely that their responses to their willingness to hire ex-offenders currently are influenced by the characteristics of ex-offenders as well.
16. It is, of course, possible that the observed correlation between tendency to check backgrounds and the hiring of blacks is not causal. In Holzer, Raphael, and Stoll (2006b), we test for whether the observed correlation remains after controlling for a wider range of employer and job characteristics, and whether it can be found in a "difference-in-difference" analysis of the effects of background checking on hiring for those who are and are not willing to hire ex-offenders. The observed relationships are robust to all such statistical tests. The analysis in that paper thus suggests a causal relationship between checking and the hiring of blacks.
17. For instance, companies such as Pinkerton Security Services, provide criminal background checking services for as little as $15.
18. Of course, we are unable to verify employer responses regarding whether they are actually required to check by law. Hence, these responses can be interpreted as employers' perception of their legal responsibility to check.
19. These tasks also include those for the use of the phone and computer, and those involved with reading, writing, and math. The results of these task variables are suppressed in table 4.4 since they were never significant and are not the focus of this analysis.
20. Of course, in these regressions it is difficult to assess whether the characteristics of firms or other employer attributes that we include have a causal effect on checking or on hiring ex-offenders. For example, employers who do background checks may be less willing to hire ex-offenders, as we document. Alternatively, background checks may objectively screen out ex-offenders, especially for those that use criminal justice agencies to do such checks. In truth, we cannot really distinguish between these two important interpretations of the results shown here. But even if the results are correlative and not causal, it is still useful to know the extent to which checking and hiring ex-offenders is associated with these employer attitudes and firm characteristics.
21. Though not shown here, we also examined whether the firm characteristics and employer attitudes differ by how and when criminal background checks are conducted, controlling for the relevant characteristics. Of firms that did background checks, manufacturing and minority-owned firms

were less likely to do so because they were legally required, whereas non-profits and unionized firms were more likely to do so for this reason. With respect to when and how employers checked criminal backgrounds, there were few differences across firms in these except that nonprofits and minority-owned firms were more likely to use criminal-justice methods.

22. See Shawn Bushway et al. (chapter 6, this volume) for a thorough examination of this question about the accuracy of criminal background checks.

23. In fact, organizations such as the Center for Employment Opportunities in New York and the Safer Foundation in Chicago, as well as America Works and the Welfare-to-Work Partnership, are now playing those roles for ex-offenders.

References

Freeman, Richard B. 1992. "Crime and the Employment of Disadvantaged Youth." In *Urban Labor Markets and Job Opportunities*, edited by George Peterson and Wayne Vroman. Washington, D.C.: Urban Institute Press.

Grogger, Jeffrey. 1995. "The Effect of Arrests on the Employment and Earnings of Young Men." *Quarterly Journal of Economics* 110(1): 51–71.

Holzer, Harry J. 1996. *What Employers Want: Job Prospects for Less-Educated Workers*. New York: Russell Sage Foundation.

Holzer, Harry J., Paul Offner, and Elaine Sorenson. 2005. "Declining Employment Among Young Black Less-Educated Men: The Role of Incarceration and Child Support." *Journal of Policy Analysis and Management* 24(2): 329–50.

Holzer, Harry J., Steven Raphael, and Michael A. Stoll. 2004. "Will Employers Hire Ex-Offenders? Employer Perceptions, Background Checks, and Their Determinants." In *The Impact of Incarceration on Families and Communities*, edited by Mary Pattillo-McCoy, David Weiman, and Bruce Western. New York: Russell Sage Foundation.

———. 2006a. "How Do Crime and Incarceration Affect the Employment Prospects of Less-Educated Young Black Men?" In *Black Males Left Behind*, edited by Ron Mincy. Washington D.C.: Urban Institute Press.

———. 2006b. "Perceived Criminality, Background Checks, and the Racial Hiring Practices of Employers?" *Journal of Law and Economics* 49(4): 451–80.

Holzer, Harry J., and Michael A. Stoll. 2001. *Employers and Welfare Recipients: The Effects of Welfare Reform in the Workplace*, San Francisco: Public Policy Institute of California.

Kling, Jeffrey. 1999. "The Effect of Prison Sentence Length on the Subsequent Employment and Earnings of Criminal Defendants." Woodrow Wilson School of Economics Discussion Paper no. 208. Princeton: Princeton University.

Kling, Jeffrey, David Weiman, and Bruce Western. 2000. "The Labor Market Consequences of Mass Incarceration." Paper presented at the Urban Institute Reentry Roundtable. (October 12 to 13).

Legal Action Center. 2004. *After Prison: Roadblocks to Reentry*. New York: Legal Action Center.

Pager, Devah. 2002. "The Mark of a Criminal Record." Paper presented at the American Sociology Association Conference. Chicago (August 15 to 19).

Pager, Devah, and Lincoln Quillian. 2005. "Walking the Talk: What Employers Say v. What They Do." *American Sociological Review* 70(3): 355–80.

Pager, Devah, and Bruce Western. 2005. "Discrimination in Low-Wage Labor Markets: Evidence from an Experimental Audit Study." Unpublished manuscript. Princeton University.

Raphael, Steven, and Michael A. Stoll. 2004. "The Effects of Prison Releases on Regional Crime Rates." *Brookings–Wharton Papers on Urban Affairs*, 5: 207–56.

U.S. Bureau of the Census. 2002. 2000 U.S. Census of Population. Washington: U.S. Department of Commerce.

U.S. Department of Justice, Bureau of Justice Statistics (BJS). 2001. Criminal Offenders Statistics. Washington: Bureau of Justice Statistics

= Chapter 5 =

Two Strikes and You're Out: The Intensification of Racial and Criminal Stigma

Devah Pager

Jerome arrived at a branch of a national restaurant chain in a suburb twenty miles from Milwaukee. He immediately sensed that he was the only black person in the place.

An employee hurried over to him. "Can I help you with something?"

"I'm here about the job you advertised," Jerome replied.

The employee nodded reluctantly and went off to produce an application form. Jerome filled out the forms, including information about his criminal record. He was given a math test and a personality test. He was then instructed to wait for the manager to speak with him. The manager came out after about ten minutes, looked over Jerome's application, and frowned when he noticed the criminal history information. Without asking any questions about the context of the conviction, the manager started to lecture: "You can't be screwing up like this at your age. A kid like you can ruin his whole life like this." Jerome began to explain that he had made a mistake and had learned his lesson, but the manager cut him off: "I'll look over your application and call if we have a position for you."[1]

Jerome could have been any one of the hundreds of thousands of young black men released from prison each year, facing bleak employment prospects as a result of their race and criminal record. In this case, Jerome happened to be working for me. He was one of four college students I had hired as "testers" for a study of employment discrimination. His assignment was to apply for entry-level job openings throughout the Milwaukee metropolitan area, presenting a fictitious profile designed to represent a realistic ex-offender. For each job opening, a second black tester also submitted an application, presenting equal ed-

151

ucational qualifications, work experience, and interpersonal skills. Everything was the same except for their criminal records.

At the same time that Jerome and his partner were working on the project, I had a second pair of white testers apply to a separate set of job openings. The contrast between their outcomes and those of Jerome and his partner point to a troubling interaction between race and criminal background in the search for employment. Among whites, those presenting a prior felony conviction were half as likely to receive a callback from employers as were those with no criminal background (17 versus 34 percent). Among blacks, those with prior felonies were only a third as likely to receive a callback relative to blacks with equal qualifications but no criminal past (5 versus 14 percent). A typical black applicant with no criminal background would thus have to apply to more than twice as many jobs as comparable whites to secure an interview, and a black applicant with a prior conviction would have to apply to nearly seven times the number of jobs to secure the same opportunities as an otherwise similarly qualified white applicant with no criminal background. These differentials suggest a powerful interaction between race and crime in the evaluation of entry-level applicants. Above and beyond the individual handicaps of minority status and criminal record, the combination of the two seems to multiply disadvantage. The limited number of employers audited in this study prevents us from making strong claims about the reliability of this interaction in the full sample; there are, however, some revealing patterns that emerge from further investigation.[2] In this chapter, I look at how the effects of race and criminal background differed depending on degree of personal contact, location, and occupation. The patterns discerned here more clearly illustrate the intensification of stigma that results when minority status and criminal background are combined.

Two Strikes and You're Out: The Intensification of Stigma for Black Ex-Offenders

Why might we expect the combined effects of race and criminal background to be larger than the sum of each effect on its own? What is it about the association between race and crime that might generate such strong reactions? According to social psychological research, the activation and application of stereotypes can be triggered by both characteristics of the individual being evaluated and the context in which the evaluation takes place. With respect to the individual being evaluated, we know that the more closely an individual matches a stereotype along multiple dimensions of the stereotype, the more powerfully that stereotype will be activated (Darley and Gross 1983; Fiske and Neuberg

1990).[3] Racial stereotypes triggered by the appearance of a young black man (already constituting an age, race, and gender profile) are further intensified by the revelation of his criminal past. Subtle and perhaps unconscious concerns about black applicants are at once confirmed, weakening any incentive to give a young black man the benefit of the doubt.

Among young white men, by contrast, the reaction is likely to be quite different. Because whites do not fit the stereotypical profile of a criminal, employers may be more willing to overlook a single prior conviction.[4] A young white man with a criminal background can more convincingly explain that he made a regrettable mistake and has learned his lesson. His prior criminal involvement is then interpreted as an isolated incident rather than an internal disposition. Of course, whites also pay a significant penalty for having a criminal background; but the results shown earlier, reinforced in the analyses presented below, indicate that a criminal conviction does not generate the same level of intensity for a white man as it does for a young black male.

At the same time, it is also important to recognize variation in the activation of stereotypes across social contexts. Although both race and criminal background show strong effects in all segments of the labor market, particular types of employers or employment interactions generate distinct patterns of responses. In the following discussion, I consider the ways in which these differences in reactions to racial and criminal stigma affect employment outcomes in various contexts.

Study Design

This study uses an experimental audit methodology to measure the extent to which race and criminal backgrounds represent barriers to employment. The basic design of an employment audit involves sending matched pairs of individuals (called testers) to apply for real job openings in order to see whether employers respond differently to applicants on the basis of selected characteristics. The current study included four male testers, two blacks and two whites, matched into two teams—the two black testers formed one team, and the two white testers formed a second team. The testers were college students from Milwaukee who were matched on the basis of age, race, physical appearance, and general style of self-presentation. The testers were assigned fictitious résumés that reflected equivalent levels of education and work experience.[5] In addition, within each team, one tester was randomly assigned a "criminal record" for the first week; the pair then alternated which member presented himself as the ex-offender for each successive week of employment searches, such that each tester served in the criminal-record condition for an equal number of cases.[6] By varying which member of the pair presented himself as having a criminal record, unobserved differences within the pairs of applicants were effectively controlled.

The testers participated in a common training program to become familiar with the details of their assumed profiles and to ensure uniform behavior in job interviews. The training period lasted for one week, during which testers participated in mock interviews with one another and practiced interviews with confederate employers. The testers were trained to respond to common interview questions in standardized ways, and were well rehearsed for a wide range of scenarios that emerge in employment situations. Frequent communication between me and the testers throughout each day of field work allowed for regular supervision and troubleshooting in the event of unexpected occurrences.

A random sample of entry-level positions (jobs requiring no previous experience and no education beyond high school) was drawn each week from the Sunday classified-advertisement section of the *Milwaukee Journal Sentinel*. In addition, I drew a supplemental sample from Jobnet, a state-sponsored website for employment listings.[7] I excluded from the sample those occupations with legal restrictions on ex-offenders, such as jobs in the health-care industry, work with children and the elderly, jobs requiring the handling of firearms (such as security guards), and jobs in the public sector. Of course, any true estimate of the collateral consequences of incarceration would also need to take account of the wide range of employment fully off-limits to individuals with prior felony convictions.

Each of the audit pairs was randomly assigned fifteen job openings each week. The white pair and the black pair were assigned separate sets of jobs, with the same-race testers applying to the same jobs. One member of the pair applied first, and the second applied one day later; whether the ex-offender was first or second was randomly varied. A total of 350 employers were audited during the course of this study: 150 by the white pair and 200 by the black pair. Additional tests were performed by the black pair because black testers received fewer callbacks on average, and there were thus fewer data points with which to draw comparisons. A larger sample size enables the calculation of more precise estimates of the effects under investigation.

Immediately following the completion of each job application, testers filled out a six-page response form that coded relevant information from the test. Important variables included type of occupation, metropolitan status, wage, size of establishment, and race and sex of employer. Additionally, testers wrote detailed narratives describing the overall interaction and recording any comments made by employers (or statements on application forms) specifically related to race or criminal records.

It is important to note that the study focused only on the first stage of the employment process. Testers visited employers, filled out applications, and proceeded as far as they could in the course of one visit. If testers were asked to interview on the spot, they did so, but in no case did they return to the employer for a second visit. My primary outcome measure then is based on the proportion of applications that elicited callbacks from employers. Individual voice mail boxes were set up for each tester to record employer responses. I focus only on this initial stage of the employment process because it is the stage likely to be most affected by the barrier of a criminal record. Early on, employers have the least individualizing information about the applicant, and are thus more likely to generalize on the basis of group-level (stereotyped) characteristics. As a parallel case, for example, a recent audit study of age discrimination found that 76 percent of the measured differential treatment occurred at this first stage of the employment process (Bendick et al. 1999). Given that both race and a criminal record, like age, are highly salient characteristics, it is likely that as much as if not more of the overall effects of race and criminal stigma will be detected at this stage.

A second advantage of the callback as our key outcome variable relative to a job offer is that it does not require employers to narrow their selection down to a single applicant. At the job offer stage, if presented with an ex-offender and an equally qualified non-offender, even employers with little concern over hiring ex-offenders would likely select the applicant with no criminal record, an arguably safer choice. Equating the two applicants could in fact magnify the impact of the criminal record, as it becomes the only remaining basis for selection between the two (Heckman 1998). The callback, by contrast, does not present such complications. Typically, employers interview multiple candidates for entry-level positions before selecting a hire. In fact, in subsequent interviews employers in this study reported interviewing an average of eight applicants for the last entry-level position filled. At the callback stage, then, employers need not yet choose between the ex-offender and non-offender. If the applicants appear well qualified, and the employer does not view the criminal record as an automatic disqualifier, she or he can interview them both.[8]

In each of the following comparisons, I look at the outcomes for white testers first, followed by a discussion of the differences in effects for blacks. White non-offenders provide a useful baseline measure of the outcomes for all applicants with a given set of human-capital characteristics. Adding race to this picture—and the interaction of race and criminal record—then demonstrates the often sharp contrast between these groups.

The Effect of Personal Contact on Callbacks

> Bill, one of the white testers, applied in person at a furniture sales company. The owner of the company was on-site to look over Bill's completed application. The owner read through the application, looked Bill up and down, then looked back at the application.
>
> "So it says here you were at the Winnebego Correctional Facility," he stated matter-of-factly, but clearly looking for an explanation.
>
> Bill gave the scripted response: "Yes, I served time for a drug conviction. I made a big mistake in my life and I'm looking to move on." The owner looked at him for a moment, seemed satisfied, and moved on to ask Bill some questions about his work experience and interests. "Well, you seem okay to me," the owner concluded. Bill seemed to have made a positive impression on him, despite the awkward beginning.

Bill's experience in this employment interaction was not the norm; more often than not, employers who commented on the testers' criminal record appeared far more disturbed by it. Employers would scrutinize the tester from head to toe, speaking volumes with their gaze even when too uncomfortable to deal with the issue directly. In other cases employers would want to know more about the conviction, as if trying to reconcile the decent-looking young man before them with their mental image of a prison inmate. The effect of these interactions on hiring outcomes is of direct interest to us here. Are employers able to look beyond a conviction when other characteristics of the applicant appear suitable? In what cases can personal interaction mediate the initial stigma of a criminal record?

One of the most direct ways in which stereotypes are activated is through personal contact with members of stereotyped groups. Interactions with members of stereotyped groups trigger an array of conscious and unconscious associations, which affect and distort the ways in which the interaction is perceived. At the same time, extensive interaction can provide the opportunity to supply personal information that is at odds with stereotyped expectations. To the extent that this information is noticed and retained, the effects of stereotypes may be weakened. A closer look at the ways in which personal contact between testers and employers shaped the outcome of the audits can help us to infer the meanings attached to race and criminal record in the minds of employers and to better understand how these views are attenuated or intensified in the course of direct interaction.

Figure 5.1   The Effect of Personal Contact (Whites)

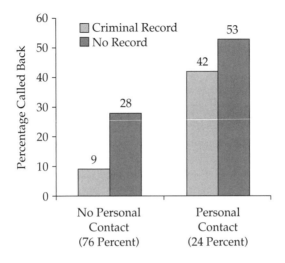

Source: Author compilation.
Note: The effects of criminal record and personal contact are significant (p < .01). The interaction between criminal record and personal contact is marginally significant (p = .07).

Given that this audit study tested only the first stage of the employment process, a majority of tests were completed without significant personal interaction with the employer. Testers were instructed to ask to speak to the person in charge of hiring, but often this person was unavailable or appeared only briefly to instruct the tester to fill out the application and wait for a callback. In these cases, only the most superficial indicators are available to the employer when making decisions about which applicants to consider.

In about one-quarter of all audits, by contrast, testers had the opportunity to engage in extensive discussions with employers. Whether such interactions were official interviews or merely informal conversations about the job, they allowed testers to demonstrate their highly effective interpersonal abilities and to convey an image of general competence. Comparing the outcomes of testers who did and did not interact with employers allows us to assess to what extent employers notice and utilize interpersonal cues in making their assessments of job applicants. Particularly in the case of applicants with criminal records, where stereotypical images are likely to dominate an employer's evaluation, the presentation of a friendly or trustworthy demeanor may be especially important.

Figure 5.1 presents the percentage of callbacks received by white testers, by criminal status and personal contact. Personal contact here includes both conversations with employers and formal interviews, as recorded by testers on their post-application data sheet.[9]

The results shown in this figure clearly indicate that personal contact is associated with a much higher likelihood of receiving a callback for all white testers. Mean callback rates for testers increased by 250 percent (from 18.5 percent to 47.5) after the testers had the opportunity to make personal contact with the person in charge of hiring.[10] This finding is consistent with two plausible and not mutually exclusive explanations. The first implies a change in the applicant's desirability following a direct personal interaction: the findings here are consistent with the interpretation that the testers' ability to make a good impression during personal interactions does in fact translate into significantly higher callback rates. On the other hand, we must also acknowledge the possibility that there may be something specific about these firms that makes them more likely to respond to all applicants. Employers who are experiencing acute labor shortages, for example, may be those who tend to be present to conduct on-the-spot interviews. This would result in an association between personal contact and hiring probabilities in the absence of any mediating effects. As we will see below, however, the fact that personal contact has a very different effect for black testers suggests that the interaction itself—rather than merely the types of employers likely to interact with job applicants—does in fact have a direct effect on hiring outcomes.

More important, these results demonstrate that the effect of a criminal record is substantially smaller in those cases where white testers had the opportunity to interact with the employer. While white ex-offenders were nearly 70 percent less likely to receive a callback in the absence of personal contact, those who did have the opportunity to interact with the employer were only 20 percent less likely to be called back relative to their non-offender partners. This finding suggests that presenting personal indicators that are at odds with the stereotypical profile of a criminal may in fact offset the negative stigma of a criminal record. As noted earlier, research on stereotypes finds that presenting individuating information can reduce the impact of stereotypical judgments (Allport 1954; Fiske and Neuberg 1990). For employers concerned that ex-offenders will be aggressive or uncouth, personal contact can effectively attenuate these associations, offering the applicant a better chance to demonstrate his capabilities.[11]

The previous results applied only to white testers. Given that personal contact may have significant implications for the mediation of racial stereotypes as well as those concerning ex-offenders, it is important to consider how this process may work differently for black applicants. Figure 5.2 presents the percentage of callbacks received by black

Figure 5.2   The Effect of Personal Contact (Blacks)

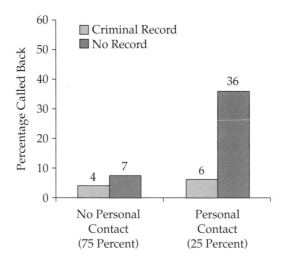

Source: Author compilation.
Note: The main effects of criminal record and personal contact are significant (p < .01). In a model including an interaction between the two, the main effect of criminal record becomes insignificant, and the interaction term demonstrates a large and marginally significant negative effect (p < .06).

testers in each condition. From these results, we see a strikingly different picture.

On the one hand, as in the case of whites, personal contact does increase the likelihood of a callback for blacks *without* criminal records. According to the numbers presented here, blacks without criminal records are more than five times more likely to receive a callback if they have had personal interaction with the employer. In this respect, interpersonal cues certainly seem to strengthen the applicant's case, perhaps mediating initial negative racial stereotypes.[12]

But in contrast to the situation with white applicants, where personal contact increased the likelihood of a callback for both testers and narrowed the gap between those with and without criminal records, for black applicants, personal contact actually widens the disparities.[13] As we can see in figure 5.2, among those who had no contact with the employer, black testers with criminal records were 43 percent less likely to be called back than those without criminal records. Among those who did have personal contact, by contrast, there was an 83 percent difference. This disparity is strikingly large. A number of possible explanations should be considered. First, it is important to remember that these three-way interactions are based on small sample sizes. Although black testers completed two hundred audits in total (or four hundred tester visits), only thirty-five tester-visits resulted in a callback. As a result, the actual proportions in these figures are based on small sample sizes: the number in each of these cells is 7, 10, 3, and 18, respectively. Small fluctuations in the number of callbacks among black ex-offenders, therefore, could make large differences in the comparison of effect sizes.

In this case, however, the disparity is large enough to warrant serious consideration. In fact, despite the small cell sizes, the interaction effect between personal contact and criminal status in a model predicting callbacks reaches statistical significance (p < .05).[14] What is it, then, that leads employers to react so differently to interactions with black applicants with and without criminal records? Although it is impossible to infer the cognitive attributions triggered by these interactions, the outcomes are consistent with the notion that the presence of multiple stigmas produces an intensification of effects. Indeed, prior research has shown that when a target matches on more than one dimension of a stereotype, negative attributions are more likely to be activated and reinforced (Darley and Gross 1983; Fiske and Neuberg 1990; Quillian and Pager 2001). Even though these testers are bright, articulate, and personable, these traits may not be sufficient to overcome the intense negative attributions that accompany the combination of minority status and criminal background. Although whites with criminal records seem to benefit a great deal from personal interaction with employers, this type of interaction does nothing to improve the chances for blacks with criminal histories. Even a bright, friendly demeanor appears immaterial relative to the profound stigma associated with race and criminal involvement. With two strikes, you're out.

The Effect of City and Suburban Location on Callbacks

> During the study, one of the young men posing as a job applicant reflected on the site of a job he'd just applied for. "There's nothing in Franklin but white people and prisoners." Franklin, a suburb on the outskirts of Milwaukee, was indeed a very white part of town. Apart from the population housed in the Franklin Correctional Facility, very few blacks lived or worked nearby. Yet it was in suburbs like these where job growth in the Milwaukee metropolitan area was most rapid. For job seekers from the central city, finding one's way to these employment opportunities required overcoming serious physical and social barriers.

A great deal of literature has described employment differentials in the city compared to the suburbs, with particular attention placed on the experiences of marginalized workers (Freeman and Holzer 1986;

Wilson 1996). Central-city employers are typically more open in their hiring practices, whereas suburban employers are often viewed as those who have escaped or avoided inner-city populations, physically distancing themselves from a less desirable applicant pool (Tilly et al. 2001). Changes in the spatial distribution of job growth has been highly consequential for the employment prospects of young urban job seekers, as job development has primarily occurred outside the city in areas generally less accessible to central-city residents. Indeed, a recent survey of employment in the Milwaukee metropolitan area found that more than 90 percent of recent job growth was in the outlying areas, compared to only 4 percent of new jobs in the central city of Milwaukee (Pawasarat and Quinn 2000). These trends are in sharp contrast to the location of job seekers, who are far more heavily concentrated in the city. Previous research has shown the spatial mismatch between job growth and job seekers to be a major source of minority disadvantage (Fernandez and Su 2004; Holzer 1991; Jencks and Mayer 1990; Kain 1992; Ihlandfeldt and Sjoquist 1998). It is not clear from the available literature, however, whether the obstacles to employment are created by distance alone (for example, problems of transportation or lack of information about distant job opportunities) or whether employers located far from minority populations actively seek to avoid minority workers (Ellwood 1986; Fernandez and Su 2004). On the one hand, the concentration of job growth in suburban areas, paired with high levels of residential segregation, implies a growing distance between black urban residents and emerging job opportunities. The cost of transportation to these jobs is often prohibitive, particularly for entry-level jobs for which compensation is minimal. Even among those willing to make the journey, information about job opportunities in the distant suburbs is less likely to make its way to central-city residents. These transportation and information barriers to access reduce the pool of black applicants for suburban jobs, with a corresponding reduction in black employment overall (Kain 1992).

This explanation remains silent on the issue of employer preferences. Racial segregation in housing and social networks contributes to segregated applicant pools, and employers simply draw from the pool that is available. Other interpretations of the spatial-mismatch hypothesis, by contrast, argue that firm location is directly related to a preferred applicant type. Employers who wish to avoid disadvantaged populations are more likely to locate themselves far from the central city. Previous research has shown suburban employers to be more reluctant to hire racial minorities, openly expressing concerns about the characteristics of black men from the central city (Kirschenman and Neckerman 1991; Wilson 1996). According to one employer quoted in William Julius Wilson's (1996) study, black inner-city men are perceived to be troublesome workers: "We have some problems with blacks . . . I find that the blacks aren't as hard workers as Hispanics and—or the Italian or whatever. . . . The black kind of has a, you-owe-me kind of an attitude" (Wilson 1996, 112). Another reported a similar sentiment: "They tend to laziness. . . . I think people are willing to give them a chance and then it's like they really don't want to work" (Wilson 1996, 118).[15] Harry Holzer (1996), in a more systematic investigation, explored characteristics of employers related to the likelihood of hiring a black worker for a recent noncollege job opening. Controlling for the racial composition of the applicant pool, suburban employers were significantly less likely to hire an African American than were employers in the city. According to these and similar studies, "The problem isn't space. It's race" (Ellwood 1986).

With respect to criminal records, there is a small amount of evidence pointing in the opposite direction. According to a survey of employer preferences, Holzer (1996, 55, 59) found suburban employers to be somewhat less resistant to hiring applicants with criminal records (and less likely to conduct criminal background checks) than their counterparts in the city. It may be the case that central-city employers are more likely to encounter ex-offenders among their applicant pool, and are therefore more sensitized to concerns about criminal backgrounds than their suburban counterparts. Whatever the case, we have little concrete information about how employers in various parts of the city respond to job applicants of varying characteristics. In fact, because of limitations in existing data sources, it has been difficult to systematically assess the relationship between employer location and applicant characteristics.

Among the biggest limitations of studies of spatial mismatch is that they have been plagued by the problems of selection, or the possibility that residents of the central city may differ from suburban residents in important unobserved ways that make them less employable (Jencks and Mayer 1990). If this is the case, the problems of mismatch have less to do with the location of jobs and job seekers and more to do with the quality of workers located near and far from new job growth. Researchers have used creative techniques to control for selective migration and individual background characteristics (see Fernandez and Su 2004 for a review); available data sources, however, are typically limited in the number and quality of control variables available, leaving open the possibility of spatial misattribution.

The design of the audit study offers a novel approach to the study of spatial mismatch. Job seekers are matched on neighborhood of residence, mode of transportation (private vehicle), source of information about job openings (classified ads), and all job-relevant characteristics. Within this model, therefore, the effects of transportation, information,

Figure 5.3   The Effect of a Criminal Record, by Location (Whites)

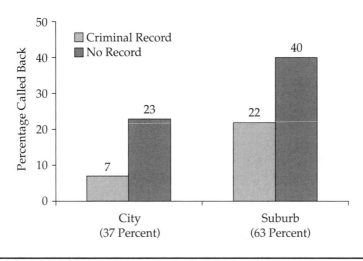

Source: Author compilation.
Note: The effects of criminal record and city are significant (p < .01). The interaction between the two is not statistically significant.

and individual selection are effectively controlled; we can then assess the degree to which employer preferences for blacks, whites, and ex-offenders vary significantly by location. The extensive controls in the current study design are perhaps overly conservative. Suburban employers with strong preferences against workers from the central city are likely to advertise through informal networks or local suburban newspapers rather than in the major metropolitan newspapers, and thus will not show up in our sample. Likewise, many suburban employers are located far from any form of public transportation, further limiting access for disadvantaged populations. We would expect, then, that the results found here may understate the degree to which suburban employers overall resist certain applicant types.

Figure 5.3 presents the callback rates for white testers by criminal status and location. The results here indicate that the overall demand for employment is substantially higher in the suburbs and surrounding counties than in the city of Milwaukee. Among white testers with and without a criminal record, the likelihood of a callback is significantly greater in suburban areas; in fact, the rate of callbacks among white ex-offenders in the suburbs is close to equal that of white non-offenders in the city. Location, therefore, is highly consequential with respect to the likelihood of finding employment.

A second important finding from this graph is that the effect of a criminal record appears to be larger among city employers than among those in the suburbs or surrounding counties. The ratio of callbacks for white non-offenders relative to offenders applying for suburban jobs is just under 2 to 1, compared to a ratio of more than 3 to 1 for those applying for city jobs. Though this interaction does not reach statistical significance in the present sample, the magnitude of the effect is nevertheless worth consideration. Although a criminal record remains a major barrier in all contexts, suburban employers appear to be somewhat less put off by evidence of a white applicant's criminal history than are city employers. This finding is consistent with evidence from Holzer (1996) that suburban employers are less likely to screen for criminal background information in their recruitment of noncollege workers. It is also consistent with general arguments about labor supply, according to which the higher overall demand for workers among suburban employers should lead to less differentiation on the basis of worker characteristics (such as criminal record). Whatever the case, it appears that the problem of spatial mismatch for white ex-offenders is not a matter of employer tastes. Though suburban jobs may be more difficult to access for ex-offenders from the central city because of limited and costly public transportation, for those who make it into the applicant pool their chances of selection by suburban employers are greater than by central-city employers.[16]

Among black testers, by contrast, the higher demand for workers in the suburbs does not seem to offer the same advantages. Figure 5.4 illustrates the callback rates among black testers, by criminal record and location. Here we see that, moving from city to suburb, the increase in callbacks for black non-offenders is less than 50 percent, compared to a jump of almost 100 percent for white non-offenders. Among blacks with criminal records, the move from city to suburb actually lowers the likelihood of a callback. In fact, the interaction between race and criminal record becomes significant among suburban employers, with black ex-offenders facing substantially worse prospects in suburban job searches than the additive effects of race and criminal record would predict.[17] Far from benefiting from the tighter labor market in the suburbs, black ex-offenders fare poorly in suburban job searches.[18]

The overall result of these disparate effects is a widening of the criminal-record effect among suburban employment. Whereas for whites the effect of a criminal record was less pronounced among suburban employers, for blacks this trend is reversed. The ratio of callbacks for black non-offenders relative to offenders is less than 2 to 1 in the city, but more than 5 to 1 in the suburbs. Callback rates remain quite low for blacks in the city, but among city employers willing to hire blacks, a criminal record presents less of an obstacle than it does in the suburban

Figure 5.4   The Effect of a Criminal Record by Location (Blacks)

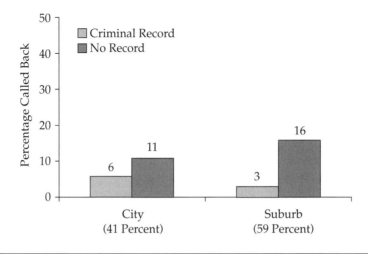

Source: Author compilation.
Note: The effect of a criminal record is significant (p < .001), whereas the effect of city location in this model is not significant. There is a large and significant positive interaction between city location and criminal record, indicating the substantial advantage to black ex-offenders in the city compared to their suburban counterparts.

context. Though suburban employers are somewhat more likely than their city counterparts to consider black non-offenders, they all but close their doors to black applicants with criminal histories.

The interaction between race, criminal record, and location suggests some interesting insights into the relative preferences of city and suburban employers. While suburban employers are generally more responsive to applicants of all kinds—reflecting the tighter labor market in suburban areas—this rule does not apply to blacks with criminal records. Spatial mismatch, therefore, is unlikely to be solely the consequence of physical distance between employers and job seekers. Suburban employers do exert different preferences for low-wage workers, with black ex-offenders ranking at the bottom of their queue. Once again we see that the combination of race and criminal record has an effect far more powerful than does either attribute on its own. In the case of suburban employers, minority status *or* criminal record may be tolerable, but the combination of the two represents almost complete grounds for exclusion. As in the case of personal contact discussed earlier, the "two strikes and you're out" phenomenon applies in the context of suburban employment as well.

Table 5.1   Percent of Applications Requesting Criminal Background Information by Occupation

	Restaurant	Production	Laborer	Service	Sales	Clerical
Percent	52%	76%	79%	81%	83%	84%
N (total)	(82)	(43)	(92)	(37)	(64)	(32)

Source: Author's calculations.

The Effect of Job Type: The Case of Restaurant Work

A third way that tester experiences differed was across occupational categories. Job types varied substantially according to the profile of workers needed, from physical stature (for jobs involving lifting and carrying) to knowledge of Milwaukee roads (for delivery drivers) to interpersonal style (for sales and customer-service positions). The norms and expectations of workers across occupational categories may likewise affect relative openness to minority applicants and applicants with criminal records.

One notable difference among occupational types was the relative frequency with which applicants were asked about their criminal histories. Among six major occupational categories, restaurant jobs stood out in particular as the least likely to request criminal history information on application forms (see table 5.1). In fact, among restaurant jobs included in this sample, just over half requested criminal history information, compared to more than 75 percent in all other occupational categories.[19] It is worth considering how this distinctive characteristic of restaurant hiring procedures may affect the hiring patterns of blacks and ex-offenders.

Restaurant jobs have a high rate of turnover and offer low fixed wages (the assumption is that a large portion of the employee's pay will be in the form of tips); the combination of these conditions often leads to the casting of a wide recruitment net and lower restrictions on candidacy. Indeed, among white testers, restaurant jobs offered one of the highest rates of callbacks for both non-offenders and offenders. Employers often seemed eager to hire applicants right away, and were perhaps therefore less concerned with the information provided about their criminal past.

Figure 5.5 presents the callback rates for white testers by criminal status for restaurant and nonrestaurant jobs. As we can see, rates of callbacks were higher among restaurant jobs for white applicants with and without criminal records, and, likewise, the gap between applicants with and without criminal records is somewhat smaller than in other occupational types.[20]

Figure 5.5   The Effect of Restaurant Jobs (Whites)

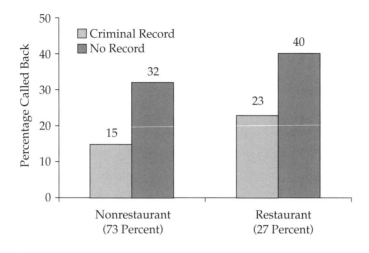

Source: Author compilation.
Note: The main effect of criminal record is significant (p < .001), and the effects of restaurant occupation and the interaction between the two are not significant.

The outcomes for blacks were quite different (see figure 5.6). Restaurant jobs were among the least likely to result in callbacks for black testers, irrespective of criminal condition; this difference is large and statistically significant, with the size of the race effect more than doubling within restaurant jobs (p < .05).[21] It is interesting that such strong racial bias would be demonstrated in such a low-wage, high-turnover job. One possible explanation is "customer discrimination"—or, rather, the employer's perception thereof: if employers believe that diners prefer white waiters to black ones, this creates an incentive to discriminate against black applicants (Becker 1971). Previous research has found strong evidence of a gender preference in restaurant hiring, with high-price restaurants significantly favoring men over women, the assumption being that high-paying customers prefer to be waited on by men (Neumark 1996). A similar type of customer discrimination may be at play with respect to race.[22] A second possibility is concern over the exchange of money between customers and employees, given that waiters handle significant amounts of cash during each shift. If employers perceive blacks to be more likely to steal, they would then demonstrate a preference for whites in hiring for positions involving the handling of cash. Indeed, a separate analysis of all jobs requiring the handling of cash (not shown here) demonstrates a similar, though less pronounced, pattern as that shown in figure 5.6. Whatever the underlying reason,

Figure 5.6   The Effect of Restaurant Jobs (Blacks)

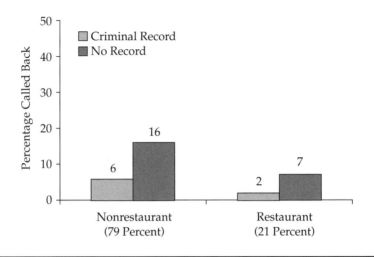

Source: Author compilation.
Note: The main effect of criminal record is significant (p < .001), and the effects of restaurant occupation and the interaction between the two are not significant.

this striking aversion to blacks among restaurant employers warrants further investigation.

As for the criminal record effect, we once again see evidence that black ex-offenders are by far the least favored group. Although there is less evidence of an interaction in this case (likely due to a floor effect), it is readily apparent that the chances of a black ex-offender finding employment in a restaurant occupation are virtually nonexistent.[23] Despite the fact that restaurants appear relatively open to white ex-offenders (and certainly demonstrate an openness on their application forms), evidence of a criminal history among blacks appears to be strong grounds for rejection. Given the fact that restaurant jobs are one of the most frequent types of entry-level job openings (representing nearly one-quarter of job openings in this sample), these findings do not bode well for the overall labor market outcomes of black ex-offenders.

Compounding Stigma: Concluding Remarks

Exploring the interaction between race and criminal record in three contexts, we detect the ways in which black ex-offenders face an intensification of stigma, above and beyond the simple additive effects of either characteristic alone. Given the small sample sizes available for these comparisons, our findings can be considered only preliminary hypotheses in need of further investigation. The consistency of effects across domains, however, provides some assurance that this phenomenon is not merely artifactual. Even in cases where demand for employment is high, employers appear unwilling to overlook the "two strikes" against black ex-offenders. If these findings hold true among applicants with effective interpersonal skills, high levels of motivation, and reliable transportation, one can only wonder what the outcomes may be for black ex-offenders with additional disadvantages. Indeed, if representative of larger trends, these results suggest some troubling conclusions for the employment prospects of blacks with criminal records. Blacks, already burdened by their disproportionate representation in prison, carry the added weight of compounding stigma. The combination of minority status and criminal record create barriers to employment that appear virtually impossible to overcome.

Notes

1. This vignette was reconstructed from the tester's field notes and conversations following the audit. The quotations are not exact reproductions of the conversation, but approximate the interaction closely.
2. The interaction between race and criminal background is not significant in the overall sample; this interaction term becomes significant, however, when we look at specific subsamples presented later.
3. Note that this discussion does not address the question of stereotype accuracy, which will likewise vary across individuals and contexts.
4. Stereotypes work to facilitate the processing of consistent information, whereas evidence not confirming to stereotypes is more easily overlooked or discounted (Rothbart, Evans, and Fulero 1978). Other research finds that subjects interpret information about a black defendant as more dispositional (i.e., more indicative of internal attributes) than equivalent information about white defendants; dispositional attributions are further activated for black defendants following exposure to media coverage of violent crime (Johnson et al. 1997).
5. Testers presented themselves as high school graduates with steady work experience in entry-level jobs.
6. The criminal record in all cases was a drug felony, possession with intent to distribute (cocaine), and eighteen months of prison time. Testers presented the information to employers by checking the "Yes" box in answer to the standard application question, "Have you ever been convicted of a crime?" As additional cues, testers also reported work experience in the correctional facility, and listed their parole officer as a reference (see Pager 2003 for a more in-depth discussion of these issues).
7. Employment services such as Jobnet have become a much more common method of finding employment in recent years, particularly for difficult-to-employ populations such as welfare recipients and ex-offenders. A survey

conducted by Harry Holzer, Michael Stoll, and Steven Raphael (2001) found that nearly half of Milwaukee employers (46 percent) use Jobnet to advertise job vacancies in their companies.

8. A more in-depth discussion of methodological concerns—including limits to generalizability, representativeness of testers, sample restrictions, and experimenter effects—is presented in Pager (2007, appendix 4A).

9. Testers often had lengthy conversations with other employees while filling out their applications. In this analysis, only conversations with the person in charge of hiring counted as having "personal contact."

10. These percentages are averages of callback rates for the group with no personal contact ([9 + 28] ÷ 2) and the group with personal contact ([42 + 53] ÷ 2).

11. Of course, personal contact will not always serve in an individual's favor. Certainly, for many ex-offenders, a demonstration of "soft skills" (or lack thereof) will further reinforce employers' negative stereotypes about this group. In the case of drug offenders, however, the range of delinquency is great. A large proportion of those incarcerated for drug offenses are first-time offenders with no history of violent behavior (Bureau of Justice Statistics 1994). These individuals are far from the image of the "hardened criminal" that employers are likely to be most concerned about.

12. Note that the rate of callbacks among black noncriminals who had personal contact with the employer (36 percent) is even higher than that among white noncriminals who had had no personal contact (28 percent). It may be the case that the appealing interpersonal abilities of these testers weighed more favorably than the mean value of interpersonal ability assigned to white testers when no direct evidence was available. It is also possible, however, as mentioned above, that the employers available to conduct on-the-spot interviews are also those most in need of new staff, in which case the higher rate of callbacks would imply differences in demand rather than the effect of any supply-side characteristics.

13. Note that the overall level of personal contact does not differ between blacks and whites. This may have to do with the small (and rather select) group of employers who do speak with candidates on the spot. In a later study, conducted in New York City, we find that a higher proportion of testers had personal contact with employers, and that whites were more likely to have personal contact than blacks (Pager and Western 2005).

14. Likewise, the interaction between race and criminal record among audits involving personal contact is statistically significant, p < .05.

15. Note, however, that interview studies often find greater expression of negative attitudes among inner-city employers than among suburban employers, despite the fact that inner-city employers are more likely to hire blacks (see Wilson 1996, 119); see also Moss and Tilly 2001, 149–52.

16. Again, though, recall that the employers in this study all advertised in the major metropolitan newspaper. More selective employers are likely to recruit through less universal channels.

17. The coefficient for the interaction term in a logistic regression predicting callbacks is –1.14 with a standard error of .59, p = .055.

18. Once again, however, it is important to acknowledge that the sample sizes

are quite small in these comparisons, and therefore the stability of these estimates is difficult to confirm. The sample sizes in figure 5.3 are 4, 13, 21, and 38, respectively; those in figure 5.4 are 5, 9, 4, and 19, respectively.

19. Note there is some slippage here between industry and occupation. The current coding scheme takes into account the fact that within industries, some employers use different screening procedures for different job types. In the present sample, roughly 75 percent of restaurant jobs were wait-staff positions, specifically. The general results reported here hold true for this more specific job category, though the statistical power declines.

20. Recall that even in cases where the application form did not explicitly request information about criminal background, testers provided cues about their criminal background by reporting work experience gained in the correctional facility and listing their parole officer as a reference in order to provide a consistent signal to all employers. In a separate analyses, I recalculated callback rates separately for employers who did and did not request criminal background information. In the case of restaurant jobs, the difference in callback rates for testers with and without criminal records would have been smaller had no unsolicited criminal background information been presented. If we assumed that testers in the criminal-record condition would have received callbacks in all cases where the noncriminal tester received a callback and where employers did not ask about criminal histories, 35 percent of testers with a criminal record would have received callbacks in restaurant jobs. This accounts for roughly 70 percent of the difference in treatment among whites in restaurant jobs.

21. In a logistic regression predicting callbacks, the coefficient for the main effect of race is −.87, with the coefficient of the interaction between race and restaurant occupation reaching −1.34. These coefficients are from a model including main effects for race, criminal record, and restaurant occupation, with interactions between race and restaurant and race and criminal record (the latter interaction is not significant).

22. By contrast, however, analyses of callback rates by race, criminal status, and a variable measuring customer contact finds no significant effects of customer contact.

23. Note once again that the sample sizes used for these comparisons are small: in figure 5.5, the sample sizes are 16, 35, 9, and 16, respectively; those for figure 5.6 are 9, 25, 1, and 3, respectively.

References

Allport, Gordon W. 1954. *The Nature of Prejudice.* Reading, Mass.: Addison-Wesley.

Becker, Gary S. 1971. *The Economics of Discrimination.* Chicago: University of Chicago Press.

Bendick, Marc, Jr., Lauren Brown, and Kennington Wall 1999. "No Foot in the Door: An Experimental Study of Employment Discrimination." *Journal of Aging and Social Policy* 10: 5–23.

Bureau of Justice Statistics. 1994. "Comparing Federal and State Inmates, 1991." Washington: U.S. Department of Justice, Bureau of Justice Statistics.

Darley, John M., and Paget H. Gross. 1983. "A Hypothesis-Confirming Bias in Labeling Effects." *Journal of Personality and Social Psychology* 44(00): 20–33.

Ellwood, David. 1986. "The Spatial Mismatch Hypothesis: Are There Teenage Jobs Missing in the Ghetto?" In *The Black Youth Employment Crisis*, edited by Richard B. Freeman and Harry J. Holzer. Chicago: University of Chicago Press.

Fernandez, Roberto, and Celina Su. 2004. "Space and the Study of Labor Markets." *Annual Review of Sociology* 30: 545–69.

Fiske, Susan, and Steven L. Neuberg. 1990. "A Continuum Model of Impression Formation: From Category-Based to Individuating Processes as a Function of Information, Motivation, and Attention." In *Advances in Experimental Psychology*, edited by Mark P. Zanna. Volume 23. Thousand Oaks, Calif.: Academic Press.

Freeman, Richard B., and Harry J. Holzer, eds. 1986. *The Black Youth Employment Crisis*. Chicago: University of Chicago Press, for National Bureau of Economic Research.

Heckman, James. 1998. "Detecting Discrimination." *Journal of Economic Perspectives* 12: 101–16.

Holzer, Harry. 1991. "The Spatial Mismatch Hypothesis: What Has the Evidence Shown?" *Urban Studies* 28(1): 105–22.

———. 1996. *What Employers Want: Job Prospects for Less Educated Workers*. New York: Russell Sage Foundation.

Holzer, Harry, Steven Raphael, and Michael Stoll. 2001. "Perceived Criminality, Criminal Background Checks and the Racial Hiring Practices of Employers." *Journal of Law and Economics* 49(2): 451–80.

Ihlandfeldt, Keith R., and David L. Sjoquist. 1998. "The Spatial Mismatch Hypothesis: A Review of Recent Studies and Their Implications for Welfare Reform." *Housing Policy Debate* 9(4): 849–92.

Jencks, Christopher S., and Susan E. Mayer. 1990. "Residential Segregation, Job Proximity, and Black Job Opportunities." In *Inner-City Poverty in the United States*, edited by Laurence E. Lynn Jr. and Michael G. H. McGeary. Washington, D.C.: National Academy Press.

Johnson, James D., Mike S. Adams, William Hall, and Leslie Ashburn. 1997. "Race, Media, and Violence: Differential Racial Effects of Exposure to Violent News Stories." *Basic and Applied Social Psychology* 19(1): 81–90.

Kain, John F. 1992. "The Spatial Mismatch Hypothesis: Three Decades Later." *Housing Policy Debate* 3(2): 371–460.

Kirschenman, Joleen, and Katherine Neckerman. 1991. "'We'd Love to Hire Them, but . . . ': The Meaning of Race for Employers," in Christopher Jencks and P. Peterson, *The Urban Underclass*, Washington, D.C.: Brookings Institute.

Moss, Philip, and Chris Tilly. 2001. *Stories Employers Tell: Race, Skill, and Hiring in America*. New York: Russell Sage Foundation.

Neumark, David. 1996. "Sex Discrimination in Restaurant Hiring: An Audit Study." *Quarterly Journal of Economics* 915–41.

Pager, Devah. 2003. "The Mark of a Criminal Record." *American Journal of Sociology* 108(5): 937–75.

———. 2007. *Marked: Race, Crime, and Finding Work in an Era of Mass Incarceration*. Chicago: University of Chicago Press.

Pager, Devah, and Bruce Western. 2005. "Discrimination in Low Wage Labor Markets." Paper presented at the Annual Meetings of the Population Association of America. Philadelphia, Pa. (April).

Pawasarat, John, and Lois M. Quinn. 2000. "Survey of Job Openings in the Milwaukee Metropolitan Area: Week of May 15, 2000." Report. Milwaukee: University of Wisconsin, Milwaukee, Employment and Training Institute, University Outreach.

Quillian, Lincoln, and Devah Pager. 2001. "Black Neighbors, Higher Crime? The Role of Racial Stereotypes in Evaluations of Neighborhood Crime." *American Journal of Sociology* 107(3): 717–67.

Rothbart, Myron, Mark Evans, and Solomon Fulero. 1978. "Recall for Confirming Events: Memory Processes and the Maintenance of Social Stereotypes." *Journal of Experimental Social Psychology* 15(4): 343–55.

Smith, Tom W. 1991. *What Americans Say about Jews*. New York: American Jewish Committee.

Tilly, Chris, Philip Moss, Joleen Kirschenman, and Ivy Kennelly. 2001. "Space as a Signal: How Employers Perceive Neighborhoods in Four Metropolitan Labor Markets." In *Urban Inequality: Evidence from Four Cities*, edited by Alice O'Connor, Chris Tilly, and Lawrence Bobo. New York: Russell Sage Foundation.

Wilson, William Julius. 1996. *When Work Disappears: The World of the New Urban Poor*. New York: Vintage Books.

== Chapter 6 ==

Private Providers of Criminal History Records: Do You Get What You Pay For?

SHAWN BUSHWAY, SHAUNA BRIGGS,
FAYE TAXMAN, MERIDITH THANNER,
AND MISCHELLE VAN BRAKLE

Individuals who have been incarcerated are significantly more likely than the never-incarcerated to have an unstable work career and low earnings potential, owing in part to the stigmatizing impact of a criminal history record.[1] Attempts to measure the negative impact on employment outcomes associated with having a criminal record have consistently shown that contact with the criminal-justice system leads to increased job instability and an average decline in income (Nagin and Waldfogel 1995; Grogger 1995; Freeman 1991; Waldfogel 1994; Lott 1992; Bushway 1998; Western 2002; Western, Kling, and Weiman 2001).[2] And compelling evidence presented in this volume suggests that employers use criminal history records to screen employees. Harry Holzer, Steven Raphael, and Michael Stoll (chapter 4, this volume) found that 65 percent of all employers would not knowingly hire an ex-offender, and between 30 and 40 percent of all employers actually checked the criminal history records of their most recently hired employees. Devah Pager (2003; chapter 5, this volume) used a matched-pair audit study to understand whether criminal history plays a role in a job applicant's getting a callback from an employer. The study showed that whites with a criminal history record had a 50 percent reduction in the probability of a callback compared to their matched partner without a criminal history record, whereas blacks had a 64 percent reduction in the probability of a callback. The finding that ex-offenders are one-half to one-third as likely to be considered by employers suggests that having a criminal record represents a major barrier to employment (Pager 2003; chapter 5, this volume).

Employers have many incentives to screen applicants for criminal history records. Some employers believe the existence of a criminal history record is indicative of a lack of trustworthiness (Hulsey 1990), while others are worried about their liability for the actions of their employees. Under the legal theory of negligent hiring, employers who know, or should have known, that an employee has had a history of criminal activity may be liable for the employee's criminal or tortious acts. Negligent-hiring actions are now recognized in most states (Craig 1987). In addition, most states require an ever-expanding list of employers to check the criminal history records of applicants and to refuse employment to anyone convicted of a crime. This is especially true of jobs in which work includes caring for children or vulnerable adults.[3]

This concern for security can be understood in the context of a post–9/11 world, but there is also a competing concern that ex-offenders whose criminal histories might restrict them from jobs might be forced to resort to further criminal activity in order to survive. This concern is supported by research published in the academic literature to the effect that the maintenance of employment is at least moderately helpful in curbing ex-offenders return to crime (see Sampson and Laub 1993; Fagan and Freeman 1999; Bushway and Reuter 2002).

As a result of concerns about both the reentry process of ex-offenders and the potential for racial discrimination, researchers who study the employment situation of ex-offenders often call for tighter controls on the release of information about criminal histories (Pager 2003; Petersilia 2003). Recent reports by national committees constructed to study the surge of background checks by nongovernment agencies routinely recommend increased rights for ex-offenders (Search Inc. 2006). But the suggestions that records be sealed or that employers should be restricted from having access to criminal history information miss the fact that state-operated repositories, used by state criminal-justice systems, or larger data repositories maintained at the federal level for use by government agencies, are no longer the sole source of information about criminal history records. Private companies also regularly provide criminal background information to employers that are based on court and prison records. A recent employer survey in Los Angeles showed that over half of all employers who check for criminal records do so through private companies (Holzer, Raphael, and Stoll 2003). Unlike public repositories, private records providers operate in a largely unregulated environment and very little information is known about the accuracy and completeness of these private background checks.

In this article we attempt to shed light on the nature of information provided by private record companies. The first step of our comprehensive search approach involved a search of the Internet, which resulted in our identifying more than four hundred private providers of criminal history records. A review of a random sample of fifty firms established that, in general, the private sector promises to provide background checks faster than public sources, with fewer restrictions. Additionally, we compared FBI rap sheets with a county-level check of court records by a private Internet company for a sample of one hundred twenty parolees and probationers in Virginia. From this review it was found that information provided by the private company was less complete than what was available from the FBI. Although a correlation was not found between the presence of a record from the private provider and employment outcomes for this sample of probationers and parolees, the high number of false negatives and the poor quality of the private records raise some troubling questions about the use of private background screening firms by employers. Policies that allow these private sources of information to become the de facto source for employers represent a missed opportunity for policymakers to help balance the competing demands of employers and ex-offenders.

Access to Criminal History Records

The Bureau of Justice Statistics (2000) conducted a review of state privacy laws in 1999 and noted that there has been an increase in the dissemination of criminal history records. This increased freedom is a relatively recent phenomenon. During the 1960s and '70s, there was much more concern over issues of privacy and a demand for a national mandate on the issue. In 1973 an amendment was added to the Omnibus Crime Control and Safe Streets Act of 1968. This amendment stated that the state and local criminal justice agencies should be in charge of collecting and disseminating criminal history information. The amendment also specified that the information "must be used only for law enforcement and other lawful purposes" (Bureau of Justice Statistics 2000, 4).

Despite this federal legislation, individual states were still allowed to set their own standards. In 1976, the U.S. Department of Justice's Law Enforcement Assistance Administration issued comprehensive information systems regulations which permitted non-criminal-justice access and use of criminal history records maintained by the states if "authorized by statute, ordinance, executive order or court rule, decision or order as construed by the appropriate state or local officials or agencies" (section 20.21 (b)(2). The net result has been a great diversity of statutory schemes across states. Currently, seventeen states either forbid access to criminal records or require employers to meet certain qualifications in order to obtain them. At the other extreme, Florida is a state that provides Internet access to anyone who wants to perform a background check (Petersilia 2003). No two states have identical statutes on practices involving access to criminal history records by non-criminal-justice agencies. States generally do not define which non-criminal-justice agencies may have access but instead "define classes or types of agencies or organizations that may obtain certain types of records for specific purposes" (Bureau of Justice Statistics 2000, 9). For employers, this inconsistency may lead to great confusion about whether they have permission to access their state's repositories. An employer who typically hires workers from more than one state may find such a process too involved and ultimately might be denied access to the records he or she needs.

The next two sections highlight the current system in place for federal and state criminal history repositories. A more thorough review of private providers of criminal history records will follow.

Federal Criminal History Records System

In the federal system, the Federal Bureau of Investigation maintains criminal history records of federal offenders and also state offenders for states that voluntarily provide the information. The technical name of the FBI database is the National Crime Information Center (Hinton 2002). The FBI offender files largely duplicate the criminal history information found in the state files but depend on the cooperation of the local authorities to forward the necessary information. In addition, the FBI maintains a national telecommunications system that allows local, state, and federal criminal-justice agencies to perform national searches of criminal records to determine whether individuals have been arrested or prosecuted in other states (Bureau of Justice Statistics 2001a). The FBI also provides criminal history record services to non-criminal-justice organizations where federal law authorizes access to criminal records by those organizations. Under certain circumstances, employers (including government agencies) may have access to these databases, but for the most part they are inaccessible to the public.

Criminal record information is also generated in federal courts; however, there is no central federal court record repository (Eisenberg et al. 2001). The federal court system is composed of ninety-four federal judicial districts clustered into twelve regional circuits throughout the United States (Hinton 2002). The district courts serve as the trial courts at the federal level. Each circuit contains a court of appeals that hears appeals in criminal cases. To gain access to criminal records, one must go to each of the individual courts.

State Criminal History Record Systems

All states and the District of Columbia have centralized criminal history record repositories. They obtain case information from law enforcement agencies, court records, and corrections records (Bureau of Justice Statistics 2001a) and serve as the link to the FBI record systems (Hinton 2002). At year-end 2001, state criminal repositories contained 64.3 million criminal history files (Bureau of Justice Statistics 2003). Not all state repositories allow public access for non-criminal-justice purposes such as employee background checks.

There are essentially three types of state repositories: open-records states allow the release of criminal history record information from the repository to the general public; intermediate states allow access to their repositories on the condition that the subject of the search signs a release form; and closed-records state repositories require statutory authority in order to allow access to criminal history record information.[4] The studies that look at employment and incarceration in this volume involve states from each of these categories. Florida (see Tyler and Kling, chapter 8, this volume) and Washington (See Pettit and Lyons, chapter 7, this volume) are open-records states. Ohio (Sabol this volume) is an intermediate state and California (Raphael and Weiman this volume) is a more restrictive state.

If one cannot access criminal record information from the state repository, one can go to local courts to retrieve the information because court records are public information in all states. A statewide search covers all counties, but it may not be up-to-date or as detailed as a county level search (Hinton 2002). This is because state repositories are dependent on the more than three thousand counties for their information. County-level searches, on the other hand, are more detailed and more recent, but cover only one county. Access to county and state records over the Internet is not widespread. The Public Record Research Library reports that only about 20 percent of public records are available on-line. Some states offer dial-up access through private commercial systems. According to the 1999 Survey of State Criminal History Information Systems (2000), approximately 89 percent of the 59,065,600 state repository records were automated. As of 1999, twenty-one state repositories had fully automated files, and the remaining twenty-nine states had a combination of both manual and automated files.

This level of automation means that many users in the criminal-justice system have almost instantaneous access through networked computer systems. But when employers wish to access the information in the repositories it tends to take more time for their request to be filled that it takes to do an official search. A survey by Shawn Bushway (1998) found that a response to the average employer request took sixteen business days. The cost is relatively modest. According to the Survey of State Criminal History Information Systems (U.S. Department of Justice 2001), the average cost of a name search through the records requested by a non-criminal-justice entity (including other government agencies) is $19.80; for a fingerprint search the cost is $13.46. Most states have detailed rules about who can conduct a name rather than a fingerprint search. Although general statements are hard to make, fingerprint searches appear to be the norm rather than the exception for employers, and they usually need to provide documentation of employee notification before a search can be performed. These requirements are intended to protect the privacy rights of the potential employee and ensure the accuracy of the subsequent report. These attempts may prove futile, however, if employers ultimately turn to private providers of background information.

The Private Criminal History Records Industry

The fact that there are now private companies disseminating public information has drastically changed an employer's ability to gather information on an applicant or current employees' past criminal record. Court records have always been public documents and therefore individuals can gain access to such information, if they are willing to go to the individual courthouses and pay a fee. Private companies, however, pay their own staff to go to courthouses and compile information into private databases. An employer can now simply choose a private provider on the Internet and search their databases without leaving his or her office.

Private providers can obtain the information in different ways. Some jurisdictions in the United States do not allow for off-site access to the data; thus, an individual must go to the courthouse. Some of the larger companies employ a network of court runners who go to a courthouse and perform the search. These data are then added to the company's larger database, which can be accessed when new requests are made. Private companies are thus able to provide employers with the option of searching records retrieved from several different counties or states, providing employers with the ability to widen the scope of their search. Thus, if they are interested in possible criminal activity in specific counties or states, they are able to add them to the search criteria without having to send someone to each individual site. The convenience factor is a major factor leading to the increased use of pre-employment screening services.

Another factor that has contributed to the rise of the private criminal history record industry is employer concern over legal liability for employees' backgrounds. A background check provides some legal protection to companies if an employee eventually performs a negligent act during his term of employment (Greg Burns, "Holes Found in Cheap Background Checks," *Chicago Tribune*, April 11, 2004, IC).

The 1997 Economic Census provides a broad-brush picture of the makeup of the investigative services industry, a broad category taking in companies that conduct criminal background checks. In 1997 the industry took in almost $2 billion in gross receipts, according to the IRS—but, surprisingly, it is dominated by smaller firms. Of a total 5,077 investigative firms the top 50 firms had 24.1 percent of the revenue and 22.3 percent of the employees. In contrast, there were only 1,588 credit bureaus and the top 4 of these firms had 59.1 percent of the revenue and 34.9 percent of the employees. Moreover, the total revenue of the credit bureau firms was two and a half times the size that of the investigative services firms. Both industry groups provide background information for a fee, but the investigative services industry appears to be more fragmented and therefore harder to regulate than the credit bureau industry.

The major concern is the transmission of inaccurate data. As stated by a National Task Force on Privacy, Technology and Criminal Justice Information, "The commercial marketplace for criminal histories may exacerbate the risk of communicating incomplete or inaccurate records" (Bureau of Justice Statistics, 2001b, 61). In fact, there is very little external or internal regulation of the industry.

Regulations

The Individual Reference Service Group (IRSG) was a private industry lobbying group, founded in 1997 by fifteen of the largest corporations that provide credit and criminal history records to employers and the public at large. The group adopted a list of self-regulatory practices in hopes of showing the government that the industry respected citizens' right to privacy. The group was interested in creating criteria and rules for operating procedures that private companies would be asked to follow in order to generate some set of standards for the industry. "The IRSG principles provide the most effective way to secure the benefits of these important information service resources while assuring effective protection of consumer privacy," (Individual Reference Service Group 1999, 4).

The Federal Trade Commission (1997), in a report to Congress in 1997, noted that many private companies have established precautions on their own websites. However, the report also expressed concern about private entities operating without sufficient oversight: "The barriers to entry for setting up a service online are remarkably low; by paying a local Internet provider as little as $19.95 per month and purchasing the information from a vendor, anyone can publish a website with whatever information she chooses" (Federal Trade Commission 1997, 7).

In response to these privacy concerns, the Federal Trade Commission encouraged the passage of the Gramm-Leach-Bliley Act, in 1999, which specified the responsibilities of background information providers. "Under these provisions, financial institutions have restrictions on when they may disclose a consumer's personal financial information to nonaffiliated third parties."[5] The Gramm-Leach-Bliley Act strictly regulated the selling of an individual's private information to a third party. For example, paragraph 1 of the act stipulates, "All financial institutions are required to provide consumers with a notice and opt-out opportunity before they may disclose information to nonaffiliated third parties."

The Individual Reference Service Group sued the FTC in an effort to prevent these regulations from taking effect. In 2001, a federal court denied the IRSG's motion for an injunction on the new regulations, pending an appeal. Following this decision the lobbying group disbanded, citing the lack of need for self-regulation. Since companies are now legally mandated to have strict privacy standards, the IRSG felt that self-regulation in this environment was no longer necessary. It is not clear to us that these restrictions are binding on the dissemination of criminal history records (nonfinancial records), although the same companies that provide financial information may also conduct criminal record checks.

However, the federal government does regulate the dissemination of criminal history information through the Fair Credit Reporting Act (FCRA), which was originally passed in 1971 and was updated most recently in 2006.[6] The Fair Credit Reporting Act is a federal statute enacted with the stated purpose of ensuring that credit information is disseminated accurately and fairly.[7] At first glance the Fair Credit Reporting Act would seem to be inapplicable to the criminal history record industry. However, the act does regulate this industry if a criminal history record vendor is considered to be a "consumer reporting agency," that is, if the vendor provides a consumer report for "employment purposes."[8] According to the act, a consumer report is used for employment purposes when it is "used in connection with a consumer report for the purpose of evaluating a consumer for employment, promotion, reassignment or retention as an employee" (Hinton 2002, 94). Consequently, a criminal history record vendor that directly gathers information regarding an individual's criminal past and then provides that information to an employer must comply with the regulations or be subject to criminal or civil penalties or both. States may also have reporting procedures that are similar to those of the Fair Credit Reporting Act and that may impose more stringent restrictions on criminal record vendors than the federal regulations. As will be shown, many Internet providers refer to the FCRA on their websites.

The FCRA places restrictions on what type of information background-check companies may provide to employers and also establishes disclosure guidelines that both employers and companies must follow. The original FCRA placed limitations on how far back in time a company could search, and a company was not allowed to provide information on arrest or convictions if the offenses occurred more than seven years prior to the time the search was requested. In November 1998, an amendment, the Consumer Reporting Employment Clarification Act, was added to the FCRA. This amendment lifted the seven-year limit for providing information on a conviction, but companies still were not permitted to provide details of arrest information if the arrest occurred farther than seven years back.

The FCRA mandates that an employer must notify a job applicant in writing that a consumer report may be used in the decision to hire. It also requires that an individual whose background is being searched consent "orally, in writing, or electronically to the procurement of the report by that person." Also, an employer must follow certain guidelines if they intend to use the criminal history record as part of a hiring decision. According to FCRA, an employer must send the individual a copy of the report and a pamphlet describing his rights in the matter. The act also requires the employer to state explicitly "that the consumer reporting agency did not make the decision to take adverse action and is unable to provide the consumer the specific reasons why the adverse action was taken" (FCRA). As will be documented, this requirement of employee notification may not always be enforced.

Many members of the industry are concerned about enforcement and the lack of standards. The background-screener industry formed an industry group in 2003, the National Association of Professional Background Screeners, and currently claims 274 members from 200 companies. The group is moving toward establishing industry standards and a certification process, but at the time of this writing, nothing has been established.

Private-Industry Growth

As previously stated, all signs indicate that the private-records industry has grown considerably since the 1980s. But it is hard to describe the growth precisely because the majority of companies are privately owned and operated and thus are not required to file financial reports

Table 6.1   Estimated Size of the "Investigation Services" Industry
            (U.S. Census Bureau)

Survey Year	Number of Establishments	Receipts ($1,000)	Number of Employees	Payroll ($1,000)
1982	3,730	$1,345,066	30,811	$533,963
1987	4,098	$1,405,796	39,327	$643,953
1992	4,631	$1,577,424	43,653	$709,245
1997	5,016	$1,855,562	50,768	$830,260

Source: All dollars are constant 1997 dollars using the Bureau of Labor Statistics Consumer Price Index. We have assumed that the "investigation services" sector, code 561611 in the North America Industry Classification System, represents a constant proportion of the overall industry code from the older standard industrial classification (SIC) code, 7381, based on the 1997 survey. This may not be an accurate assumption and will lead to an overestimate of the industry size in the early years, given the rapid growth in the industry in recent years.

with government agencies such as the Securities and Exchange Commission. The U.S. Census Bureau does, however, collect information that allows us to get some idea of the growth of the industry. The Economic Census, which is conducted every five years (U.S. Census Bureau 2000), provides data on industry growth and decline based on reported industrial classification codes. The categories in the original standard industrial classification (SIC) code, established in 1987, were very broad, and the criminal history records industry was used in the 1982, 1987, and 1992 economic censuses. In 1997, the Census Bureau moved to a more precise categorization, the North America Industry Classification System (NAICS).

In 1997, data for industries in both the SIC and NAICS code categories were reported, and it could be determined what percentage of the larger SIC code is represented by investigation services. In 1997, 40 percent of all establishments in the larger SIC category fell under investigation services; this business activity represented 15 percent of the total revenue and about 10 percent of the total payroll in this larger category. If we assume, for analytical purposes, that investigation services have remained a constant percentage of the larger industry category, we can calculate a conservative estimate of industry growth in background investigations. This analysis is reported in table 6.1.

In constant 1997 dollars, we estimated a 38 percent increase in revenue and a 55 percent increase in payroll in the investigative services industry since 1982. This growth has not been constant: The revenue increase from 1982 until 1987 was only 4.5 percent, but the growth from 1992 to 1997 was 17.5 percent. We speculate that this acceleration is likely due to the growth of Internet background-search services.

To address this issue of growth another way, Holzer, Raphael, and

Stoll (2003) compared data that they gathered from employers in Los Angeles from the years 1992 to 1994 to data he gathered from employers in Los Angeles for the year 2001. As a part of the survey on employers' hiring practices, the researchers directly asked employers their policy on running a background check, and found that "the employer data for 1992 to 1994 shows that approximately 32 percent of employers in the sample say that they always check" (Holzer, Raphael, and Stoll 2003, 15). This percentage rose to 44 percent by the year 2001. Holzer, Raphael, and Stoll then carried this further to assess whether it was certain types of employers, and not the industry as a whole, that were driving this number upward. They found that the practice of conducting background checks become more common in the retail trade, among large companies employing over one hundred workers, in the manufacturing sector, and among companies located in suburban areas.

Holzer, Raphael, and Stoll (2003) also reviewed data from a 2001 survey that directly asked employers what type of service they used to get background checks (these data were not available for the earlier surveys). Nearly 50 percent of the employers stated that they used a private contractor. The survey also found that the employers were most likely to conduct the background check prior to the hiring decision. Holzer, Raphael, and Stoll (2003) summarized the findings thus: "The availability of low-cost criminal background checking services has played a part in the increase in checking over time, especially since there were few such services to do this checking in the early 1990s" (19).

Qualitative Analysis

The next step of analysis includes a review of surveys conducted with a sample of firms offering Internet-based background checks. To assure a representative sample, the population of companies advertising Internet services was defined. This was done after we conducted a number of searches using different Internet search engines (see appendix 6A). This is not a complete listing of all providers of criminal history records, but is a reasonable estimate of companies who maintain a website on the Internet. A random sample of fifty (N = 50) companies was drawn for the analysis. Appendix 6B is a list of the randomly selected fifty companies reviewed for this analysis.

The goal of the analysis is to describe the different kinds of information available, the costs and timelines of the searches, and the privacy protections provided by the companies, especially with respect to compliance with the FCRA. Each of the fifty companies' websites was visited and the available data were collected. The survey results are limited to the information that is available on the companies' websites.

Many of the companies do not disclose certain information until a customer has submitted a request or entered payment information. As a result, not all information was able to be collected on all fifty companies, as shown in table 6.2.

Results

As expected, these record searches are fairly inexpensive, ranging from $13.50 to $50. The average cost of a one-county search was $24 dollars—higher than the average cost, $13.46, of a name search in the public repositories, but the private search is considerably faster than the typical public-repository search. Four companies said they could do the search in one day, and forty-five companies said they could provide the information within a week.

Data were also collected on the type of courts from which the companies gathered data—county, state, or federal—in addition to the number of states from which records were obtained. Of the companies in our sample, 51 percent stated that they had access to county, state, and federal court records; 36 percent had access only to county and state courts; and 13 percent advertised access to only one type of court. Most sites did not claim national coverage, and the average number of states covered is twenty-one (information not in table.) Most companies do not limit themselves to conviction data or felonies: 97 percent of the firms provide information on both misdemeanors and felonies, and 77 percent claimed access to both arrest and conviction data. There was little evidence on these websites that the records would include information on final disposition for all cases. The overall picture is of data that is limited in geographic and jurisdictional scope, but fairly broad in terms of the type of criminal activity recorded. Additionally, arrests for misdemeanor offenses that are ultimately dismissed are also included in most record searches.[9]

The websites were also split fairly evenly with respect to the source of their information. Sixty-one percent of the companies that provided the information report using court runners to gather the data, meaning that an actual person goes to the courthouse(s) of interest and looks for records on a given individual. These types of searches are thought to be more accurate and up-to-date than searches using wholesale databases made from prison and court data. Not surprisingly, the "runner" searchers are also significantly more expensive ($27.04 versus $19.58, $p = .07$, $N = 19$). Since a runner is required for each jurisdiction, this type of search, while more accurate, will not be as comprehensive as a search of a centralized state repository.

The next stage of the analysis focused on data we gathered on the companies' policies concerning privacy rights of the individuals being

Table 6.2   Survey of Fifty Internet Providers

Variable	N	Descriptive Information (Standard Deviation)
Cost of a one-county search	24	Average = $24.03 ($9)
Average response times	29 days	
One day or less		13.8% (4)
Two to seven days		82.7% (24)
More than seven days		3.4% (1)
Scope of searches	47	
Federal, state, and county court		51.1% (24)
County and state courts		36.17% (17)
other		12.8% (6)
Number who use court runners, not just vended databases	33	60.6% (20)
Provide information about FCRA guidelines on disclosure of personal information on website	50	56% (28)
Provide disclaimer about search accuracy	50	36% (18)
Reports include arrests and convictions	30	76.7% (23)
Reports include felonies and misdemeanors	36	97.2% (1)
Length of record search	28	
Seven years or less		42.9% (12)
More than seven years		57.1% (16)
Website has form to notify candidate about search	50	40% (20)
Required information about employee	28	
Name only		21.4% (6)
Name, date of birth		17.9% (5)
Name, Date of birth, and social security number	60.7% (17)	

Source: Authors' calculations.

searched. Only 56 percent of the firms provided information on their websites regarding FCRA rules for the allowable uses of the data. In most cases, the sites make it clear that it is the employer's responsibility to comply with the FCRA, and the companies maintaining the sites take no responsibility to make sure the information is used correctly. As a result, it is perhaps not surprising that there were no significant relationships between posting a notice about the Fair Credit Reporting Act and the type and nature of the data provided. For example, the FCRA states that arrest records cannot be searched farther back than seven years; 57 percent of the firms, however, stated that they can search more than seven years back, and five of the firms that do post information on the FCRA also state that they can provide arrest and conviction information for more than seven years back. Only 40 percent of the firms post a form for disclosure to the job candidate. Fifteen of the firms that post the FCRA regulations do not post a form for disclosure, despite the FCRA requirement to do so. Although it is possible that the forms are provided at a later point in the transaction, evidence that the record providers seriously fulfill FCRA requirements is not strong.

There was a striking contrast between public repositories' obvious concern about accuracy of the information they dispense and the lack of such concern on the part of the private companies. Ironically, some of the websites provided detailed information as to ways in which the data may be inaccurate. A primary source of inaccuracy involves the type of identification used for the search. Most public repositories require fingerprints for background checks (Search Inc. 2006). In contrast, six of the twenty-eight firms that do background checks require only a name, and another five require only name and date of birth. The remainder also required a Social Security number but none that we are aware of require a fingerprint check. Only 36 percent of the Internet sites reviewed in this analysis provided some type of disclaimer concerning the accuracy of the data provided. The absence of absolutely reliable identification procedures raises the possibility of serious mistakes based on scrambled identities.[10]

In summary, this qualitative review of a sample of fifty Internet checking sites provides a picture of how to obtain a fairly inexpensive and quick but not particularly comprehensive or accurate background check. Though the firms appeared to have some awareness of the FCRA, we found little evidence that the regulations were being followed rigorously.

Our next analysis was of 120 parolees and probationers in Virginia. The FBI and a private company were asked to find records on these individuals, and we did a detailed comparison of the results, to obtain another perspective on the differences between private and public repositories. The design of our project only allows us to investigate false negatives (when an individual with a criminal history is recorded as not having a record) and not false positives (when an individual without a record is reported as having a record) because our sample only includes those people who are already known to have criminal history records. In general, prior research on the problems with criminal history records suggest that the false-negative rate should be higher than the false-positive rate (Geerken 1994). In principle, many more people are potential false positives than false negatives because anyone without a criminal history record could theoretically be false positive, while only those who actually have a criminal history record can be false negative. It is not clear which error affects more people; future research should focus on identifying the prevalence of false positives.

Virginia Offenders

Two of the authors of this paper are involved in a study to examine the impact of different types of drug treatment services to offenders in a community supervision setting. As part of this randomized trial (see Taxman and Thanner 2006; Thanner and Taxman 2003; Weisburd and Taxman 2000; Taxman and Yates 2001 for a description of the overall study), the researchers used criminal history to identify whether offenders had been rearrested in the post-randomization period. Criminal history records for the offenders in our study were obtained from the FBI. In reviewing these records, we observed that often the crime for which the offender was placed on probation or parole was not on the FBI record. Because two of the study sites were located in Virginia, Alexandria and Prince William County, we sought to obtain local information on arrests in the state of Virginia. We were denied access to the statewide Virginia Criminal Information Network because procedures for granting access to researchers had not yet been established. We sought the assistance of a private company to obtain the criminal histories and were then able to compare these records to those previously provided by the FBI.[11]

The company was selected after a review of several companies identified through an Internet search. We reviewed the information from four companies and determined that the company we selected offered the most comprehensive services. The decision was made in light of our knowledge of the type of information provided on the FBI records: this particular company provided similar criminal history information.

Of the 120 records requested from both sources, the FBI returned records on 87 (72 percent) clients, even though everyone in our sample was on probation or parole, and thus had at a minimum of one arrest and one criminal conviction—in fact, the average number of prior arrests for our sample was seven, and nearly 70 percent of the individuals had been incarcerated in the previous twelve months. This result was not entirely a surprise—previous research has documented that centralized rap sheets have a relatively high rate of false negatives as a result of communication problems between local and state agencies (Geerken 1994).

When we requested records on the same 120 individuals from the private company, information was returned on only fifty-six clients (47 percent), substantially fewer than from the FBI. Eleven of the records we got were for offenders that the FBI did not return any information on. We obtained records from both the FBI and the private company for only forty-two clients. Both the FBI and the private provider had a significant problem of false negatives—records were not returned when they should have been—although the problem was considerably larger for the private provider than for the FBI. We also learned that the systems are also not completely redundant—the private provider search found records in about 33 percent of the cases that the FBI did not find.

We also compared the content of the forty-two records that were found by both the FBI and the private company, with respect to consistency of arrest activity reported—specifically, overall number of arrests, dates of arrest, and arrest charges. Since the FBI has access to records from jurisdictions nationwide whereas the local records are only from the Prince William jurisdiction, we anticipated some inconsistency, so we also noted the number of arrest events listed on the FBI records as having occurred in Prince William. Table 6.3 presents information on the consistency of the information provided by the two record sources, by client.

In this comparison, the time frame was limited to arrests that have occurred in the past ten years, because the private company only provided information as far back as ten years. So even though the FBI records provided a fuller history of arrest information, only arrest information provided by the FBI within the past ten years was included. Even limiting this comparative review to arrests that occurred in Prince William County with the preceding ten years, the group of 120 clients has an extensive criminal offending history: 227 arrests were reported in the FBI files over the past ten years in Prince William County, an average of 5.4 arrests per client. The average would be much higher if all prior arrests, including those beyond the ten-year limit and those outside Prince William County, were counted.

Even with the imposed ten-year time limit, arrest information from the FBI is much more comprehensive than information obtained from the private company, particularly with respect to information provided on arrests in Prince William County (see table 6.3). Although the private-company records indicated one to five arrest events in each of the forty-two cases, the FBI records reflected the same number of events in

Table 6.3   Comparison of Arrest Information Generated From FBI Records and Private Company Search of Courthouse Records[a]

	FBI Record		Private Record	Number of
Client	Number of Total Arrests	Number of Arrests in Prince William	Number of Arrests in Prince William	Arrest Events in Both FBI and Private Records
1	8	5	2	1
2	4	1	1	0
3	4	0	1	0
4	7	2	1	0
5	1	0	1	0
6	5	2	1	0
7	7	7	1	0
8	4	1	1	0
9	9	0	1	0
10	4	2	1	0
11	5	2	2	1
12	6	0	1	0
13	2	0	1	0
14	7	1	1	0
15	3	2	1	0
16	3	0	1	0
17	3	0	1	0
18	5	2	1	1
19	8	4	1	0
20	11	4	1	0
21	6	3	1	0
22	7	4	4	1
23	2	1	1	0
24	1	0	1	0
25	13	9	3	1
26	5	4	1	0
27	2	0	1	0
28	6	6	1	0
29	6	2	3	1
30	5	1	1	0
31	2	1	1	0
32	2	1	1	0
33	9	8	1	1
34	4	0	1	0
35	2	2	1	1
36	10	9	3	0
37	6	2	1	1
38	10	10	1	1
39	4	0	3	0
40	8	8	1	0
41	5	4	5	3
42	6	1	1	0
TOTAL	227	111	59	13

Source: Authors' calculations.
[a]Prince William County, Virginia; information was for the ten years prior to date of search.

thirteen cases, in addition to numerous other arrests in Prince William, ranging from one to nine additional arrests.

Thus, the FBI records captured more arrests overall and, more important, more arrests occurring within Prince William. Of a total number of 157 arrest events occurring in Prince William reported for this sample from both sources, 111 of these events (or 71 percent) were captured by the FBI records and only 59 (or 38 percent) were captured by the private company.[12] In several cases, the private record provided information on an arrest in Prince William when the FBI record indicated no arrests. Overall, the consistency rate between the two sources was only 8 percent.[13] Even where the information on the basic fact of an arrest matched, information on details of the arrest events often did not. Where basic arrest information matched, both sources provided information on arrest dates and arrest charge. The FBI records did not provide information on disposition or sentence, whereas most of the records from the private company included this information. In general, we do not have a great deal of confidence that the information provided by either source represents an accurate description of the criminal activity of the offenders. It is hard for us to imagine how this information can lead to the type of nuanced interpretation often recommended by policymakers about the relevance of the offense for the job in question.

The high rate of false negatives gives us an opportunity to explore the potential impact of criminal history records on actual job searches. Since these participants were on probation or parole, they were all required to pursue employment. Moreover, as part of the larger study we have information on their employment within two months of their release, and roughly one year later. If the performance of the private-record provider in our study was typical of other such providers, we would expect that clients whose searches result in false negatives from the private record provider would have a competitive advantage in the labor market over clients whose searches produced true positives. Therefore, during the follow-up period, we compared clients who got false negatives with those who got the true positives, on a number of labor-market outcomes—including employment status, hours worked, daily pay, and earnings growth over the follow-up year. We found no evidence that having a true positive record in the private database had any impact on these employment outcomes.

There are several interpretations of these results. First, as parolees and probationers, these individuals may have followed what is fairly common advice and made their ex-offender status clear to their potential employer. Second, these individuals were working at fairly low-wage jobs, often in the gray market as day laborers or car washers. These are exactly the type of jobs for which criminal backgrounds often are immaterial. Finally, it is possible that employers have other ways of finding out about criminal history records that are unrelated to the information gathered by the particular company we chose.

Conclusion

Increasing numbers of ex-offenders being released from prisons and the rise in the number of offenders under correctional control in jail and probation or parole make it necessary to identify strategies to help ex-offenders maintain a productive life in the community. Over the last fifteen years there has been an explosion in the growth of private companies that conduct background checks, which allow employers to circumvent barriers to public repositories. One interpretation of this growth is that these companies provide a service by taking pressure off of overwhelmed public agencies designed to deal with the criminal-justice system and not with employers.

These companies are not organized by state, and are not regulated by the same state laws that govern access to records by the public repositories. Thus, these companies are not subject to restrictions on the nature of the records that they can retrieve, nor must they follow guidelines on the process for handling complex criminal justice issues such as expungement of records and for differentiating among various types of law violations, for example, misdemeanor, felony, and so on. There are only fifty public repositories but there are well over four hundred companies providing background checks. Even though private companies are regulated by the provisions of the federal Fair Credit Reporting Act, enforcement of these rules appears spotty at best.

Another problem with private companies concerns available remedies for incorrect information. If someone has been arrested in New York, and he believes that there is a potential error in that record, he can deal with one and only one public agency to fix the error. This is not true in the private system, where each company is essentially an independent operator with no obligation to update or otherwise audit the accuracy of the records it has gathered and is using. An individual who wants to correct an error in the private system would have to deal with each and every company who provides information on background checks, a nearly impossible task. This feature of the industry also means that expungement and sealing orders, often used by states to facilitate rehabilitation, are virtually unenforceable in the private system. Once the information is publicly available and disseminated by the data venders, there is no mechanism for correcting or altering that piece of information.

Indeed, our review demonstrated that there is reason to be concerned about the accuracy of the information in the private record sphere. People who were convicted were not captured by the data (false negatives), and there was little correspondence between what we gathered from the FBI and what we gathered from the private system.

We believe that our research supports several policy recommendations. First, policymakers should not equate a background check conducted through a state repository with a background check conducted by a private company. Some states, such as Maryland, appear to make that analogy by allowing background checks for nursing homes to be conducted by private companies while requiring that background checks for workers in other sensitive industries be conducted at the state repository. This practice, requested by the repository itself, implies an equivalency that simply does not exist. Despite their faults, government repositories constitute the best source for accurate information about criminal history records and they have the best existing mechanisms for the responsible dissemination of that information.

Second, we believe to be archaic distinctions between the sources of requests for background information: those coming from the criminal-justice system and those coming from employers and other entities. Criminal history repositories originally existed strictly for criminal-justice purposes, and repositories continue to view the criminal-justice system as their primary client. But policymakers have increasing tasked the repositories with non-criminal-justice functions, namely, background checks for employment. And, in point of fact, the issues surrounding any background check (accuracy, privacy) are the same, regardless of the reason for the check. Why should someone under investigation have the right to identification whose accuracy is ensured via a fingerprint search, but someone applying for a job only has the right to unreliable identification by name, or by name and birthday? Policymakers who believe criminal history records are valuable information for purposes other than criminal investigations should fund repositories so that they can carry out this broader service effectively and provide individuals with the necessary protection of their basic rights. Convenient access to accurate information at the repository level would virtually eliminate the need for private companies, and it would facilitate easier regulation and control over the information in question.[14]

Finally, we believe that the dissemination of criminal history record information that lacks the personal, individual context of the subject of the search is difficult to defend. Rap sheets are difficult to read. Despite our experience with the criminal-justice system, we at times found it difficult to interpret the information we obtained from the background checks, since there is tremendous variation in the nature of offenses, different criminal-justice actions (including arrest, nolle, sentencing information, and so forth). The current position of the repository systems is to place the burden directly on the employers to interpret this complex web of information. But we know that not all information about criminal history records is equally informative or relevant to assessing the likelihood of an ex-offender's committing a future crime; elapsed time since the offense, the nature of the offense, and other factors all help predict the probability of reoffending in the future. The government can and, we believe, should play a role in interpreting this information and presenting it clearly. For example, six states now provide certificates of rehabilitation to ex-offenders after they demonstrate, through a variety of actions, their commitment to a constructive lifestyle. It may also be possible to provide more continuous information. It is not hard to imagine instituting a credit-score-like number that summarizes an individual's risk of offending. This number, which would have the advantage of being affected by the individual's actions, could be based on statistical analysis of information currently available in the criminal history record repositories. We see no reason why employers would not be willing to pay for accurate, up-to-date information that summarizes and quantifies an individual's risk of reoffending.

The public nature of court records always leaves open the possibility that employers and others can make an end run around public repositories if given the incentive to do so, despite the fact that, in our opinion, this private system is much worse for both employers and ex-offenders. We believe that policymakers must also pay attention to factors such as negligent-hiring case law that motivate some employers to avoid ex-offenders. Decreasing some of the demand for background checks would provide breathing room for the system to develop solutions to its current problems.

Appendix 6A

Several different Internet searches were conducted to obtain a sample of companies offering background checks for a fee. The initial searches were done through Lexis Nexis and the Ebsco Academic Universe, using the search terms "criminal history record checks," "background checks," and "criminal record companies." These searches yielded some information but did not provide a comprehensive list of companies that conduct criminal record checks. The focus then shifted to searching for the companies on the Internet by using the Yahoo and Google search engines.

Varying the search terms also helped increase the hit rate for finding companies. For example, typing in the phrase "background check" produced approximately 3,210,000 hits in the Yahoo search engine and 3,280,000 hits from Google. The sheer volume of hits made it impossible to zero in on the type of list we needed, so we refined the search, using the search terms "public record vendor," "public record wholesaler," "public records," "public record resources," "public records research," "employment screening," "investigative services," and "background verification." This yielded additional companies. After cross-checking the additional lists with the list from the Public Record Sources site, we compiled a tentative list of 472 companies that conducted criminal history record checks. For the detailed analysis we drew a random sample of fifty (N = 50) companies. A list of the 472 companies is available from the authors upon request.

Appendix 6B: Names of Background-Search Companies with Internet sites

1stPublic Records.com

A Matter of Fact

Accurate Credit Bureau

AccuScreen Systems

Achievement Tec

ADREM Profiles Inc.

Advance Credit Reports Inc.

Applicant-Screening.Com, Inc.

Background Bureau Inc.

Background Check

BackgroundFerret.com

Backgrounds USA

Bearak Reports

Case Breakers

Check-Mate

CICS Employment Services

ConcentraCheck.com

Corporate Screening Svcs

Data Quest Ltd.

DDI Inc.

DDS Online

Discreet Research

DMV Driving Record Search

Docusearch

EBI

Employment Research Services

ERS Hire

FABCO

FactsFinder.com

Fairfield Information Services & Associates

First Check

Florida Asset Locators, Inc.— USA Background.com

GiS (General Information Services Inc.)

HireRight

InfoCheck, Inc.

Insights Corporate Selection Systems Inc.

Intellichoice

Logan Registration Service

Merlin's Data Research

Nation Wide Record Search

Property Owners Exchange Inc.

Record Search America Inc.

RefCheck

Staftrack Inc.

Superior Information Services

The Screening Network   VeriCORP Inc.

US Search Screening Services   Verifacts
   Inc.
                                         WJP & Associates

Notes

1. Criminal history records are "cumulative, name-indexed histories of an individual's involvement in the criminal justice system"; they generally include conviction information and nonconviction information such as arrests (Belair 1989).
2. The size and length of time of the impact of incarceration on employment for ex-offenders is somewhat ambiguous (Western 2002). Evidence from Jeffrey Grogger (1995) and Jeffrey Kling (2006) using official data suggests that the impact of incarceration on employment is small and transitory. The chapters in this volume (see Pettit and Lyons, chapter 7; Tyler and Kling, chapter 8; and Sabol, chapter 9) actually document a short-term gain in employment and earnings immediately following incarceration, perhaps because of supervision requirements, before an eventual return to employment rates and earnings roughly equal to those before incarceration. What is not known is whether the rather low employment and earnings of offenders would increase absent incarceration; see, for example, the increases for the GED control group in John H. Tyler and Jeffrey Kling (chapter 8, this volume).
3. For an overview of legislation requiring the use of criminal history records, see J. Hahn (1991).
4. States that allow general public access to criminal records are Colorado, Florida, Iowa, Kansas, Massachusetts, Minnesota, Montana, Oregon, Pennsylvania, Texas, Wisconsin, Connecticut, Hawaii, Idaho, Maine, Michigan, Missouri, Nebraska, Oklahoma, South Carolina, and Washington.

   States that require some form of release for access to criminal records by the general public are Alabama, Arkansas, Delaware, the District of Columbia, Illinois, Maryland, Nevada, New Hampshire, New Mexico, North Dakota, Ohio, South Dakota, Utah, West Virginia, and Wyoming.

   States that require statutory authority for access to criminal history records are Alaska, Arizona, California, Georgia, Indiana, Kentucky, Louisiana, Mississippi, New Jersey, New York, North Carolina, Rhode Island, Tennessee, Vermont, and Virginia (all from Hinton 2002).
5. Paragraph 1 of the Gramm-Leach-Bliley Privacy of Consumer Financial Information Act. The complete text is available on-line at http://www.ftc.gov/privacy/privacyinitiatives/glbact.html.
6. Fair Credit Reporting Act (FCRA), 15 U.S.C. § 1681 et seq. [[The FCRA cited in this paper is complete as of January 7, 2002, and contains the amendments to the act promulgated in the Consumer Credit Reporting Reform Act of 1996 (Public Law 104–208, Omnibus Consolidated Appropriations Act for Fiscal Year 1997, title II, subtitle D, chapter 1); section 311 of the Intelligence Authorization for Fiscal Year 1998 (public law 105–107);

the Consumer Reporting Employment Clarification Act of 1998 (public law 105–347); section 506 of the Gramm-Leach-Bliley Act (public law 106–102); and sections 358(g) and 505(c) of the Uniting and Strengthening America by Providing Appropriate Tools Required to Intercept and Obstruct Terrorism Act of 2001 (USA PATRIOT Act, public law 107–56).]) The most recently updated text of the Fair Credit Reporting Act (July 30, 2004) is available at http://www.ftc.gov/os/statutes/031224fcra.pdf.

7. See Fair Credit Reporting Act, § 602, "Congressional findings and statement of purpose [15 U.S. Code, paragraph 1681], http://www.ftc.gov/os/statutes/031224fcra.pdf, p. 3.

8. See Fair Credit Reporting Act, http://www.ftc.gov/os/statutes/031224fcra.pdf, pages 5: "§ 603(f): The term consumer reporting agency means any person which for monetary fees, dues, or on a cooperative nonprofit basis regularly engages in whole or in part in the practice of assembling or evaluating consumer credit information or other information on consumers for the purpose of furnishing consumer reports to third parties, and which uses any means or facility of interstate commerce for the purpose of preparing or furnishing consumer reports.

"§ 603(d) Consumer report. (1) In general, the term 'consumer report' means any written, oral, or other communication of any information by a consumer reporting agency bearing on a consumer's credit worthiness, credit standing, credit capacity, character, general reputation, personal characteristics, or mode of living, which is used or expected to be used or collected in whole or in part for the purpose of serving as a factor in establishing the consumer's eligibility for credit or insurance to be used primarily for personal, family, or household purposes; employment purposes; or any other purpose authorized under section 604 [§ 1681b]."

9. Since disposition information is often not explicitly included in court records, arrest information without conviction need not be interpreted as an acquittal or dismissal.

10. While completing a background check for another project, one of the authors of this paper once conducted an analysis on a pair of criminally involved twins. One agency reported the record for both individuals in the report for each, thus indicating the presence of an alias.

11. Record requests from the FBI were free as part of a research agreement between the FBI and the University of Maryland. Checks conducted by the private company cost $14 per search of the Prince William County courthouse records.

12. Percentages were calculated by dividing 157, the total number of arrest events reported in Prince William County by both sources, by 59, the number of arrest events recorded by the private company ($59 \div 157 = .38$).

13. Calculated by adding the number of all reported arrests in the FBI records (111) and the private company (59) and then subtracting the number of overlap arrest events (13): $111 + 59 - 13 = 157$.

14. For example, in Florida, which provides on-line access to its records, private companies simply connect directly to the state repository and thus do not need to create a second data set for their own use.

References

Belair, Robert. 1989. "Public Access to Criminal History Record Information." Search, Inc., Criminal Justice Information Series, NCJ 111458. Washington: U.S. Department of Justice, Bureau of Justice Statistics.

Bureau of Justice Statistics. 2000. "Compendium of State Privacy and Security Legislation: 1999 Overview." Report no. NCJ 182294, prepared by Search Inc. (National Consortium for Justice Information and Statistics). Washington: U.S. Department of Justice, Bureau of Justice Statistics.

Bureau of Justice Statistics. 2001a. "Use and Management of Criminal History Record Information: A Comprehensive Report." Update, NCJ 187670. Washington: U.S. Department of Justice, Bureau of Justice Statistics.

Bureau of Justice Statistics. 2001b. "Report of the National Task Force on Privacy, and Criminal Justice Information." Report, no. NCJ 187669. Washington: U.S. Department of Justice, Bureau of Justice Statistics.

Bureau of Justice Statistics. 2003. "Survey of State Criminal History Information Systems, 2001." Report, no. NCJ 200343. Washington: U.S. Department of Justice, Bureau of Justice Statistics.

Burton, Velmer, Jr., Francis Cullen, and Lawrence Travis III. 1987. "The Collateral Consequences of a Felony Conviction: A National Study of State Statutes." *Federal Probation* 51: 52–60.

Bushway, Shawn. 1998. "The Impact of an Arrest on the Job Stability of Young White American Men." *Journal of Research in Crime and Delinquency* 35: 454–79.

Bushway, Shawn, and Peter Reuter. 2002. "Labor Markets and Crime Risk Factors." In *Evidence-Based Crime Prevention*, edited by Lawrence Sherman, David P. Farrington, Brandon C. Welsh, and Doris Layton MacKenzie. New York: Rutledge Press.

Craig, Scott. 1987. "Negligent Hiring: Guilt by Association." *Personnel Administrator*, October 32–34.

Eisenberg, Deborah, Chris Rahl, Marcia Reinke, and Warren Weaver. 2001. "State and Federal Policy on Electronic Access to Court Records." Report. Available at http://www.courts.state.md.us/access/states7-5-01.pdf.

Fagan, Jeffrey, and Richard B. Freeman. 1999. "Crime and Work." In *Crime and Justice: A Review of Research*, edited by Michael Tonry. Volume 25. Chicago: University of Chicago Press.

Federal Trade Commission. 1997. *Individual Reference Services: A Report to Congress.* Available at http://www.ftc.gov/os/1997/12/irs.pdf.

Freeman, Richard. 1991. "Crime and the Employment of Disadvantaged Youth." NBER working paper no. 3875. Washington, D.C.: National Bureau of Economic Research.

Geerken, Michael. 1994. "Rap Sheets in Criminological Research Considerations and Caveats." *Journal of Quantitative Criminology* 10(1): 3–21.

Grogger, Jeffrey. 1995. "The Effect of Arrests on the Employment and Earnings of Young Men." *Quarterly Journal of Economics* 110(1): 51–71.

Hahn, Jeffrey. 1991. "Pre-Employment Information Services: Employers Beware?" *Employee Relations Law Journal* 17(1): 45–69.

Hinton, Derek. 2002. *Criminal Records Book*. Tempe, Ariz.: Facts on Demand Press.

Holzer, Harry J. 1996. *What Employers Want: Job Prospects for Less-Educated Workers*. New York: Sage.

Holzer, Harry, Steven Raphael, and Michael Stoll. 2003. "Employer Demand for Ex-Offenders: Recent Evidence from Los Angeles." Working paper. University of California, Los Angeles.

Hulsey, Lonnie. 1990. "Attitudes of Employers with Respect to Hiring Released Prisoners." Ph.D. diss., Texas A & M University.

Individual Reference Service Group. 1999. "On Elements of Effective Self-Regulation for the Protection of Privacy and Questions Related to Online Privacy." Comments submitted to the Department of Commerce, July 6, 1998. Available at http://www.ntia.doc.gov/ntiahome/privacy/mail/disk/irsgcom.html.

———. 2001. "IRSG Information." Available at http://www.dnis.com/irsg.asp (accessed January 8, 2007).

Kling, Jeffrey R. 2006. "Incarceration Length, Employment and Earnings." *The American Economic Review* 96(3): 863–76.

Laudon, Ken. 1986. *Dossier Society: Value Choices in the Design of National Information Systems*. New York: Columbia University Press.

Lott, John. 1992. "Do We Punish High-Income Criminals Too Heavily?" *Economic Inquiry* 30: 583–608.

Nagin, Daniel, and Joel Waldfogel. 1995. "The Effects of Criminality and Conviction on the Labor Market Status of Young British Offenders." *International Review of Law and Economics* 15(1): 109–26.

Pager, Devah. 2003. "The Mark of a Criminal Record." *American Journal of Sociology* 108(5): 937–75.

Petersilia, Joan. 2003. *When Prisoners Come Home*. Oxford: Oxford University Press.

Rubin, Sal. 1971. "The Man with a Record: A Civil Rights Problem." *Federal Probation* 35(00): 3–7.

Sampson, Robert, and John Laub. 1993. *Crime in the Making*. Cambridge: Harvard University Press.

Schwartz, Richard, and Jerome Skolnick. 1962. "Two Studies of Legal Stigma." *Social Problems* 10(2): 133–38.

Search, Inc. 2006. "Report of the National Task Force on the Criminal Backgrounding of America." Sacramento, Calif.: Search, Inc.

Taxman, Faye S., and Meridith Thanner. 2006. "Risk, Need, and Responsivity: It All Depends." *Crime and Delinquency* 52(1): 28–52.

Taxman, Faye S., and Brian Yates. 2001. "Quantitative Exploration of Pandora's Box of Treatment and Supervision: What Goes on Between Costs In and Outcomes Out." In *Preventing Crime: Economic Costs and Benefits*, edited by David P. Farrington, Brandon C. Walsh, and Lawrence Sherman. Boulder: Westview Press.

Thanner, Meridith, and Faye Taxman. 2003. "Responsivity: The Value of Providing Intensive Services to High-Risk Offenders." *Journal of Substance Abuse Treatment* 24: 137–47.

U.S. Census Bureau. 2000. *History of the 1997 Economic Census*. Bulletin no.

POL/00-HEC, July 2000. Available at http://www.census.gov/prod/ec997/pol100-hec.pdf.

Waldfogel, Joel. 1994. "The Effect of Criminal Conviction on Income and the 'Trust Reposed in the Workmen.'" *Journal of Human Resources* 29(1): 62–81.

Weisburd, David, and Faye S. Taxman. 2000. "Developing a Multicenter Randomized Trial in Criminology: The Case Study of HIDTA." *Journal of Quantitative Criminology* 16(3): 315–40.

Western, Bruce. 2002. "The Impact of Incarceration on Wage Mobility and Inequality." *American Sociological Review* 67(4): 526–46.

Western, Bruce, Jeffrey R. Kling, and David F. Weiman. 2001. "The Labor Market Consequences of Incarceration." *Crime and Delinquency* 47(3): 410–27.

= Part III =

From Prison to the Labor Market and Back?

= Chapter 7 =

Status and the Stigma of Incarceration: The Labor-Market Effects of Incarceration, by Race, Class, and Criminal Involvement

BECKY PETTIT AND
CHRISTOPHER J. LYONS

Prison growth over the last quarter of the twentieth century is notable not only for its magnitude but also for the fact that it has disproportionately affected already disadvantaged segments of the population. The prison buildup generates three important observations about inequalities related to incarceration. African Americans are seven times more likely than whites to serve time in prison; educational disproportionality in exposure to the criminal-justice system has increased; and nonviolent offenders represent a growing proportion of prison inmates (Pettit and Western 2004; Mauer 1999).

Criminal offenders and prison inmates face poor labor-market opportunities. Employers express a reluctance to hire ex-inmates (Pager 2003; Holzer 1996), and ex-inmates face earnings penalties of between 10 and 30 percent (Western, Kling, and Weiman 2001). Research that finds persistent incarceration penalties, even when controlling for indicators of productivity and criminal embeddedness, suggests the causal relevance of the stigma of incarceration. Explanations for incarceration effects that emphasize the stigma of contact with the criminal-justice system claim that individuals are typed or labeled as "essentially deviant" by formal agents of the criminal-justice system. Exposure to the criminal-justice system precedes the existence of any secondary or more positive characteristics of an individual, and the general consequence of being labeled essentially deviant means that one is viewed as less trustworthy and rule-abiding (Becker 1963).

Although there is clear evidence of disproportionality in exposure to the criminal-justice system, we know relatively little about how the effects of incarceration vary by race, class, or criminal involvement. The ubiquity of incarceration among low-skilled minority men leads us to reconsider the relevance of social stigma for the economic fortunes of inmates. In an environment of "mass incarceration" (Garland 2001), stigma effects may be less severe, as incarceration may not provide a clear signal of trustworthiness or future productivity to employers. Harry J. Holzer, Steven Raphael, and Michael Stoll (2003) argue that the effects of incarceration may be minimized because employers statistically discriminate against groups with high rates of incarceration (for example, young black low-skilled men). Similarly situated young men already face poor job prospects due to structural divisions within labor markets that relegate low-skilled workers to jobs with low wages and little chance for earnings growth (Bernhardt et al. 2001).

This chapter examines how the effects of incarceration on post-release employment and wages depend on offender characteristics. In order to investigate this question we assembled an administrative data set containing information on individuals who were in a Washington State prison between 1990 and 2000, linked to demographic, education, and earnings records. We use these data to examine post-release employment and wages in jobs covered by unemployment insurance (UI). We investigate how the effects of spending time in prison vary by race, education, and a general measure of criminal severity.

We find that incarceration has mixed effects on post-release employment. Offenders experience temporary gains in UI-covered employment in the first year after release from prison, although the effect declines with time out of prison. Incarceration is consistently associated with declines in post-release wages. Subgroup differences in incarceration effects emphasize the significance of social stigma explanations, particularly for high-status offenders. The negative effects of incarceration on wages are greatest for those who are least likely to spend time in prison and for whom spending time in prison is strongly counternormative. Racial differences in post-release employment and wages highlight race as a "master status" and suggest that incarceration effects must be considered in relation to growing inequality in labor-market outcomes generated by structural divisions in labor markets.

Prison incarceration has become a common occurrence among young low-skilled men in recent cohorts, and the penal system has taken on growing significance in accounts of inequality. Men at high risk of incarceration (for example, low-skilled, black) are not more heavily penalized for spending time in prison than other offenders. However, all ex-inmates experience post-release declines in wages, and declines are enduring for blacks. Further, even small wage penalties, when considered in relation to high rates of incarceration among disadvantaged men, deepen inequality and reinforce the growing cleavage between the economic opportunities of men involved in the criminal-justice system and those outside of it.

The Stigma of Incarceration

Spending time in prison adheres a deviant label to ex-convicts. Labeling theory contends that some labels acquire greater significance than others, and previous research studying incarceration effects indicates that the deviant label associated with spending time in prison trumps other more positive characteristics of individuals when they are being considered for jobs in the paid labor force. According to the theory of social stigma, criminal offenders are unattractive employees because their criminal records signal that they cannot be trusted (Schwartz and Skolnick 1962). The stigma of incarceration takes on legal significance in some jurisdictions where a felony conviction creates legal prohibitions on some categories of employment (Kuzma 1996).

Research on the prevalence of social stigma and the labor market suggests that at least some employers use criminal history records when making hiring decisions. Holzer (1996) reports that between 30 and 40 percent of employers sampled in a survey of five major U.S. cities checked the criminal history records of their most recently hired employee, and about 65 percent of employers stated that they "would not knowingly hire an ex-offender," regardless of the offense, preferring instead to hire other marginalized workers such as welfare recipients over ex-criminals. Experimental studies using criminal and noncriminal job applications also suggest that employers discriminate against individuals with criminal records (Boshier and Johnson 1974; Schwartz and Skolnick 1962; Pager 2003). In addition to the negative association between criminal conviction and employment, support for the social stigma interpretation is provided by studies that show that the effects of conviction on earnings are especially large for those in occupations with high incomes or requiring significant trust (Lott 1990; Waldfogel 1994).

As prison time has become a routine event in the life course of disadvantaged men, it is increasingly important to understand how incarceration affects their employment opportunities and earnings. We might expect incarceration to have little consequence on the later life outcomes of low-skilled minority men because employers discriminate either on the basis of taste or anticipated productivity against men who fit a certain image and are at high risk of spending time in prison (for example, young black low-skilled men). Structural divisions within labor markets may also position men at risk of incarceration in low-wage jobs with flat earnings profiles at the bottom of the wage hierarchy where there is little opportunity for additional wage declines. Finally, men at high risk of incarceration, with multiple prior convictions and deeply embedded in criminal networks, may have few ties to the legitimate labor market and have little economic standing to lose.

Race

Wage convergence between black and white men in the 1960s and 1970s was widely attributed to equal employment opportunity (Burstein 1979; Heckman 1989; Darity and Myers 1998, 44–45). The Civil Rights Act (1964) barred discrimination in employment, and equal employment opportunity and affirmative action measures further reduced black-white earnings inequality through the 1970s (Donohue and Heckman 1991; Chay 1998). However, persistent racial differences in employment and earnings leads some researchers to argue that discrimination has a continuing effect on labor-market inequality (Cancio, Evans, and Maume 1996; Darity and Mason 1998). The implication of continued discrimination in the labor market is that rather than evaluating individual potential of possible future (or current) employees on the basis of anticipated (or observed) productivity and adjusting job and wage offers accordingly, employers make employment decisions on the basis of preferences for, or anticipated productivity of, whole demographic groups. Whether employers have a taste for discrimination and are willing to pay more for certain types of workers or statistically discriminate on the basis of anticipated productivity, continued discrimination means the economic fortunes of individual workers are bound up with those of others with whom they share observable social and demographic characteristics.

Dramatic differences in the risk of incarceration by race may be linked to variation in the effects of incarceration. High rates of incarceration among black men may make it difficult for employers to distinguish black ex-convicts from other blacks and employers may view all black, especially low-skilled, men as potential criminals (for example, Holzer, Raphael, and Stoll 2003). Among whites, in contrast, incarceration is less common and employers may view exposure to the criminal justice system as a clear indicator of untrustworthiness, low productivity, or future criminality. If race serves as a "master status," all blacks will experience lower returns in the labor market than we expect on the basis of their observable human capital, and incarceration will not necessarily have any additional negative effect on employment or wage outcomes. In contrast, white ex-convicts will experience more salient discrimination associated with spending time in prison because employers distinguish white ex-inmates from non-inmates (for example, on the basis of time spent in prison, references from corrections officers, work experience gained in prison) and adjust employment offers and wages accordingly.

Research on racial variation in incarceration effects finds evidence of race differences in the effect of incarceration on employment, but not on wages. Evidence shows that blacks are much less likely to be called for interviews than even white ex-convicts, all else equal. However, the effect of convict status on the likelihood of callbacks is much larger (absolutely) for whites than for blacks (Pager 2003). When examining racial differences in post-prison employment, Samuel L. Myers (1983) finds that blacks are more responsive to post-release work incentives than whites and suggests that employers may find black ex-offenders indistinguishable from black non-offenders. However, research examining post-release wages finds no race differences in the effects of incarceration on post-release wages or wage trajectories (Western 2002).

A priori we expect to find the incarceration penalty to be smaller for blacks than for whites, although we also expect to observe higher levels of unemployment among blacks both before and after incarceration. That is, we expect that after incarceration blacks will have a harder time finding employment than whites (negative black effect), but that the incarceration effect will be smaller for blacks than for whites (positive interaction between black and incarceration). If the same mechanism is at work, the effects of incarceration by race should be the same for wages as for employment.

Class

Growing inequality in earnings through the 1980s and 1990s was coupled with job instability and declines in long-term wage growth among men without college education (Bernhardt et al. 2001). Annette Bernhardt and her colleagues (2001) claim that declines in the manufacturing sector and growth in the service economy explain high turnover and slow wage growth among low-skilled workers. Structural shifts led to changes in the character of jobs available to low-skilled workers as high-paying career jobs in manufacturing were replaced with low-paying service jobs with few returns to seniority.

Increasing stratification in the labor market leads us to expect different incarceration effects for men in jobs with high wages and strong earnings growth and in jobs with low wages and flat earnings profiles. The existence of a criminal record can undermine reputations based on trust and responsibility. These qualities are often highly valued in white-collar jobs and the experience of incarceration can shift ex-inmates from professional jobs with high wages to low-skilled jobs with lower wages. The post-release wages of low-wage men may be protected because they are already at the wage floor, a minimum threshold below which wages in the legitimate labor market will not fall.

Research examining class-based differences in the effects of incarceration finds that men convicted of white-collar offenses are more likely to find employment after incarceration than street-level offenders (Kerley and Copes 2004), but men in high-status jobs experience greater earnings penalties than other offenders (Lott 1990; Waldfogel 1994). These somewhat divergent findings highlight different mechanisms operating for ex-offenders in securing employment and wages. High-status offenders may be able to secure jobs through using their extensive social and human capital, but they experience large wage penalties.

Although we expect men with high levels of education to be more likely to secure jobs after release from prison than less educated men, we expect to find larger declines in wages for men with some college than men with lower levels of education. Men with high levels of education may be displaced from career jobs with high wages, or their human and social capital may depreciate more dramatically as they spend time in prison. Men with less education are concentrated in low-skilled jobs, where there are few rewards associated with seniority, so we expect time out of the labor force will matter less for their post-release wages.

Criminal Involvement

Spending time in prison is no longer reserved for the most incorrigible or heinous offenders, and the prison boom of the late twentieth century disproportionately affected low-skilled men convicted of drug and property crimes. Intensified criminalization of drug use swelled state and federal prison populations by escalating arrest rates, increasing the risk of imprisonment for those who were arrested, and lengthening sentences for drug crimes through the 1980s (Tonry 1995; Mauer 1999). At the end of the 1970s, over 50 percent of all state inmates were spending time in prison for violent offenses. By 2000, the percentage of inmates incarcerated for violent crimes had fallen to 27.4 percent (Bureau of Justice Statistics 2001).

Previous research shows a strong relationship between criminal involvement and its effects on labor-market involvement. Men who are deeply ensconced in criminal networks and have few ties to the legitimate labor market are at high risk of incarceration and reincarceration (Hagan 1993). However, research shows that as men develop attachments to work and family, they are increasingly likely to desist from crime (Sampson and Laub 1990, 1993). The expansion of custodial sentences to nonviolent, property, and drug offenders suggests that the level of criminal involvement of offenders is quite heterogeneous and may be related to post-release employment outcomes. On the one hand, offenders with extensive criminal records and strong ties to the criminal-justice system may experience harsher employment and wage penalties upon release from prison because employers regard them more suspiciously. On the other hand, high-risk offenders may have few ties to the legitimate labor market and may be relegated to the lowest sectors of the economy both before and after incarceration. If the latter is the case, we will find smaller employment and wage penalties among high-risk (repeat) offenders than among low-risk offenders.

Very little research has examined post-release employment and earnings by the extent of previous criminal involvement. A study of British inmates finds that serious (repeat) offenders exhibit the greatest effects of an employment intervention (Soothill, Francis, and Ackerley 1997). Keith Soothill, Brian Francis, and Elizabeth Ackerley (1997) argue that serious offenders were particularly motivated to stay out of future trouble and thus were responsive to programs to help them find employment.

Ex ante, we don't have strong expectations about differences in the effects of incarceration by involvement with the criminal justice system. We might expect that men who are at high risk of (re)incarceration are deeply embedded in criminal networks and have few ties to the legitimate labor market and thus have very poor employment and wage outcomes. However, we might also expect that, given their location in the occupational and stratification hierarchy, we will find relatively small incarceration effects compared with those of lower-risk offenders.

In summary, although a growing body of research indicates that imprisonment has negative consequences on the labor-market experiences of ex-inmates, we know little about how the effects of incarceration are related to demographic characteristics. Both theories of social stigma and structural divisions within labor markets lead us to expect that the consequences of incarceration should differ across demographic groups.

Data and Methodology

To investigate our research questions we assembled an administrative data set containing information on men who were admitted to and released from a Washington State prison between 1990 and 2000, linked to demographic, education, and earnings records. We compile data for over fourteen years, from 1988 through 2001, for 10,477 individuals.[1] Our data collection strategy ensures that we observe individuals for at least two years (eight quarters) before their first complete stay in a Washington State prison in the decade. We also have at least two years of employment and wage data for each individual after his release from prison.

The data are organized into quarterly observations. Each quarterly observation contains information on whether the individual was incarcerated during that quarter, whether he was employed in a UI-covered job, and if he was employed, what his average hourly wage in the quarter was. Observations also include information on race, education, and criminal severity as well as conditions of the most recent incarceration and a host of demographic covariates.

These data are used to estimate the effect of incarceration on employment and hourly wages in jobs covered by unemployment insurance and to examine how incarceration effects vary by subgroup. An individual is coded as being employed if he has positive reported earnings within a quarter. Hourly wages are calculated by dividing quarterly earnings by reported hours. In approximately 4 percent of cases where there are positive quarterly wages, the hours data are either missing or misreported. We find few systematic differences in the misreporting of hours, and for the wage analysis we exclude all cases with zero reported wages. Wage data are in constant dollars, indexed to 1995.

All of the individuals in our sample have completed at least one incarceration in a Washington State prison in the observation period. A person is coded as currently incarcerated if he is in state prison at any time during the quarterly observation. We are primarily interested in the effects of having been incarcerated on employment and wages. Therefore, all quarters after an incarceration indicate the individual had a prior incarceration. We also examine the effects of length of last incarceration (measured in quarters) and the amount of time, in quarters, since the last incarceration.

In addition to the effects of incarceration, time of incapacitation, and time since last incarceration, our examination of the effects of incarceration on post-release employment and wages includes available demographic covariates and information about the conditions of confinement. Our models include information on race, education, and level of service inventory classification, log of age, offense type (violent, drug, property, or other), whether the individual was involved in a work-release program at his last incarceration, age at last admission (measured in five-year intervals), and previous work experience (measured as a percentage of prior quarters employed). Models estimating post-release wages include industry dummies, and all models include year dummies.

Key descriptive statistics for Washington State inmates are shown in table 7.1. Just over 50 percent of inmates are employed in UI-covered jobs for one and two years prior to prison admission, and their average wage is between $7.59 and $7.40 per hour. Sixty-four percent of inmates are employed in the first year following release from prison, but the employment rate of former inmates falls to only 45 percent in the sec-

Table 7.1   Key Descriptive Statistics of Washington State Inmates (N = 10,477 Individuals)

Type of Data Variables	First Year	Second Year
Employment experiences prior to admission		
Employment	50.37%	50.75
Hourly wage	$7.40	$7.59
Total earnings	$8,403.03	$7,876.20
Industry (last job)		
Service	29.06%	
Retail	23.40%	
Agriculture-Mining	6.86%	
Transportation	3.83%	
Wholesale trade	4.31%	
Construction	15.27%	
Financial–public administration	2.84%	
Manufacturing	14.43%	
Employment experiences post-release		
Employment	64.25	45.65
Hourly wage	$10.33	$9.26
Total earnings	$12,984.34	$11,145.63
Industry (first job)		
Service	32.56%	
Retail	23.70%	
Agriculture, mning	3.90%	
Transportation	2.78%	
Wholesale trade	4.57%	
Construction	12.78%	
Financial–public administration	2.03%	
Manufacturing	17.68%	
Key covariates		
Race		
White	59.7%	
Black	27.1%	
Hispanic	8.1%	
Other	5.1%	
Education		
Less than high school	40.2%	
High school diploma or GED	55.1%	
Some college	4.7%	
Criminal history		
Three or more prior arrests	23.1%	
Arrest prior to age sixteen	39.7%	

(Table continues on p. 212)

Table 7.1   *Continued*

Type of Data Variables	First Year	Second Year
Other covariates		
Average age at admission	29.55 years	
Eighteen to twenty	14.04%	
Twenty-one to twenty-five	24.17%	
Twenty-six to thirty	19.80%	
Thirty-one to thirty-five	17.18%	
Thirty-six to forty	12.80%	
Over forty	11.18%	
Characteristics of admission[a]		
Length of spell		6.3 quarters
Violent offense		41.6
Drug offense		29.1
Property offense		26.7
Other offense type		2.5
Program participation in prison		
GED in prison		11.8
Work release		32.1
Recidivism	9.79%	15.96%

Source: Authors' calculations.
[a]Admission data refer to first admission observed between 1990 and 2000.

ond year following release. Wages average $10.33 in the first year after incarceration and drop to $9.26 in the second year after incarceration.

Descriptives for key subgroup covariates are also shown in table 7.1. Whites are the largest racial-ethnic category of our inmate sample (59.7 percent), followed by blacks (27.1 percent), Hispanics (8 percent), and other race or ethnicity (5 percent). Although inmates may acquire additional education while in prison, we treat education as fixed, since we do not have reliable time-varying measures of educational attainment. Over 40 percent of the sample has not completed high school, and less than 5 percent have some college experience. The remaining 55 percent have a high school degree or equivalent. About 40 percent of inmates are classified as high-risk offenders, 35 percent are medium-risk, and 25 percent are low-risk.[2]

Table 7.1 also includes descriptives for other variables included in the model. The average age at admission is twenty-nine, and the modal age of admission is between ages twenty-one and twenty-five. The table also shows that the average length of imprisonment is just over six quarters, two-fifths of inmates served time for violent offenses, 29 percent served time for drug offenses, and 26 percent served time for property crimes. In addition, nearly a third of inmates were released from a work-release program.

Finally, table 7.1 includes a few additional variables not included in our analysis in order to compare our sample with those used in other studies in this volume that also use administrative data. For example, 11.8 percent of inmates earned a GED (general equivalency diploma) in prison, 23 percent of inmates had three or more prior convictions as adults, and two-fifths were arrested before they turned sixteen. We also find that just under 10 percent of inmates were readmitted to state prison within one year and an additional 16 percent were readmitted in the second year after release.

Method

We analyze the effects of incarceration on employment and wages, using pooled cross-sectional time series data. We use a conditional fixed-effects logit model to estimate the effects of incarceration on post-release employment, and a fixed-effects regression to estimate log hourly wages. We first estimate models for all inmates and then estimate models separately by race, education, and criminal severity.

Much of the research on the effects of incarceration on labor-market outcomes is concerned with how selection into prison affects estimates of incarceration effects. We attempt to deal with this concern in two ways. First, we include controls that influence both the likelihood of incarceration and employment outcomes. Second, we estimate models using individual fixed effects to take account of time-invariant observed and unobserved characteristics that vary across individuals.

The fixed-effects models do not estimate coefficients for time-invariant characteristics such as race, education, and LSI categories.[3] Thus, to explore whether the effects of incarceration vary across these groups, we estimate separate fixed-effects models for each race, education, and LSI subgroup. To test the difference between regression coefficients across models we use a Z-test (Paternoster et al. 1998; Clogg, Petkova, and Haritou 1995),

$$Z = (b_1 - b_2) / \sqrt{(SEb_1^2 + SEb_2^2)}$$

where b_1 and b_2 are the betas and SEb_1^2 and SEb_2^2 are the coefficient variances associated with the first and second groups, respectively.

Results

Table 7.2 shows key results from multivariate regression models of quarterly employment. Having been incarcerated is associated with a

Table 7.2   Unstandardized Coefficients from the Regression of Employment on Incarceration

Variables	All (Standard Error)
Prior incarceration	0.5063**
	(0.0179)
Quarters since incarceration	−0.0509**
	(0.0010)
Quarters incarcerated	0.0487**
	(0.0016)
Fixed effects	Yes
N, observations	453,523
N, respondents	9,566

Source: Authors' calculations.
Note: Models include controls for age of admission in five-year intervals, offense type, involvement in work-release program, prior work experience, log age, and year dummies.
**$p < .01$

temporary increase in the probability of employment after release from state prison. Initial increases in employment in the immediate post-release period are followed by steep declines, as indicated by the negative effect of time out of prison. The return to pre-incarceration employment level occurs within ten quarters after release, and then continues to fall below pre-incarceration levels. Temporary increases in employment in the first years following incarceration are somewhat surprising, but have been replicated in other studies that also rely on administrative data (Tyler and Kling, chapter 8, this volume; Sabol, chapter 9, this volume).[4]

The temporary increase in employment after release from prison suggests that the positive post-release employment effect may be related to Washington State's extensive post-release supervision program. Over 70 percent of inmates released in 2002 had mandatory post-prison community supervision for one year. Unfortunately we cannot identify which inmates receive post-release supervision, but we suspect that at least some of the positive post-release employment effect is due to conditions of release, including job placements. Supervisory personnel may engage in positive labeling of ex-convicts, and employers may be encouraged by supervisory personnel to employ recently released inmates. In addition, ex-inmates assigned to community supervision also have access to a network of potential employers and employment contacts through the supervisory program.

Trends in post-release employment are shared by inmates with work experience in the year prior to incarceration and those without prior work experience. We find that 77.6 percent of men employed in the

Table 7.3   Unstandardized Coefficients from the Regression of Log
Hourly Wages on Incarceration

Variables	All (Standard Error)
Prior incarceration	–0.0440**
	(0.0044)
Quarters since incarceration	0.0023**
	(0.0003)
Quarters incarcerated	0.0039**
	(0.0004)
Intercept	–2.6475**
	(.1183)
Fixed effects	Yes
R2	0.1905
N, observations	12,6547
N, respondents	9,532

Source: Authors' calculation.
Note: Models include controls for age of admission in five-year intervals, offense type, involvement in work-release program, prior work experience, log age, industry, and year dummies.
**p < .01

year before incarceration are employed in the year following incarceration and 57.8 percent are employed in the second year after incarceration. Among men not employed in the year prior to incarceration, we find that 50.6 percent are employed at some point in the first year following release and 33.3 percent are employed in the second year after release. Both groups experience relatively steep declines in post-release employment after the first year out of prison. We also find that the length of time incarcerated has positive effects on the probability of employment after release.

Table 7.3 shows clear evidence of a negative effect of prior incarceration on post-release wages. Inmates experience a 4.5 percent wage penalty after release from prison ($\exp^{-0.0440}$). On average, the wage penalty persists for about five years after release (indicated by a positive coefficient on quarters since incarceration). The amount of time spent in prison is positively associated with wages.

In summary, the temporary positive post-release employment effect is puzzling, though it is consistent with results using administrative data in other states (Sabol, chapter 9, this volume; Tyler and Kling, chapter 8, this volume). At least some of the employment gains experienced by ex-inmates in Washington State are likely due to extensive patterns of post-release community supervision in Washington. This conjecture is supported by the observation that the increase in employment declines over time, and within thirty months after release employment falls below pre-incarceration levels.

Wage models indicate a small, though more persistent, wage penalty after incarceration. Inmates earn less, on average, after release from prison than they did before entering prison. This is particularly noteworthy given that we control for human-capital differences, length of stay, and conditions of confinement, including participation in work-release programs. Although the wage effects we find here are smaller than those found in other research, they indicate a direct and negative effect of incarceration on post-release wages and lend support for explanations of incarceration effects that focus on the importance of the stigma of contact with the criminal-justice system. Significant subgroup differences in the effects of prior incarceration on employment and wages, shown in Tables 7.4 to 7.6, further examine the importance of stigma explanations, but also highlight other important processes affecting incarceration effects.[5]

Race

Blacks experience the largest increases in immediate post-release employment, but they also experience the steepest declines over time. The top panel of table 7.4 shows that blacks are significantly more likely to be employed after incarceration, while whites and Hispanics experience significant, though smaller, gains in employment. Tests of significance confirm that black employment gains are significantly larger than those of whites, and both blacks and whites experience larger employment gains after incarceration than Hispanics. However, results also indicate that blacks experience the steepest declines in employment with time out of prison.

Large, significant, racial differences in employment after release from prison suggest that black men may be particularly isolated from jobs in the legitimate labor market prior to incarceration. Spending time in prison links them to a network of employers, possibly through community corrections officers, that affords them employment in UI-covered employment at least for a short while after release from prison. That black men experience steeper declines in employment with time out of prison may reflect that they are strongly motivated to be employed in the legitimate labor market in the short term after release, but cannot maintain employment in this labor market.

The bottom panel of table 7.4 shows that the wage penalty associated with incarceration is half as large for blacks as it is for whites. The incarceration penalty is nearly 5 percent for whites, just over 3 percent for Hispanics, and 1.8 percent for blacks. Formal tests indicate that the difference between whites and blacks in the effect of incarceration is

Table 7.4   Race-Specific Direct Effects of Incarceration on Employment and Wages (Standard Errors in Parentheses)

Employment	Whites	Blacks	Hispanics
Prior incarceration[a,b,c]	0.5095***	0.6528***	0.3000***
	(0.0020)	(0.0359)	(0.0698)
Quarters since incarceration[a,b]	−0.0459***	−0.0661***	−0.0449***
	(0.0013)	(0.0021)	(0.0041)
Quarters incarcerated[a,b,c]	0.0548***	0.0353***	0.0217***
	(0.0020)	(0.0033)	(0.0064)
Fixed effects	Yes	Yes	Yes
N, observations	280,393	116,792	32,999
N, respondents	5,871	2,515	689
Wages	**Whites**	**Blacks**	**Hispanics**
Prior incarceration[a]	−0.0497***	−0.0186*	−0.0318***
	(0.0050)	(0.0088)	(0.0150)
Quarters since incarceration[a,b]	0.0030***	−0.0002	0.0030***
	(0.0005)	(0.0005)	(0.0009)
Quarters incarcerated	0.0040***	0.0040***	0.0070***
	(0.0005)	(0.0009)	(0.0015)
Intercept	−3.496***	−1.9209***	−0.7818***
	(0.1480)	(0.2762)	(0.2950)
Fixed effects	Yes	Yes	Yes
R^2	0.1993	0.2124	0.1722
N, observations	84,191	27,793	8,636
N, respondents	5,856	2,496	687

Source: Authors' calculation.
Note: Employment models include controls for age of admission in five-year intervals, offense type, involvement in work-release program, prior work experience, log age, and year dummies. Wage models include controls included in employment models in addition to industry.
*$p < .10$; ***$p < .01$
[a]Significant difference between whites and blacks
[b]Significant difference between blacks and hispanics
[c]Significant difference between whites and hispanics

statistically significant. Among both whites and Hispanics the effect declines with time out of prison and is indistinguishable from zero within three years. For blacks, however, the effect of incarceration persists. Although they experience a smaller penalty than other groups immediately post-release, there is no evidence that the effect of this penalty for prior incarceration on the wages of black men declines over time.

Significant racial differences in the effect of incarceration on wages suggest that black ex-inmates aren't differentiated from non-inmates to the same extent that white and Hispanic ex-inmates are differentiated from non-inmates. This finding lends suggestive support for arguments

Table 7.5   Education-Specific Direct Effects of Incarceration on Employment and Wages (Standard Errors in Parentheses)

Employment	Less Than High School	High School	Some College
Prior incarceration[b,c]	0.4873**	0.5016**	0.7107**
	(0.0299)	(0.0231)	(0.0868)
Quarters since incarceration[c]	−0.0470**	−0.0520**	−0.0626**
	(0.0017)	(0.0014)	(0.0057)
Quarters incarcerated[b,c]	0.0486**	0.0512**	0.0317**
	(0.0027)	(0.0020)	(0.0070)
Fixed effects	Yes	Yes	Yes
N, observations	172,752	262,684	21,879
N, respondents	3,672	5,583	461

Wages	Less Than High School	High School	Some College
Prior incarceration[b,c]	−0.0430**	−0.0419**	−0.1308**
	(0.0075)	(0.0055)	(0.0224)
Quarters since incarceration[a]	0.0033**	0.0017**	0.0037*
	(0.0004)	(0.0003)	(0.0016)
Quarters incarcerated	0.0039**	0.0040**	0.0059**
	(0.0007)	(0.0005)	(0.0017)
Intercept	−1.7013**	−3.1786**	−4.3260**
	(0.1860)	(0.1571)	(0.7606)
Fixed effects	Yes	Yes	Yes
R^2	0.1996	0.2104	0.1281
N, observations	42,200	78,621	6,888
N, respondents	3658	5579	461

Source: Authors' calculation.
Note: Employment models include controls for age of admission in five-year intervals, offense type, involvement in work-release program, prior work experience, log age, and year dummies. Wage models include controls included in employment models in addition to industry.
*$p < .05$; **$p < .01$
[a]Significant difference between "Less Than High School" and "High School"
[b]Significant difference between "High School" and "Some College"
[c]Significant difference between "Less Than High School" and "Some College"

emphasizing the presence of ongoing discrimination in the labor market. Ex-convict status leads to significant wage penalties for whites, Hispanics, and blacks, but evidence also suggests that race serves as a "master status" among blacks.

Class

Former inmates who have some college education experience the greatest increases in employment post-release. The top panel of table 7.5

Table 7.6   LSI-Specific Direct Effects of Incarceration on Employment and
Wages (Standard Errors in Parentheses)

Employment	LSI Low	LSI Medium	LSI High
Prior incarceration	0.5520**	0.5530**	0.4859**
	(0.0386)	(0.0312)	(0.0293)
Quarters since incarceration[b,c]	−0.0602**	−0.0550**	−0.0445**
	(0.0023)	(0.0019)	(0.0017)
Quarters incarcerated	0.0494**	0.0527**	0.0464**
	(0.0032)	(0.0029)	(0.0028)
Fixed effects	Yes	Yes	Yes
N, observations	109,372	155,169	178,180
N, respondents	2,581	3,813	4,428

Wages	LSI Low	LSI Medium	LSI High
Prior incarceration[c]	−0.0596**	−0.0422**	−0.0322**
	(0.0086)	(0.0074)	(0.0076)
Quarters since incarceration[c]	0.0018**	0.0021**	0.0032**
	(0.0005)	(0.0004)	(0.0004)
Quarters incarcerated[b]	0.0035**	0.0054**	0.0033**
	(0.0007)	(0.0007)	(0.0008)
Intercept	−3.6353**	−2.3165**	−2.3156**
	(0.2261)	(0.1993)	(0.2064)
Fixed effects	Yes	Yes	Yes
R^2	0.1659	0.2633	0.2714
N, observations	37,036	45,526	43,956
N, respondents	2,669	3,977	4,527

Source: Authors' calculations.
Note: Employment models include controls for age of admission in five-year intervals,
offense type, involvement in work-release program, prior work experience, log age, and
year dummies. Wage models include controls included in employment models in addition to industry.
[b]Significant difference between LSI-med and LSI-high
[c]Significant difference between LSI-low and LSI-high
**$p < .01$

shows that men who have dropped out of high school experience an
increase in the probability of being employed in the first quarter after
release from prison. The negative coefficient on quarters since incarceration indicates that the effect declines over time and, on average, employment falls to pre-incarceration levels within ten quarters of release.
The effect is similar among men with a high school diploma or a GED
(general equivalency diploma), but men with some college experience
a much larger initial increase in employment after release from prison.
    Without regard for job quality, men who have some college educa-

tion are better able to capitalize on spending time in prison than their less-educated counterparts. Previous researchers have argued that white-collar offenders are able to rebound after incarceration by capitalizing on their economic resources and social and occupational networks (Kerley and Copes 2004). Well-educated men may also experience spending time in prison more harshly than less-educated men and be highly motivated to get and keep jobs in the legitimate labor market.

Analysis of post-release wages, however, shows that although college-educated men are more likely to find jobs after spending time in prison, they experience significant wage penalties. Men who have gone to college experience a nearly 14 percent decline in hourly wages after release from prison.

This is a striking effect considering the observation that the wage penalty is 4 to 5 percent for school dropouts and high school graduates. We find that the wage penalty persists throughout our observation period for college men. For dropouts, the wage penalty lasts approximately three years, and for high school graduates it lasts approximately six years.

Previous research has suggested that more-educated men should experience greater wage penalties upon release from prison than low-skilled men. Well-educated men may experience large wage declines after spending time in prison because they are more likely to be in jobs that require trust, and contact with the criminal-justice system may undermine relationships based on trust (Lott 1990; Waldfogel 1994). It may also be possible that if incarceration shifts men from career jobs with strong earnings trajectories to low-wage jobs with flat earnings profiles (Nagin and Waldfogel 1998; Western 2002), we should find larger wage declines for men who worked in career jobs prior to incapacitation. Although we don't have specific information on occupation prior to incarceration, it seems reasonable that college-educated men were working in career jobs prior to incarceration.

Criminal Involvement

Using information from the Level of Service Inventory—Revised (LSI-R) as a proxy for criminal involvement, we find no difference by criminal involvement in the probability of securing employment after release, but important differences in wage outcomes. The top panel of table 7.6 shows that all groups of ex-inmates experience sizable, though temporary, increases in post-release employment. There are, however, no statistically significant differences by level of criminal involvement in the effect of incarceration on employment. Employment gains persist the longest for high-risk offenders, and the likelihood of employment recovers to pre-incarceration levels fastest for low- and medium-risk offenders.

The bottom panel of table 7.6 shows that low-risk offenders experience the largest negative effect of incarceration on post-release wages. Wages among low-LSI offenders eventually recover to pre-incarceration levels, but they recover relatively slowly. The wage penalty for spending time in prison is significantly smaller for high-risk offenders, and high-risk offenders experience the quickest return to pre-incarceration wages.

We also examined employment and wage outcomes using three or more prior incarcerations as a proxy for criminal involvement. If we limit our analysis only to those who have one or two priors, we find the effect on employment of having spent time in prison is smaller than for the full sample. The effect of incarceration on wages, however, is slightly larger for the first-time sample than for the full sample. It appears that men with fewer previous contacts with the criminal-justice system do relatively poorly upon re-entry.

Previous research has argued that serious (that is, repeat) offenders are most responsive to post-release employment opportunities (Soothill et al. 1997). Although it may be the case that high-risk offenders are highly motivated to get and keep jobs in order to stay out of prison, that doesn't explain why the wages of high-risk offenders fall less, and recover more quickly, than the wages of low-risk offenders. We suspect instead that high-risk offenders are already involved in segments of the labor market with high turnover and slow, or no, wage growth. As a consequence, we should find little effect of incarceration on their wages after release from prison because they are already at or near the wage floor. Low-risk offenders are less likely to have prior offenses and have fewer concomitant predictors of risk, and they are also more likely to come from career jobs where they are at risk of more sizable and enduring wage penalties.

Discussion and Conclusion

Using a unique data set with a rich array of covariate information, we find spending time in prison leads to significant, though temporary, gains in post-release employment and significant and more enduring losses in post-release wages. Although post-release employment increases have not been found using self-report data, other research using administrative data has also found temporary increases in employment in UI-covered jobs after release from prison (Tyler and Kling, chapter 8, this volume; Sabol, chapter 9, this volume). We speculate that post-release employment gains are at least partly driven by community supervision, and observed declines in employment with time out of prison are consistent with this conjecture. The existence of a sizable wage penalty, even when controlling for prior work experience, conditions of confinement, and individual fixed effects, implies that the experience of incarceration has direct effects on men's wages. Incarceration could adversely affect employers' assessment of potential productivity, or shift men from career jobs with the potential for earnings growth into temporary or low-skilled jobs with low wages and few returns to seniority.

Significant subgroup differences in the effects of incarceration lend support to arguments that emphasize the stigma of criminal-justice contact and highlight structural divisions in labor-market opportunities. Stigma arguments lead us to expect that high-status offenders experience the largest penalties following incarceration. This is indeed what we find. Highly educated and low-risk offenders experience the largest wage declines after incarceration. For these men, incarceration is strongly counternormative and carries with it an enduring stigma. Although incarceration has little impact on the employment of highly educated and low-risk offenders, it has detrimental effects on wages and may prohibit them from employment in industries (and jobs) with greater job security and strong earnings growth. Smaller, though still significant, wage penalties among black and low-skilled men provide suggestive evidence of race as a "master status," and are consistent with the idea that there is little room in low-wage segments of the economy for additional wage penalties. The finding that blacks suffer a smaller wage penalty does not mean that ex-offender status isn't important for the economic fortunes of black men. On the contrary, it may mean that employers use race as a proxy for criminal involvement, view all blacks as potential criminals, and statistically discriminate on the basis of race.

Participation in the legitimate labor market is a crucial part of the reintegration of ex-inmates into mainstream society. Previous research has found that ex-inmates who become employed are less likely to re-offend than similar inmates who cannot find jobs (Uggen 2000). An examination of the relationship between post-release employment and recidivism using data on inmates in Washington State provides additional evidence that being employed after release is strongly and negatively related to reincarceration at any point in the post-release observation period. The effects of first-year employment are quite dramatic, but employment in the second year after release is even more strongly (negatively) predictive of recidivism.

However, our research indicates that many inmates' connections to the legitimate labor market are tenuous before spending time in prison, and even more so afterward. Prior to incarceration, criminal offenders are infrequently employed in jobs covered by unemployment insurance, and their wages are relatively low. Although employment rates rebound immediately after incarceration, the jobs ex-inmates get offer low wages and may discourage continuous employment.

Consistent with the demographics of state inmates nationwide, Washington State inmates are disproportionately minority and low-skilled, and less than half are serving time for violent offenses. As the prison population escalated through the last quarter of the twentieth century, the economic prospects of young low-skilled men declined and the penal system has taken on growing significance in explanations of recent trends in inequality. Criminal offenders represent an extremely disadvantaged segment of the labor market and our research suggests that spending time in prison only disadvantages them further. However, subgroup differences in the effects of incarceration on employment outcomes reveal that the consequences of incarceration must be considered in relation to persistent racial discrimination and structural changes in the economy that have already diminished the economic opportunities of low-skilled men.

We thank Elizabeth Drake, Carmen Grose, Jeff Jacksich, Michael Scroggins, and Peggy Smith for assistance with data acquisition, and Patty Glynn for help with the data analysis. This research was supported by a grant from the Russell Sage Foundation.

Notes

1. Corrections and demographic data come from the Washington State Department of Corrections; employment and earnings data come from the Washington State Employment Securities Department; and education data, including GED (general equivalency diploma) receipt come from the State Board of Community and Technical Colleges.
2. Criminal history information is derived from an inventory used to assess the risk of recidivism. In the mid-1990s Washington initiated the use of a risk-needs assessment tool called the Level of Service Inventory—Revised (LSI-R). Widely used in corrections in Canada, the LSI-R is emblematic of a risk-needs instrument that assesses dynamic measures of criminogenic needs (for example, feelings of hostility and anger, substance abuse) (Andrews and Bonta 1995; Bonta and Cormier 1999). The LSI-R has strong predictive validity for adult male recidivism (Gendreau, Little, and Goggin 1996) and recidivism among women and minority populations (Bonta 1989; Coulson et al. 1996). We use this inventory to gauge the importance of previously unmeasured factors that may jointly influence one's propensity for criminal activity and for specific labor-market outcomes. The fifty-four-item LSI-R inventory includes information on criminal history, education and employment, finances, family and marriage, living arrangements, leisure, companions, alcohol and drugs, emotional and personal problems, and attitudes toward crime. We focus on nine LSI items that measure capacity for self-control, previous criminal activity, and involvement with delinquent peers. These items specifically include information on prior incarcerations as an adult

(three or more), arrest prior to age sixteen, the presence of some criminal friends, the absence of pro-social acquaintances, self-reported drug problems, active psychosis, clinically diagnosed mental illness, attitudes supportive of crime, and negative attitudes toward convention. We sum these dichotomous items to create a total risk score ranging from 0 to 9 and then divide the sample into high-, medium-, and low-risk offenders. Offenders are classified as high risk if they have four to nine of the indicated risk factors, medium risk if they have three or risk factors, and low risk if they have two or fewer risk factors. Although individuals may have completed the LSI more than once in our observation period, we classify individuals as high-, medium-, and low-risk offenders on the basis of their first recorded LSI.

3. For information on LSI, see previous note.

4. We tested several alternative nonlinear specifications on time out of prison on employment models. We find clear evidence of nonlinearities in the time since incarceration on employment. There is a strong positive effect of incarceration on post-release employment in the first year and modest positive effects by the second year out of prison. The effect is dramatically negative for three or more years out. We find similar effects if we model time out of prison by including both a linear and quadratic term.

5. We also estimate the effect of incarceration on wages for men with observed wages in the year prior to admission, which is a proxy for stable employment. For this subsample we find a marginally smaller effect of incarceration on wages than for the whole sample. This combination of results, though not definitive, suggests there is negative selection into employment after incarceration; marginal workers get employed in the short-term after incarceration, which leads to deflated wages and an overestimate of the incarceration effect. It is remarkable, however, that even focusing on those previously employed, we find a large and significant wage penalty associated with incarceration.

References

Andrews, Donald A., and James Bonta. 1995. *LSI-R: The Level of Service Inventory, Revised*. Toronto: Multi-Health Systems, Inc.

Becker, Howard S. 1963. *Outsiders: Studies in the Sociology of Deviance*. New York: Free Press.

Bernhardt, Annette, Martina Morris, Mark Handcock, and Marc Scott. 2001. *Divergent Paths: Economic Mobility in the New American Labor Market*. New York: Russell Sage Foundation.

Bonta, James. 1989. "Native inmates: Institutional Response, Risk, and Needs." *Canadian Journal of Criminology* 31(1):49–62.

Bonta, James, and Robert B. Cormier. 1999. "Corrections Research in Canada: Impressive Progress and Promising Prospects." *Canadian Journal of Criminology* 41(2):235–47.

Boshier, Roger, and Derek Johnson. 1974. "Does Conviction Affect Employment Opportunities?" *British Journal of Criminology* 14(3): 264–68.

Bureau of Justice Statistics. 2001. "Prison and Jail Inmates at Mid-Year 2000."

Report, no. NCJ 185989. Washington: U.S. Department of Justice, Bureau of Justice Statistics.

Burstein, Paul. 1979. "Equal Employment Opportunity Legislation and the Income of Women and Non-whites." *American Sociological Review* 44(3): 367–91.

Cancio, A. Silvia, T. David Evans, and David J. Maume. 1996. "Reconsidering the Declining Significance of Race: Racial Differences in Early Career Wages." *American Sociological Review* 61(4): 541–56.

Chay, Kenneth Y. 1998. "The Impact of Federal Civil Rights Policy on Black Economic Progress: Evidence from the Equal Employment Opportunity Act of 1972." *Industrial and Labor Relations Review* 51(4): 608–32.

Clogg, Clifford, Eva Petkova, and Adamantios Haritou. 1995. "Statistical Methods for Comparing Regression Coefficients Between Models." *American Journal of Sociology* 100(5): 1261–93.

Coulson, Grant, Giorgio Ilacqua, Verna Nutbrown, Diana Giulekas, and Francis Cudjoe. 1996. "Predictive Utility of the LIS for Incarcerated Female Offenders." *Criminal Justice and Behavior* 23(3): 427–39.

Darity, William A., and Patrick L. Mason. 1998. "Evidence on Discrimination in Employment: Codes of Color, Codes of Gender." *Journal of Economic Perspectives* 12(2): 63–90.

Darity, William A., and Samuel L. Myers. 1998. *Persistent Disparity: Race and Economic Inequality in the United States Since 1945*. Northampton, Mass.: Elgar.

Donohue, John J., and James Heckman. 1991. "Continuous Versus Episodic Change: The Impact of Civil Rights Policy on the Economic Status of Blacks." *Journal of Economic Literature* 29(4): 1603–43.

Garland, David. 2001. *Culture of Control: Crime and Social Order in Contemporary Society*. Chicago: University of Chicago Press.

Gendreau, Paul, Tracy Little, and Claire Goggin. 1996. "A Meta-Analysis of the Predictors of Adult Offender Recidivism: What Works?" *Criminology* 34(4): 575–607.

Hagan, John. 1993. "The Social Embeddedness of Crime and Unemployment." *Criminology* 31(4): 465–91.

Heckman, James. 1989. "The Impact of Government on the Economic Status of African Americans." In *The Question of Discrimination*, edited by Steven Shulman, William Darity, and Robert Higgs. Middletown, Conn.: Wesleyan University Press.

Holzer, Harry. 1996. *What Employers Want: Job Prospects for Less-Educated Workers*. New York: Russell Sage Foundation.

Holzer, Harry, Steven Raphael, and Michael Stoll. 2003. "Employment Barriers Facing Ex-Offenders." Paper prepared for Reentry Roundtable on "The Employment Dimensions of Prisoner Reentry: Understanding the Nexus Between Prisoner Reentry and Work." New York University (May 19–20).

Kerley, Kent, and Heith Copes. 2004. "The Effects of Criminal Justice Contact on Employment Stability for White-Collar and Street-Level Offenders." *International Journal of Offender Therapy and Comparative Criminology* 48(1): 65–84.

Kuzma, Susan. 1996. *Civil Disabilities of Convicted Felons: A State-by-State Survey*. Washington: U.S. Department of Justice, Office of the Pardon Attorney.

Lott, John R. 1990. "The Effect of Conviction on the Legitimate Income of Criminals." *Economics Letters* 34(4): 381–85.

Mauer, Marc. 1999. *Race to Incarcerate*. New York: New Press.

Myers, Samuel L. 1983. "Racial Differences in Postprison Employment." *Social Science Quarterly* 64(3): 655–69.

Nagin, Daniel, and Joel Waldfogel. 1998. "The Effect of Conviction on Income Through the Life Cycle." *International Review of Law and Economics* 18(1): 25–40.

Pager, Devah. 2003. "The Mark of a Criminal Record." *American Journal of Sociology* 108(5): 937–75.

Paternoster, Raymond, Robert Brame, Paul Mazerolle, and Alex Piquero. 1998. "Using the Correct Statistical Test for the Equality of Regression Coefficients." *Criminology* 36(4): 859–66.

Pettit, Becky, and Bruce Western. 2004. "Mass Imprisonment and the Life Course: Race and Class Inequality in U.S. Incarceration." *American Sociological Review* 69(2): 151–69.

Sampson, Robert J., and John H. Laub. 1990. "Crime and Deviance over the Life Course: The Salience of Adult Social Bonds." *American Sociological Review* 55(5): 609–27.

———. 1993. *Crime in the Making: Pathways and Turning Points Through Life.* Cambridge, Mass.: Harvard University Press.

Schwartz, Richard D., and Jerome H. Skolnick. 1962. "Two Studies of Legal Stigma." *Social Problems* 10(2): 133–42.

Soothill, Keith, Brian Francis, and Elizabeth Ackerley. 1997. "The Value of Finding Employment for White-Collar Ex-Offenders." *British Journal of Criminology* 37(4):582–92.

Tonry, Michael H. 1995. *Malign Neglect: Race, Crime, and Punishment in America.* New York: Oxford University Press.

Uggen, Christopher. 2000. "Work as a Turning Point in the Life Course of Criminals: A Duration Model of Age, Employment and Recidivism." *American Sociological Review* 65(4): 529–46.

Waldfogel, Joel. 1994. "The Effect of Criminal Conviction on Income and the Trust 'Reposed in the Workmen.'" *Journal of Human Resources* 29(1): 62–81.

Western, Bruce. 2002. "The Impact of Incarceration on Wage Mobility and Inequality." *American Sociological Review* 67(4):526–46.

Western, Bruce, Jeffrey R. Kling, and David F. Weiman. 2001. "The Labor Market Consequences of Incarceration." *Crime and Delinquency* 47(3): 410–27.

= Chapter 8 =

Prison-Based Education and Reentry into the Mainstream Labor Market

John H. Tyler and Jeffrey R. Kling

A troubling fact associated with the historically high incarceration rates of the last twenty years is that they have had a disproportionate effect on disadvantaged and minority men, individuals who have traditionally maintained marginal positions in the mainstream labor market. An important question, therefore, concerns the extent to which education and training programs generally available in correctional facilities help criminal offenders successfully reintegrate into the mainstream labor market. One of the most ubiquitous education opportunities available to inmates who lack a high school diploma is the ability to study for and obtain a general educational development (GED) credential.[1]

Prior research on the effects of "prison GEDs" on post-release outcomes is relatively limited in spite of the fact that the 2000 Census of State and Federal Correctional Facilities (Bureau of Justice Statistics 2003) showed that 83 percent of the state correctional facilities in the United States offered "secondary education programs," of which the primary type are GED preparation programs. Furthermore, virtually all of the previous research has examined the relationship between obtaining a GED and the probability of recidivating but have given little attention to whether or not prison GEDs are related to post-release labor-market outcomes. The widespread availability of the GED credentialing program for incarcerated individuals raises the question of whether there are, in fact, any post-release economic benefits associated with participation in a prison-based GED program.[2]

Past research on prison-based education programs has been plagued by the fierce selection issues that determine who participates in these programs and data that have been largely unsuited to addressing these issues. Furthermore, prior work in this area has considered only a single counterfactual: What is the impact of participating in prison-based education as compared to not participating? We advance the line of inquiry in two ways. First, we are able to utilize a much richer and more appropriate data set than has previously been available for examining the impact of prison-based education programs. Second, we examine prison-based GED programs relative to two separate and policy-relevant counterfactuals.

The first research question we examine is the post-release economic value to inmates of having a prison-based GED program. The research here compares the outcomes of inmates who obtained a prison-based GED to those of dropout offenders who did not participate in any prison-related GED education. This exercise deals with the question of what we would expect if there were no prison-based secondary education program. On this question we find that nonwhite offenders who obtained a "prison GED" had earnings gains of about 15 percent in the first two years post-release over observationally similar nonwhite offenders who did not participate in GED-related education programs while in prison. We find no post-release benefits for white offenders, and we also find that any earnings gains for nonwhite offenders dissipate after two years.

Our second research question is whether or not there is any value in obtaining a "prison GED" relative to participating in prison-based GED education, but leaving prison without the credential. This parameter approximates the post-release signaling value of the GED in the labor market. We find, at most, only weak evidence of a signaling effect of the GED credential and only for non-white offenders.

To conduct this research, we worked with the Department of Corrections in Florida to create a unique administrative data set containing information on individuals who were in a Florida state prison at any time between 1994 and 1999, linked to demographics, education program participation, and earnings records. Our earnings measures are based on working in the mainstream economy (specifically, jobs covered by unemployment insurance, the earnings from which are commonly referred to as UI earnings). We do not attempt to study total income, but rather focus on the more proximate objective of most public policy directed toward former inmates—legitimate taxpaying employment—for which we can construct a panel of data for individuals for years both before and after prison spells. Using these data we estimate separate models for white and nonwhite offenders because we believe there are important differences in the background characteristics of these groups that could affect their post-release labor-market potential.[3]

We have no clear exogenous source of variation in GED status in our sample, and as a result we suggest caution in attaching a strictly causal explanation to our findings. Although we control for all time-invariant heterogeneity, it could be the case that unmeasured, time-varying differences between offenders who do and do not obtain a prison-based GED lend an unknown bias to our results. For example, if offenders for whom the prison experience is a positive, life-altering transformation also tend to obtain a GED, our findings overestimate the causal impact of a GED on post-release earnings. If, on the other hand, inmates who become more criminally socialized while in prison tend to enroll in GED programs to curry favor with prison officials, our findings would underestimate the causal impact of prison GEDs. Nevertheless, we believe that our estimates give the best look to date at the effectiveness of this major prison-based education program. Furthermore, since we show that our preferred estimates are substantially smaller than estimates mirroring prior research, we believe it likely that earlier work in this area has overestimated the benefits of prison-based education programs.

The next section of this chapter describes our conceptual framework. In later sections we discuss our data, present our analytical methods, present descriptive statistics, and report regression results.

Conceptual Framework

There are at least two mechanisms through which the GED could increase wages or employment for incarcerated individuals.[4] First, to the extent that individuals have to study and learn new skills to pass the GED exams, they may increase their human capital, which in turn may lead to increased wages (Becker 1993). This may be an especially important avenue for incarcerated GED candidates, since their pre-GED skill levels are likely lower than those of dropouts outside, in the "free world." Second, the GED may serve as a "labor-market signal," allowing employers to identify individuals, within the pool of dropout job applicants, whom they suspect of having productive attributes such as higher cognitive skills or motivation levels (Spence 1973).[5]

A key issue in studying the effect of the GED on labor-market outcomes is the omitted-variable problem: individuals who obtain GEDs in prison may have attributes that would have led to superior labor-market outcomes than non-GED holders even if they did not have a GED. For example, a GED may simply be a proxy for intelligence or motivation, which would have led to greater employment and earnings anyway, with no causal role for the GED itself.

Attention to omitted variables in studying the effects of correctional education on subsequent outcomes has been limited. A 1999 survey of the literature by David B. Wilson et al. (1999) cited eight studies that included an evaluation of the relationship between the GED or the GED plus some additional Adult Basic Education classes and the likelihood of returning to prison—the principal outcome in nearly all studies of the impacts of correctional education. Five of the eight studies found that offenders who obtained a GED were less likely to recidivate than those who did not. However, the authors of the research review point out that "all of these studies had weak research methodologies, simply comparing either participants with nonparticipants or program non-completers, with little to no control or adjustment for selection bias" (Wilson et al. 1999, 14). A review that directly discussed the models used to study the impact of correctional education programs on outcomes states, "The control variables were generally restricted to gender, race, and age [and only one study] controlled for important sources of selection bias between participants and nonparticipants, such as prior criminal history, in the analysis of recidivism" (Wilson, Gallagher, and MacKenzie 2000, 355).

We are aware of only one study that focused specifically on the linkage between prison-based education programs and labor market outcomes. The work of Stephen Steurer, Linda Smith, and Alice Tracy (2001) found higher subsequent earnings among education program participants.[6] Unfortunately, this study does not separate participation in GED preparation programs from participation in other prison-based education programs such as Adult Basic Education and English as a Second Language classes, so it is not clear what we learn from it about the GED.

Wilson et al. (2000) point to several potential selection mechanisms that could lend an upward bias to the estimated impact of correctional education programs on post-release outcomes. Selection mechanisms in the prison setting could work through both individual choices and administrative procedures, since enrollment in correctional education programs is predicated on variables such as good behavior and time to release. Fixed characteristics of the individual such as self-control or motivation that might affect post-release outcomes could also affect placement in a GED program through both self- and administrative selection processes. More transitory characteristics such as motivation toward positive life changes and attitudes toward society and work could have similar effects.[7]

Certain unobserved fixed and transient factors could lead to underestimates of the causal impact of GED program participation. For example, in interviews of offenders just prior to release Steurer, Smith, and Tracy (2001) found that prison-education program participants had lower levels of motivation in regard to several labor-market activities, including the "motivation to get a job, a better job, or higher pay" or the "motivation to improve job performance" than did program non-participants. At the same time, offenders in that study who participated in prison-based education programs indicated a higher motivation to both "look good to prison or parole officials to get out" and to "get a better situation in prison" than did offenders who did not participate in education programs while in prison.[8] Thus, in their study participation in education programming seemed to be driven more by a desire to impress prison and parole officials and improve one's situation in prison than by a desire to impact one's post-release labor-market outcomes.

One consistent lesson from the prior research on prison-based education programs is that the positive effects found in the literature are perhaps compromised by research designs that fail to account, even in the most rudimentary ways, for unobserved heterogeneity between program participants and nonparticipants. We attempt to address these shortcomings both through our use of rich data and through fixed-effects estimation that has not been previously employed.

Data

To determine whether ex-convicts who acquire a GED while in prison fare better in the mainstream labor market than former offenders who do not possess the credential, we use a unique data set constructed for this project by the Florida Department of Corrections, the Florida Department of Law Enforcement, and the Florida Education and Training Placement Information Program. About 10,000 of the approximately 144,000 dropouts who entered a Florida prison at some time between 1992 and 2000 obtained a GED while they were incarcerated.[9] The master data set from Florida contains basic demographic, criminal justice, and test-score information, along with the quarterly earnings for males who were incarcerated in Florida state prisons at any time between 1994 and 2000. Quarterly earnings for the sample come from the Florida Unemployment Insurance (UI) system and cover the third quarter of 1993 through the first quarter of 2002. All earnings are deflated to 2002 constant dollars using the CPI-U deflator.

We include in our analysis individuals who had a new commitment to a Florida prison after October 1994 and who had expected release dates that allowed for at least twelve quarters of post-release data.[10] The master data set from which we formed our analytic sample contained information on 24,764 males who fit this criterion. Among these individuals were 2,957 offenders who obtained a GED while incarcerated in a Florida prison at some time between October 1994 and March 1999. We were able to use data on 1,967 GED holders who had valid Social Security numbers (discussed in a later section) and were not missing values on key variables used in the analysis. We also analyzed 10,989 offenders who both lacked a high school diploma when they entered prison and did not obtain a GED while incarcerated and whose calendar quarters of entry into prison and forecasted release quarter from prison were the same as that of at least one GED holder.

Using information on all movements of individuals in the Florida Department of Corrections system we are able to construct distinct prison spells for each individual based on the date of incarceration for a new commitment and the date of prison release.[11] In analyzing the impact of the GED on the post-release outcomes of offenders, we defined as the "target spell" the prison spell in which the GED holder obtained his credential. The years and quarters in which all observed target spells began formed the basis for searching the database for uncredentialed dropouts who entered prison at approximately the same times.[12]

We will employ two different comparison groups in order to answer our two different research questions. The first group is composed of offenders who entered prison without a high school diploma and who either attempted but failed the GED exams or who took GED preparation classes but never attempted the GED exams. For convenience we will call this group the GED "attempters," even though a substantial portion of this group only attempted GED course work and never attempted the GED exams. Comparisons between GED passers and the dropout "attempters" approximate the signaling value of the GED on post-release earnings. We note that to the extent that the GED passers acquire more prison-related human capital than the attempters, contrasts between these groups will, of course, overstate the signaling value of the GED.

A second comparison group is composed of offenders who entered prison without a high school diploma and who were never enrolled in any GED preparation courses. These are the GED program nonparticipants. A third potential comparison group we could use is offenders who entered prison with a high school diploma. All preliminary investigations of the data indicate that GED holders (and all other dropout offenders) had consistently worse outcomes than did regular high school graduates, both before prison entry and upon release from prison. This matches what Stephen V. Cameron and James J. Heckman (1993) and others have found for "free world" GEDs when compared to regular high school graduates. As a result we focus in this paper on comparisons between offenders who obtain a GED while in prison and the two comparison groups of dropout offenders who do not obtain a GED while incarcerated.

Social Security numbers were used to link the Florida Department of Corrections data to the UI earnings data. All Social Security numbers in our data were verified by programmers at the federal Social Security

Administration based on standard verification algorithms used by the Employment Verification Service, which matched Department of Corrections data on the digits of the Social Security number, date of birth, sex, and name to Social Security Administration records, with some tolerance for clerical error. As might be expected in data on criminal offenders, about 19 percent of the sample lacks a valid Social Security number. Individuals with invalid Social Security numbers are more likely to be nonwhite, non-Florida residents, and unemployed at the time of arrest. Slightly over 20 percent of the potential non-attempting dropouts have invalid Social Security numbers, while only 15 to 16 percent of the other three groups (GED passers, GED attempters, and high school graduates) have invalid Social Security numbers.

Analytical Methods

Our analyses will primarily be concerned with measuring post-release quarterly earnings as measured by unemployment insurance (UI) wage records and post-release employment as inferred by non-zero UI quarterly earnings. Since UI earnings are recorded quarterly, we account for time in calendar quarters. Previous research has analyzed outcomes using time since actual release from prison as the post-release time metric. However, our regression models are specified in terms of covariates and constructs of time that are known at the time the prison spell begins. Because of the ability of prisoners to affect their release date through "good behavior" and program participation, actual release date is endogenous, and not predetermined. We deal with this issue by measuring release time relative to the forecasted release date, rather than time relative to when the offender was actually released. Although this issue is important in principle, we find in practice that obtaining a GED has little association with the deviation of actual release date from forecasted release date, and consequently the use of forecasted versus actual release dates has little impact on our results.[13]

We use three definitions of time in our analysis. Time in quarters relative to the start of an individual's target incarceration spell is indexed by "s" and we refer to it as "s-time." Thus, $s = -1$ refers to the calendar quarter before the entry of an individual to his target spell in prison. Time relative to the forecasted release date of an offender based upon sentencing information in our data is indexed by "r" and we refer to it as "r-time." For example, $r = 1$ refers to the calendar quarter after the forecasted release date of an offender from prison. We designate the quarter of actual release by "t" and refer to the release time as "t-time." Some of our regression analyses pool data from s-time and r-time, such as the four quarters before incarceration and the four quarters after forecasted release. We use these two concepts of time because we believe it is more meaningful for analysis of pre-prison outcomes to pool results around the beginning of incarceration and for analysis of post-prison outcomes to pool results around the time of forecasted release date, rather than to have a single anchor point in time.[14]

Our empirical analyses focus on post-release labor-market outcomes. We will compare the post-release outcomes of offenders who obtain a GED while in prison to the post-release outcomes of the two dropout comparison groups. Although we have no clear source of exogenous variation in GED status in these data, we do have a substantially richer set of available covariates to bring to the analysis than to previous studies, and the longitudinal UI earnings data allow us to fit models that control for individual, time-invariant fixed effects. We use the following definitions of variables:

Y_{it} = quarterly UI earnings for individual i in time (year and quarter) t.[15]

GED_i = a (0,1) indicator for whether individual i obtained a GED while incarcerated.

AGE = a set of two variables containing age and age squared when Y is measured.

YRQTR = a set of dummies for the year and quarter in which Y is measured.

X_i = a set of covariates that includes the following

- EDUC (a set of indicators for years of completed schooling)
- Predicted sentence length
- Marital status and number of dependents upon prison spell entry
- Years in Florida prior to prison spell
- Whether or not a Florida resident at prison entry
- State or region of birth
- Whether or not employed prior to arrest and conviction
- Industry and occupation of employment prior to arrest and conviction
- Whether or not an English speaker
- Whether or not a confirmed U.S. citizen or alien
- Cumulative years in prison prior to the target spell
- Number of disciplinary reports ever accumulated in prison prior to the target spell
- Type of offense for target spell in prison
- A measure of cognitive skills at the beginning of the target spell[16]

A regression model for the simplest model of mean differences between GED and non-GED holders is given in equation 8.1.

$$Y_{it} = \beta_1 + GED_{it}\delta_1 + \varepsilon_{1it},\tag{8.1}$$

To match the typical model found in the literature on prison-based interventions the first regression adjusted estimating equation we employ is

$$Y_{it} = \beta_{20} + GED_{it}\delta_2 + AGE_{it}\beta_{21} + YRQTR_{it}\beta_{22} + EDUC_i\beta_{23} + \varepsilon_{2it},\tag{8.2}$$

where i indexes person. We fit equation 8.2 on a stacked four quarters of r-time earnings data: $r = 1$ through $r = 4$ in one instance, $r = 5$ through $r = 8$ next, and then $r = 9$ through $r = 12$. This allows us to estimate δ_2 for the first, second, and third year after the forecasted release date. Using ordinary least squares (OLS), we fit equation 8.2 separately for the two different comparison groups. We also fit separate models for white offenders and nonwhite offenders. Estimates of δ_2 provide estimates of the average difference in quarterly earnings between GED holders and uncredentialed dropouts in the first, second, and third years, respectively, after prison release, depending on what r-times are used.

In a third model we include the other control variables described previously, bringing to bear considerably more information than has heretofore been used in studying prison-based education programs. Equation 8.3 illustrates the additional variables,

$$Y_{it} = \beta_{30} + GED_{it}\delta_3 + AGE_{it}\beta_{31} + YRQTR_{it}\beta_{32} + X_i\beta_{33} + \varepsilon_{3it},\tag{8.3}$$

where X contains the variables discussed previously.

Equation 8.3 offers substantial advantages over prior research on prison education programs, utilizing as it does the rich set of control variables available in our Florida data. We can, however, use the longitudinal nature of the UI earnings data to push the analysis a step further by estimating the fixed-effects model of equation 8.4:

$$Y_{it} = AFT_{it}\beta_{40} + GED_{it}\delta_4 + AGE_{it}\beta_{41} + YRQTR_{it}\beta_{42} + AFT_{it} * X_i\beta_{43} + \alpha_i + \varepsilon_{4it},\tag{8.4}$$

Equation 8.4 is fit using pre–prison spell earnings or employment data from quarters $s = -4$ through $s = -1$ stacked with post-release earnings: $r = 1$ through $r = 4$ in one instance, $r = 5$ through $r = 8$ in a second estimation, and $r = 9$ through $r = 12$ in a third estimation. A time-invariant, fixed effect for each individual is captured in α_i. In this setting the variable AFT equals 0 in the s-time quarters and one in the r-time quarters, and it captures the main effect of being in the labor market in post-release period relative to the period before prison entry. The interaction of AFT and X essentially allows main effects of X in the regression for changes in the outcome within individuals over time.[17] GED in equation 8.4 equals 0 for everyone in s-time, switching to 1 in r-time for those who obtained a prison-GED. In computing standard errors in all three models, we account for dependence of the errors within persons, across time.

We also considered using a regression discontinuity design to study the impact of a prison-GED, since a sharp cutoff on GED test scores determines who does or does not obtain a GED. Our discussions with Florida Department of Corrections officials who administer the GED program suggest, however, that such a design could yield upwardly biased estimates of the impact of the GED. Inmates in Florida are widely discouraged from taking the GED exams until there is a very good chance, as indicated by scores on GED practice exams, that they will achieve a passing score. Given this severe screening of who takes the GED exams in Florida's prisons, we believe that the 5 percent who do take the exams without passing are not comparable to those above the passing threshold, even after controlling for the linear component of the GED test score.[18]

Descriptive Statistics

Table 8.1 compares basic descriptive statistics across GED holders and the two comparison groups in the earnings-employment sample. GED holders are substantially more likely to be white than are the two uncredentialed dropout groups. About 60 percent of the GED holders are white, compared to roughly 45 percent in the two uncredentialed dropout groups. Mean years of completed schooling at prison entry are very similar across the groups, but GED passers and attempters tend to be younger than the program nonparticipants, who received no GED-related education while in prison.

In terms of criminal-justice–related factors, offenders who obtain a GED during the prison spell under study appear to be substantially more likely to have had a previous stay in prison than the uncredentialed dropouts (about 24 percent, compared to 14 and 18 percent for the latter groups).[19] However, some portion of this difference is partly an artifact of the way we selected the two dropout comparison groups. Since for these individuals we used their first spell that matched a spell where there was also one GED holder, we do not include future spells they may have had in calculating this percentage. Offenders who obtained a GED while in prison had slightly more disciplinary reports on their records (9.7) than did dropouts with some prison-based GED education (5.6) and dropouts with no prison-based GED education (5.9). GED holders are more likely than the uncredentialed dropout groups to be in prison this spell for a property offense and less likely to be in prison for a drug-related offense.

Interestingly, GED attempters have higher rates of participation in prison work-release programs (24 percent) than either GED holders (20 percent) or dropouts (16 percent). Also, a higher percentage of GED attempters spent some time in prison GED preparation programs (93 percent) than did offenders who took and passed the GED exams (68 percent). Meanwhile, offenders who obtained a GED while in prison participated in vocational training programs at higher rates than the two comparison groups. All groups had roughly similar participation rates in academic courses and work in prison industries.

In order to make comparisons of our Florida-based sample to offenders to another state studied in this volume, we have also examined some key differences in the inmate populations of Florida and Washington State.[20] Although the age at admission is similar in both groups, offenders in Florida are much more likely to be African American (46 percent in Florida and 27 percent in Washington) and much less likely to be white (46 percent versus 56 percent). Offenders in our Florida-based sample served, on average, about a year less than did offenders in Washington State, and they were less likely to be in prison for a drug offense and more likely to be in prison for a property offense. Also, offenders in Florida participated in work-release programs half as much as offenders in Washington (16 percent versus 32 percent).

The most striking differences between the two samples are in labor-market outcomes. The mean annual earnings of inmates in our Florida sample in the year immediately preceding the studied prison spell were half the earnings of those in Washington ($2,240 versus $4,230). A large portion of this difference is explained by the lower pre-prison employment in the Florida sample (32 percent) than in the Washington-based sample (50 percent). The first-year post-release differences are as disparate. Mean earnings in the first year after release from prison were $4,000 in the Florida sample and $8,342 in the Washington sample, and employment differences were 40 percent and 64 percent, respectively. Some of the post-release differences can be explained by higher recidivism rates observed in the Florida sample. In the first year after release 16 percent of the offenders in Florida had been convicted of a crime resulting in a return to prison or probation, whereas the recidivism rate in Washington in the first year is only 10 percent. Recidivism rates in the second year in Florida and Washington were 26 and 16 percent, respectively.

The most obvious explanation for the observed differences in labor-market outcomes is the different racial compositions of the two samples. The extent to which racial differences in the two samples can fully

Table 8.1 Descriptive Statistics of Offenders Without High School Diplomas (Sample Standard Deviations in Parentheses)

	Dropouts Who Leave Prison with a GED	Uncredentialed GED "Attempters"	Uncredentialed Dropout Offenders with No GED-Related Education	Total Sample: All Offenders Without High School Diplomas
N	1,967	1,400	9,589	12,956
Percentage white	60	47	45	47
Percentage black	32	45	46	44
Percentage Hispanic	7	7	8	8
Percentage other race	0.3	0.5	0.3	0.3
Mean years of education	9.7	9.5	9.5	9.5
	(1.3)	(1.3)	(1.4)	(1.4)
Mean age at admission	25.6	25.0	29.4	28.3
	(8.0)	(7.5)	(9.2)	(8.8)
Percentage age eighteen to twenty at admission	28	31	15	19
Percentage age twenty-one to twenty-five at admission	28	31	24	25
Percentage age twenty-six to thirty at admission	15	12	18	17
Percentage age thirty-one to thirty-five at admission	11	10	16	15
Percentage age thirty-six to forty at admission	7	6	13	11
Percentage age over forty at admission	6	5	12	10
Percentage with prior incarceration spell	24	13	18	18
Percentage with prior disciplinary report	10	6	6	7

Percentage with violent-crime offense this spell	39	39	36	37
Percentage with property-crime offense this spell	41	37	36	37
Percentage with drug-crime offense this spell	16	21	24	22
Percentage with other crime offense this spell	4	4	4	4
Percentage participating in work-release program	20	24	14	16
Mean days in work release for participants	171	172	165	166
	(103)	(98)	(98)	(98)
Percentage with hours in GED classes this spell	68	93	0	20
Percentage with hours in vocational training this spell	28	19	10	14
Percentage with hours in academic classes this spell[a]	28	27	29	29
Percentage with hours working in prison industry this spell	3	2	3	3
Mean sentence length in months this spell	19.9	17.7	14.4	15.6
	(10.5)	(9.6)	(9.0)	(9.3)
Percentage who recidivate within one year	17	16	16	16
Percentage who recidivate within two years	26	27	25	25
Percentage who recidivate within three years	33	36	32	33
Percentage employed one year before prison entry	32	32	31	31
Percentage employed one year after release	44	41	37	38
Quarterly wage one year before prison entry	$560	$526	$577	$569
	($1,364)	($1,336)	($1,401)	($1,388)
Quarterly wage one year after release	$1,200	$1,132	$982	$1,031
	($2,108)	($2,827)	($2,092)	($2,175)

Source: Authors' calculations.
[a] Represents non-GED-related academic course work.

explain the differences—especially post-release differences in out-comes—is worthy of further study.

Returning to table 8.1, there are essentially no differences in earnings or employment prior to entry into this prison spell in terms of variables related to the dependent variables that will be used in the analyses. In the post-release period, GED holders have a higher probability of being employed than do members of the dropout group who received no GED-related education while in prison (44 percent versus 37 percent), and they have higher mean quarterly earnings one year after release ($1,200 versus $982). Meanwhile, the GED attempters' post-release em-ployment and earnings figures lie between those of the GED holders and the no-education group of dropouts.

Though the differences are small, comparisons across groups in the last rows of table 8.1 are consistent with a hypothesis that obtaining a GED is effective in improving the post-release outcomes of offenders. The fact that there are observable differences between offenders who obtain a GED while in prison and those who do not leads one to cau-tion against making too much of the raw earnings and employment differences. In some instances GED holders have average characteristics that would be an advantage in the labor market. In particularly, they are more likely to be white. Criminal-justice outcomes, however, look less favorable for offenders who obtain a GED. They were more likely to have had a prior stay in prison and that stay was longer; they tended to have more disciplinary reports on their record; and they are more likely to have committed property crimes.[21] The empirical analyses that follow attempt to account for these and other potential differences between dropout offenders who do and do not obtain a GED while in prison.

Figures 8.1, 8.2, and 8.3 display mean quarterly earnings around the time of release based on t-time (figure 8.1), r-time (figure 8.2), and s-time (figure 8.3). In these figures we include offenders who entered prison with a regular high school diploma to illustrate the fact that these offenders have substantially different outcomes than do dropout offenders with or without a prison-based GED. In figures 8.1 and 8.2 the zero quarter represents the release-date quarter. In figure 8.1 this represents the quarter in which individuals were actually released from prison, and in figure 8.2 this represents the forecasted release-date quarter. The patterns in these two graphs are roughly similar.

Figures 8.1 and 8.2 indicate that even during quarters when most individuals are in prison (t-time and r-time just before zero), there are non-zero quarterly earnings. Non-zero earnings during prison result primarily from employment emanating from prison work-release cen-ters. For example, about 17 percent of the offenders in our data were in work-release centers at $r = -1$, working an average of sixty-seven days during that quarter.

Figure 8.1   **Raw Earnings Around the Actual Prison Release Quarter, by Education**

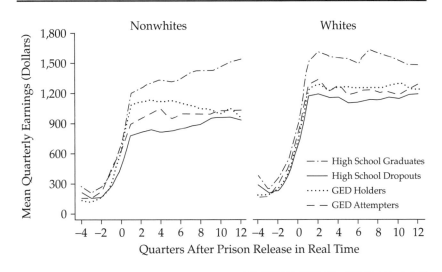

Source: Authors' calculations.

Figure 8.2   **Raw Earnings Around the Forecasted Prison Release Quarter, by Education**

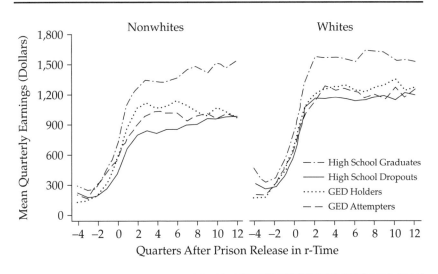

Source: Authors' calculations.

Figure 8.3   **Raw Earnings Profiles Around the Prison Entry Quarter, by Education**

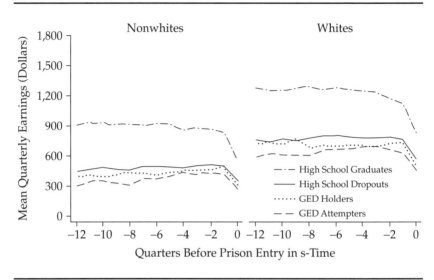

Source: Authors' calculations.

Figure 8.3 shows that the earnings of all dropout groups are substantially lower than the pre-target-spell earnings of high school graduates. Also in figure 8.3, the pre-target-spell earnings of all dropout groups are similar, offering some evidence that there are no substantial "pretreatment" differences between those who will and will not obtain a prison GED. An implication of this fact is that accounting for earnings prior to prison (as in our fixed-effects model in equation 8.4) will have little impact on GED coefficients. Our hypothesis that GED program participants would have higher earnings prior to participation than other dropouts was not confirmed, suggesting that the selection process of GED participation was not simply one in which those with better labor-market prospects were also those who participated.

Figures 8.1 and 8.2 offer, at best, weak evidence that dropouts who earned a GED while in prison have post-prison-spell earnings that are different from dropouts who do not leave prison with a GED. Figures 8.1 and 8.2 do not, however, account for the role played by observable factors that may affect earnings and the other outcomes of interest.

Results

We first discuss results from a model that most closely resembles models used in prior research on the effectiveness of prison-based education programs, and we examine what happens to these estimates across specifications with increasing controls for observable factors. Simple estimates of the "effects" of prison-based education programs in the literature simply compare program participants and nonparticipants. In this spirit, our simplest estimates compare all offenders who leave prison with a GED to those who do not, pooling all uncredentialed dropouts together, both the GED attempters in our data and those who did not participate in some GED-related education while in prison. Estimates from this rudimentary specification, our equation 8.1, are in the first column of panel A in table 8.2, and they indicate that in the first year GED holders have mean quarterly earnings $181 higher than those of uncredentialed dropout offenders. The GED advantage is $180 in the second year, and $109 in the third year; all three estimates are statistically significant.[22] These mean earnings estimates are similar to the estimates for participation in prison education programs by Steurer, Smith, and Tracy (2001) discussed earlier, including the pattern of decreasing differences in the third year.

The first innovations we bring to the topic are to allow differential GED effects for whites and nonwhites. The second and third columns of panel A suggest that estimated mean differences based on a pooled sample, as in the first column, mask differential GED effects by race and ethnicity. Only the first-year estimates in panel A are statistically different for white and nonwhite dropouts. The point estimate for nonwhites in the second year is, however, twice as large as the estimate for whites, and so we will continue to explore differences by race and ethnicity in the analyses that follow. Another reason for displaying results by race and ethnicity is an exploration of the declining GED "effects" in the third year for nonwhites seen in panel A.

Panel B of table 8.2 presents results from equation 8.2. The results here indicate that the simplest estimates of panel A are little changed by adding controls for basic characteristics such as age and education level. We continue to find the only statistically significant results for nonwhite offenders in the results on stratified samples in columns 2 and 3, and it is only the first-year estimates of the GED earnings advantage that are statistically different by race.[23]

The second innovation we bring to this line of research is our ability to include a much richer set of covariates than has heretofore been employed in research on prison-based education programs. OLS estimates from equation 8.3 are shown in panel C of table 8.2. The personal characteristics—including marital status, alien status, and state of residence and employment characteristics at the time of arrest—and prior criminal-justice history that are controlled for in equation 8.3 substantially reduce the estimated GED earnings advantage between panels B and C. Reductions in the GED earnings premium occur for both white and

Table 8.2   Comparison of Quarterly Earnings of GED Holders and Uncredentialed Dropouts

Years after Release	All (1)	Whites (2)	Nonwhites (3)
Panel A: Controlling for nothing			
First year	181**	55	243**
	(41)	(55)	(63)
Second year	180**	95	208**
	(48)	(65)	(72)
Third year	109**	101	39
	(51)	(71)	(72)
Panel B: Controlling for age, year and quarter, education			
First year	161**	9	214**
	(40)	(54)	(63)
Second year	183**	72	203**
	(49)	(66)	(73)
Third year	125	67	65
	(52)	(73)	(75)
Panel C: Controlling for age, year and quarter, x			
First year	13	−87	121**
	(45)	(58)	(71)
Second year	70	−16	180*
	(55)	(74)	(82)
Third year	22	−9	26
	(58)	(80)	(85)
Panel D: Controlling for age, year and quarter, x, α_i			
First year	57	−27	164**
	(50)	(68)	(77)
Second year	114*	45	224*
	(60)	(82)	(88)
Third year	69	58	72
	(63)	(87)	(90)
N	12,956	6,138	6,818

Source: Authors' calculations.
Note: Panels A, B, C, and D contain GED coefficient estimates δ_1, δ_2, δ_3, *and* δ_4, from equations 8.1, 8.2, 8.3, and 8.4, respectively. All entries in column 1 are from models that also control for race/ethnicity. The dependent variable is quarterly earnings in 2002 dollars, including zeros. Standard errors are in parentheses, adjusted for clustering within individuals over time.
*p < 0.05; **p < 0.10

nonwhite offenders, except for the nonwhites' estimate in the second year after release, where there is only a 10 percent reduction in the estimate from panel B to panel C ($203 to $180).

The third innovation we bring to this line of research is an ability to estimate models that control for individual fixed effects, as in equation 8.4. The estimates in panel D of table 8.2 indicate that once we control for the variables in the X vector in equation 8.3, there is little to be gained from fixed-effects estimation. The estimates in panels C and D are similar across groups and years.[24]

A first lesson from these estimates is that any credible research on the effects of prison-based programs has to be able to control for more factors than has been the norm in this line of research. The inclusion of the additional covariates in the X vector of equation 8.3 drives the simplest estimates in column 1 to close to zero. Nevertheless, even with the richer control variable set, we continue to estimate differences between GED holders and all uncredentialed dropouts among nonwhite offenders. Thus, a second lesson is that research on prison-based programs should pay attention to the possibility that estimated program effects may be different for white and nonwhite offenders. Remarkably, within the nonwhites there is little difference between the results that control for nothing in panel A and the results that control for a rich set of covariates and fixed effects in panel D.

Results in table 8.2 allow for an examination of estimates of correctional education programs compared to what one would estimate allowing for differential effects by race and ethnicity and controlling for important observable differences between treatment-group and comparison-group individuals. These results allow one to judge the results from typical prison education research relative to what one would find when sets of desirable control variables are included. Our primary interest, however, lies in answering our two research questions. First, what is the impact on subsequent earnings of obtaining a GED relative to not having a GED program in prison at all? And second, is there value in actually obtaining the GED credential while in prison beyond effects of preparing for the exam itself? The estimates in table 8.3 bring information to bear on these questions.

The entries in the first two columns of table 8.3 contrast the post-release quarterly earnings of offenders who obtained a GED to those of dropout offenders who did not participate in any GED preparation classes. In the ideal, the comparison group here estimate the counterfactual of what would have been the earnings of GED holders if there had been no prison GED program.

Estimates in column 1 of panel A show no measurable differences between the unadjusted earnings of white GED holders and white dropouts with no prison-based secondary education. Meanwhile, the

Table 8.3   Quarterly Earnings of GED Holders, GED-Program Nonparticipants, and GED "Attempters," by Race-Ethnicity

Years After Release	Comparison to Dropouts with No GED-Related Education		Comparison to GED "Attempters"	
	Whites (1)	Nonwhites (2)	Whites (3)	Nonwhites (4)
Panel A: Controlling for nothing				
First year	58	259***	34	122
	(56)	(63)	(84)	(85)
Second year	103	221***	42	116
	(66)	(72)	(99)	(93)
Third year	105	39	79	36
	(72)	(73)	(106)	(98)
Panel B: Controlling for age, year and quarter, education				
First year	11	237***	−37	16
	(56)	(64)	(82)	(84)
Second year	77	216***	18	56
	(68)	(75)	(99)	(93)
Third year	56	68	71	20
	(75)	(77)	(105)	(99)
Panel C: Controlling for age, year and quarter, x				
First year	−100	141*	−19	28
	(61)	(77)	(87)	(84)
Second year	−5	190*	33	125
	(74)	(91)	(109)	(96)
Third year	−28	−8	99	89
	(83)	(95)	(112)	(103)
Panel D: Controlling for age, year and quarter, x, α_i				
First year	−26	176**	−28	98
	(71)	(84)	(96)	(96)
Second year	71	228**	19	190*
	(84)	(97)	(116)	(109)
Third year	57	34	83	156
	(91)	(100)	(120)	(116)
N	5,475	6,081	1,849	1,518

Source: Authors' calculations.

Note: Panels A, B, C, and D contain GED coefficient estimates δ_1, δ_2, δ_3, *and* δ_4, from equations 8.1, 8.2, 8.3, and 8.4, respectively. The dependent variable is quarterly earnings in 2002 dollars, including zeros. Standard errors are in parentheses, adjusted for clustering within individuals over time.

*p < 0.10; **p < 0.05; ***p < .01

simple contrasts among nonwhites (column 2) show that GED holders earn about $220 to $260 more per quarter in the first two years after release, but that this earnings advantage falls off sharply and approaches zero in the third post-release year. These same basic observations hold as we move down columns 1 and 2 through the different specifications. In particular, even the fixed-effects estimates in panel D are relatively similar to the unadjusted estimates of panel A, showing no GED benefits for whites, and a GED earnings advantage of around $200 for nonwhites in the first two post-release years, falling to almost statistical insignificance in the third post-release year. Thus, the estimates for the nonwhites are not diminished very much, even after controlling for a rich set of covariates and for fixed effects.

The overarching story of the first two columns is that determining the value of a prison GED program depends highly on the group used to evaluate that question. It appears that white offenders have little to gain from a prison-based GED program; there are no statistically significant earnings differences by GED status and all of the point estimates are relatively small in magnitude. Meanwhile, nonwhites who obtain a GED show consistently higher post-release earnings than non-white dropout offenders with no prison-based GED-related education in the first two post-release years, an earnings advantage that consistently falls to near zero after the second year.[25]

We note that other work on the returns to a free-world GED has found that all of the impact is at the bottom end of the skill distribution: the GED seems to have large earnings effects for the least skilled dropouts and none for high skilled dropouts (Tyler 2003). Using TABE test scores and TABE test versions to construct several different definitions of "low skilled" and "high skilled" dropouts, we do not find a similar pattern of differential GED effects by skill level for prison GEDs.

Entries in columns 3 and 4 of Table 8.3 bear on the question of the additional value of obtaining a prison-based GED once you have participated in secondary education programs in prison. These estimates compare the post-release quarterly earnings of the same GED holders used in columns 1 and 2 to those of dropout offenders who participated in correctional GED programs but who left prison without the credential. Fourteen percent of the comparison group attempted, but failed, the GED exams, while the other 86 percent never attempted the exams during their time in prison. A common reason for having GED course hours but no record of attempting the GED exams is that these inmates have not achieved literacy and numeracy levels that would give a reasonable expectation of passing the GED exams at the time of their release from prison. To the extent that the GED coefficient in this analysis is positive, it will in principle contain both the signaling value of the GED and the additional human capital that GED holders garner relative to offenders who study for but do not obtain a GED while in prison. Results not shown in the table indicate that there is little relationship between GED test score and subsequent earnings among GED holders, however, so we infer that the GED coefficients in columns 3 and 4 primarily represent a signaling effect.

Even though we expected lower average skills in the comparison group than among GED holders, the estimates in columns 3 and 4 of table 8.3 provide no consistent evidence of post-release earnings differences between the two groups. In particular, the set of estimates for white offenders indicate no substantive or statistically significant GED earnings advantage. The fixed-effects estimates for nonwhite offenders yield the only evidence that GED holders fare better than offenders who obtain some prison-based education but no GED credential. The second-year estimate for nonwhite offenders is about as large as the second-year estimate for nonwhite offenders in column 2, and it is marginally statistically significant.

In interpreting these results, note that our data contain no clear source of exogenous variation in GED status. This is particularly problematic in a prison setting, where there are fierce selection issues at both the administrative and the individual level. We try to address heterogeneity issues as best we can by using both an unusually rich data set on criminal justice offenders and by fitting fixed-effects models that control for time-invariant heterogeneity. Nevertheless, since we have no transparent manner of controlling for potential time-varying heterogeneity, caution should be exercised in attaching causal inferences to our estimates. We do think that the fixed-effects estimates in this paper represent the most vigorous attempt to date to obtain good estimates of the impact of obtaining a GED while in prison on later outcomes.

We note that participation in prison-based GED programs may generate not only better earnings but also noneconomic benefits that we have not examined.[26] Also, it could be that obtaining a GED confers post-release benefits that are not directly connected to the labor market such as the ability to be a better parent or more effectively to engage in the civic life of the free world. Were this systematically the case, however, one would expect GED holders to recidivate at lower rates, something we did not find. In short, there may be advantages to corrections-based GED programs not examined in this paper.

Conclusion

The convergence of two trends has made an understanding of the effects of prison-based interventions such as the GED increasingly important. At the same time that low-skilled individuals are facing increasingly dim economic prospects, there has been a dramatic increase in the U.S. prison population, driven primarily by the incarceration of low-skilled males. The result is a historically large proportion of inmates who, upon release, will face steep obstacles as they try to reintegrate into the mainstream labor market. A primary vehicle used to help prepare offenders for reentry into society and the mainstream labor market has been the corrections-based GED program. In spite of the widespread use of this program, however, there has been scant research on how effective it actually is in meeting the desired goals. Past research showing positive benefits of corrections-based education programs has been less than convincing, often because it has been based on inappropriate data. We utilize a unique and particularly rich data set on individuals who were in Florida prisons during the 1990s to produce the following main findings on one of the most important prison education programs, the GED:

1. There is virtually no evidence that the earnings of white GED holders are higher than the post-release earnings of white dropout offenders without a GED. This is true when comparisons are made against dropouts who have and have not had any prison-based secondary education.

2. There is some evidence that having a GED program benefits nonwhite offenders. When compared to nonwhite offenders who never participated in GED-related education, nonwhite offenders with a GED had quarterly earnings that were approximately $200 higher in the first two years after release from prison. This represents about a 20 percent increase in earnings.

3. There is very little evidence that, conditional on participating in GED-related education, there is extra benefit to actually acquiring the credential.

4. Any benefits that accrue to nonwhite offenders from obtaining a GED appear to fade substantially after the second year.

The two most robust findings are the racial and ethnic differences in any returns to a prison GED and the fall off in any GED benefits for nonwhite offenders after the second year. Both results show up in the point estimates of virtually all models and regardless of the samples used in the estimation. Participation in education programming may be driven more by a desire to impress prison and parole officials and improve one's situation in prison than by a desire to improve one's post-release labor-market outcomes.[27] To the extent that this is the case in our Florida data, and to the extent that this rationale for participation in prison-based education programming is more prevalent among white offenders, this could help explain the differential results we see by race and ethnicity. It is also plausible that the negative effects of criminal conviction on hiring, which Devah Pager (chapter 5, this volume) finds to be much stronger for blacks than for whites, are partially offset by the GED educational credential. Unfortunately there is no information in our data that would allow us to explore these possibilities.

The virtual disappearance of any GED effect between the second and third years after release for nonwhite offenders is also puzzling. In analysis not shown here but available from the authors, we use a smaller sample of offenders for whom we have sixteen full quarters of post-release earnings data. The downward trend of the estimated GED effect on the earnings of nonwhite offenders also appears in year 3 in these data and continues to diminish in year 4 after release. In trying to understand this puzzling trend we can rule out differential recidivism rates and post-release community supervision rates as possible explanations, since separate analyses not shown in this paper show no effects of a prison GED on either recidivism or post-release community supervision.[28] We can also rule out as an explanation a simple mechanical relationship between recidivism and the diminished GED effect over time that we find. Since everyone who returns to prison has approximately the same (zero) earnings regardless of GED status, as more and more certified and non-GED-certified offenders recidivate, the average estimated GED effect on earnings incorporates more zero earnings for both GED and non-GED offenders and thus is diminished over time. We find that this mechanical relationship can explain very little of the downward trend in the GED effect we estimate, since refitting the models represented in table 8.2 using only individuals who have not returned to prison generates results that are similar to the full-sample estimates we present in the table. Regarding the downward trend in the GED earnings effect, we note that the same downward trend, after initial positive effects, was found by Steurer, Smith, and Tracy (2001), and is a result worthy of further study.

The authors wish to thank William Bales, John L. Lewis, Brian Hays, and Stephanie Bontrager of the Florida Department of Corrections and Duane Whitfield of the Florida Education and Training Placement Information Program for providing the data; and Aaron Sparrow and Thu Vu for invaluable research assistance. We also thank seminar participants at the University of Michigan, the University of Illinois, Massachusetts Institute of Technology, University of California, Los Angeles, the RAND Institute, the University of Maryland, Case Western Reserve University, and the University of California, Berkeley and Davis, for helpful comments. This research was partially supported with grants from the Russell Sage Foundation. Additional support was provided by the National Science Foundation (grant number SBE-9876337), the Princeton Office of Population Research (grant number NICHD 5P30-HD32030), the National Center for the Study of Adult Learning and Literacy, and the Princeton Industrial Relations Section.

Notes

1. To obtain a GED, individuals have to pass exams that cover math, science, social studies, reading, and writing. All of the test items are multiple choice except for a section in the writing exam that requires GED candidates to write an essay. The total test time if all tests are taken at the same time is about seven and three-quarters hours.

2. Although there has been little research examining the potential effects of passing the exams and obtaining a GED in prison or jail, there has been substantial work in the past ten years on the general labor-market effects of obtaining a GED. Stephen V. Cameron and James J. Heckman (1993) showed that GED holders were not the labor-market equivalents of regular high school graduates. Recent work has tended to indicate that dropouts who leave school with very low skills benefit from obtaining a GED, but that there are no payoffs to the credential for dropouts who leave school with higher skills (Murnane, Willett, and Boudett 1999; Murnane, Willett, and Tyler 2000; Tyler, Murnane, and Willett 2000). Estimates from these studies generally show that after about five years, the earnings of low-skilled dropouts who obtain a GED are 15 to 20 percent higher than those of low-skilled uncredentialed dropouts. Heckman, Jingjing Hsse, and Yona Rubinstein (2000) do not find the same pattern as the aforementioned studies. An important difference in the two sets of findings is that the latter findings do not allow time for the effects of the GED to accrue, a result that the other authors found to be important.

3. In particular, nonwhite offenders tend to be younger and are more likely to be in prison for a drug-related offense than the white offenders in our data. The median age of nonwhite offenders upon prison entry is twenty-four, while the white offenders in our data are twenty-eight when we observe them entering the prison spell of interest. In terms of offense type, 13 percent of the minority offenders in our data are in prison on a drug-related charge, while only 5 percent of the white offenders are in prison for crimes related to drug use or distribution. Meanwhile, 19 percent of the white offenders are in prison for crimes related to property theft or burglary, whereas only 10 percent of the minority offenders are incarcerated for property-related crimes. Overall, the distribution of minority offenders in Florida's prisons in the middle to late 1990s is different from that for white offenders in ways that may be related to labor-market potential, to the prison GED experience, or to both. For our purposes, "nonwhites" refers to everyone who is not coded as "white, non-Hispanic" in the data.

4. In principle, the GED could positively impact labor-market outcomes if inmates use their GED to obtain post-incarceration higher education or training, but this is not likely to be an important mechanism since the data indicate

that GED holders obtain very little post–secondary education or company-provided training (Boudett 2000; Murnane, Willett, and Tyler 2001).

5. The negative signal of criminal conviction may be more salient than a positive signal about education. See Harry Holzer, Steven Raphael, and Michael Stoll (chapter 4, this volume) for a discussion of the use of criminal history background checks.

6. This study uses prison records linked to UI earnings, as we do. Relative to offenders with no participation in prison-based education programs, unconditional estimates indicated that the "treatment" group of offenders who received some prison-based educational services had lower estimated recidivism rates three years after release, though the differences were not statistically significant. The treatment group also had higher annual earnings in the first, second, and third years after release. Only the first-year earnings differences were statistically significant ($7,775 versus $5,980), and the estimated differences declined over time. There were no discernible differences in employment rates between those who did and did not receive education programming while in prison.

7. Robert J. Sampson and John H. Laub (1993) and T. P. Thornberry and R. L. Christenson (1984) suggest that program participants may have a higher level of social bond to conventional, noncriminal society than do program nonparticipants. These authors posit that program participants may be more likely to be married, to have children with whom they are in contact, to have had a job before incarceration, and so on. Assuming such factors lead to more positive post-release outcomes, failure to control for such attributes will lead to overestimates of the effect of education program participation on outcomes. E. Zamble and F. J. Porporino (1988) offer a conjecture that a sentence to prison may act as a critical life event for some offenders, resulting in a change in motivation to both participate in correctional programs and conduct one's life in a more positive manner post-release. In this model, any estimated program effects could simply be measures of the commitment of program participants to a life away from crime rather than of effects of the program itself on outcomes.

8. Neither of these differences between the treatment and comparison group was statistically significant at the .01 level, but the mean differences on the five-point Likert scale variables were nontrivial. On the question "motivation to look good to prison or parole officials to get out," the mean for education program participants was 2.77 and that for the comparison group was 2.65. On the question "motivation to get a better situation in prison," the respective results were 2.55 and 2.45 (Steurer, Smith, and Tracy 2001). The only question in the "motivation survey" of Stephen Steurer, Linda Smith, and Alice Tracy (2001) that showed a statistically significant response at the .01 level was a question about the "motivation to feel better about self" where the comparison group scored .11 mean points higher, suggesting that the responses cited above were likely close to statistical significance, something that cannot be determined from the reported results in the paper.

9. In Florida, offenders housed in virtually all state prisons have the opportunity to test for the GED, provided they follow certain guidelines. We note

that the count of 144,000 dropouts includes individuals for whom information on education level is missing. When the statistics are limited to individuals for whom education level is known, there are about 108,000 dropouts who entered Florida prisons between 1992 and 2000.

10. As a result of the twelve-quarter criterion, no one in our analytic data set entered prison after March 1999. Individuals admitted to a Florida prison prior to December 1994 were eligible for "control release." Control release is an administrative function that was used to manage the state prison population within lawful capacity. In the era of control release many inmates were not in prison long enough to participate in academic programs, and those who were likely differed in important ways from prisoners who were being granted control release. As a result, we have limited our analysis to individuals who were admitted to Florida prisons after control release was terminated. We actually use people who were admitted on or after October 1, 1994, because in our data no offenders admitted during October and November of 1994 were given a control release.

11. Our spells begin upon entry to jail for an eventual prison spell. Specifically, we impute a spell beginning date using prison entry date minus jail credit days. In our definition, a spell must last more than one day and it is assumed to continue until a permanent release that lasts for more than one day is observed. If there is a subsequent entry into prison for that individual, a second spell begins and ends according to the same guidelines.

12. We analyze one spell per individual, selecting the earliest one (if any) where there was at least one GED holder who entered prison in the same calendar quarter and had the same prison sentence length (rounded to half years).

13. Offenders who leave prison with a GED and those who never take any GED courses spend on average about a month and a half longer in prison than their forecasted release date would predict, while offenders who take GED courses but do not obtain the credential spend about two months longer than their predicted sentence.

14. As a concrete example, consider individuals X and Y who entered prison at the same time and who have forecasted sentence lengths of eight quarters and sixteen quarters, respectively. Analysis in s-time is most useful for pre-prison outcomes. At $s = -2$, both offenders have not yet begun their incarceration spell, so we can meaningfully compare their pre-prison outcomes. Pooling results on post-spell outcomes at time $s = 10$ is not very meaningful because Y will likely still be in prison. Analysis in r-time is most useful for post-prison outcomes. At $r = 2$, it is likely that both offenders will have recently reentered mainstream society, so we use r-time for post-spell analyses pooling individuals in r-time. At $r = -10$, X is not in prison, but Y is in prison, so the pre-prison outcome is not observed.

15. UI earnings are not available for out-of-state earnings or for jobs that are not usually covered by the UI system, such as self-employment, work that may be "off the books" such as domestic service or informal child care, or for employers who do not report earnings. Thus, UI earnings may understate "true" earnings. A comparison of data from UI earnings and more complete data from the Social Security Administration (SSA) found that average earnings from SSA data were about 25 percent higher. Self-

reported earnings for adult men were 30 percent higher than UI reports, with the additional difference apparently due mainly to uncovered jobs rather than out-of-state jobs; in an evaluation of JTPA training, the differences between the treatment and control groups were similar for survey and UI employment rates, suggesting that between-group differences may remain quite informative, even when levels differ (Kornfeld and Bloom 1999).

16. The measure of cognitive skills that we employ is the Test of Adult Basic Education (TABE). The first stop for offenders entering the Florida prison system is the "reception center" where they are processed. While at the reception center, all offenders are administered the survey test battery of the TABE. The data resulting from this test are particularly appropriate for our use because it is administered before any prison interventions. Since different versions of the TABE tests were administered during the period we cover, and since TABE scores are not necessarily equitable across versions, we created a vector of 58 TABE score by version indicators. We control for TABE scores with this vector of indicators.

17. For example, if there were one observation of the outcome before prison and one after, an interaction of *AFT* and *X* in a fixed-effects model would control for changes in the outcome related to time-invariant characteristics like type of conviction offense. Time-varying coefficients for time-invariant characteristics has also been used by Louis S. Jacobson, Robert J. Lalonde, and Daniel G. Sullivan (1993) in the context of evaluating the effect of job loss on later earnings and by Orley Ashenfelter and Dean Hyslop (2001) in measuring the effects of arbitration on wages.

18. This policy is reflected in the fact that of all the individuals in our data with a record of ever taking the GED exams while in prison, only 5 percent never achieved a passing score. This compares with about a 25 percent non-pass rate among free-world GED candidates in Florida over the same period, based on our calculations using free-world GED data from Florida. In regression discontinuity estimates we do find that offenders who score just above the passing threshold, and obtain a GED, have quarterly earnings by the second year that are a statistically significant $400 greater than those who score just below the threshold. However, we do not believe the conditions hold to interpret this as the causal impact of the GED.

19. GED holders who had prior prison experience spent longer amounts of time in prison prior to this spell than the other groups—about 450 days for eventual GED holders compared to about 380 days for the other dropout groups (these results not shown here).

20. We make the comparison to Washington State because of the use of data from this state in chapter 7, this volume, by Becky Pettit and Christopher Lyons.

21. Steurer, Smith, and Tracy (2001) also found that offenders who obtain prison-based educational programming look somewhat worse on some criminal-justice–related measures than offenders who received no educational programming while in prison.

22. While simplistic from the point of view of estimating the effect of a GED for an individual, the estimates in Panel A may be relevant from the point of view of an employer with little information—say, only dropout and conviction status—trying to infer the expected productivity of GED and non-GED holders.

23. We test this hypothesis in a model that constrains the effects of the other independent variables to be the same for whites and nonwhites. The p value on the interaction between the GED indicator and a dummy variable indicator for being white is .056 in the first-year regression.

24. The point estimates are slightly higher in panel D than in panel C of table 8.2. The reason for this is that the regression-adjusted GED coefficient for the four quarters prior to the beginning of the prison spell (using equation 3) is insignificant but negative in sign. Conditional on observable Xs, GED holders had slightly lower earnings prior to prison.

25. In the fixed-effects estimates of panel D, it is only in the first year that the nonwhite results are statistically different from the results estimated over whites.

26. For example, security considerations are of paramount importance in correctional institutions, and it could be that participation in a GED preparation program leads to an inmate's better behavior while he is incarcerated. Certainly this is possible, but we did not find that GED program participants in our data had fewer disciplinary reports during the target spell than did the comparison groups. Still, given the importance of security issues, this is an area that deserves a closer look.

27. In a survey administered to offenders by Steurer, Smith, and Tracy (2001) just prior to release in 1997 and 1998, they find that compared to offenders with no prison-based educational programming, offenders who had participated in education programs while in prison reported a consistently lower motivation in regard to several labor-market activities, including the "motivation to get a job, a better job, or higher pay" or the "motivation to improve job performance." Though none of the differences between those who did and did not participate in prison education were statistically significant (at the .01 level), the point estimates consistently pointed to a negative correlation between prison-based education participation and labor-market motivation. On the other hand, offenders in the study conducted by Steurer, Smith, and Tracy who participated in prison-based education programs indicated a higher motivation to both "look good to prison or parole officials to get out" and to "get a better situation in prison" than did offenders who did not participate in education programming while in prison.

28. In this analysis we define recidivism as being convicted of a crime within three years of the forecasted release date that results in a return to prison or probation.

References

Ashenfelter, Orley, and Dean Hyslop. 2001. "Measuring the Effect of Arbitration on Wage Levels: The Case of Police Officers." *Industrial and Labor Relations Review* 54(1): 316–28.

Becker, Gary S. 1993. *Human Capital: A Theoretical and Empirical Analysis with Special Reference to Education.* Chicago: University of Chicago Press.

Boudett, Kathryn Parker. 2000. "'Second Chance' Strategies for Women Who Drop Out of School." *Monthly Labor Review*, December, 19–31.

Bureau of Justice Statistics. 2003. "Census of State and Federal Correctional Facilities, 2000." NCJ 198272. Washington: U.S. Department of Justice.

Cameron, Stephen V., and James J. Heckman. 1993. "The Nonequivalence of High School Equivalents." *Journal of Labor Economics* 11(1): 1–47.

Heckman, James J., Jingjing Hsse, and Yona Rubinstein. 2000. "The GED is a 'Mixed Signal': The Effect of Cognitive and Non-Cognitive Skills on Human Capital and Labor Market Outcomes." Unpublished manuscript. University of Chicago.

Jacobson, Louis S., Robert J. Lalonde, and Daniel G. Sullivan. 1993. "Earnings Losses of Displaced Workers." *American Economic Review* 83(4): 685–709.

Kornfeld, Robert, and Howard Bloom. 1999. "Measuring Program Impacts on Earnings and Employment: Do Unemployment Insurance Wage Records Agree with Survey Reports of Individuals?" *Journal of Labor Economics* 17(1): 168–97.

Murnane, Richard J., John B. Willett, and Kathryn Parker Boudett. 1999. "Do Male Dropouts Benefit from Obtaining a GED, Postsecondary Education, and Training?" *Evaluation Review* 22(5): 475–502.

Murnane, Richard J., John B. Willett, and John H. Tyler. 2000. "Who Benefits from a GED? Evidence from High School and Beyond." *Review of Economics and Statistics* 82(1): 23–37.

Sampson, Robert J., and John H. Laub. 1993. *Crime in the Making: Pathways and Turning Points Through Life.* Cambridge, Mass.: Harvard University Press.

Spence, Michael. 1973. "Job Market Signaling." *Quarterly Journal of Economics* 87(3): 355–74.

Steurer, Stephen, Linda Smith, and Alice Tracy. 2001. "Three-State Recidivism Study." Report. Washington: U.S. Department of Education, Office of Correctional Education.

Thornberry, Terrence P., and R. L. Christenson. 1984. "Unemployment and Criminal Involvement: An Investigation of Reciprocal Causal Structures." *American Sociological Review* 49: 398–411.

Tyler, John H. 2001. "So You Want a GED? Estimating the Impact of the GED on the Earnings of Dropouts." *Brown University Department of Economics Working Paper No. 01–34.*

———. 2003. "The Economic Benefits of the GED: Lessons from Recent Research." *Review of Educational Research* 73(3): 369–403.

Tyler, John H., Richard J. Murnane, and John B. Willett. 2000. "Estimating the Labor Market Signaling Value of the GED." *Quarterly Journal of Economics* 115(2): 431–68.

Wilson, David B., Catherine A. Gallagher, Mark B. Coggeshall, and Doris L. MacKenzie. 1999. "A Quantitative Review and Description of Corrections-Based Education, Vocation, and Work Programs." *Corrections Management Quarterly* 3(4): 8–18.

Wilson, David B., Catherine A. Gallagher, and Doris L. MacKenzie. 2000. "A Meta-Analysis of Corrections-Based Education, Vocation, and Work Programs for Adult Offenders." *Journal of Research in Crime and Delinquency* 37(4): 347–68.

Zamble, E., and F. J. Porporino. 1988. *Coping, Behavior, and Adaptation in Prison Inmates.* New York: Springer-Verlag.

= Chapter 9 =

Local Labor-Market Conditions and Post-Prison Employment Experiences of Offenders Released from Ohio State Prisons

WILLIAM J. SABOL

I n this chapter we examine the impacts of local labor-market conditions on the post-prison employment experiences of offenders released from Ohio state prisons during 1999 and 2000. It uses administrative data from the state's department of correction that are linked
to data from the state's unemployment insurance claims to track ex-
prisoner employment experiences for two years following release from
prison. We first use discrete duration models to analyze the impacts of
county labor-market conditions on the probability that ex-prisoners will
find a job upon release, conditional upon the length of time that they
are unemployed when they are released from prison. Second, we use
individual-level fixed-effects models to estimate the impact of county
labor-market conditions on the probability of employment during the
first two years following release from prison.

Following Steven Raphael and David Weiman (chapter 10, this volume) in their analysis of the impacts of local labor-market conditions
on recidivism, and Hilary Williamson Hoynes (2000) and John M. Fitzgerald (1995) in their analyses of exits from welfare, we use county
unemployment rates as the measure of local labor-market conditions.
It allows these rates to vary over time so as to measure the effect of
changing labor-market conditions on post-prison employment experiences. We also measure a variety of individual offenders' attributes,
such as type of offense, length of stay, prior incarcerations, participa-

tion in prison programs, pre-prison employment experiences, and demographic attributes, and assesses their impacts on post-prison employment experiences.

We found, first, that county unemployment rates are negatively associated with the time to find a first job upon release from prison. The marginal effect of a 1 percent increase (or decrease) in county unemployment rates is to decrease (or increase) the probability of exiting the initial spell of unemployment and finding a job by about two percentage points, from a baseline exit rate of 16 percent. Despite the effects of local labor-market conditions, more than one-third of the ex-prisoners in the sample had not found a first job by the end of the eighth quarter after release. In addition, pre-prison employment experiences are found to have larger and more enduring effects on the probability of exiting the initial spell of unemployment than do local labor-market conditions, as one additional quarter of pre-prison employment (having had two quarters of employment during the year prior to incarceration instead of one quarter) increases the probability of exiting unemployment by 6 percent.

Post-prison employment during the first two years following release is also affected by local labor-market conditions, as increases in county unemployment rates lead to decreases in quarterly post-prison employment probabilities. The estimated marginal effect of a 1 percent change in unemployment (evaluated at the mean level) is to reduce the probability that an ex-offender will be employed by about 4 percentage points (on an average employment probability of 36 percent). Here again, pre-prison employment has comparatively larger effects on post-prison employment outcomes than does variation in local labor markets. An additional quarter of employment during the year prior to incarceration can increase the probability that an offender is employed during the two years following release by about 10 percentage points.

In both analyses, participation in prison programs is shown not to increase post-prison employment, but post-prison supervision is shown to increase both the probability of exiting unemployment upon release from prison and post-prison employment. Prior incarcerations lower post-prison employment probabilities, and black offenders were slightly more likely to be employed than white offenders, as were older offenders.

Together, the findings about post-prison employment suggest that while employment prospects of ex-offenders are enhanced by local labor-market conditions, that offenders' pre-prison attachments to labor markets appear to be more important in determining post-prison outcomes than in-prison participation in vocational training programs or policies that affect aggregate demand for labor. While these findings are consistent with employer demands for ex-prisoners with work experience (for example, Holzer, Raphael, and Stoll 2003, 2004), a limitation of this study is that the covariates available in the administrative data that were analyzed are insufficiently rich to adequately measure individual offender characteristics that may be associated with pre-prison employment experiences, and therefore, the study is unable to fully isolate the causal effects of pre-prison employment from other, unmeasured, offender attributes that may be associated with post-prison employment.

Background: Local Labor-Market Conditions and Post-Prison Employment

Evidence for considering a relationship between macroeconomic conditions and post-prison employment comes from several sources. First, there is evidence to suggest that the economic conditions are related to aggregate crime rates, especially property crimes (Grogger 1998; Gould, Weinberg, and Mustard 2002). Raphael and Rudolf Winter-Ember (2001) also show that state and county property crime rates are lower when unemployment is lower. That an aggregate relationship between unemployment and crime holds for the general offender population is suggestive that it might also hold for the ex-prisoner population.

However, while the associations between aggregate unemployment and crime are consistent with the view that labor-market conditions might affect the criminal activities of released prisoners, this proposition has not been directly tested. Moreover, aggregate relationships between unemployment and prisoner recidivism suggest that ex-prisoners may be less responsive to macro-economic conditions than other offenders. Richard Freeman (2003), for example, uses two Bureau of Justice Statistics studies of the recidivism rates of offenders released from state prisons, in 1983 and 1994, to show that the sample of prisoners released during 1994 had a higher rate of return to prison within three years of release from prison than did the 1983 sample: 51 percent of the 1994 sample returned to prison within three years, as compared to 41 percent of the 1983 sample (Beck and Shipley 1989; Langan and Levin 2002). It is significant that labor-market conditions in 1994 were much tighter than those in 1983. For example, during 1983, the average unemployment rate was near 10 percent, whereas in 1994 it was between 5 percent and 6 percent. Thus, Freeman argues, if aggregate demand for labor affects recidivism through offenders' employment, one would expect the 1994 sample to have lower recidivism rates than the 1983 sample. The implication of this, as Freeman (2003) points out, is that the 1990s job market did not reduce recidivism of ex-prisoners, even though it contributed to the reduction in aggregate crime rates during the same period.

Further, as Raphael and Weiman (chapter 10, this volume) point out, the aggregate relationship between unemployment and crime and the recidivism rates of ex-prisoners over time are both consistent with an interpretation that so-called hardened offenders (such as ex-prisoners) are insensitive to labor-market conditions, and the changes in crime rates are driven by offenders who have not been incarcerated or are on parole. Jeffrey Grogger's (1995) finding that sanctions short of prison, such as probation or fines, do not have longer-run impacts on employment and earnings of offenders is also consistent with this interpretation.

With these considerations in mind, local labor-market conditions can affect the post-prison employment of ex-prisoners in several ways. On the supply side, they can affect offenders' decisions to engage in legitimate activities. On the demand side, they can affect employers' demands for low-skilled ex-prisoner labor.

If ex-prisoners are presumed to make choices between crime, leisure, and legitimate labor-market activities based upon the relative risks and returns to each activity, then lower local unemployment rates coupled with job growth and increases in wages would increase the relative attractiveness of legitimate labor-market activities. Ex-prisoners' willingness to seek work and continue to apply for jobs even if initially turned down should increase under these conditions, provided the demand for their labor and the returns to legitimate labor are high enough. Nationwide, about 55 percent of prisoners reported being employed full-time prior to their incarceration, and one-third reported being unemployed. In addition, most ex-offenders have multiple barriers to employment, including low skills and literacy, poor work histories, and behavioral and health issues. Changes in local labor-market conditions cannot directly enhance the skills and abilities of ex-prisoners to perform work until or unless they are employed. But if employers demand a certain level of skill and experience prior to hiring, even when labor markets are tight, the likelihood that ex-prisoners are hired may be lowered by their comparatively low levels of skills and work experience.

Tight labor markets can also affect the demand for ex-prisoner labor. Presumably, as unemployment rates lower, especially in low-skill sectors, employers will demand more ex-prisoner labor. During the boom of the 1990s, for example, employers consistently reported that they could not hire or retain unskilled workers. These same surveys revealed, however, that employers tended to hire welfare recipients, immigrants, and persons without high school diplomas to fill these positions, rather than ex-offenders. Harry Holzer, Raphael, and Michael Stoll (2003) speculate that as the 1990s boom went on, anecdotal evidence suggested that an increasing number of employers were willing to hire ex-offenders.

Employer preferences for ex-prisoner labor may be affected by a variety of factors. For example, ex-prisoners' involvement with the criminal-justice system and the attendant stigma associated with their criminal-justice experiences may make them undesirable in the eyes of employers. The stigma of a criminal conviction (Schwartz and Skolnick 1962; Western, Kling, and Weiman 2001) suggests that individuals can be labeled or categorized by the criminal-justice system as "essentially deviant" or untrustworthy and less likely to abide by rules. Other institutions react to the criminal-justice system's labeling of individuals as deviant and use the label as a signal of the person's status, rather than searching for and obtaining additional information that might change the status indicated by the label. To the extent that employers need workers to fill positions of trust and employers respond to the stigma of a record, they may continue to seek other sources of low-skilled labor to meet their needs, even when labor markets are tight.

Time in prison may contribute to the erosion of the limited human capital that most offenders bring with them upon entry into prison. For example, more than 40 percent of prisoners nationwide have not completed high school or its equivalent (Harlow 2003). Further, upwards of 20 percent of prisoners have some mental or physical problems that limit their ability to work. This is about twice the level of all persons who report such conditions nationwide (Freeman 2003). For men with limited human capital to begin with, prison can contribute to the erosion of what skills and habits they possess that are productivity related, and hence, contribute to lowering post-prison employment. Imprisonment may also undermine the development of human capital and the acquisition of skills. In some respects, prison vocational training programs attempt to mitigate these effects. More generally, at a time when most young persons are starting their employment careers, learning skills, and developing social job connections, young persons who are incarcerated do not develop these skills and networks, thereby lessening their value to the labor market (Waldfogel 1994). For jobs that require training or specific capabilities, time spent out of the labor force reduces a worker's competence in relevant areas.

Ex-prisoners may experience difficulty developing and maintaining attachments to labor markets. Robert J. Sampson and John H. Laub (1993, 1997) argue that periods of incarceration, particularly those that occur during the transition from adolescence to adulthood, can disrupt young men's transition to stable career employment. Early incarceration can contribute to an accumulation of disadvantage that eventually leads to poor performance in school, weak attachments and bonds to labor markets, and increasing crime in adult life. Young males whose lives have been punctuated by periods of incarceration can find career jobs inaccessible for several reasons: The stigma of incarceration can make ex-offenders unattractive for entry-level or union jobs that require high levels of trust; civil disabilities (that is, legal exclusions and prohibitions to work) can affect ex-prisoners' access to career employment in the skilled trades or public sector; and employers may be unwilling to invest in developing the specific skills required for long-term employment in a particular sector for ex-offenders. All of these factors contribute to segmenting ex-offenders into spot and secondary labor markets with few prospects for earnings growth (Western 2000, 2002; Nagin and Waldfogel 1998).

This brief review suggests that for labor markets to affect post-prison employment, they must be especially tight, or there must be some mechanisms that can facilitate post-prison employment prospects. However, apart from Raphael and Weiman's derived estimates of the effects of local labor-market conditions on post-prison employment, there have been no recent direct tests of these effects. This paper provides such a test.

Empirical Model: The Duration of Initial Unemployment

The paper analyzes two dependent variables: the duration of the initial period of unemployment upon release from prison and quarterly employment during the first two years after release from prison.

Discrete-Hazard Model of the Time to a First Job Post-Release

In this first analysis, the dependent variable is conceptualized as a discrete event: the conditional probability of exiting the initial spell of unemployment that occurs upon release from prison and finding a job. These conditional probabilities are referred to as hazards, or exit rates. The paper analyzes only the first observed (complete, or right-censored) spell of unemployment for the exit-rate hazards.[1]

Using the hazard rate, it is possible to construct the duration distribution (or the probability that an individual experiences a spell of length t) and the survivor function (or the probability that an individual will experience a spell of at least t periods. Both of these distributions are conditional on the covariates and on initial entry into a state, in this case, exiting unemployment by obtaining a first job. As Hoynes (2000) and David W. Hosmer and Stanley Lemeshow (1989) show, for a given specification of the transition probability and the covariates, the parameters of the model can be estimated using conventional maximum-likelihood methods.

The models are estimated with several sets of covariates, which are described in detail in the next section, on the data used in the analysis. Key variables in the models include time-varying (quarterly) county unemployment rates (the measure of local labor-market conditions), pre-prison employment experiences, type of offense, offense severity, prior incarcerations, length of stay, prison program participation, post-prison supervision, and demographic variables such as age and race.[2]

Quarterly Employment During the First Two Post-Release Years

A second set of analyses address the question of the impact of local labor-market conditions on post-prison employment during the first two years (eight quarters) following release from prison. The dependent variable is the probability of employment in a quarter. Released prisoners are tracked for the same length of time, thereby allowing changes in local labor-market conditions to affect the post-prison employment experiences of the ex-offenders who obtain a job in, say, the first or second quarter of release. This exposes all offenders to local labor-market conditions, as the analysis allows the quarterly probability of being employed to vary with the quarterly county unemployment rates.

This analysis of post-prison employment uses longitudinal data on individual offenders, and therefore it is expected that the observations will be correlated within individuals. This clustering within individuals along with the fact that there are also inevitably unobserved factors that may influence the quarterly employment probabilities leads to the use of individual-level fixed-effects models to address unobserved heterogeneity and produce robust standard errors. The array of covariates that were used to assess initial employment outcomes are pressed into duty here to look at quarterly employment outcomes.

Description of the Ohio Data and Description of the Sample

The paper relies upon a rich source of data for its analysis. The principal data sources for this analysis are administrative records from the Ohio Department of Rehabilitation (ODRC) and Corrections and the Ohio Department of Jobs and Family Services (ODJFS). The ODRC data are individual-level offender records of 46,000 offenders released from Ohio state prisons during 1999 and 2000. These records contain demographic information about offenders, along with information about their offense at commitment, sentences imposed and time served, methods of release, and form of supervision. In addition, the ODRC data include a Social Security number for each offender. The Social Security numbers were used to link ODRC offender records with ODJFS unemployment insurance records.[3] Information on all of the jobs recorded in the ODJFS data for the period from 1993 through 2002 was appended to each offender record for which there was a match.

The availability of UI (unemployment insurance) wage data imposed a limitation on the construction of the data set. The UI wage data were available only back to 1993. This meant that offenders who were admitted into prison prior to 1993 did not have pre-prison employment data, and consequently they were also omitted from the analysis data set. To allow for one year of pre-prison employment experience, the sample of offenders who were included in the "employment sample" for analysis was limited to offenders admitted to prison during or after 1994. This limits the analysis to offenders who left prison during 1999 and 2000 but who entered prison in 1994 or later. For the most part, the maximum length of sentence served by offenders in the employment sample was seven years in prison net of jail credits. Based on the time frames needed to obtain pre- and post-prison employment records, more than 39,000 offender records were available for analysis.[4]

The UI wage data provide information about the number of jobs and earnings per quarter. They do not provide data on the dates that jobs were obtained or on the number of hours worked. This and other limitations of UI wage data have been analyzed elsewhere (Kornfeld and Bloom 1999), by researchers who found that for the purposes of comparing impacts of employment and training programs, UI wage data and survey data were generally comparable. Survey data on earnings were generally higher than earnings reported in UI wage data. This difference may arise from the fact that UI wage data provide information on employment only in formal labor markets and in sectors covered by unemployment insurance. To the extent that ex-offenders find employment in informal or secondary labor markets that operate on cash or barter, their employment is unobserved by UI wage data. To the extent that there are large numbers of uncovered sectors, potentially large numbers of legitimate jobs can go uncounted. In Ohio, more than 99 percent of jobs are covered by unemployment insurance. Despite the possibility that ex-prisoners obtain employment in informal labor markets, this analysis of participation in formal labor markets is important, as it provides a measure of the extent to which ex-prisoners are reintegrated into mainstream, legitimate institutions.

The UI wage data provide indications of whether persons were employed during a quarter, the number of jobs held during a quarter, the industrial sectors in which the employment occurred, and quarterly earnings in each job.[5] From this information were constructed variables that indicated whether a person had at least one job in a specific quarter, the number of jobs in a quarter, total quarterly earnings, and the sector of employment having the largest quarterly earnings. Quarterly employment and earnings data are available until the end of 2002, so that each offender has a minimum of eight quarters of employment post-prison.

Construction of the Dependent Variables

From the UI wage data two dependent variables were constructed. The first dependent variable is the time (or duration) until ex-prisoners obtained their first job upon release from prison, conditional upon the length of their initial spell of unemployment. Technically, this is measured as the probability of exiting unemployment, conditional upon the length of unemployment. The durations for both finding a job and length of unemployment were measured in quarters, consistent with the nature of the ODJFS data.

The second dependent analyzed is quarterly employment rates. Figure 9.1 shows the dependent variable for the 34,081 offenders in the employment sample of offenders released during 1999 and 2000. The hazard rate represents the probability of exiting unemployment and finding a job for those at risk of finding an initial job. Thus, offenders who found an initial job in quarter 1 are omitted from the probability calculations in quarter 2, and so on.[6] The initial spell of unemployment is defined by the number of quarters until an offender finds his first job or until his observation is censored. Offenders who obtain employment in the quarter of release are coded as taking one quarter to find their first job. Offenders' initial spell of unemployment is censored if they have not found a job by the end of the 2002. For offenders released during 2000, this amounts to eight full quarters of data; for those released during 1999, this amounts to twelve quarters of data. There are only minor differences in the hazard rate in the first quarter for those released in 1999 as compared to those released in 2000.

In figure 9.1, the hazard rates decline relatively rapidly after the end of the second quarter after release. The conditional probability of finding a job hovers at about 31 or 32 percent during the first two quarters, but by the end of the third quarter it declines to less than 15 percent. By one year after release, the offenders who still have not found a job, had less than a 10 percent chance of finding a job. By the end of two years, the chances of finding a job, given that an offender still did not have a job, were about 3 percent.

Figure 9.2 shows the survivor function, or the size of the pool of ex-prisoners who are still at risk of finding their first job, that is, who have not exited unemployment. By the end of the second post-release quar-

Figure 9.1   Hazard Rate, or Probability of Exiting the Initial Spell of Unemployment (Finding a Job) upon Release from Prison, Conditional upon the Length of Unemployment

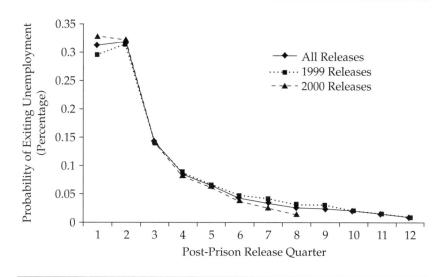

Source: Author's analysis of ODRC data.

ter, 53 percent of the release cohort had survived, that is, had not yet exited the initial spell of unemployment. By one year after release, 42.5 percent of the cohort remained unemployed; and by the eighth post-release quarter, 33 percent of the release cohort was still unemployed. Thus, while the hazard rate shows that by the fourth quarter (or one year) following release from prison, the probability of exiting the spell of unemployment that occurred upon release from prison had declined to less than 10 percent, and 42.5 percent of ex-prisoners still had not found their first job by the end of year 1.

The second dependent variable analyzed is quarterly employment rates. Figures 9.3 and 9.4 show the quarterly employment rates pre- and post-prison. The data are organized by quarter, so that the pre-prison quarters refer to the quarter prior to admission, regardless of the year in which an offender was admitted, and the post-prison quarters refer to the quarters following release, regardless of the date of release. The periods labeled "pre-Q01" and "post-Q01" refer to the quarters of admission into prison and quarters of release, respectively. Note that the employment rate does not fall to zero after admission into prison.[7]

The UI wage data obtained from the ODJFS were organized by quar-

Figure 9.2   **Survivor Function, or Percentage of Releases Still in the Pool of Offenders Who Have Not Yet Found a First Job Following Release, by Quarter Since Release from Prison**

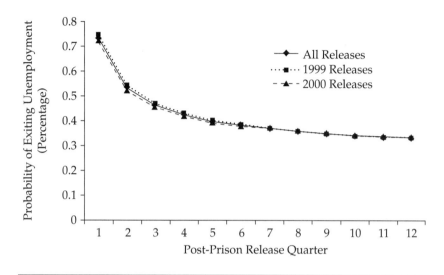

Source: Author's analysis of ODRC data.

ter of employment, and they did not contain information about the actual date of an ex-offender's employment, whereas the ODRC data contain the actual date of release. By linking actual release dates to quarterly UI data, it is possible to identify the quarter of release from prison in the UI data, and from there, to identify each offender's employment history. The quarter "post-Q01" refers to the quarter in which the prisoner was released, or his first post-prison quarter in the UI data. However, it is not possible to measure the actual length of time from release to employment during the first post-prison quarter for offenders who were employed during the first post-prison quarter. Analysis of the release dates in the ODRC data indicate that during the quarter of release (post-Q01), about one-third of offenders were released during each of the quarter's three months. (In the regressions, dummy variables for the month of release during the quarter are introduced to control for variation among offenders in the duration of time on the street during the quarter of release.)

Figure 9.3 shows an increase in the percent of offenders employed in the second post-prison quarter, as compared to the pre-prison average. The post-prison quarterly employment rates are shown in two ways: the number employed in a quarter is divided by all releases,

Figure 9.3   Percentage of Offenders Released During 1999 and 2000 Who Were Employed During any Quarter, by Pre- and Post-Prison Quarters

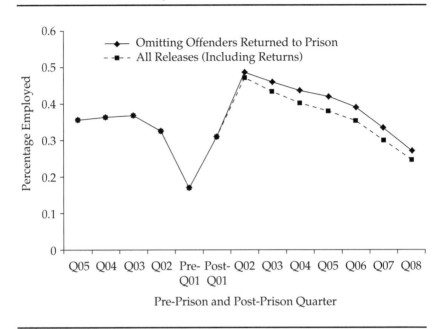

Pre-Prison and Post-Prison Quarter

Source: Author's analysis of ODRC data.

regardless of whether an offender had been observed as returning to prison; and the number employed is divided by the number of offenders "at risk" of employment, in that the ODRC data did not yet record them as having returned to an Ohio prison.[8] Both measures of post-prison employment show short-term employment gains, followed by longer-run returns to pre-prison employment levels.

In the 5 quarters prior to prison admission, about 35 percent to 37 percent of the release cohort was employed in any quarter. In the second quarter post-release the employment rate reaches almost 50 percent (using either measure of quarterly employment), but by the sixth quarter post-release it falls by 10 percentage points, to 40 percent, the rate based on omitting returning prisoners from the employment-rate calculation. And on the basis of calculations using the entire cohort, by the eighteenth month after release, the quarterly employment rates are below their pre-prison level of 35 percent.

The roughly 35 percent pre-prison employment rate obtained from the UI wage data is lower than the 45 percent employment rate reported by the 1996 *Intake Study* of offenders entering Ohio's prisons,

Figure 9.4   Pre- and Post-Prison Mean Quarterly Earnings, by Year of Release: Offenders with Positive Earnings During the Quarter; Offenders Who Served Seven or Fewer Years

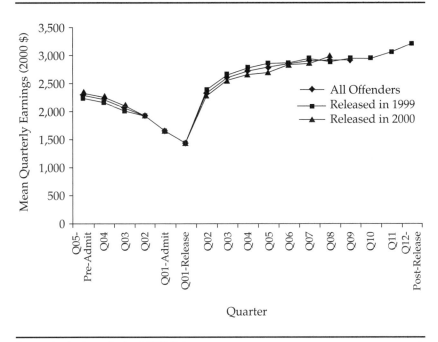

Quarter

Source: Author's analysis of ODRC data.

which was conducted by the ODRC (Norton 1998). The differences in unemployment rates between the UI data and the data in the *Intake Study* arise from two sources: First the *Intake Study* uses self-report employment data (not the official UI wage data), and the self-report employment data could include self-employment jobs that are not reported in the UI wage data. The *Intake Study* did not attempt to verify the self-report data against wage data. Second, the *Intake Study* reports on the 1996 entering cohort, whereas the data in figure 9.3 are based on data from members of several cohorts that entered prison before and after 1996. The selectivity of admissions years can lead to differences in employment measures.

The pattern of a short-term gain in offender employment rates early in the post-release period followed by a longer-run decline to pre-prison employment rate levels was also observed by Becky Pettit and Christopher Lyons (chapter 7, this volume) in their analysis of employment of ex-offenders in Washington State in the 1990s, as well as Jeffrey R. Kling's (2002) data for federal criminal defendants in California in the 1990s. In the Washington data, the quarterly pre-prison employment rates were reported to be about 29 percent, and the early-period post-release quarterly employment rates reached 50 percent. But the post-release employment rates declined from 50 percent to their pre-prison levels of 29 percent within two years. In the California federal defendant sample, post-prison employment levels rose to or exceeded pre-prison levels by within a year of release from prison. And as occurred in Ohio and Washington, the post-prison employment levels of the California defendants also fall over time.

Speculations as to why the post-prison employment rates increase rise above the pre-prison rates include the effects of post-prison supervision in the community. In Ohio as well as in Washington State, supervised offenders are required at least to make efforts to find employment, and this may contribute to the short-run increase in employment rates.

For illustrative purposes, the data in figure 9.4 show the quarterly earnings of employed offenders, pre- and post-prison. All data are in constant (year 2000) dollars. Overall, ex-prisoners earnings are comparatively low, averaging less than $2,500 per quarter prior to admission and reaching nearly $3,000 per quarter for the less than one-third of ex-prisoners who are employed by the eighth post-prison quarter. The pattern of a post-prison increase in earnings is also consistent with the pattern in Pettit and Lyons's data from Washington State (chapter 7, this volume). The earnings for all Ohio prisoners are higher than those reported by John H. Tyler and Jeffrey Kling (chapter 8, this volume) for their sample of GED participants and high school graduates. The increase in post-prison earnings over time may largely be due to the selectivity of those who retain jobs several quarters after release from prison. As discussed above, by the second year following release, less than one-third of the Ohio release cohort was employed, down from the almost half of all offenders employed during the second post-release quarter.

Local Labor-Market Conditions
(County Unemployment Rates)

The ODRC data provide information on the county of sentencing. This variable is used as a proxy for the county of release, a variable that is otherwise only recently and sporadically available in the ODRC data. Support for this use of county of sentencing as a proxy for county of release comes from two sources. First, in the ODRC data the address of release is available only for offenders who are released into supervision. More than 60 percent of the release cohort in this study was released into some form of post-prison supervision. Data on the address of release were geocoded for supervised offenders released into five counties that are the main counties of the Cleveland metropolitan area. For this subset of offenders, county of sentencing and county of release corresponded in over 90 percent of the cases. Further support for the use of the county of sentencing as a proxy for county of release comes from Raphael and Weiman (chapter 10, this volume), who report that in the California data that they used, only 10 percent of parolees were returned to a county other than the county of sentencing.

Another reason why county of sentencing is important is that it, along with the date of release, provides the variables to link ex-offenders to county unemployment rates at a specific point in time. County unemployment rates are one of the key explanatory variables, providing a measure of the local demand for labor. In the analysis, quarterly average county unemployment rates are constructed from the three-month county unemployment rates. Quarterly county unemployment rates are linked to individual offender records on the basis of the date (quarter) of release and county of sentencing. Data on up to twelve quarters post-release are appended, depending on the length of time that an offender is in the sample.

During the late 1990s, local labor-market conditions varied widely both within and among Ohio's eighty-eight counties (figure 9.5). This variation is used to assess the impact of local labor-market conditions on post-prison employment. Quarterly unemployment rates are computed as the average of the unemployment rates for the three months making up a quarter. Monthly unemployment data from the Ohio Department of Jobs and Family Services Local Area Unemployment Statistics are used in the calculations.[9]

Given that labor-market conditions varied within counties over time, and given our interest in variation in local labor-market effects, quarterly unemployment rates for each quarter subsequent to the quarter of release in the county of release were calculated and appended to each offender's release record. The quarterly unemployment rates begin with the quarter of release and continue through the next eight quarters. In the duration models, these are entered as time-varying covariates. Thus, each offender record has up to eight quarters of data on county unemployment rates, starting with the month of the individual's release.

Figure 9.5 shows the quarterly county unemployment rates for selected Ohio counties. Cuyahoga, Franklin, and Hamilton counties contain Ohio's three largest cities (Cleveland, Columbus, and Cincinnati, respectively). Adams and Monroe are two counties with smaller populations. The unemployment rates in the larger counties are less than those in the smaller counties, and they follow a relatively common pattern: During 1999 and 2000, the unemployment rates tended to exhibit

Figure 9.5   Quarterly Unemployment Rates for Selected Ohio Counties, 1999: First Quarter Through 2002: Second Quarter

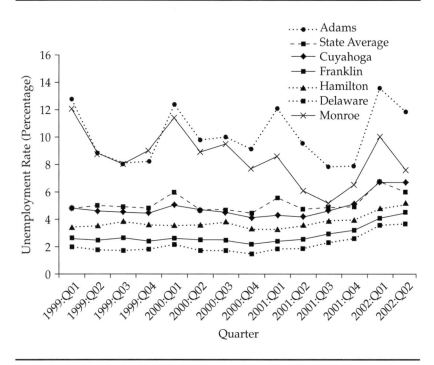

Source: Author's analysis of LAMS data.

minor fluctuations around a comparatively low level. After 2000, the rates increased, and by the end of 2002, the unemployment rates had increased by from 50 to 100 percent, depending upon the county. For example, in Cuyahoga County, the 1999 unemployment rate was slightly more than 4 percent; by 2000 it declined to 4 percent, but by 2002, it increased to 7 percent. In the smaller counties, the unemployment rates fluctuated somewhat widely around much higher average levels than the average levels in the larger counties.

In the analysis that follows, the time path of county unemployment rates are permitted to vary over time with the quarters since release from prison. This time-varying measure of unemployment differs from the fixed measure of unemployment at exit from prison that Raphael and Weiman (chapter 10, this volume) used in their analysis of the impact of labor-market conditions on recidivism. In their model, they emphasized the importance of the enduring effects of the labor-market conditions that an offender encounters upon his release from prison.

Two additional issues arise with using county unemployment rates to approximate local economic conditions. First, there may be errors in the measurements of quarterly county unemployment rates; these would attenuate estimates of the effects of county unemployment on ex-offender post-prison employment and this would likely result in underestimates of the effects of this variable. Clearly, the availability of reliable, quarterly county unemployment data is desirable. The LAUS (Local Area Unemployment Statistics, compiled by the Bureau of Labor Statistics) used in this analysis also are used for administrative purposes (such as identifying labor-surplus areas, public works programs, waivers to food stamp time limits for able-bodied workers, emergency food and shelter assistance, and so forth)—so at least the measurement error is correlated with allocations of federal funds. But this argument does not justify their scientific use.

One solution would be to include additional measures of quarterly local labor-market conditions, such as labor-force or sector employment; however, these also would have to be drawn from the LAUS data, so including these other measures would not eliminate problems associated with measurement error. However, effects of county unemployment on welfare exits were found by research on labor-market effects on welfare exits (Fitzgerald 1995) that used multiple measures of local labor-market conditions such as unemployment, county per capita income, and county retail sales from other data sources. This suggests that even though this variable may be measured with error, effects can be estimated. Also, to minimize effects of measurement error with the quarterly data, models are estimated, using county unemployment rates at the time of release from prison as a fixed covariate prior to estimating effects while allowing county unemployment to vary across quarters.

The second problem is that ex-prisoners may not reside in the county of release, and if they move to, say, lower-unemployment counties, the effects of county unemployment on post-prison employment may be biased. Several factors contribute to minimizing the possible effects of post-release migration of ex-offenders. About 60 percent of offenders are released with some form of post-prison supervision, and the supervision requirements impose some limitations on supervised offenders' mobility. For example, supervised offenders are required to keep supervising officers informed of residence and employment and to obtain permission before leaving the state (La Vigne and Thompson 2003).

The geography of Ohio may minimize the possible effects of ex-prisoner mobility, especially out of state. Several large counties—Cuyahoga (Cleveland), Franklin (Columbus), Summit (Akron), and Hamilton (Cincinnati)—accounted for more than one-half of all releases from prison during the sample period. Cuyahoga, Franklin, and Summit are internal counties, which reduces the chances of ex-prisoners' migrating over the state line, whereas Hamilton borders Kentucky and there is a chance that ex-offenders may migrate to Kentucky. A study of the job market in the Cleveland area found that the city of Cleveland experienced almost no job growth during the 1990s, but the surrounding suburbs within Cuyahoga County did experience job growth (Bania, Coulton, and Leete 2000). This suggests, for Cuyahoga County, at least, that if ex-offenders are mobile, they may remain within the county. To the extent that these conditions apply to the other counties, a similar conclusion could be drawn. Finally, though there is little research on post-release mobility of ex-offenders, researchers at the Urban Institute have compared the residences of offenders at the time of admission into prison and at the time of release for a cohort of Illinois state prisoners. Their data for Cook County (Chicago) show that even though offenders returned to different residences from their residence at admission, their mobility was within the county (between census tracts) and not between counties.

Measures of Corrections Policy Variables and Offender Characteristics

The ODRC data contain a rich set of potential covariates that can be used to control for observable differences among offenders, as we attempt to isolate the effects of variation in county unemployment on post-prison employment. Table 9.1 shows the means for these variables.

The ODRC data describe the most serious offense at admission, which is identified by the offense having the longest sentence. The most serious offenses are categorized into fairly homogeneous classes: homicide, rape, aggravated assault, robbery, other violent, burglary, theft, other property, drug trafficking, drug abuse, weapons, and public order.[10] These classes are coded as dummy variables equal to 1 to represent a class.[11] About a quarter of the sample members were sentenced for a violent offense; 33 percent of these had a drug offense as their most serious offense; 31 percent were property offenders; and the remainder of the sample had other offenses.

The degree of the felony level of the most serious offense is also indicated. In Ohio, the lower the number associated with a felony level the higher the severity of the offense; thus felony 1 offenses are more severe than felony 5 offenses. Felony 1 and life sentences are combined into the "felony 1" category. Thirty-five percent of offenders were released from prison with a fifth-degree felony, making this the modal offense category; 30 percent of the sample were fourth-degree felons; 17 percent were third-degree; 13 percent were second-degree; and 5 percent were first-degree felons.[12]

Prior prison admissions are measured in two ways, by means of a

Table 9.1   Descriptive Statistics for Estimation Sample Used in the Analysis of Exits from the Initial Spell of Unemployment upon Release from Prison

Variable	Definition	Mean
Labor-marktet variables		
County unemployment rate	Time varying county unemployment rate, quarterly	4.37
Number of pre-prison quarters	Number of quarters worked, one year plus one quarter prior to admission	0.96
Second month of quarter	Dummy variable indicating release in second month of quarter of release	0.33
Third month of quarter	Dummy variable indicating release in third month of quarter of release	0.35
Prior prison		
Prior incarcerations	Number of prior incarcerations	0.93
First-term group	Dummy variable = 1 if admit is first on a term	0.94
Form of release and supervision		
Parole supervision	Dummy variable = 1 if release was onto parole	0.19
Post-release control (PRC) supervision	Dummy variable = 1 if release was onto PRC	0.29
Judicial release	Dummy variable = 1 if release was judicial	0.09
Type and length of sentence		
TIS sentence	Dummy variable = 1 if sentence on most serious offense was TIS	0.71
Time served	Total length of time served in prison plus jail credit	24.33
Offense severity level		
Felony one	Dummy = 1 if offense was a first-degree felony or life	0.05
Felony two	Dummy = 1 if offense was a second-degree felony	0.13
Felony three	Dummy = 1 if offense was a third-degree felony	0.17
Felony four	Dummy = 1 if offense was a fourth-degree felony	0.30
Felony five	Omitted offense severity level category	0.35

(Table continues on p. 276)

Table 9.1   *Continued*

Variable	Definition	Mean
Offense type		
Homicide (manslaughter)	Dummy = 1 if offense was homicide	0.01
Rape	Dummy = 1 if offense was rape	0.03
Aggravated assault	Dummy = 1 if offense was aggravated assault	0.11
Robbery	Dummy = 1 if offense was robbery	0.08
Other violent	Dummy = 1 if offense was other violent	0.02
Burglary	Dummy = 1 if offense was burglary	0.12
Theft	Dummy = 1 if offense was theft	0.09
Other property	Dummy = 1 if offense was other property	0.10
Drugs	Omitted offense category	0.33
Weapons	Dummy = 1 if offense was weapons	0.03
Public order or other	Dummy = 1 if offense was public order	0.09
Education level and prison program participation		
TABE total score	Total TABE test score	7.06
Vocational program graduate or certificate	Dummy = 1 if offender received the vocational training certificate	0.03
Vocational work assignments	Dummy = 1 if offender participated in work assignments	0.03
GED in prison	Dummy = 1 if offender obtained a GED in prison	0.07
Substance abuse program	Dummy = 1 if offender participated in a substance abuse program	0.07
Race and age		
Black	Dummy = 1 if offender was black	0.56
Less than or equal to twenty	Dummy = 1 if offender was twenty or under at release	0.08
Twenty-one through twenty-five	Dummy = 1 if offender was twenty-one through twenty-five at release	0.22
Twenty-six through thirty	Dummy = 1 if offender was twenty-six through thirty at release	0.18

Table 9.1   *Continued*

Variable	Definition	Mean
Thirty-one through thirty-five	Dummy = 1 if offender was thirty-one through thirty-five at release	0.15
Thirty-six through forty	Dummy = 1 if offender was thirty-six through forty at release	0.15
Over forty-one	Omitted age category	0.23
Release year		
Released during 1999	Dummy = 1 if offender was re-leased during 1999	0.57
Number of observations		144,196

Source: Author's analysis of Ohio Department of Corrections (ODRC) data and Local Area Unemployment (LAUS) data.

count of the number of prior incarcerations, and by creating an indicator variable to distinguish whether a release is from a first term (or admission to prison on a conviction for a new crime) or a subsequent release from a term (that is, a release from a commitment as a conditional release violator).[13] The mean number of prior incarcerations was 0.92, and 94 percent of the release cohort was released on their first term on a commitment.

The ODRC data provide indications of the method of release and the form of post-prison supervision. Ohio sentencing laws changed in 1996, as a result of reforms begun in the early 1990s that came to be known as senate bill 2 (or SB2), for the original legislation that proposed the reforms. These reforms introduced "truth in sentencing" (or TIS), which was associated with the elimination of parole release decisions and indeterminate sentences. Under TIS sentences, offenders were required to serve all or most (97 percent) of their imposed terms, as they could receive only small amounts of good time reductions. TIS sentences replaced the "old law" system of indeterminate sentences with parole release. Parole supervision was replaced with "post-release control" (or PRC) supervision. Under TIS, offenders are released by expiration of sentence and are required to be supervised by PRC if they were sentenced for a first- or second-degree felony or if they committed a sex or violent offense that was a third-degree felony. Offenders who committed third-degree nonviolent offenses or fourth- or fifth-degree felonies that were not sex offenses are eligible for PRC, but supervision for these offenders is discretionary.[14] The length of PRC supervision terms varies from three to five years. About 20 percent of offenders were released to parole, and 29 percent were released to PRC.

Ohio has another form of release, known as judicial release, under which eligible offenders may apply for release. When a judicial release is granted, offenders are placed under community supervision by the probation department. The court reserves the right to reimpose the sentence that was reduced pursuant to the judicial release if the offender violates the sanction. Under judicial release, the period of community supervision is limited to a maximum of five years; this term may be reduced by the time offenders spend in prison or jail.[15] Nine percent of offenders were released judicially.

Length of stay in prison is calculated as the difference between dates of admission and release, plus jail-time credits, which are reported in a separate variable. The inclusion of jail-time credit provides a measure of the total time that an offender is incarcerated and away from society. Average time served was slightly more than twenty-four months.

In addition to information on these criminal-justice measures, the ODRC data provide several education-related measures. The ODRC examines each inmate shortly after admission, using the Test of Adult Basic Education (or TABE) test to determine whether an offender can qualify for the GED (general equivalency degree), as well as to make classifications for participation in particular types of training programs. The TABE scores are appropriate for this analysis because the TABE tests are administered prior to any prison program interventions. The TABE test scores are generally associated with a grade level—a TABE score of 9 can be thought of as the equivalent of a ninth-grade education. The mean TABE test score level of the sample members was 7.

The ODRC data indicate whether an offender completed a GED during prison, as opposed to entering prison with the GED. Seven percent of offenders completed a GED in prison.

The ODRC data contain several indicators of offenders' involvement in prison programs, including education, substance abuse, and vocational training programs. The ODRC data also identify inmates who obtained certificates upon completion of an ODRC apprenticeship vocational training program. For these inmates, the date of certification is available. For all other program participants, the only data that are available are indicators that an inmate participated in a particular type of program. No data are available on the extent of participation in these programs. About 3 percent of the sample graduated from the vocational training program and obtained a certificate, another 3 percent participated in work assignments, and 7 percent participated in substance abuse programs.

The race, age at release, and date of release are also available. Fifty-four percent of the release cohort was black, 42 percent was white, and the remainder belonged to other groups. There was a bimodal distribution of age, as about 21 percent of the sample members were over forty at admission and 21 percent were between twenty-one and twenty-five. Less than 8 percent were under twenty years of age. Offenders twenty-five to thirty years of age made up 18 percent of the sample; those thirty-one to thirty-five, 17 percent; and those thirty-six to forty, 16 percent.

The Ohio sample of releases differs in many respects from the Washington State sample (see chapter 7, this volume). The time periods differ, as the Washington sample covers admissions and releases throughout the 1990s, whereas the Ohio sample covers releases for 1999 and 2000. A majority of the Ohio prisoners are black (56 percent), compared to the slightly more than one-quarter of the Washington prisoners who are black. Both samples excluded women from their analysis. The fraction of older offenders in the Ohio sample (21 percent are over forty) is twice that of the Washington sample. The shares of Ohio offenders convicted for violent and drug crimes exceed these shares for Washington. While pre- and post-prison employment rates are roughly similar, average earnings in the Ohio sample are larger (but this may be due to the more recent time period for which they were observed). Larger shares of the Ohio sample were employed pre-prison in the service sector than in the Washington sample (42 percent versus 29 percent), but the shares of the Washington sample employed pre-prison in construction and agriculture (15 percent and 7 percent) exceeded the Ohio shares (7 percent and 2 percent). Shares employed post-prison in various sectors were more similar than the pre-prison shares, but the Ohio sample still had larger shares employed in the service sector (42 percent) as compared to 33 percent for Washington, whereas Washington still maintained a larger share employed in construction (13 percent) compared to Ohio (8 percent).

Results on the Probability of Exiting Unemployment and Finding a First Job

The results of the analysis of the duration of initial unemployment are described in two parts. First, the effects of labor-market variables—county unemployment rates and pre-prison employment—on the probability of exiting unemployment (and getting a job) are discussed; second, the effects of the other variables in the models are discussed.

Table 9.2 shows the length of the initial spells of unemployment; these spells are measured in quarters. Spells longer than eight quarters are treated in the analysis as censored.

Table 9.3 shows the parameters for four models of the effects of the labor-market variables and the other, individual-level variables described previously on the duration of initial unemployment. It also reports the marginal effects of each variable, with all other variables eval-

Table 9.2   Spells of Initial Unemployment upon Release from Prison

Number of Quarters	Cumulative Percentage Complete	Survival Probability (Percentage)
1	44.8	73.2
2	76.3	53.3
3	85.8	46.3
4	90.7	42.5
5	94.1	39.9
6	96.2	38.2
7	97.6	37.0
8	98.5	36.0
9	99.2	35.1
10	99.7	34.4
11	99.9	33.9
12	100.0	33.5
Count	25,764	

Source: Author's analysis of ODRC data.

uated at their mean levels. County unemployment rates enter these models as time-varying covariates. Pre-prison employment appears in the models in two different ways—as a count of the number of quarters in which the ex-inmate held at least one job, and as a set of dummy variables that indicate whether a person was employed in a particular quarter. models 1 and 2 show results without county fixed effects, and models 3 and 4 are estimated with county fixed effects.

Effects of Labor-Market Variables

Turning first to the effects of county unemployment rates, models 1 and 2 show a highly significant and negative coefficient (–0.0358 and –0.0427, respectively) on the time-varying county unemployment rate.[16] These findings are consistent with predictions that local labor-market demand would affect post-prison employment, and as county unemployment rates increased the conditional probability of exiting the spell of initial unemployment at release would decrease. Evaluated at the means of all variables, a one-percentage-point increase in county unemployment rates leads to about a half-percentage-point decrease in the probability of exiting the initial spell of unemployment and finding a job.

The difference between these two estimates is that model 2 includes a dummy variable if an offender's release county was one of the six largest counties in Ohio. Including this term slightly increases the effect of county unemployment rates on the probability that an ex-offender

Table 9.3   Parameter Estimates of Discrete Duration Model of the Probability of Exiting the Initial Spell of Unemployment upon Release from Prison

	Model (1)		Model (2)		Model (3)		Model (4)	
Variable	Parameter	Change in exit rate[a]	Parameter	Change in exit rate[a]	Parameter	Change in exit rate[a]	Parameter	Change in exit rate[a]
Intercept	−3.4291***		−3.3596***		−0.2871***		−2.9631***	
Labor market variables								
County unemployment rate	−0.0358***	−0.5%	−0.0427***	−0.6%	−0.1347***	−1.8%	−0.1340***	−1.8%
Number of pre-prison quarters	0.4194***	5.6%	0.4184***	5.6%	0.4186***	5.6%	0.4277***	5.7%
N of pre-prison by time interaction							−0.0060*	−0.1%
Second month in quarter of release	−0.1037***	−1.4%	−0.1052***	−1.4%	−0.1076***	−1.4%	−0.1078	−1.4%
Third month in quarter of release	−0.2988***	−4.0%	−0.2998***	−4.0%	−0.3034***	−4.1%	−0.3036	−4.1%
Big county dummy			−0.0934***	−1.3%				
Prior prison admissions								
Prior incarcerations	0.0243***	0.3%	0.0261***	0.4%	0.0259***	0.3%	0.0263***	0.4%
First-term group	−0.0925*	−1.2%	−0.0846*	−1.1%	−0.0836*	−1.1%	−0.0881*	−1.2%
Form of supervision or release								
Parole supervision	0.4242***	5.7%	0.4255***	5.7%	0.4204***	5.7%	0.4181***	5.6%
PRC supervision	0.1687***	2.3%	0.1657***	2.2%	0.1637***	2.2%	0.1634***	2.2%
Judicial release	0.2275***	3.1%	0.2114***	2.8%	0.2067***	2.8%	0.2060***	2.8%

(Table continues on p. 282)

Table 9.3 *Continued*

Variable	Model (1)		Model (2)		Model (3)		Model (4)	
	Parameter	Change in exit rate[a]	Parameter	Change in exit rate[a]	Parameter	Change in exit rate[a]	Parameter	Change in exit rate[a]
Type and length of sentence served								
TIS sentence	-0.1537***	-2.1%	-0.1496***	-2.0%	-0.1500***	-2.0%	-0.1541***	-2.1%
Time served	0.0217***	0.3%	0.0214***	0.3%	0.0213***	0.3%	0.0214***	0.3%
Time served squared	-0.0004***	0.0%	-0.0004***	0.0%	-0.0004***	0.0%	-0.0004***	0.0%
Education level and prison program variables								
TABE total score	0.0060*	0.1%	0.0054*	0.1%	0.0052*	0.1%	0.0050*	0.1%
Vocation program graduate or certificate	-0.1160*	-1.6%	-0.1204*	-1.6%	-0.1197*	-1.6%	-0.1200*	-1.6%
Vocational work assignments	-0.0327	-0.4%	-0.0325	-0.4%	-0.0344	-0.5%	-0.0316	-0.4%
GED in prison	0.0004	0.0%	0.0020	0.0%	0.0011	0.0%	0.0004	0.0%
Substance abuse program	0.0289	0.4%	0.0261	0.4%	0.0291	0.4%	0.0268	0.4%

	Model 1		Model 2		Model 3		Model 4	
Race and age								
Black	0.0330*	0.4%	0.0657***	0.9%	0.0521*	0.7%	0.0487*	0.7%
Less than or equal to twenty	0.2794***	3.8%	0.2760***	3.7%	0.2796***	3.8%	0.2830***	3.8%
Twenty-one through twenty-five	0.3488***	4.7%	0.3450***	4.6%	0.3480***	4.7%	0.3522***	4.7%
Twenty-six through thirty	0.2677***	3.6%	0.2661***	3.6%	0.2684***	3.6%	0.2689***	3.6%
Thirty-one through thirty-five	0.2779***	3.7%	0.2787***	3.7%	0.2816***	3.8%	0.2833***	3.8%
Thirty-six through forty	0.2337***	3.1%	0.2354***	3.2%	0.2386***	3.2%	0.2457	3.3%
Release year								
Released during 1999	0.0260	0.3%	0.0283*	0.4%	0.0361*	0.5%	0.0293	0.4%
Duration dummies	Yes		Yes		Yes		Yes	
County effects			Yes		Yes		Yes	
Log likelihood	−49456		−49443		−49348		−49302	

Source: Author's analysis of ODRC data.

Note: Each regression also includes four dummy variables for the felony severity level of the offense (that is, felony 1 through felony 4), and ten dummy variables for offense categories (manslaughter, rape, aggravated assault, robbery, other violent, burglary, theft, other property, weapons, and public order or other).

[a]Exit rate change based on mean levels

* = 5%; *** = 0.01%

exits unemployment. This term also shows that the duration of unemployment upon release from prison was slightly lower for offenders released into one of the six largest counties than those released into other counties.

Unmeasured attributes of counties may also be associated with ex-offender employment prospects. To account for these, models 3 and 4 introduce county-fixed effects. When unmeasured aspects of counties are taken into account, the magnitude of the effects of county unemployment rates increase in absolute value. For example, in models 3 and 4, the estimated coefficients on the county unemployment rate are −0.1347 and −0.1340, respectively. By comparison, the estimated coefficient on the county unemployment rates in model 1 was −0.0358. In the county-fixed-effects models, the estimated marginal effects of a one-percentage-point increase in the county unemployment rate on the probability of exiting the initial spell of unemployment is close to 2 percent, which is almost four times the magnitude of its estimated marginal effect in model 1.[17]

This suggests that some unobserved component within counties is correlated with county unemployment, and introducing the county dummies picks up this unobserved component. Ohio counties may differ on unobserved characteristics that could be correlated with unemployment rate. One possible unobservable is the set of federal programs that are associated with county unemployment rates. As indicated previously, the LAUS data are used to determine allocations for selected federal support programs, such as determining labor-surplus areas, public works programs, and emergency assistance. The federal allocations are based on unemployment rates in local areas relative to national unemployment rates. Some Ohio cities, such as Cleveland, Akron, and Cincinnati, often are identified as labor-surplus areas by the Department of Labor rules, and this designation may provide employers in the counties that contain these cities with preferences in bidding on federal procurement contracts. Though designation as a surplus labor-area may change over time, the benefits from contracts obtained could represent an unmeasured difference among counties that could affect ex-offender employment prospects. In addition, Ohio counties may also differ in the scope of programs that they implement to assist ex-offenders. Such county-level programs could also be correlated with county unemployment rates, for tax revenues fall off when unemployment rates rise, and declines in county revenues could lead to reductions in the size or scope of programs.

Although the focus of this paper is primarily on local labor-market effects, all four specifications include estimates of the effects of pre-prison employment experiences on the probability of exiting unemployment, and in all four models, the estimate effects are larger than

0.4. In addition, introducing other, primarily criminal-justice-related co-variates (for instance, supervision type, prior commitments, prison program participation, and so forth) does not change the estimated effects of pre-prison employment. Regressions that estimated the effects only of pre-prison employment and county unemployment rates on exit probabilities also generated estimated effects of pre-prison employment of greater than 0.4.[18] In addition, adding a term that interacts the number of pre-prison quarters of employment with time (post-prison quarter) shows that the effects of pre-prison employment diminish only very slightly over time.

The data used in this study do not contain other measures of individual characteristics that may be correlated with both pre- and post-prison employment. For example, if there is a spatial mismatch between the locations of residences of ex-offenders and the locations of jobs, then the estimated effects of pre-prison employment on post-prison employment could be an artifact of lack of available data. Nevertheless, including measures of pre-prison employment in the regressions does not affect estimates of the effects of county unemployment rates, which is the main focus of this paper.

The effects of county unemployment rates on post-prison employment are nonlinear. Figure 9.6 shows the simulated survivor curves for various levels of county unemployment. The survivor curves represent the simulated percentages of offenders who survive in their initial spell of unemployment. The simulations are based on the estimated coefficients in model 3 and the means of the variables. The figure shows the estimated percentages surviving in the initial spell of unemployment for durations of up to two, four, six, and eight quarters for various levels of county unemployment rates.

The mean unemployment rate across counties and periods was slightly more than 4 percent, so in figure 9.6, the line representing the 4 percent county unemployment rate provides basis for comparison with the other levels. An increase in county unemployment rates from 4 to 8 percent would increase the four-quarter percentage surviving from 42 to 49 percent, and it would increase the eight-quarter percentage surviving from 36 to 42 percent.

In sum, these regressions show that local labor-market conditions affect the timing of ex-prisoners' efforts to find a first job upon release from prison. A one-percentage-point change in county unemployment rates, from about 4 percent to 5 percent (with all other variables evaluated at their mean levels) results in about a two-percentage-point change in the baseline probability of exiting the initial spell of unemployment (where the baseline probability was 16 percent). These county-level unemployment effects emerge most strongly when controls (county dummies) for the structural differences between counties

Figure 9.6   Simulated Survivor Functions: Percentage Who Did Not Find a Job, by Quarter and County Unemployment Rate

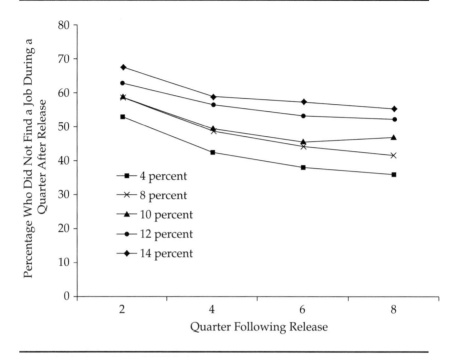

Source: Author's analysis of ODRC data.

in the level of unemployment are introduced. These findings suggest that efforts designed to improve local labor-market demand for labor and efforts to attach potential prisoners to labor markets prior to their incarceration can have beneficial longer-run outcomes for their post-release employment experiences.

Effects of Sentencing and Corrections' Policy Variables and Individual Offender Attributes

The parameter estimates for the other variables included in the models (except for felony severity level and type of offense) are shown in table 9.3. First, across these three models the estimated effects of the other variables do not change when the labor-market variables are introduced into the models in different ways; nor do the effects of the other variables change when the county fixed effects are estimated. These results are not too surprising, given that the other variables generally measure the attributes of individual offenders that offenders brought with them as they entered prison, or represent attributes that were assigned to offenders in prison. For example, prior incarcerations and type of offense are attributes that offenders brought with them upon entry; type of supervision into which offenders were released represent variables that were assigned to them, as are the types of prison programs in which they were involved. None of these variables are necessarily expected to correlate with the time paths of county unemployment rates within counties; hence, it comes as no surprise that their estimated values do not change across specifications.

Interest here centers on prison policy variables that can affect post-prison employment, such as the form of release and type of supervision variables, the type and length of sentence, and the education and prison program participation variables, and the type of offense. The form of supervision and type of release variables all are significant and positive, indicating that supervised offenders have higher probabilities of exiting the initial spell of unemployment more quickly than unsupervised offenders. In Ohio, supervised offenders generally fall into two categories, pre–truth-in-sentencing (TIS)prisoners who were released onto parole for offenses committed prior to July 1996, and post-TIS prisoners who committed less serious felonies. Unsupervised TIS offenders consist largely of drug offenders, and drug offenders are generally younger than other offenders. Although not required, a condition of post-prison supervision may be to get a job, or at least to look earnestly for one (La Vigne and Thompson 2003).

The typical length of supervision, regardless of the form of supervision, is at least three years. Hence, all of the ex-prisoners were observed during periods while they were supervised. The observed changes in the hazard rates of exiting the initial spell of unemployment therefore are not due to the end of supervision. Rather, supervision appears to affect only the levels of the hazards of exiting unemployment, and not the underlying shape.

Of all released ex-inmates, parolees have the highest probability of exiting unemployment, followed by offenders who have obtain judicial release and TIS offenders who were released into post-release control. For parolees, the marginal effect is five to six percentage points; for offenders released judicially or into PRC, the marginal effect is between two and three percentage points. It was expected that offenders released judicially might have the highest probability of exiting unemployment, given that these offenders must petition the court for their release, but in fact, despite the differences among supervision types, in general offenders released into some form of post-prison supervision had better initial employment outcomes than unsupervised offenders. These differences may arise from either side of the supervision process: parole officers may be able to help offenders find jobs, or offenders may be more motivated to quickly find a job if they are under supervision.

Offense severity and criminal history variables have differing effects on the probability of exiting the initial spell of unemployment. Prior incarcerations increase this probability, whereas belonging to the first-term group lowers it. This may be due to the fact that offenders in the first-term group are less likely to be supervised than offenders with prior admissions, and the effects of supervision may outweigh the effects of membership in a prior prison category.

The type and length of sentence are correlated with the time to first job. Offenders are classified into TIS and pre-TIS sentences, and the length of stay is measured. New law offenders sentenced under Ohio's TIS laws are less likely to exit the initial spell of unemployment than are those sentenced under the old law.

Holzer, Raphael, and Stoll (2003; chapter 4, this volume) suggest that employers prefer drug offenders over violent and property offenders. The offense-type variables from the employer surveys provide mixed support for this conclusion. Serious violent offenders, such as rapists, are less likely to exit the initial spell of unemployment than are drug offenders (the excluded category of offense types), but offenders convicted of assault and robbery are more likely than drug offenders to exit initial unemployment. However, in this Ohio sample, offense type correlates with supervision status, as drug offenders are less likely to be supervised than are ex-prisoners who were convicted of robbery and aggravated assault.[19] In addition, ex-prisoners who were convicted of robbery and aggravated assault were also more likely to be released on parole than were drug and other offenders, and parole supervision had the largest positive effect on the probability of exiting the initial spell of unemployment.

Conversely, burglars also have higher initial employment probabilities than drug offenders. For the other offense types, there are no statistically significant differences in the time to finding a first job upon release from prison.

Prison education and vocational training programs have been viewed as important mechanisms for improving the skills of prisoners and for connecting ex-prisoners to labor markets, so the effects of prison program variables on post-prison employment outcomes are of interest. In these Ohio data, the effects of participation in prison programs are generally null, or in the case of obtaining a certificate for completing the vocational training program, perverse. Included among the education variables are the TABE scores. These are observed shortly after offenders arrive in prison, so they can be considered as measures of pre-prison human capital. Among the education and prison program variables, only the TABE scores have significant and correctly signed effects on the probability of exiting unemployment. Although these effects are small, they suggest that offenders with higher levels of education do better at finding jobs after prison than those with lower levels of education.

Conversely, participation in vocation work assignments, obtaining a GED in prison, and participation in substance abuse programs do not affect the post-prison probability of exiting unemployment.[20] In addition, the estimate on the variable that indicates whether an offender completed the ODRC vocational training program and obtained a certificate for completing the program is negative and significant, indicating that completing the vocational training program is associated with decreases in the probability of obtaining a job.

In a separate analysis of the Ohio data, William J. Sabol (2007) explored these perverse effects of completing the ODRC vocational training program in more detail. Using propensity scoring methods, he matched offenders on their propensity to complete the vocational training program, given the array of covariates shown in this paper, and he compared post-prison employment outcomes for offenders who actually completed the program with those who did not complete it but had similar propensities to complete the ODRC vocational training program. The results from that propensity score analysis are consistent with the estimated coefficients on the vocational training program reported here, in that offenders who did not participate in the vocational training program generally had more favorable post-prison employment outcomes than comparable offenders who completed the training program.

The negative effects of completing the vocation program on employment outcomes may be explained by different factors. There may be a "spatial mismatch" between the occupations and trades in which offenders are trained and the demand for these trades in the local labor markets into which offenders are released. Or, in a relatively heavily unionized state such as Ohio, ex-offenders who were trained to finish drywall or do other construction work may be forced to compete with skilled unionized workers who have the same skill set. Furthermore, for some trades there may be legal barriers to entry. For example, offenders trained in barbering and cosmetology may require licenses to practice, but it is not clear that they would be able to readily obtain a license, given their criminal conviction.

Another reason is that the vocational training program may be designed primarily to serve internal, correctional labor markets, rather than external markets, and consequently, the timing of the completion of the program is not coordinated with the timing of an offender's release from prison. Offenders who obtained the vocation certificate served an average of thirty months from the date they graduated until they were released from prison. This two-and-a-half-year post-vocational certification period in prison may be viewed by employers as more of a detriment to hiring than the certificate is a plus. Finally, the negative effects on the vocational training certificate could also be explained by offender choice. Offenders who obtain certificates may view themselves as specialists, and consequently, they may look only for jobs related to their training. Such a search strategy could reduce their overall chances of finding a job.

The perverse effects of the vocational training program variable run counter to other research. For example, the literature contains some strong evidence from nonexperimental studies that suggest that prison programs improve post-prison employment outcomes (Saylor and Gaes 1997). More generally, meta-analyses of adult correctional programs suggest that the programs may work modestly, though they are promising, but also that the research designs are flawed in ways that create uncertainty about the findings (Wilson 2001). One possible reason for the failure to find positive effects for the vocational training program variable here is that in this study, the available data permitted measuring this variable only as a binary indicator of having completed the certificate. Alternative measures (such as number of attempts to complete, number of hours in the program) could provide better measures of the training actually received, and these measures could produce other results.

Finally, Tyler and Kling's (chapter 8, this volume) analysis of the effects of obtaining a GED in prison on post-prison employment and earnings produces findings that are consistent with the null findings on the prison GED in this analysis. Tyler and Kling compare those who obtained the GED in prison with other, more similar, groups, such as those who left prison without a GED. Using sufficient control variables to adequately control for pre-existing differences between the GED earners and comparable offenders, they are able to show that the post-prison employment and earnings of the GED earners are indistinguishable from those who left prison without a GED. This finding is consistent with the null finding on the GED variable in the Ohio sample.

Summing Up

This analysis of the duration of the initial spell of unemployment suggests that local labor-market conditions can affect post-prison employment opportunities for ex-prisoners and can affect them in the expected direction: when labor markets are tight, employers may dip into the ex-prisoner pool to meet their demands for labor and hire ex-prisoners. The marginal effects of a one-percentage-point change in local unemployment rates on the duration of the initial spell of unemployment experienced by ex-prisoners is to decrease it by two percentage points around a base exit rate of 16 percent. This finding also suggests that policies that aim to increase the aggregate demand for labor have the additional benefit of increasing the demand for ex-prison labor. Hence, if policy debates revolve around the merits of specialized programs for ex-prisoners, as opposed to programs for other deserving groups, the finding that increasing the demand for labor also increases the demand for ex-prisoner labor gives policymakers one option that avoids those potentially contentious debates.

A second finding of this analysis is that the duration of the initial spell of post-prison unemployment is related to pre-prison employment experiences of offenders. Offenders with even one quarter of pre-prison employment find jobs much more quickly than those with no pre-prison employment experiences, and each additional quarter of pre-prison employment further increases the chances that an ex-prisoner will quickly find a job upon release. Although pre-prison employment may be representing several unmeasured individual characteristics, it, along with the results from the TABE score variable, also indicate that the level of human capital that prisoners bring with them when they enter prison may be more important than what they learn while in prison (as indicated by the results on the GED variable; see Tyler and Kling, chapter 8, this volume).

Among prison and corrections practices, only post-prison supervision has positive effects on the duration of the initial spell of post-prison unemployment. Supervising offenders lessens the duration of the initial spell of unemployment, which may be due to the quality of the supervision, the work requirements, or other factors. Otherwise, prison programs had no effects or had perverse effects on the duration of unemployment. With respect to the perverse effects of the vocational training program, more work needs to be done to determine whether the hypotheses regarding these effects are valid, and if they are, what kind of programming should be undertaken to attempt to address them.

Post-Prison Quarterly Employment Results

The final set of analyses was direct to the issue of post-prison quarterly employment during the first two years following release from prison. Here, the dependent variable is dichotomous (whether the ex-offender is employed in a specific quarter or not). Employment experiences of all ex-prisoners were tracked for eight quarters; those returning to prison during this period were counted as unemployed beginning with the quarter of their return to prison.

Table 9.4 shows the characteristics of the sample of male offenders whose post-prison employment outcomes were analyzed. Across the

Table 9.4   Descriptive Statistics for Sample Used in Post-Prison Employment Analysis

Variable	Mean	Standard Deviation
Post-prison employment probability	0.359	0.480
Labor market variables		
County unemployment rate (quarterly)	4.381	1.297
Number of quarters employed pre-prison	1.601	1.683
Offense severity level		
Felony one	0.041	0.198
Felony two	0.129	0.335
Felony three	0.175	0.380
Felony four	0.306	0.461
Offense type		
Homicide	0.005	0.069
Rape	0.027	0.162
Aggravated assault	0.120	0.325
Robbery	0.079	0.269
Other violent	0.024	0.154
Burglary	0.130	0.336
Theft	0.080	0.272
Other property	0.093	0.291
Weapons	0.031	0.173
Public order or other	0.095	0.293
Prior prison		
Prior incarcerations	0.883	1.346
First-term group	0.949	0.219
Type and length of sentence		
TIS sentence	0.734	0.442
Time served	22.672	21.590
Release type and form of supervision		
Judicial release	0.100	0.299
Parole	0.170	0.375
Education and program participation		
Substance abuse program	0.069	0.254
Vocational program certificate	0.028	0.164
GED in prison	0.073	0.260
TABE total test score	7.088	3.428
Race and age at release		
Black	0.544	0.498
Twenty and under	0.083	0.277
Twenty-one to twenty-five	0.249	0.432
Twenty-six to thirty	0.180	0.384

Table 9.4   *Continued*

Variable	Mean	Standard Deviation
Thirty-one to thirty-five	0.154	0.361
Thirty-six to forty	0.146	0.353
Release year		
Released during 1999	0.472	0.499
Number of observations	34,081	

Source: Author's analysis of ODRC data.

eight quarters their average employment probability was about 36 percent. Their average characteristics were otherwise similar to the means and proportions in table 9.2, with some minor differences that were due to the differences in the ways that the samples were constructed.

Table 9.5 shows the parameter estimates for three models of the effect of county unemployment rates on post-prison employment. As was done in the analysis of the duration of unemployment, county unemployment rates are permitted to vary across quarters. Except for the lagged value of post-prison employment, all other variables are as described previously. Table 9.5 also shows the parameter estimates, significance levels, and estimated marginal effects of variables, with other variables evaluated at their mean levels. Models 1 and 2 in table 9.5 assess effects for all released prisons, but model 2 includes a lagged value (by one quarter) of post-prison employment. Model 3 assesses effects for only the sample of offenders who had at least one pre-prison quarter of employment. All models are estimated with county-level fixed effects.

As occurred in the results of the analysis of the spells of initial unemployment, county unemployment rates are inversely associated with the probability of post-prison employment. The results are fairly robust across the three specifications in table 9.5, as the differences in the magnitudes of the estimated coefficients on the county unemployment rates are small, and the marginal effect of a 1 percent increase in county unemployment rates ranges from five percentage points, in model 1, to six percentage points, in model 3.

These estimated marginal effects of county unemployment rates on post-prison employment probabilities are larger than those reported by Raphael and Weiman (chapter 10, this volume). They used an estimate from Holzer and Paul Offner (2002) that showed that a 1 percent increase in the local area unemployment rate decreases the probability that less-educated black males are employed by 2.7 percent. While the estimates for the Ohio sample are around the same order of magnitude

Table 9.5   Parameter Estimates of the Probability of Post-Prison Employment of Male Offenders[a]

Variable	Model 2 All Releases		Model 3 Lagged Employment		Model 4 Pre-Prison Employed	
	Parameter	Marginal Effect on Employment Probability	Parameter	Marginal Effect on Employment Probability	Parameter	Marginal Effect on Employment Probability
Intercept	-0.0732***		-0.7168***		-0.3496***	
Quarterly county unemployment rate	-0.2156***	-5.0%	-0.2240***	-5.2%	-0.2378***	-5.9%
Lagged post-prison employment			0.1024***	2.4%	0.0371**	0.9%
Number of pre-prison quarters employed	0.4645***	10.8%	0.4732***	11.1%	0.3818***	9.5%
Felony one	0.1823**	4.2%	0.1915**	4.5%	0.3023*	7.6%
Felony two	0.1797**	4.2%	0.2159**	5.1%	0.2513*	6.3%
Felony three	0.0680*	1.6%	0.0833*	2.0%	0.1156*	2.9%
Felony four	0.0012	0.0%	0.0133	0.3%	0.0353*	0.9%
Homicide	0.2242*	5.2%	0.2523*	5.9%	0.3223*	8.1%
Rape	-0.1580**	-3.7%	-0.1431**	-3.4%	-0.0509	-1.3%
Aggravated assault	0.1718**	4.0%	0.1686**	4.0%	0.2223*	5.6%
Robbery	0.1047*	2.4%	0.0822*	1.9%	0.0762	1.9%
Other violent	0.0568	1.3%	0.0623	1.5%	0.0626	1.6%
Burglary	0.0671	1.6%	0.0571	1.3%	0.0461	1.2%
Theft	0.0106	0.2%	0.0040	0.1%	-0.0259	-0.6%
Other property	-0.0548	-1.3%	-0.0768	-1.8%	-0.0516	-1.3%
Weapons	-0.1114*	-2.6%	-0.1122*	-2.6%	-0.1116	-2.8%
Public order or other	-0.0487	1.1%	0.0431	1.0%	0.0892**	2.2%

	(1)		(2)		(3)	
Prior incarcerations	−0.0434*	−1.0%	−0.0570*	−1.3%	−0.0920**	−2.3%
First-term group	0.2164*	5.0%	−0.2648*	6.2%	0.4319**	2.8%
TIS sentence	−0.1323*	−3.1%	−0.1355*	−3.2%	0.1101*	−2.8%
Time served	−0.0152**	0.4%	−0.0130**	0.3%	−0.0019	0.0%
Time served squared	−0.0003**	0.0%	−0.0002**	0.0%	0.0001	0.0%
Judicial release	0.1397***	3.2%	0.1598***	3.7%	0.1500**	3.7%
Parole	0.2469***	5.7%	0.2074***	4.9%	0.0978*	2.4%
Substance abuse program	0.0013	0.0%	0.0020	0.0%	−0.0155	−0.4%
Vocational program certificate	−0.1111*	−2.6%	−0.1113*	−2.6%	−0.0601	1.5%
GED in prison	−0.0086	−0.2%	−0.0113	0.3%	−0.0158	−0.4%
TABE total test score	0.0049**	0.1%	0.0056**	0.1%	0.0031	0.1%
Black	0.0326*	0.8%	0.0388*	0.9%	0.0543**	1.4%
Less than twenty at release	−0.0846	2.0%	0.1194	2.8%	0.2607*	6.5%
Twenty-one through twenty-five	0.0585	1.4%	0.0341	0.8%	−0.0833	−2.1%
Twenty-six through thirty	0.0851	2.0%	0.0798	1.9%	−0.0321	−0.8%
Thirty-one through thirty-five	0.1301*	3.0%	0.1189*	2.8%	−0.0059	−0.1%
Thirty-six through forty	0.1582**	3.7%	0.1429**	3.3%	0.0687	1.7%
Released during 1999	0.1848**	4.3%	0.2239**	5.2%	0.3338	8.3%
Time (quarterly) dummies	Yes		Yes		Yes	
County dummies	Yes		Yes		Yes	
Number of observations	262,674		229,391		135,820	
Log likelihood	−150335		−131159		−85639	
Mean probability of employment	36.7%		37.5%		49.9%	

Source: Author's analysis of ODRC data.

[a]Male offenders released during 1999 and 2000 and tracked for eight post-release quarters. Within subject (offender) fixed effects in all models; robust standard errors.

* = 5%; ** = 1%; *** = 0.01%

as the Holzer and Offner estimates, the differences in samples and methods may account for the differences in magnitudes. Alternatively, the men in the Ohio ex-prisoner sample may generally be more employable than less-educated black men.

Also, as occurred in the analysis of the spells of unemployment, the effects of pre-prison employment on the probability of post-prison employment are larger than the effects of county unemployment rates. In models 1 and 2, the marginal effect of an additional quarter of pre-prison employment is to increase the probability of post-prison employment by about 11 percent.

Lagged post-prison employment (model 2) also increases the probability of employment in the current quarter, indicating that offenders who were employed in a prior quarter are more likely to be employed in a current quarter than offenders who were not employed in a prior quarter. However, the marginal effects of lagged post-prison employment are about four-fifths those of pre-prison employment.

In models 1 and 2, the effects of type of crime, length of stay, and other individual attributes of offenders are generally similar to those found in the analysis of the duration of the initial spells of unemployment. Post-prison supervision increases the probability of post-prison employment. In models 1 and 2—without and with lagged post-prison employment—the marginal effect of these two types of supervision ranges from three to five percentage points. Also as before, obtaining the vocational training program certificate reduces the probability of post-prison employment. Obtaining the prison GED has no effect. Black offenders have slightly higher probabilities of being employed post-prison than do white offenders, but this result obtains only when controls for pre-prison employment are included in the models.

Finally, model 3 assesses the post-prison employment experiences of the sample of offenders who had at least one pre-prison quarter of employment. For these offenders, the effects of county unemployment mirror its effects for the entire sample of offenders. The persistence of the effect of county unemployment rates between models 1 and 2 suggests that demand for ex-prison labor is not limited only to offenders with some pre-prison employment. Otherwise, in model 3 the effects of pre-prison employment are smaller than in model 2, but this arises from the omission of the comparison with offenders having no pre-prison employment. As occurred in models 1 and 2, black offenders with pre-prison employment are more likely to be employed post-prison than white offenders with some pre-prison employment. But in the model 3 sample (limited to those with at least one pre-prison employment quarter in the year prior to admission), the racial differences are larger than appear among the sample of all released prisoners.

Summary and Conclusions

Across the two post-prison employment outcome variables, several patterns of relationships emerged. First, local labor-market conditions, as measured by county unemployment rates, seem to matter by affecting the chances that ex-prisoners find jobs. In the analysis of the initial spell of unemployment, the marginal effect of county unemployment rates on the probability of exiting the initial spell was two percentage points; in the analysis of quarterly employment, the marginal effect reached six percentage points. County unemployment rates equally affected the post-prison employment probabilities for offenders with no pre-prison employment and those with some pre-prison employment. Thus, in these Ohio data at least, the speculation that tight labor markets can improve employment opportunities for ex-prisoners finds some support.

These findings are tentative, however. Despite the support for the central thesis—that local unemployment rates matter—the unemployment rates observed during much of this period were relatively low. This suggests that the results that were obtained may have come primarily from increases in unemployment leading to job loss, rather than the other way around. If the Ohio prisoners released during 1999 and 2000 benefited from the relatively tight labor-market conditions at the time, which have not been observed since 2000, then this period may represent the maximum gains for ex-prisoner employment that can be obtained from decreases in unemployment. This limitation can be studied by collecting data on post-prison employment experiences for longer periods of time. Once the original investment is made in linking corrections data to UI wage data, the marginal costs of obtaining additional years of data are small.

Along these same lines, the use of UI wage data by corrections departments to track employment outcomes seems to be a plausible and relatively inexpensive method for obtaining outcome data on ex-prisoners. States that collect prisoners' social security numbers, such as Ohio, are in the position to develop relationships with their UI claims departments, and they can enter into computer record matching agreements that permit them to link offender records to the UI wage records. Such arrangements to obtain data can lead to the development of inexpensive, ongoing systems to monitor post-prison outcomes. They also can contribute to the development of research databases. To the extent that several states develop these systems, the various research databases can allow for comparative analyses of post-prison employment outcomes.

The speculations about post-prison outcomes also highlight one limitation of this analysis: its reliance only on unemployment rates to measure local labor-market conditions. Future research should expand upon the measure of local labor-market conditions to include factors such as the size of the labor force, the sectoral composition, new job growth, wages, and other measures of the supply of and demand for labor. These analyses might give more clues as to whether and how ex-prisoners can be absorbed when labor markets are not as tight as they were throughout much of this period. Analyses of sectoral demand for labor, for example, can be accomplished by using the industry information in the UI wage records.

A second finding is that the accumulation of pre-prison human capital—as indicated by pre-prison employment—seems to facilitate post-prison employment. Ex-prisoners with as little as one-quarter of employment in the year prior to admission into prison exited their initial post-prison unemployment more quickly than offenders with no pre-prison employment during the year prior to admission, and their post-prison employment probabilities were as much as 10 percent higher than those with no pre-prison employment.

Third, the poor performance of prison programs in this analysis is perplexing and discouraging and merits additional work to better measure program outcomes. The negative outcomes for the vocation certificate recipients can be understood in terms of their role in the prison, the possibility of a spatial mismatch between the trades in which they are trained and local demands for these skills, and the discounting of prison labor by employers. To better understand the program participation outcomes, both better measures of program participation and different methods to isolate causal mechanisms are required. If the results found here were to hold after additional analyses, they would suggest that prison programming does little to enhance the capacity of offenders to compete in local labor markets unless these offenders already possess labor-market skills and experiences. For example, if prison vocation programs focus only on offenders who have prior work experiences, they not only "cream off" the offenders who are most likely to succeed but also fail to serve the majority of offenders who have little to no pre-prison labor-market experience.

The combination of the findings about pre-prison employment and education experiences and the absence of findings of beneficial effects of prison program participation also suggest more generally that the current focus on prisoner reentry efforts may be somewhat misplaced, if it focuses too intently on what happens in prison to prepare offenders for release. Without discounting the importance of the need to prepare offenders for reentry, these analyses show that pre-prison work experience and education are much more important in determining post-prison outcomes than what goes on in prison to prepare offenders for release. This perspective also suggests that broader labor-market policies can have beneficial effects, both for the general labor force and for ex-prisoners.

Finally, post-prison supervision also turns out to be positively related to post-prison employment. Whether this arises from offenders' attempting to comply with conditions of supervision or from parole officers' efforts to locate jobs and help in the reintegration effort is not known. Even though states have turned away from using parole-release decisions, there is still relatively widespread use of different forms of post-prison supervision. The Ohio (and Washington State) cases suggest that continuing to use some form of post-prison supervision can be beneficial in improving post-prison employment. The downside to post-prison supervision is exemplified by California, where more than two-thirds of prison admissions are of persons who have returned to prison due to technical violations of conditions of supervision. While the California case does refute the view that supervision can be beneficial, it suggests that the type and character of supervision may be important. In future research, administrative data such as that used in this paper needs to be supplemented with additional data on post-prison supervision experiences in order to better understand how supervision contributes to post-prison employment and recidivism outcomes.

The views expressed are those of the author and do not reflect the views of the Bureau of Justice Statistics or the U.S. Department of Justice. Partial support for this research was provided by the Russell Sage Foundation (grant number 85-01-06). The support of the Ohio Department of Rehabilitation and Correction and the Ohio Department of Jobs and Family Services in providing the data for this project is gratefully acknowledged. In particular, the efforts of Steve Van Dine and Brian Martin in organizing the Ohio Department of Rehabilitation effort and preparing the data are acknowledged.

Notes

1. The basic element of the discrete duration model is the hazard rate, or transition probability, $P(t, X)$, which captures the probability of leaving a state in the tth period, given continuous participation in that state for the last t-1 periods and a group of covariates, X. The hazard rate is modeled as a logit probability:

$$P(t, X) = [\exp(\alpha_t + \beta X)] / \{1 + [\exp(\alpha_t + \beta' X)]\}$$

This specification of exits from spells has been used in the literature on the duration of welfare spells (Bane and Ellwood 1983; Blank and Ruggles 1996; Hoynes 2000), and it is attractive because it allows for time varying covariates and a flexible form for the effects of time in the spell on exits. The αt are dummy variables for the length of spell to date, and they account, nonparametrically, for the basic duration properties of the model. These duration effects create a baseline hazard, and the covariates (X) scale the exit probabilities up or down uniformly.

2. Note that the sample analyzed excludes female offenders because program participation data were not available for them.

3. The Social Security numbers were used only for linking purposes and in accordance with Internal Review Board protocols maintained at Case Western Reserve University, where this research was conducted. The Social Security numbers were eliminated from analysis files after the ODRC and ODJFS data were linked.

4. Subsequently, missing data on prison program participation and other key variables reduced the analysis sample size to about 35,000 offenders.

5. UI wage data do not provide information on occupations.

6. In addition, offenders who returned to prison prior to finding a job are removed from the set of offenders at risk of exiting unemployment and finding a job.

7. As described by Kling (2002), who used UI wage data to examine the effect of sentence length on earnings, there are several reasons why employment rates do not drop to zero after admission into prison. First, with the UI data, we have only quarters of employment; it is therefore likely that some offenders entered or were released from prison during the same quarter that their UI wage data were recorded. Second, there may be some individuals who are working for private employers while in prison and their earnings are recorded in the state's UI data. Third, earnings may be reported by individuals who use an offender's Social Security number, inadvertently or fraudulently, or because an offender either fraudulently or inadvertently used another persons Social Security number.

8. The denominator in this calculation shown by the solid line still overestimates the number at risk, as the ODRC data provided for this project did not record all offenders returned for new crimes. In addition, offenders who moved out of state should be excluded, but then again, they also could be employed in their new state of residence.

9. For a description of the methodology used by ODJFS to calculate the local area unemployment statistics, see: http://198.234.34.242/LAUS/LAUS-Concepts.htm.

10. Most of the homicides among the offenders in the employment sample (admitted and released between 1994 and 2000) were manslaughter or other less-serious homicides, as opposed to first-degree murder.

11. In the regressions that follow, drug offenses are the excluded classes of offenses.

12. A comparison of the felony levels of entering cohorts of prisoners gives a very different distribution of offense-severity levels, particularly when one looks at entering cohorts arriving after the 1996 change in Ohio sentencing law (discussed in the next section of the chapter text).

13. The idea for this measure came from Raphael and Weiman (2002).

14. For more on Ohio's law changes and supervision, see La Vigne and Thompson (2003).

15. The conditions of supervision are similar across forms of release. The Adult Parole Authority supervises ex-prisoners. According to La Vigne and Thompson (2003), ex-prisoners are supervised at different levels—Intensive, Basic High, Basic Medium, Basic Low, and Monitoring Time. The different levels of supervision have different reporting requirements and may require additional requirements. Additionally, supervised offenders with special conditions may be required to take drug tests. The ODRC data provided for this analysis do not contain information about the level of detail of supervision.

16. Not shown, but available upon request from the author, are results using the county unemployment rate at the time of release from prison as a fixed covariate. The results from these regressions show that when county unemployment is introduced as fixed at the time of release, its effects on the probability of exiting unemployment at release are smaller (in absolute value) than the effects of county unemployment as a time-varying covariate.

17. All of the models in table 9.3 were estimated with county unemployment rates entering the model as time-varying covariates. Alternative models were estimated with the county unemployment rate at the time of release from prison held constant. This latter approach is consistent with the approach taken by Raphael and Weiman (2002) in their efforts to estimate the effects of county unemployment on recidivism. In general, the size of the effects of the county unemployment rates fixed at the time of release from prison on the probability of exiting the initial spell of unemployment are smaller than the effects reported in table 9.3. These results are not shown here but they are available from the author.

18. These results are not shown here but are available from the author.

19. Regressions in which interactions between supervision status and the degree of the felony, prior incarcerations, and first-term group are added to the model support this contention. In general, the interaction between these offense and offender history statuses and supervision are positive and generally significant. These are available from the author.

20. The author's preliminary analysis of the relationship between prison program participation and return to prison for technical violations of conditions of supervision suggest that participation in substance abuse programs decreases the probability of returning to prison. Thus, though substance abuse program participation does not affect post-prison employment in the models in table 9.3, it may have other beneficial effects.

References

Bane, Mary Jo, and David Ellwood. 1983. "The Dynamics of Dependence: The Routes to Self Sufficiency." Washington: U.S. Department of Health and Human Services, Office of the Assistant Secretary for Planning and Evaluation.

Bania, Neil, Claudia Coulton, and Laura Leete. 2000. "Welfare Reform and Access to Job Opportunities in the Cleveland Metropolitan Area." Working paper. Case Western Reserve University, Center on Urban Poverty and Social Change.

Beck, Allen J., and Bernard E. Shipley. 1989. "Recidivism of Prisoners Released in 1983." Special report, no. NCJ 116261. Washington: U.S. Department of Justice, Bureau of Justice Statistics.

Blank, Rebecca, and Patricia Ruggles. 1996. "When Do Women Use AFDC and

Food Stamps? The Dynamics of Eligibility Versus Participation." *Journal of Human Resources* 31: 57–89.

Fitzgerald, John M. 1995. "Local Labor Markets and Local Area Effects on Welfare Duration." *Journal of Policy Analysis and Management* 14(1): 43–67.

Freeman, Richard. 2003. "Can We Close the Revolving Door? Recidivism vs. Employment of Ex-Offenders in the U.S." Paper presented at the Urban Institute Reentry Roundtable, Employment Dimensions of Reentry: Understanding the Nexus between Prisoner Reentry and Work. New York University Law School (May 19–20).

Gould, Eric D., Bruce A. Weinberg, and David B. Mustard. 2000. "Crime Rates and Local Labor Market Opportunities in the United States: 1977–1997." *Review of Economics and Statistics* 84(1): 45–61.

Grogger, Jeffrey. 1995. "The Effects of Arrests on the Employment and Earnings of Young Men." *Quarterly Journal of Economics* V 110: 51–71.

———. 1998. "Market Wages and Youth Crime." *Journal of Labor Economics* 16(4): 756–91.

Harlow, Caroline Wolf. 2003. "Education and Correctional Populations." Special report, no. NCJ 195670. Washington: U.S. Department of Justice, Bureau of Justice Statistics.

Holzer, Harry, and Paul Offner. 2002. "Employment Trends Among Less-Skilled Young Men." Unpublished manuscript. Georgetown University. Washington D.C.

Holzer, Harry, Steven Raphael, and Michael Stoll. 2003. "Employment Barriers Facing Ex-Offenders." Paper presented at the Urban Institute Reentry Roundtable, Employment Dimensions of Reentry: Understanding the Nexus between Prisoner Reentry and Work. New York University Law School (May 19–20).

———. 2004. "Will Employers Hire Ex-Offenders? Employer Preferences, Background Checks and Their Determinants." In *The Impact of Incarceration on Families and Communities*, edited by Mary Pattillo, David Weiman, and Bruce Western. New York: Russell Sage Foundation.

Hosmer, David W., Jr., and Stanley Lemeshow. 1989. *Applied Logistic Regression.* New York: Wiley.

Hoynes, Hilary Williamson. 2000. "Local Labor Markets and Welfare Spells: Do Demand Conditions Matter?" *Review of Economics and Statistics* 82(3): 351–68.

Kling, Jeffrey R. 2002. "The Effect of Prison Sentence Length on the Subsequent Employment and Earnings of Criminal Defendants." Unpublished manuscript. Princeton University.

Kornfeld, Robert, and Howard S. Bloom. 1999. "Measuring Program Impacts on Earnings and Employment: Do Unemployment Insurance Wage Reports from Employers Agree with Surveys of Individuals?" *Journal of Labor Economics* 17(1): 168–97.

Langan, Patrick A., and David J. Levin. 2002. "Recidivism of Prisoners Released in 1994." Special report, no. NCJ 193427. Washington: U.S. Department of Justice, Bureau of Justice Statistics.

La Vigne, Nancy, and Gillian L. Thompson. 2003. "A Portrait of Reentry in Ohio." Research Report. November. Washington D.C.: The Urban Institute

Nagin, Daniel, and Joel Waldfogel. 1998. "The Effect of Conviction on Income Through the Life Cycle." *International Review of Law and Economics* 18(1): 25–40.

Norton, Lee. 1998. *1996 Intake Study: Final Report*. Columbus: Ohio Department of Rehabilitation and Correction.

Pastore, Ann L., and Kathleen Maguire. 2000. *Sourcebook of Criminal Justice Statistics*. Available at http://www.albany.edu/sourcebook (accessed January 2007).

Pettit, Becky, and Christopher Lyons. 2002. "The Consequences of Incarceration on Employment and Earnings: Evidence from Washington State." Unpublished manuscript. University of Washington, Seattle.

Raphael, Steven, and David F. Weiman. 2002. "The Impact of Local Labor Market Conditions on the Likelihood that Parolees are Returned to Custody." Unpublished manuscript. Columbia University.

Raphael, Steven, and Rudolf Winter–Ember. 2001. "Identifying the Effect of Unemployment on Crime." *Journal of Law and Economics* 44(1): 259–84.

Rosenbaum, P. R., and Donald B. Rubin. 1984. "Reducing Bias in Observational Studies Using Subclassification on the Propensity Score." *Journal of the American Statistical Association* 79(00): 516–24.

Sabol, William J. "Local Labor Market Conditions, Participation in Prison Programs, and Post-prison Employment: Evidence from Ohio." Paper presented to the Institute for Excellence in Justice, Ohio Department of Rehabilitation and Correction, June 1, 2007, Columbus, Ohio.

Sampson, Robert J., and John H. Laub. 1993. *Crime in the Making: Pathways and Turning Points Through Life*. Cambridge, Mass.: Harvard University Press.

———. 1997. "A Life-course Theory of Cumulative Disadvantage and the Stability of Delinquency." *Advances in Criminological Theory* 7: 133–61.

Saylor, William G., and Gerald G. Gaes. 1997. "Training Inmates Through Industrial Work Participation and Vocational Apprenticeship Instruction." *Corrections Management Quarterly* 1: 32–43.

Schwartz, Richard D., and Jerome H. Skolnick. 1962. "Two Studies of Legal Stigma." *Social Problems* 10: 133–42.

Tyler, John H., and Jeffrey R. Kling. 2002. "What is the Value of a 'Prison GED'?" Unpublished manuscript. National Bureau of Economic Research, Cambridge, Mass.

Uggen, Christopher. 2000. "Work as a Turning Point in the Life Course of Criminals: A Duration Model of Age, Employment, and Recidivism." *American Sociological Review* 65: 529–46.

Waldfogel, Joel. 1994. "The Effect of Criminal Conviction on Income and the Trust 'Reposed in the Workmen.'" *Journal of Human Resources* 29: 62–81.

Western, Bruce. 2000. "The Impact of Incarceration on Earnings and Inequality." Paper presented at the annual meetings of the American Sociological Association. Washington, D.C. (August 16—19).

———. 2002. "The Impact of Incarceration on Wage Mobility and Inequality." *American Sociological Review* 67(4): 526–46.

Western, Bruce, Jeffrey R. Kling, and David F. Weiman. 2001. "The Labor Market Consequences of Incarceration." *Crime and Delinquency* 47: 410–27.

Wilson, David B., Catherine A. Gallagher, and Doris L. MacKenzie. 2001. "A Meta-Analysis of Corrections-Based Education, Vocation, and Work Programs for Adult Offenders." *Journal on Research in Crime and Delinquency* 37: 347–68.

= Chapter 10 =

The Impact of Local Labor-Market Conditions on the Likelihood that Parolees Are Returned to Custody

STEVEN RAPHAEL AND DAVID F. WEIMAN

Tне post-release employment experience of a paroled ex-offender is frequently offered as an important determinant of whether the individual successfully completes his or her term of community supervision. Support for this proposition comes from research demonstrating a positive relationship between labor-market conditions and crime rates, and evaluations of parolee employment programs showing significant associations between program participation, employment, and recidivism. However, drawing inferences from this empirical evidence about the effect of employment interventions on recidivism and parole violations is problematic for several reasons. Research that demonstrates an aggregate impact of unemployment on crime does not demonstrate that the criminal behavior of released prison inmates is sensitive to available employment opportunities. One might argue that such offenders are a particularly hardened group, and that the supply of ex-offenders to both the legitimate labor market as well as to criminal activity is likely to be inelastic.

Concerning the evaluation evidence of targeted program interventions, very little of this research is based on careful experimental or quasi-experimental research methods. Program participation is rarely determined by random assignment and hence it is impossible to distinguish programmatic effects from unobserved differences in motivation or determination. In light of these weak methodological designs, two recent reviews of this research have concluded that while suggestive, this research does not offer conclusive evidence that intervention impacts the post-release outcomes of ex-offenders (Bushway and Reuter 2002; Wilson, Gallagher, and MacKenzie 2000).

In this chapter, we assess whether the availability of employment opportunities impacts the likelihood that a paroled ex-offender is returned to custody, using a source of variation in employment conditions that is unlikely to be related to unobserved differences in motivation. Using administrative data from the California State Department of Corrections, we assess whether the likelihood that a paroled offender is returned to prison depends on the local labor-market conditions in the county where the offender is released at the time of release. We test for overall effects of local labor-market conditions on all individuals paroled during the 1990s and for groups of parolees stratified by variables that are highly correlated with the likelihood of being returned to custody.

We find moderate effects of county unemployment rates at the time of release on the likelihood that a paroled offender is returned to custody. The difference in return rates between those paroled to low-unemployment counties and those paroled to high-unemployment counties widens as the period analyzed increases—in other words, there is little impact on the likelihood of returning within six months, a larger impact on returning within twelve months, and a larger effect on returning within twenty-four months. When we stratify by offender characteristics, we find that the impact of employment conditions on the likelihood of reincarceration is larger for offenders that are relatively less likely to violate the imposed parole terms. Hence, the post-release criminal activity of the most problematic parolees is least impacted by local labor-market conditions.

Combined with findings from research on the impact of local unemployment rates on the employment probabilities of low-skilled workers (Sabol, chapter 9, this volume; Holzer and Offner 2002), our results imply that the impact of being employed on the probability of being returned to custody is small for the average parolee, on the order of one to two percentage points. However, our results also indicate that the employment effects for parolees that are at relatively low-risk of violating parole are fairly large. For the lowest-risk parolees, our results suggest that having a job reduces the likelihood of being returned to custody on a parole violation by six to twelve percentage points (13 to 26 percent of the three-year recidivism rate for low-risk releases). Thus, targeted workforce development efforts may be quite effective at reducing the return-to-custody rates among subgroups of former inmates.

Parole in the United States and in California and Its Impact on Employment Opportunities

Parole is technically defined as a period of conditional supervision following release from prison. An inmate can be paroled either at the discretion of state parole boards (referred to as discretionary parole) or via statutory requirements (referred to as mandatory parole). Over the last two decades, the proportion of parolees released at the discretion of state parole boards has declined considerably, from roughly 55 percent in 1980 to 25 percent in 1999. Comparable figures for mandatory parole are 20 percent in 1980 and 42 percent in 1999. Roughly 70 percent of released prison inmates enter state parole systems. Of the remaining 30 percent, approximately 20 percent are released as a result of the expiration of their sentence (in which case they receive no post-release supervision), and 10 percent are released for other reasons, such as commutations or release to probation (Hughes, Wilson, and Beck 2001).

The conditions of parole often vary with the offender. At a minimum, parolees are required to maintain contact with a supervising parole agent, not to abuse drugs, and not to engage in criminal activity of any kind. However, additional conditions may be placed on certain offenders, such as prohibitions against alcohol consumption, requirements that the ex-offender stay away from victims, and requirements that the parolee make restitution to victims. Parole violations can result in a number of alternative sanctions. For example, a parolee who fails a drug test may be fined, may be required to attend a substance abuse program, or in some instances may be returned to prison (Legislative Analyst's Office of California 1998). In general, length of time on parole does not exceed three years and the average parole term is slightly over a year.[1]

California's parole system differs from that of many other states along several dimensions. To start, practically all offenders released from California prisons are subject to parole supervision. This is not the case in other states. For example, William Sabol (chapter 9, this volume) reports that roughly 60 percent of releases in Ohio during the late 1990s were conditionally released. Nationwide, roughly 70 percent of released inmates are conditionally released. This relatively intensive use of parole is due to several factors. First, determinate sentencing legislation passed in 1977 increased the proportion of convicted offenders sentenced to prison terms while reducing the discretion of the Board of Prison Terms (BPT), the California state parole board, over who is or isn't paroled. Second, during the early 1990s, the BPT dropped the practice of reviewing the files of soon-to-be-released prison inmates for possible unconditional discharge (Legislative Analyst's Office of California 1998). Given this intensive use of parole and the size of the state, nearly one in five parolees in the United States reside in California (Travis and Lawrence 2002).

California punishes parole violators more harshly than other states. This can be seen in higher parole failure rates, differences in the composition of the population of parole violators currently in state prison custody, and an increasing proportion of parole violators in state prison admissions. For instance, only 20 percent of California's ex-offenders released to parole in 1999 successfully completed their terms of community supervision, compared to 42 percent nationally. Among parole violators incarcerated in state prisons, 23 percent of California's inmates were returned to custody for public-order violations (in other words, a technical violation such as missing an appointment with a probation officer) compared to 13 percent nationally. The California and national figures for parolees being returned to custody were 27 and 23 percent for drug violations, 25 and 30 percent for property crimes, and 24 and 34 percent for violent crimes (Hughes, Wilson, and Beck 2001). These patterns indicate that parole violators in California prisons are incarcerated for less serious infractions than parole violators returned to custody in other states.

Finally, parole violators account for an unusually large proportion of prison admission in California. In 1999, nearly 70 percent of admissions to California state prisons were attributable to parole violations (see figure 10.4). The California figure exceeds not only the national average of 35 percent but the rate of every other state in the nation, with Utah a distant second at 55 percent (Hughes et al. 2001).[2]

The potential impact of local labor-market conditions on the likelihood that parolees violate the terms of their supervised release depends on both the demand side of the market for ex-offenders as well as the supply side behavior of ex-offenders themselves. Concerning the supply side, to the extent that paroled ex-offenders are responsive to changes in incentives, one would predict that better labor-market conditions would reduce the likelihood of being returned to custody. Lower unemployment rates coincide with higher wages (Blanchflower and Oswald 1995) and a higher likelihood of finding gainful employment in legitimate activities. In this regard, a tighter labor market increases the expected value of the return to playing it straight and decreases the relative attractiveness of engaging in criminal activity. As long as the labor-supply elasticity of ex-offenders is greater than zero,[3] an ex-offender released under favorable labor-market conditions should be more likely to seek legitimate employment and less likely to engage in crime for personal gain than an otherwise similar ex-offender released under less favorable conditions. Any factor that reduces the likelihood of committing a crime is likely to reduce the likelihood of a parole violation.

In addition to the economic incentives that may deter a parole violation, gainful employment occupies a parolee's time, keeping the parolee off the streets and probabilistically reducing the likelihood that the ex-offender encounters high-risk situations. A job may also provide daily structure and regimentation, factors that may be particularly important for ex-offenders whose social contacts to those outside of prison have deteriorated during the recently served prison term.

To be sure, whether parolees are more likely to be employed post-release when labor-market conditions are favorable will depend crucially on the demand side of the labor market. Surveys of employers of low-skilled workers consistently show that employers are quite averse to hiring ex-offenders and quite frequently check the criminal history records of job applicants (Holzer, Raphael, and Stoll 2002a; chapter 4, this volume). While there is little research assessing how employer demand for ex-offenders varies with the business cycle, the one study that does attempt to investigate this question (Holzer, Raphael, and Stoll 2002a) finds little evidence of increased hiring of ex-offenders when labor markets are tight. This may be due in part to the fact that a fairly large proportion of employers who indicate that they are unlikely to hire ex-offenders are prohibited by law from doing so (Holzer, Raphael, and Stoll, chapter 4, this volume).

However, there is evidence that employer willingness to hire applicants with criminal history records depends to a certain extent on the severity of the offense committed (Holzer, Raphael, and Stoll, chapter 4, this volume). Specifically, employers are least willing to hire ex-offenders who have committed violent crimes and property crimes (in that order). In contrast, employers are more willing to hire applicants who have served time for a drug offense. Hence, the extent to which employer demand for ex-offenders varies with labor-market conditions is likely to depend on the characteristics of the ex-offender.

There is aggregate evidence that tight labor markets coincide with lower crime levels. Steven Raphael and Rudolf Winter-Ember (2001) as well as Eric Gould, Bruce A. Weinberg, and David B. Mustard (2002) show that state and county-level property crime rates are lower when unemployment is lower. Moreover, the magnitude of the unemployment effect is sufficiently large to explain a fair portion of the decline in property-crime rates occurring during the 1990s. Such evidence is consistent with an impact of labor-market conditions on the criminal activity of parolees and, by extension, the likelihood that ex-offenders violate the terms of parole.

Whether these unemployment effects are being driven in part by lower offending by parolees, however, will depend in part on the extent to which parolees are on the margin between offending and not offending (or, less restrictively, that the amount of offending is sensitive to relative returns). The studies cited above cannot assess this question since data on crime attributable to parolees is not separately available. Hence, the aggregate evidence is also consistent with the behavior of hardened offenders (such as those on parole) being completely insensitive to labor-market conditions. In this instance, the aggregate relationship between unemployment and crime would be driven entirely by the responsiveness of less serious offenders to variation in legitimate economic opportunities. Evaluations of state employment programs tailored to paroled ex-offenders provide more direct evidence of the impact of employment on the likelihood that an ex-offender violates parole. Evaluations of earlier state interventions reviewed by Shawn Bushway and Peter Reuter (2002) arrived at quite pessimistic conclusions regarding the ability of training and job search assistance to lower the recidivism of parolees. Evaluations of more recent state programs, however, are uniformly more positive. In a review of recent research, Joan Petersilia (2002) cites several evaluations that find program effects on the likelihood that parolees find employment on the order of twenty percentage points, and effects on the likelihood of rearrest and being returned to prison custody on the order of ten percentage points. A review of nineteen studies by David B. Wilson, Catherine A. Gallagher, and Doris L. MacKenzie (2000) finds similar program effects.[4]

The difference between the results from earlier and later research may be driven by several factors. For one, the large increase in incarceration rates since the early 1970s (the period corresponding to the earlier wave of research) likely implies that the United States is incarcerating people for increasingly less-serious offenses, and that such individuals are more responsive to the services offered by state programs. That is to say, with a low incarceration rate (such as that of the 1970s) the average prisoner may be more difficult to serve than the average prisoner when incarceration rates are high. Alternatively, the larger impacts of more recent evaluations may be due to flaws in the methodological design of these more recent evaluations. Bushway and Reuter (2002) as well as Wilson, Gallagher, and MacKenzie (2000) note that few of the program evaluations are based on randomized designs where program participation is determined by random assignment rather than self-selection. Moreover, many of the evaluations do not control for differences in offender characteristics that may simultaneously explain program participation and recidivism and parole violation rates. Hence, although this research is suggestive, the estimated program effects are likely to be upper-bound estimates of the potential for policy intervention to increase employment and reduce recidivism among paroled ex-offenders.

Description of the California Data and the Empirical Strategy

The research on the relationship between unemployment and criminal activity discussed above only partially informs the question of whether employment prospects are related to the likelihood that parolees are returned to custody. The aggregate research fails to directly test for a relationship between economic conditions and the behavior of paroled ex-offenders. The program evaluations directly analyze the outcomes for parolees, but program participation itself is likely to be determined by unobserved factors such as motivation or determination not to be sent back to prison. Such factors are also likely to influence the probability that an ex-offender successfully completes his or her parole term; consequently the estimates from this research are likely to be biased upwards.

In this project, we assess the impact of employment conditions on the likelihood that paroled inmates in California are returned to custody, using a source of variation in labor-market conditions that is unlikely to be correlated with unobserved offender characteristics. Specifically, we assess whether the labor-market conditions in the county of release at the time that the offender is released influences the likelihood of a parole violation. Our empirical strategy requires that we construct a parole violation measure as well as characterize the local labor-market conditions that an individual parolee is exposed to upon release. Before discussing our estimation strategy, a discussion of the structure of the data used to create the dependent and independent variables of analysis is needed.

Constructing Parole Violation Measures

Our principal data source comes from administrative records maintained by the California Department of Corrections (CDC). We use these records to construct four parole violations measures that serve as our dependent variables. We requested data on all commitments with prison terms beginning during the period from January 1, 1990, to December 31, 1999. A prison term corresponds to a specific spell served in a California state prison, and a prison commitment refers to a specific prison sentence associated with the commission of and conviction for a felony offense. An individual offender can (and often does) serve multiple terms for a single commitment. Ex-offenders are returned to prison for subsequent terms on the same commitment when they violate the terms of their parole. An ex-offender who commits a new felony while on parole is prosecuted and (if found guilty) sent to prison on a new commitment.[5]

Figure 10.1   Number of Prison Admissions, Individual Commitments, and
Individual Offenders Entering the California State Prison
System, 1990 to 1999

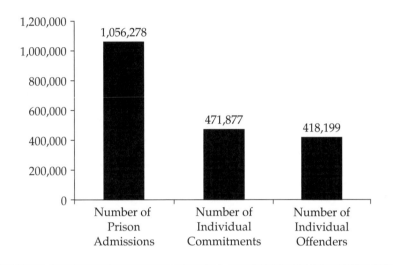

Source: Authors' tabulations of CDC administrative data.

In the data provided to us, each record corresponds to an individual
term. Included in each record is a term counter that increases within a
given commitment (first term, second term, third term, and so forth), a
unique commitment identification variable, unique identifiers for individual offenders, basic demographic information, information on the
offense committed, the county of commitment, and, most important,
the start and end dates for each term.[6] Over 95 percent of the terms
beginning during the 1990s end during the 1990s, with a median term
length of roughly twelve months. For all terms ending during the decade, the inmate is discharged to parole status.

Figures 10.1 through 10.4 summarize several aspects of the California
prison term data. Collectively, these figures document the extremely high
incidence of parole violations that result in the ex-offenders' being returned to custody, as well as the high contribution of parole violations
to prison admissions in California. Figure 10.1 shows the number of
terms (the number of records in our data set), the number of unique
court commitments, and the number of individual offenders. The fact
that the number of commitments is only slightly greater than the number of offenders indicates that a relatively small proportion of offenders
were prosecuted and sentenced more than once during the decade.
Conversely, the fact that the number of terms is more than double the

Figure 10.2   Distribution of Court Commitments by the Number of Terms Served, Commitments with Any Time Served During the 1990s

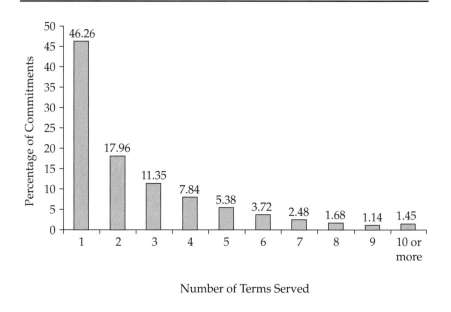

Number of Terms Served

Source: Authors' tabulations of CDC Administrative data.

number of commitments indicates that the lion's share of repeat spells in California prisons is due to parole violations rather than new felony offenses.

Figures 10.2 and 10.3 reinforce this interpretation. Figure 10.2 presents the relative frequency distribution for the 471,877 individual commitments by the number of terms served, and figure 10.3 presents the relative frequency distribution for the 418,199 offenders by the number of commitments incurred during the decade. As can be seen, multiple terms are served on over half of the commitments. On the other hand, 90 percent of offenders accumulate only one commitment during the time period observed.

Finally, figure 10.4 summarizes the number of new admissions to the state prison system by whether the new admission is the first term of a new commitment or the second or higher term on an existing commitment.[7] First-term admissions give the number of new commitments to the state prison system, and the number of second or higher term admissions provide the number of admissions that are due to parole violations. Over the decade, the proportion of admissions accounted

Figure 10.3   Distribution of Offenders Entering the California State Prison System by the Number of Individual Commitments, 1990 to 1999

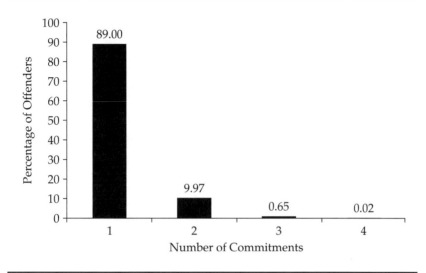

Source: Authors' tabulations of CDC administrative data.

for by parole violators increased from approximately 60 percent to 70 percent of all admissions. These figures are high for California (relative to past years) and relative to other states.

We use the administrative records to construct our parole-violation measures in the following manner. We first restrict the term records to those terms that end during the 1990s. This ensures that all base terms correspond to a subsequent period on parole. We then sort the term records by the unique commitment identification number and the term counter variable (the variable that counts terms within a commitment). For each commitment, we identify the total number of terms served on the commitment and attach this figure to each term record within a given commitment.[8] If the term-counter code number is less than the total number of terms served on the commitment, than we know that the current term is followed by a subsequent prison spell resulting from a parole violation. For such observations, we merge the in dates for the subsequent terms and calculate the time (in months) between the release date from the base term and the in date for the new term. If, on the other hand, the term-counter identification for a given term record equals the value of the total terms served, then the term is the last term served. For such observations, we set the variable measuring the time between terms to an arbitrarily large number.[9]

Figure 10.4   Total New Admissions, Admissions Due to Parole Violations, Admissions Due to New Commitments, 1990 to 1999

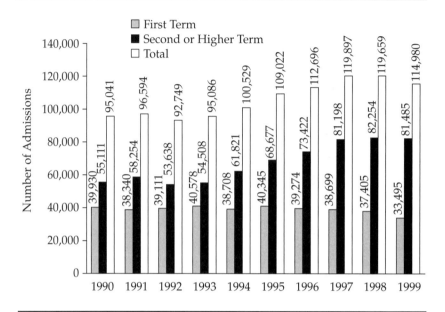

Source: Authors' tabulations of CDC administrative data.

Using this variable, we construct four dependent variables that are indicative of a parole violation resulting in a return to custody: dummy variables that indicate that the offender is returned to custody within six, twelve, twenty-four, and thirty-six months of release from the previous term.[10] For the six- and twelve-month return-to-custody variable, we restrict the sample to terms ending prior to 1999. This restriction ensures that we have at least one year post-release to observe whether the parolee is returned to custody. Similarly, for the twenty-four-month variable, we restrict the sample to terms with end dates prior to 1998, whereas for the thirty-six-month variable we restrict the sample to terms ending prior to 1997.

Figure 10.5 presents average values for the return-to-custody dummies, by year, for the period 1990 to 1998. The proportion of parolees returning within six months varies between 30 and 40 percent, and the proportion returning within one year varies from a low of 48 percent to a high of 61 percent. Between one and two years post-release, the proportion returning to prison on a parole violation increases by roughly ten percentage points, with 60 to 70 percent returning within

Figure 10.5   The Proportion of Parolees Returning to Prison Within Six, Twelve, Twenty-Four, and Thirty-Six Months of Release, by Year of Release

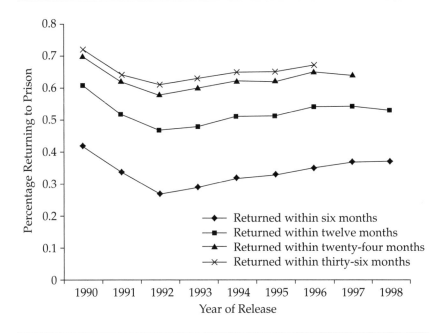

Source: Authors' tabulations of CDC administrative data.

two years. Finally, between two and three years, there are small increases in the proportion returning to custody on a parole violation. These California return-to-custody rates are exceptionally high when compared to those of other states. For example, John Tyler and Jeffrey Kling (chapter 8, this volume) report that roughly 16 percent of Florida prison releases recidivate within one year, and 26 percent recidivate within two years (these numbers are less than half of the estimates presented in figure 10.5).

The return-to-custody rates exhibit clear time trends. Between 1990 and 1993, all return rates decline by roughly ten percentage points. The Legislative Analyst's Office of California (1998) attributes this decrease to a standardization of parolee monitoring procedures and standards for parole revocation across the four geographic divisions of the Department of Corrections Parole Services Division. Furthermore, between 1993 and 1998 all return rates trend upwards, with increases on the order of five percentage points. This second trend is often attributed to the increased influence of the California Board of Prison Terms in determining whether to revoke the parole of violators.

Table 10.1 presents average values for the parole violations measures for the entire period when the sample of terms is stratified by offender characteristics. There are several notable differences across the groups defined in the table. Male parolees are more likely to violate parole and be returned to prison than female parolees. White and black offenders have considerably higher return rates than Hispanic and Asian offenders. Concerning difference by offense committed, the lowest return rates are observed for convicted murderers, sex offenders, and inmates serving time for driving under the influence. The highest return rates occur for escapees and those convicted of a robbery, a burglary, a weapons-possession charge, a theft, fraud, or some other property crime.

Particularly large differences in return rates are observed for those released from their first term when compared to those released from a second or higher term. For example, the proportion of offenders who are returned within three years increases from 0.52 for first-time releases to 0.67 for second-time releases, to 0.73 for parolees being releases from their third or higher term.

Another notable characteristic shown in table 10.1 is the absence of a consistent relationship between age at time of release and the likelihood of returning to prison on a parole violation. Previous research on the relationship between age and criminal activity would predict that the likelihood of successfully completing one's term of parole should increase with age, and thus the likelihood of being returned to custody should decrease (Greenberg 1985; Grogger 1998). Although there is some evidence of such a relationship in table 10.1, the impact of age is not monotonic and the differences between younger and older parolees are small.

The figures reported in the first column can be used to characterize the average person released from prison during the 1990s in California.[11] Although these numbers do not provide averages for the state's incarcerated population at a point in time, they do reveal some of the differences between California and other states. For example, California releases are roughly evenly split between Hispanics, African Americans, and white offenders. This stands in stark contrast to the tabulations for Washington in Pettit and Lyons (Chapter 7, this volume), which reveal a predominantly white prison population, and Sabol's (chapter 9, this volume) for Ohio, which reveal a predominantly black population. Furthermore, only 36 percent of releases in California are being released from the first term on a commitment, compared with roughly 95 percent for Ohio (Sabol, chapter 9, in this volume).

Table 10.1   **Proportion of Terms Where the Parolee is Returned to Custody Within Six, Twelve, Twenty-four, and Thirty-six Months of Release, by Offender Characteristics[a]**

Offender Characteristics	Proportion of Terms	Returns to Prison Within . . .			
		Six Months	Twelve Months	Twenty-four Months[b]	Thirty-six Months[c]
All terms	1.00	0.34	0.52	0.62	0.64
Age at time of release					
Eighteen to twenty	0.02	0.30	0.50	0.61	0.64
Twenty-one to twenty-five	0.16	0.32	0.51	0.62	0.64
Twenty-six to thirty	0.23	0.34	0.52	0.63	0.65
Thirty-one to thirty-five	0.23	0.35	0.54	0.64	0.66
Thirty-six to forty	0.18	0.35	0.54	0.63	0.65
Forty-one plus	0.18	0.32	0.58	0.58	0.60
Male	0.90	0.34	0.53	0.63	0.65
Female	0.10	0.27	0.45	0.56	0.59
White	0.33	0.35	0.54	0.64	0.66
Black	0.34	0.38	0.57	0.68	0.70
Hispanic	0.30	0.28	0.45	0.54	0.57
Asian	0.01	0.20	0.33	0.43	0.46
Other	0.02	0.29	0.45	0.54	0.56
Offense committed					
Murder or manslaughter	0.01	0.20	0.33	0.44	0.47
Robbery	0.08	0.31	0.49	0.59	0.61
Assault	0.07	0.31	0.49	0.60	0.63
Sex crimes	0.03	0.28	0.41	0.50	0.53
Kidnap	0.00	0.26	0.39	0.49	0.52
Burglary	0.14	0.38	0.56	0.66	0.68
Theft, Fraud, other property	0.22	0.38	0.58	0.68	0.70
Drug crimes	0.36	0.33	0.51	0.61	0.63
Escape	0.00	0.50	0.66	0.74	0.76
DUI	0.04	0.20	0.34	0.44	0.46
Arson	0.00	0.31	0.46	0.55	0.58
Weapons possession	0.04	0.34	0.54	0.66	0.69
Other	0.01	0.32	0.48	0.59	0.62
Term group					
First	0.36	0.21	0.37	0.49	0.52
Second	0.21	0.34	0.54	0.65	0.67
Third or higher	0.44	0.44	0.63	0.72	0.73

Source: Estimated using administration records from the California Department of Corrections.

[a] Data refer to all terms served in California beginning during the 1990s and with an outdate occurring prior to 1999.

[b] Sample is restricted to commitments with first terms ending prior to 1998.

[c] Sample is restricted to commitments with first terms ending prior to 1998.

Figure 10.6   Average Monthly Unemployment Rate in County of Release, by Year

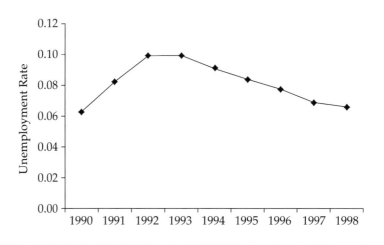

Source: California Department of Finance.

Characterizing Local Labor-Market Conditions

Upon release from prison, the overwhelming majority of California parolees are returned to the controlling county—the county that prosecuted the parolee for the initial offense.[12] Paroled ex-offenders are required to remain in the county of commitment and to maintain contact with parole authorities. During the 1990s, local labor-market conditions varied considerably both within and between the state's 58 counties. We use this variation to identify the impact of local labor-market conditions on the likelihood that the offender's parole status is revoked.

Specifically, for each offender we attach the average monthly unemployment rate for the offender's controlling county for the six-month period beginning with the month that the offender is paroled into the community. We do so using county monthly unemployment rate data from the California Employment Development Department Labor Market Information Division. This average monthly unemployment rate, anchored to a county and a specific time period defined by the offender's date of release, is our key explanatory variables.

Figure 10.6 presents the average local unemployment rate in the county of release by year of release. Labor-market prospects diminished between 1990 and 1993 as the state economy slipped into a particularly deep recession and then improved between 1993 and 1998 with improvements in the national economy. The time path of average unemployment rates is such that local unemployment rates are increasing when parole violation rates are decreasing, and are decreasing when parole violation rates are increasing. We have already noted that the changes over time in return-to-custody rates are being driven in large part by institutional forces internal to California corrections. Thus, the patterns in figures 10.5 and 10.6 may lead to the false conclusion that ex-offenders are more likely to fail on parole when the unemployment rate is low. To adjust for potentially confounding institutional influences, we include year effects in all models estimated below.

Empirical Strategy

We assess the impact of local labor-market conditions on the likelihood that an offender violates the conditions of parole and is returned to custody by regressing each of our four measures of parole failure on our measure of local unemployment rates. To the extent that local labor-market conditions impact the likelihood that an ex-offender finds a job, and to the extent that having a job impacts the likelihood of violating parole, local unemployment rates should impact the likelihood of a parole violation. Technically, the coefficient on the local unemployment rate in our models will equal the effect of local unemployment rates on the probability that a parolee finds employment, times the effect of being employed on the probability of violating parole and being returned to custody.[13] We hypothesize a priori that both effects are negative, and thus, that the reduced-form unemployment effect should be positive.

Concerning the magnitude of the empirical relationships that we estimate, a small unemployment effect is consistent with either a small effect of labor-market conditions on ex-offender employment prospects, a small effect of being employed on the likelihood of violating parole, or both. Absent offender-specific information on post-release employment status, we cannot disentangle these two structural parameters. However, in summarizing our results we will draw on estimates from existing labor-market research concerning the impact of local labor-market conditions on the employment rate of relatively marginalized workers to provide ballpark estimates of the impact of employment on the likelihood of being returned to custody that is implied by our reduced-form results.

To be sure, the population of paroled ex-offenders is heterogeneous, and as a result, one might suspect that the impact of local labor-market conditions on the likelihood of successfully completing one's parole term is heterogeneous as well. For instance, Holzer, Raphael, and Stoll (chapter 4, this volume) show that the demand for low-risk, nonviolent offenders is greater than employer demand for violent offenders. In terms of the impact of labor-market conditions, one might suspect that in tight labor markets employers would be more likely to take a chance with such low-risk offenders. If this were the case, the effect of local conditions on the likelihood of finding a job would be greater for such offenders. Holding all else constant, this would translate into a larger reduced-form impact of local unemployment rates on the likelihood of violating parole. Moreover, one might also argue that the impact of employment on the likelihood that one commits a parole violation may be larger for certain offenders, thus also contributing to heterogeneity in the effect of labor-market conditions.

We explore such heterogeneity in the following manner. Our first strategy is based on the proposition that parolees at the highest risk of violating parole will be returned to custody relatively soon. Thus, as the time since release increases, the pool of remaining parolees is likely to be increasingly positively selected with respect to such characteristics as employability and adaptability to noninstitutional life. By estimating separate models for the likelihood of returning within a short period of time versus returning within a longer period of time, we can assess whether local labor-market conditions matter more or less for relatively high-risk offenders. For example, if the short-period unemployment effect is less than the long-period unemployment effect, one might infer that employment conditions have little impact on those who are quickly returned to custody, yet have larger impacts on those who are likely to survive the first few months of parole.

An alternative manner for testing whether the impact of labor-market conditions is heterogeneous would be to stratify the sample along dimensions correlated with the likelihood of being returned to custody and to estimate separate models for the subsamples. Below, we do this by using a simple imputation procedure to classify offenders into risk-of-subsequent-term quartiles and estimate separate models for each group. We discuss this imputation in detail in the next section.

Estimation of Impact of Local Labor-Market Conditions on Parolees

In this section we present our principal estimates of the impact of local labor-market conditions on the likelihood that paroled offenders are returned to custody in California. We begin with base estimates using the entire population of paroled ex-offenders. We then explore whether the effect of labor-market conditions varies with the relative risk of being returned to custody. Specifically, we impute the risk of being returned to custody among parolees and then estimate separate models for parolees in alternative risk groups.

Table 10.2   **Linear Probability Models of the Likelihood of Returning to Prison Within Six, Twelve, Twenty-four, and Thirty-six Months of Release, All Terms (Standard Errors in Parentheses)**

	Returns to Prison Within . . .			
	Six Months	Twelve Months	Twenty-four Months	Thirty-six Months
Unemployment Rate	0.017	0.025	0.059	0.055
	(0.018)	(0.019)	(0.020)	(0.022)
Female	−0.067	−0.077	−0.066	−0.057
	(0.002)	(0.001)	(0.002)	(0.002)
Black	0.025	0.035	0.042	0.044
	(0.001)	(0.001)	(0.001)	(0.002)
Hispanic	−0.043	−0.064	−0.072	−0.068
	(0.001)	(0.001)	(0.001)	(0.002)
Asian	−0.114	−0.171	−0.174	−0.158
	(0.007)	(0.007)	(0.008)	(0.008)
Other	−0.038	−0.060	−0.072	−0.070
	(0.003)	(0.003)	(0.003)	(0.004)
N	831,216	831,216	708,913	592,351

Source: Estimated using administrative records from the California Department of Corrections.
Note: Each regression includes 390 fixed effects, defined by the thirteen offense categories, six age categories, and five categories describing the terms of release (terms 1 through 4 and fifth or higher). The regressions also include a third-order polynomial of the spell length of the most recent term served, a complete set of year dummies, dummy variables for parole regions, and complete interactions between the parole regions and year dummies. For the twenty-four-month model, the sample is restricted to terms ending prior to 1998. For the thirty-six-month model, the sample is restricted to terms ending prior to 1997.

Base Estimates Using the Entire Population of Parolees

Table 10.2 presents parameter estimates from linear-probability regression models of the likelihood that a paroled ex-offender is returned to prison. The first column presents estimation results where the dependent variable is a dummy indicating a return to custody within six months, the next column presents the results for the twelve month dependent variable, and the third and fourth columns present the results for the twenty-four- and thirty-six-months dependent variables, respectively.

In addition to the explanatory variables shown in the table, each regression model includes 390 fixed effects for all possible combinations of the thirteen possible offenses committed, listed in table 10.1, the six age categories (both listed in table 10.1), and five term-group possibilities (released from the first-, second-, third-, fourth-, or fifth- or higher term). The models also include a set of dummy variables for year of release, dummy variables for which state parole division the offender is released into, and a complete set of interaction terms between the year dummies and the parole division dummies.[14] Finally each model includes controls for a third-order polynomial of the length of the most recent term served. Again, the unemployment-rate variable equals the average monthly unemployment rate in the county of release for the six-month period beginning with the month in which the offender is paroled into the community.

Beginning with the impact of local labor-market conditions, there is no measurable effect of local unemployment rates on the likelihood of returning within six months, a small marginally significant effect on the likelihood of returning within twelve months, and larger and highly significant (at the 1 percent level of confidence) effects on the likelihood of returning to custody within twenty-four and thirty-six months. These effects, while significant, are extremely small. Converting these estimates into elasticities indicates that a 1 percent increase in the local unemployment rate would cause an increase in the likelihood of being returned to custody on a parole violation of between 0.004 and 0.008 percent, depending on the length of time analyzed. An alternative manner of characterizing the magnitudes is to calculate the change in the likelihood of returning to prison caused by a one-percentage-point increase in the local unemployment rate. The estimated effects suggest that a one-percentage-point increase in the unemployment rate results in a 0.00017 to 0.00059 percentage point increase in the likelihood of returning to custody. Again, these relatively small effects may be attributable to either a small impact of labor-market conditions on the employment prospects of ex-offenders, a small effect of employment on parole violations, or both.

Nonetheless, the effects are significant and suggest that employment policy may contribute to combating parole violations among ex-offenders. Moreover, the generally larger effects for longer time periods indicate that employment conditions at time of release are more important for offenders who survive the first few months on parole relative to offenders who are returned to custody within a short time of release. Concerning the patterns observed for the other explanatory variables listed in table 10.2, women are consistently less likely than men to be returned to custody, although the gender difference narrows as the time period analyzed increases. Blacks and whites (the omitted race category) are the most likely and Hispanics, Asians, and others are the least likely to be returned to custody. The racial-ethnic differences in return rates tend to increase markedly after six months on parole.

A More General Stratification by Risk of Return

To reiterate, the impact of employment conditions is likely to vary by offender characteristics. Employers prefer those guilty of less serious offenses, so the demand for such ex-offenders should be particularly sensitive to labor-market conditions. Moreover, less serious offenders may be easier to divert from activities that result in parole violations and subsequent reincarceration. Hence, having a job may have a larger marginal effect for low-risk parolees on the likelihood of violating parole. Both factors would increase the reduced-form estimates of the impact of labor-market conditions that we are investigating here.

In this section we explore heterogeneity in the impact of local unemployment rates on the likelihood of being returned to custody. First, we impute the risk of returning to prison on a parole violation for each prison discharge, taking into account the relationship between all of the observed explanatory variables and the likelihood of being returned to custody. We then use this imputed risk measure to stratify the population of paroled offenders into risk quartiles and estimate separate models accordingly. Our imputation procedure is similar to that used in an alternative context by David Card (1996) and Raphael (2000). First, we estimate a flexibly specified linear-probability model, where the dependent variable is a dummy variable indicating a return to custody within twelve months and the explanatory variables include all those employed in the specifications in table 10.2 (with the exception of the unemployment rate which is omitted from this first stage regression). Next, we use the coefficient estimates from this model to calculate a predicted probability of returning within one year of release. We then stratify the sample into the quartiles of the empirical distribution of this imputed probability. We refer to parolees in the bottom quartile as low-risk parolees, those in the second quartile as low-to-medium risk, those in the third quartile as high-to-medium risk, and those in the top quartile as high-risk parolees.

Table 10.3 presents average return rates as well as average values for all of the variables listed in table 10.1 for each of the four risk groups. As can be seen, there are pronounced differences in return-to-custody rates across risk groups. For example, 16 percent of low-risk parolees are returned to custody for a parole violation within six months of release while the comparable figure for high-risk parolees is 50 percent. The corresponding figures for returning within three years are 46 percent and 79 percent. Concerning offender characteristics,

Table 10.3   Average Characteristics of Released Prisoners, by Predicted Risk of a Parole Violation and Subsequent Return to Custody[a]

	Low Risk	Low to Medium Risk	High to Medium Risk	High Risk
Returns within				
Six months	0.163	0.288	0.391	0.504
Twelve months	0.308	0.484	0.597	0.690
Twenty-four months	0.420	0.610	0.705	0.773
Thirty-six months	0.457	0.644	0.727	0.786
Age at end of term				
Eighteen to twenty	0.017	0.029	0.016	0.009
Twenty-one to twenty-five	0.170	0.198	0.148	0.138
Twenty-six to thirty	0.222	0.230	0.232	0.239
Thirty-one to thirty-five	0.200	0.224	0.241	0.269
Thirty-six to forty	0.155	0.165	0.187	0.202
Forty-one plus	0.236	0.154	0.176	0.143
Male	0.840	0.887	0.909	0.965
Female	0.160	0.113	0.091	0.035
White	0.271	0.328	0.339	0.373
Black	0.195	0.301	0.364	0.510
Hispanic	0.480	0.337	0.273	0.108
Asian	0.015	0.006	0.001	0.000
Other	0.039	0.028	0.023	0.009
Offense committed				
Murder or manslaughter	0.030	0.012	0.003	0.000
Robbery	0.083	0.103	0.085	0.032
Assault	0.086	0.089	0.082	0.039
Sex crimes	0.057	0.035	0.018	0.003
Kidnap	0.005	0.003	0.001	0.000
Burglary	0.065	0.152	0.162	0.175
Theft, fraud, or other	0.095	0.207	0.241	0.334
Drug crime	0.432	0.306	0.322	0.358
Escape	0.000	0.002	0.004	0.008
DUI	0.101	0.029	0.018	0.004
Arson	0.005	0.003	0.003	0.001
Weapons possession	0.019	0.046	0.046	0.034
Other	0.022	0.013	0.015	0.012
Term group				
First	0.895	0.458	0.066	0.004
Second	0.080	0.306	0.333	0.113
Third or higher	0.025	0.236	0.601	0.883

Source: Estimated using administrative records from the California Department of Corrections.

[a]Risk categories are defined by the quartiles of a predicted probability of returning to custody within twelve months. See the text (page 323) for a description of the model used to estimate the probability of returning to custody.

Table 10.4   Estimates of the Effect of Local Unemployment Rates on the Likelihood of Returning to Custody Within Six, Twelve, Twenty-four, and Thirty-six Months of Release, by Predicted Probability of Violating Parole (Standard Errors are in Parentheses)

| | Returns to Custody Within . . . | | | |
Predicted Risk of Violating Parole	Six Months	Twelve Months	Twenty-four Months	Thirty-six Months
Low risk	0.102	0.156	0.270	0.321
	(0.033)	(0.041)	(0.047)	(0.052)
Low-to-medium risk	0.024	0.052	0.128	0.113
	(0.037)	(0.040)	(0.044)	(0.047)
High-to-medium risk	0.080	0.073	0.053	0.032
	(0.037)	(0.037)	(0.038)	(0.041)
High risk	−0.109	−0.141	−0.154	−0.195
	(0.037)	(0.034)	(0.034)	(0.039)

Source: Estimated using administrative records from the California Department of Corrections.
Note: Each figure is the coefficient on the average monthly unemployment rate for the six-month period following release in the county of release. Each regression includes 390 fixed effects, defined by the thirteen offense categories, six age categories, and five categories describing the terms of release (terms 1 through 4 and fifth or higher). The regressions also include a third-order polynomial of the spell length of the most recent term served, a complete set of year dummies, dummy variables for parole regions, and complete interactions between the parole regions and year dummies. For the twenty-four-month model, the sample is restricted to terms ending prior to 1998. For the thirty-six-month model, the sample is restricted to terms ending prior to 1997.

there are no uniform patterns concerning age (other than that the oldest offenders are most represented in the low-risk group), but there are pronounced patterns for gender, race-ethnicity, offense, and term served. Female parolees are disproportionately represented in the low-risk group and male parolees are disproportionately represented in the high-risk group. Blacks and whites are disproportionately high-risk parolees, and Hispanics and Asians are disproportionately low-risk. Finally, parolees released from their first term are concentrated in the low-risk quartiles and offenders released from second or higher terms are concentrated in the high-risk quartiles.

We use these risk groupings to assess more generally whether the effect of local labor-market conditions on the likelihood of being returned to prison on a parole violation varies across offender types. Table 10.4 presents the results of this exercise. The rows of table 10.4 correspond to risk groups and the columns correspond to the four different dependent variables. Each figure in the table is the coefficient on the local unemployment rate from a separate regression for each risk group and for each dependent variable. The results clearly indicate that the impact of local labor-market conditions varies by risk group. For low-risk offenders, the coefficients on local unemployment rates are positive and statistically significant at the 1 percent level in all models. Moreover, the point estimates are anywhere from five to six times the average effects that we estimate for the population of paroled ex-offenders overall (the estimates in table 10.2).

For low-to-medium-risk offenders, the effects are positive for all models but are significant only for the twenty-four-month and thirty-six-month equations. The magnitudes of the effects for the two significant estimates are much smaller than those observed for low-risk offenders. Local labor conditions exert significant effects for the six-month and twelve-month outcome variables for high-to-medium risk parolees, but not for the longer periods analyzed. Finally, there is no evidence of an impact of local labor-market conditions for high-risk offenders. In fact, for this group the coefficients are the wrong sign and statistically significant.

Putting These Results into Perspective

The results of this study are several. To start, we find that the likelihood of being returned to custody on a parole violation is sensitive to variation in the local labor-market conditions into which a paroled offender is released. This result indicates that criminal behavior even among the most serious offenders in society (those who have been incarcerated in state prisons for their offenses) is responsive to economic incentives. Thus, there is clearly a role for employment policy interventions in smoothing the reentry of ex-offenders into the community. Moreover, our findings indicate that local labor-market conditions are particularly important for offenders who are at lower overall risk of being returned to custody. This suggests that the marginal product of employment interventions in terms of reducing the inflow into prison of parole violators would be greatest if such intervention were targeted at certain offenders. Such targeting may free up the time and effort of parole officers, who would then be able to concentrate their monitoring efforts on more high-risk parolees. Such efficiency gains are clearly needed in the state under study in light of the unusually high incidence of parole violations and the consequent reincarceration documented here.

One shortcoming of our research design is that we are unable to generate estimates of the impact of being employed on the likelihood of violating parole and being returned to prison. This follows from the fact that we are unable to observe the employment status of paroled ex-offenders. Thus, our reduced-form estimates of the local-area unemployment effect represent the product of two structural effects: the effect of local unemployment rates on the probability that the parolee finds a job, and the effect of having a job on the likelihood of violating parole. Moreover, having reliable estimates of the second effect is particularly important, since a number of public-sector demand-side interventions, such as public-service employment, wage subsidies, or indemnifying employers against negligent-hiring lawsuits, could be tapped to augment employment among parolees.

With our data alone we cannot estimate the impact of being employed on the likelihood of being returned to prison, but by combining it with the findings from research on the effect of unemployment on employment rates, we can present ballpark estimates of the employment-parole violation effects that our estimates imply. For example, if we were to divide our reduced-form estimate of the unemployment effect by an external estimate of the effect of unemployment on the likelihood that an ex-offender is employed, the result would be an estimate of the structural effect of employment on parole violation and incarceration based on variation in employment associated with local labor-market conditions.[15]

To make this imputation, we employ the empirical estimates of the effect of local unemployment rates on employment probabilities from two studies. First, Sabol (chapter 9, this volume) estimates the effect of local unemployment rates and the likelihood that recently released offenders in the state of Ohio will show up in state unemployment insurance records as having earned income during a given calendar quarter. Sabol finds that a one-percentage-point increase in the unemployment rate decreases the likelihood of being employed among released offenders by five percentage points.

The second estimate comes from Holzer and Paul Offner (2002). Using cross-sectional and longitudinal variation in regional unemployment rates, the authors estimate that every one-percentage-point increase in the local-area unemployment rate decreases the probability that less-educated black males are employed by 2.7 percentage points. Given that less-educated black males are disproportionately represented among prison parolees, this parameter serves as an alternative.

Note, since the effect of employment on the likelihood of going to prison is imputed by dividing our reduced-form estimates by the estimated effect of local unemployment rates on the likelihood of having a job, the larger the employment-unemployment effect, the smaller the imputed employment–returned-to-custody effect. Thus, the parameter estimate from Sabol serves to provide our lower-bound estimate of the

Table 10.5   **Predicted Effect of Being Employed on the Likelihood of Being Returned to Custody, Based on the Local Labor Market Conditions Effect Estimates in Tables 2 through 5**

Unemployment-Effect Estimates Used	Predicted Effect of Employment on Likelihood of Returning to Prison Within ...			
	Six Months	Twelve Months	Twenty-four Months	Thirty-six Months
Overall effects (table 10.2)				
Lower bound	−0.003	−0.005	−0.012	−0.011
Upper bound	−0.006	−0.009	−0.022	−0.020
Effects for first-term parolees (table 10.3)				
Lower bound	−0.008	−0.015	−0.036	−0.048
Upper bound	−0.014	−0.027	−0.067	−0.088
Effects for low-risk parolees (table 10.4)				
Lower bound	−0.020	−0.031	−0.054	−0.064
Upper bound	−0.038	−0.058	−0.100	−0.119

Source: Estimated using administrative records from the California Department of Corrections.

Note: The figures in the table are calculated as follows: The coefficient on local unemployment rates in the linear probability model is theoretically equal to the product of the effect of local unemployment rates on the probability of being employed times the effect of being employed on the probability of being returned to custody. To isolate the employment effect on parole violations, one needs to divide the point estimates in tables 10.2 through 10.4 by an estimate of the effect of unemployment rates on the probability of being employed. In linear probability models where the dependent variable is a dummy variable equal to one if a person is employed, Holzer and Offner (2002) find that the coefficient on unemployment for a regression restricted to less-educated black males is equal to −2.7. Sabol (Chapter 9, this volume) finds a marginal effect of a one-percentage-point change in the unemployment rate on the employment probabilities for recent released prisoners of five percentage points. We use this point estimate to calculate the figures in the table. We use the Holzer and Offner estimate to calculate the upper-bound employment-effect estimate and the Sabol parameter to compute the lower-bound estimates. The figures in the table should be interpreted as estimates of the effect of having a job on the likelihood of being returned to custody within the given time frame.

effect of having a job on the likelihood of being returned to prison, and the parameter estimate from Holzer and Offner is used to calculate the upper bound.[16]

Table 10.5 presents estimates of the effect of being employed on the likelihood of being returned to prison on a parole violation that are based on the reduced-form unemployment effects that we present here and on the employment–unemployment-rate effects borrowed from the literature. The table presents employment-effect estimates for all parolees, parolees released from their first term, and low-risk parolees.

Finding a job reduces the likelihood that the average parolee is returned to custody within three years by only one to two percentage points. This amounts to at most 3 percent of the average probability of being returned within three years. This is a much smaller effect than the ten-percentage-point estimate that is commonly reported in nonexperimental evaluations of job programs reviewed above. Hence, our study suggests that the findings from existing evaluation research are biased upwards by the unobserved differences between program participants and nonparticipants.

However, for parolees who are at a lower risk of being returned to custody, the implied effects are quite substantial. For offenders being released from their first terms, our estimates imply that those with jobs are five to nine percentage points less likely to be returned to custody within three years. For parolees who are in the bottom quartile of the risk distribution, our estimates imply that employed parolees are six to twelve percentage points less likely to be returned to custody within three years. For these two low-risk groups, the implied reduction in the three-year return probability associated with having a job amounts to 10 to 17 percent of the proportion of first-term parolees who are returned on average and 12 to 26 percent of the proportion of low-risk parolees who are returned on average. These are clearly sizable effects.

Whether employment interventions are cost-effective will depend on the social saving associated with diverting parolees from future terms of incarceration as well as the cost saving associated with reduced criminal behavior. We have not attempted to quantify the relative costs and benefits of such interventions, but the large implied effects for low-risk offenders suggests that focusing public resources on employment aspects of prisoner reentry may very well be a cost-effective strategy, at least for low-risk parolees.

We would like to thank the California Department of Corrections for graciously providing the data integral to this research project and the Russell Sage Foundation for their generous financial support.

Notes

1. A small proportion of offenders are subjected to longer parole terms. In some cases such as ex-offenders paroled from a life sentence, parole terms may be indefinite.

    Parole and probation are different statuses of community supervision. Probation is generally an alternative to incarceration, so those on probation

are rarely ex-offenders discharged from state prisons. The probation population in 2001 was more than five times the parole population (Glaze 2002).

2. The Legislative Analyst's Office of California attributes the harsher punishment of parole violators and the relatively high return-to-custody rates to
policy choices of the state Board of Prison Terms (BPT). During the 1990s,
the BPT increased the number of parole infractions that must be reported
to the BPT by parole officers, thus reducing the discretion of parole officers
to fashion alternative sanctions to new prison terms. In addition, among
those parole violations reviewed by the BPT, the proportion of reviews
where parole was revoked and the parolee returned to prison increased.
Specifically, in 1993, 65 percent of parole violators reviewed by the BPT
were returned to custody and 35 percent were continued on parole. In 1997,
by contrast, 90 percent of parole violators were returned to custody and 10
percent were continued on parole (Legislative Analyst's Office of California
1998).

3. An equivalent condition for responsiveness is that the supply of ex-offenders to criminal activity not be perfectly inelastic. For a thorough discussion
of this economic model of crime see Richard Freeman (1996).

4. For detailed descriptions of three state level job training and placement
programs, see Peter Finn (1998a, 1998b, and 1998c).

5. In the review of California's parole system, the Legislative Analyst's Office
of California (1998) reports that local prosecutors often forgo prosecuting
new offenses when the prison sanction associated with the parole violation
is likely to exceed the sentence length of a newly committed felony. Hence,
among the population of ex-offenders sent back to prison for subsequent
terms based on parole violations, many will have committed new felony
offenses. Nonetheless, surveys of incarcerated parole offenders in California indicate that a large fraction of such offenders are paroles for "public
order offenses"—that is, technical violations of the conditions of parole—
and nearly half of incarcerated parole violators are sent back to prison for
a drug violation (Hughes, Wilson, and Beck 2001).

6. We were provided with a unique CDC offender identification code, Social
Security numbers, and names.

7. These figures are tabulated by summing records within year by the beginning date of the term served.

8. Given that the term counter identifies the term number served within the
commitment, we can identify the maximum number of terms served for
commitments whose first terms began prior to the 1990s as well.

9. Our key dependent variables are whether the parolee is returned to custody within set time periods, the largest being thirty-six months. Thus, for
releases that do not receive a subsequent term, we set the time between
terms variables to a value greater than thirty-six. This ensures a value of
zero for all returned-to-custody dummy variables.

10. Parole terms can last no longer than three years. Hence, if an offender has
not been sent back within three years, in all likelihood he has successfully
completed the parole term.

11. Note that the figures in the proportion-of-terms column should be interpreted as the distribution of offender characteristics across terms rather than

across offenders, given that many offenders serve multiple terms and that the unit of observation in the data set used to calculate the figures in table 10.1 is a prison term.

12. Approximately 10 percent of parolees are returned to other counties. We do not have information on the county of release for this group.

13. This can best be illustrated with a simple two-equation empirical model. Suppose that the likelihood of being returned to custody is determined according to the equation $RTC_i = \alpha_0 + \alpha_1 E_i + \alpha_2 X_i + \varepsilon_i$, where RTC is a dummy variable indicating being returned to custody, E is a dummy variable indicating whether one is employed, X is a vector of control variables, α_0 through α_2 are parameters, and ε is a mean-zero error term. Furthermore, assume that whether one is employed is determined by the equation $E_i = \beta_0 + \beta_1 U_i + \beta_2 X_i + \eta_i$, where U is the local area unemployment rate, β_0 through β_2 are parameters, and η is a mean-zero random disturbance. Substituting the equation for employment determination into the return-to-custody equation gives the reduced form, $RTC_i = (\alpha_0 + \alpha_1\beta_0) + \alpha_1\beta_1 U_i + (\alpha_2 + \alpha_1\beta_2)X_i + (\varepsilon_i + \alpha_1\eta_i)$. As can be seen, the coefficient on the local unemployment rate is equal to the effect of the unemployment rate on the likelihood of being employed times the effect of being employed on the likelihood of being returned to custody.

14. The state is divided into four parole divisions: two for Southern California (one for the county of Los Angeles and one for the remaining counties to the east and south of Los Angeles), and two for central and northern California; of the latter, one encompasses all counties along the coast to the north of Los Angeles and one takes in all remaining inland counties.

15. This is theoretically equivalent to a split-sample two-stage least-squares estimate of the employment-parole violation effect, using local unemployment rates as an instrument for predicting whether the offender is employed. For a discussion of such estimators, see Raphael and David Riker (1999).

16. To be sure, the effect of the local-area unemployment rate on the likelihood of being employed is likely to vary across released offenders, defined by the risk groups employed in this study. We are basically assigning a similar value for this elasticity to all risk groups (with an implicit assumption that is likely to be violated in practice). Unfortunately, in the absence of micro-level information on employment status among released offenders, we are constrained to assuming a constant employment-unemployment effect for all offenders.

References

Blanchflower, David B., and Andrew L. Oswald. 1995. "An Introduction to the Wage Curve." *Journal of Economic Perspectives* 9(3): 153–67.

Bushway, Shawn, and Peter Reuter. 2002. "Labor Markets and Crime." In *Crime: Public Policies for Crime Control*, edited by James Q. Wilson and Joan Petersilia. Oakland, Calif.: Institute for Contemporary Studies Press.

Card, David. 1996. "The Effect of Unions on the Structure of Wages: A Longitudinal Analysis." *Econometrica* 64(4): 957–79.

Finn, Peter. 1998a. *Chicago's Safer Foundation: A Road Back for Ex-Offenders*, Washington, D.C.: National Institute of Justice.

———. 1998b. *Successful Job Placement for Ex-Offenders: The Center for Employment Opportunities*. Washington, D.C.: National Institute of Justice.

———. 1998c. *Texas' Project RIO (Re-integrating of Offenders)*. Washington, D.C.: National Institute of Justice.

Freeman, Richard B. 1996. "Why Do So Many Young Men Commit Crimes and What Might We Do About It?" *Journal of Economics Perspectives* 10(1): 25–42.

Glaze, Lauren E. 2002. *Probation and Parole in the United States, 2001*. Washington: Bureau of Justice Statistics.

Gould, Eric D., Bruce A. Weinberg, and David B. Mustard. 2002. "Crime Rates and Local Labor Market Opportunities in the United States: 1977–1997." *Review of Economics and Statistics* 84(1): 45–61.

Greenberg, David F. 1985. "Age, Crime, and Social Explanation." *American Journal of Sociology*, 91(00): 1–21.

Grogger, Jeffrey. 1998. "Market Wages and Youth Crime." *Journal of Labor Economics* 16(00): 756–91.

Holzer, Harry, and Paul Offner. 2002. "Employment Trends Among Less-Skilled Young Men." Unpublished manuscript. Georgetown University.

Holzer, Harry J., Steven Raphael, and Michael A. Stoll. 2004. "Will Employers Hire Ex-Offenders? Employer Preferences, Background Checks, and Their Determinants." In *The Impact of Incarceration on Families and Communities*, edited by Mary Pattillo-McCoy, David Weiman and Bruce Western. New York: Russell Sage Foundation.

Hughes, Timothy A., Doris J. Wilson, and Allen J. Beck. 2001. *Trends in State Parole, 1990–2000*. Washington: Bureau of Justice Statistics.

Langan, Patrick A., and David J. Levine. 2002. *Recidivism of Prisoners Released in 1994*. Washington: Bureau of Justice Statistics.

Legislative Analyst's Office of California. 1998. "Reforming California's Adult Parole System." LAO Analysis of the 1998–99 Budget Bill. Available at http://www.lao.ca.gov/analysis_1998/crim_justice_crosscutting_an198.html (accessed January 12, 2007).

Petersilia, Joan. 2002. "Community Corrections." In *Crime: Public Policies for Crime Control*, edited by James Q. Wilson and Joan Petersilia. Oakland: Calif.: Institute for Contemporary Studies Press.

Raphael, Steven. 2000. "Estimating the Union Earnings Effect Using a Sample of Displaced Workers." *Industrial and Labor Relations Review* 53(3): 503–21.

Raphael, Steven, and David Riker. 1999. "Geographic Mobility, Race, and Wage Differentials." *Journal of Urban Economics* 45(1): 17–46.

Raphael, Steven, and Rudolf Winter-Ember. 2001. "Identifying the Effect of Unemployment on Crime." *Journal of Law and Economics* 44(1): 259–84.

Travis, Jeremy, and Sarah Lawrence. 2002. *California's Parole Experiment*. Washington, D.C.: Urban Institute Justice Policy Center.

Wilson, David B., Catherine A. Gallagher, and Doris L. MacKenzie. 2000. "A Meta-Analysis of Corrections-Based Education, Vocation, and Work Programs for Adult Offenders." *Journal on Research in Crime and Delinquency* 37(4): 347–68.

= Part IV =

Does Prison Work?

= Chapter 11 =

The Penal System and the Labor Market

Bruce Western

The chapters in this volume are part of a burgeoning research literature that studies the social and economic effects of imprisonment. Earlier work on the effects of incarceration focused on the recidivism of those coming out of prison and jail. Recent research, however, also examines how imprisonment affects the socioeconomic life of prisoners and the poor urban communities to which they return (for example, Braman 2003; Western 2006; Clear, forthcoming; Wacquant, forthcoming).

New research on the social consequences of incarceration is motivated by the facts of mass imprisonment. The American incarceration rate—historically high by U.S. standards, surpassing that of some former Soviet republics, and an order of magnitude higher than in the affluent democracies of Western Europe—is a vivid symbol of social inequality. For young male high school dropouts, particularly African Americans, imprisonment has become a routine life event. A young black man born in the late 1960s is more likely to have a prison record than a bachelor's degree, and over half of young black male dropouts born in the late 1960s will go to prison at some point their lives (Pettit and Western 2004). Statistics like these have focused the attention of students of poverty, race, and urban problems on the penal system as a novel feature of a distinctively American pattern of social inequality.

Research on the social impact of incarceration suggests that policy has a role, not just in reducing crime but in improving the economic and family life of those drawn into the penal system. Policies designed to repair the economic and family life of ex-prisoners serve several goals. First, steady work and a stable family are keys to desistance from crime (Sampson and Laub 1993; Uggen 2000; Warr 1998). A good job provides structure to daily life, draws a man out of his peer networks that form the context for criminal offending, and offers a wage, which weakens the temptations of an illegal income. Beyond the effects on crime, policies that smooth the reentry of ex-offenders into their homes and jobs may have large redistributive effects. Because incarceration rates are now so high among young men with little schooling, measures that improve employment and family life among ex-prisoners may also raise the economic standing of those at the bottom of American society. In the era of mass imprisonment, social supports for ex-prisoners provide new tools for reducing poverty.

The papers in this volume study the links between the penal system and the American labor market. In this chapter I connect this research on prisons and the labor market to policies that can help ex-prisoners find work after coming out of prison.

The Political and Economic Origins of Mass Imprisonment

To understand the impact of employment policy on returning prisoners, we need first to consider the historical origins of the prison boom. Mass imprisonment of the late 1990s can be traced two basic shifts in politics and economics. The growth of harsh sentencing policies and a punitive approach to drug control began with a rightward shift in American politics, first visible at the national level in the mid-1960s. Barry Goldwater's fated presidential run in 1964 is seen as pivotal (Beckett 1997; Gest 2001). Goldwater, in accepting the Republican nomination, warned that crime and disorder were threats to human freedom and freedom must be "balanced so that liberty lacking order will not become the license of the mob and of the jungle." The Republican campaign of 1964 linked the problem of street crime to civil rights protest and the growing unease among whites about racial violence. Although Goldwater was roundly defeated by Lyndon Johnson, conservatives within the Republican Party had brought to the national stage a new kind of politics. Historically, responsibilities for crime control were divided mostly between state and local agencies. The Republicans had placed the issue of crime squarely on the national agenda. What's more, by treating civil rights protest as a strain of social disorder, veiled connections were drawn between the crime problem on the one hand and social protest by and on behalf of African Americans on the other.

Despite Goldwater's defeat, the law-and-order message resonated, particularly among southern whites and northern working-class voters of Irish, Italian, and German descent who turned away from the Democratic Party in the 1970s (Edsall and Edsall 1991). The social problem of crime became a reality as murder rates and incidence of other violence escalated in the decade following the 1964 election. Through the 1960s, urban riots in Los Angeles, New York, Newark, Detroit, and dozens of other cities provided a socially ambiguous mixture of disorder and politics.

Elevated crime rates and the realigned race relations of the post–civil rights period provided a receptive context for the law-and-order themes of the Republican Party. In state politics, Republican governors and legislators increased their representation through the South and West, and placed themselves in the vanguard of the movements for mandatory minimum sentences, sentence enhancements for repeat offenders, and expanded prison capacity (Western 2006; Davey 1998; Jacobs and Carmichael 2001). Quantitative analyses show that incarceration rates grew fastest under Republican governors and state legislators (Western 2006, chapter 3). Republicans were quick to promote prison expansion and tough new criminal sentences, but Democrats also came to support punitive criminal justice policy. Perhaps the clearest signal that Democrats too were tough on crime was sent by President Clinton's Violent Crime Control and Law Enforcement Act (1994). The Clinton crime bill earmarked $9.9 billion for prison construction and added life terms for third-time federal felons (Windelsham 1998, 104–7). By the 1990s, Democrats and Republicans had come to support the sentencing policies and capital construction campaigns that grew the penal population.

Urban deindustrialization eroded the labor market for unskilled young men while punitive politics gained momentum in the 1970s and 1980s. William Julius Wilson's (1987) study, *The Truly Disadvantaged*, provides the classic analysis. The decline of manufacturing-industry employment in the Midwest and the Northeast coupled with the exodus of middle-class and working-class blacks from inner cities produced pockets of severe unemployment in poor urban neighborhoods. From 1969 to 1979, central cities recorded enormous declines in manufacturing and blue-collar employment. For example, New York lost 170,000 blue-collar jobs through the 1970s, in Chicago another 120,000 jobs were shed, and blue-collar employment in Detroit fell by 90,000 jobs (Kasarda 1989, 29). For young men in metropolitan areas, employment rates dropped by 30 percent among black high school dropouts and nearly 20 percent among black high school graduates. Job loss was only a third as large among young noncollege whites (Bound and Holzer 1993, 390). Following the development of antidiscrimination law, affirmative action, and gains to earnings and employment among African Americans through the mid-1970s, the labor economists John Bound and Richard Freeman (1992) were led to ask what had gone wrong in the 1980s with the promise of opportunity for young black men.

Idle young men in poor minority neighborhoods supplied a large share of the inmates that drove the prison boom. The path from concentrated economic disadvantage to mass imprisonment runs partly through the mechanism of crime, but policy also played a vital role. At any given point in time, crime among young disadvantaged men is higher than in the rest of the population. For example, the murder rate—the rates of both victimization and offending—are about twenty-five times higher for black men aged eighteen to twenty-four than for white men aged twenty-five and older (Pastore and Maguire 2006, tables 3.126.2004 and 3.128.2004). Violent crime is also a more serious problem in poor communities than affluent (for example, Sampson 1987; see also the review by Braithwaite 1979). The criminal involvement of young, economically disadvantaged men makes them more likely at a given point in time to go to prison than others who are less involved in crime. Crime cannot explain, however, why disadvantaged young men were so much more likely to go to prison by the end of the 1990s than two decades earlier. Indeed, survey data show that poor male youths were much less involved in crime at the height of the prison boom, in 2000, than at its inception, in 1980. To explain the growing risk of imprisonment over time, the role of policy is decisive. Because the system of criminal sentencing had come to rely so heavily on incarceration, an arrest in the late 1990s was far more likely to lead to prison time than it was at the beginning of the prison boom, in 1980 (Blumstein and Beck 1999).

As Weiman, Stoll, and Bushway showed in this volume, the drug trade plays a special role in this story. The drug trade itself became a source of economic opportunity in the jobless ghetto. Ethnographers paint striking pictures of how the inner-city drug trade becomes a focal point for the problems of economic disadvantage, violence, and state control. Sudhir Venkatesh and Steven Levitt (2000) describe how drug trafficking thrived in the vacuum of legitimate employment in Chicago's Southside neighborhoods. Chicago youths spoke to Venkatesh and Levitt of their "gang affiliation and their drive to earn income in ways that resonated with representations of work in the mainstream corporate firm. Many approached [gang] involvement as an institutionalized path of socioeconomic mobility for down-and-out youth" (Venkatesh and Levitt 2000, 447). In Elijah Anderson's (1999) account, violence follows the drug trade as crime becomes a voracious force in the poor neighborhoods of Philadelphia (134):

> Surrounded by violence and by indifference to the innocent victims of drug dealers and users alike, the decent people are finding it harder and harder to maintain a sense of community. Thus violence comes to regulate life in the drug-infested neighborhoods and the putative neighborhood leaders are increasingly the people who control the violence.

The picture drawn by the ethnographic research is of poor neighborhoods, chronically short of legitimate work, and embedded in a violent and illegal market for drugs.

High rates of joblessness and crime and a flourishing street trade in illegal drugs combined with harsher criminal penalties and intensified urban policing to produce high incarceration rates among young unskilled men in inner cities. In the twenty-five years from 1980, the incarceration rate tripled among white men in their twenties, but fewer than 2 percent were behind bars by 2004. Imprisonment rates for young black men increased less quickly, but one in seven (14.2 percent) were in custody by 2004. Incarceration rates are much higher among male high school dropouts in their twenties. Threefold growth in the imprisonment of young white male dropouts left 7 percent in prison or jail by 2004. The incarceration rate for young low-education black men rose by 22 points in the two decades after 1980. Incredibly, on an average day in 2004, 34 percent of all young black male high school dropouts were in prison or jail, an incarceration rate forty times the national average.

Variation in imprisonment is closely linked to variation in wages and employment. Weekly earnings for young low-education men declined through the 1980s and 1990s, while imprisonment rates were rising. Among black men, unemployment increased steeply with declining education. One study estimates that if wages and employment had not declined among low-education men since the early 1980s, growth in prison admission rates would have been reduced by as much as 25 percent by 2001 (Western, Kleykamp, and Rosenfeld 2006).

The urban deindustrialization that produced the raw material for the prison boom was as much a failure of institutions as a failure of markets. Large job losses in the mid-1970s and early 1980s were concentrated in unionized industries (Farber and Western 2001). Deunionization thus joined manufacturing decline to drive down the incomes of unskilled inner-city workers. Besides unemployment insurance, which provided only temporary assistance, few social programs were available to supplement the incomes of, retrain, or mobilize young able-bodied men into new jobs. The welfare system was also poorly equipped to handle the social problems linked to unemployment. Drug addiction, petty offending, and public idleness all afflicted the neighborhoods of concentrated disadvantage. Tough sentences for drug and repeat offenders, strict policing and prosecution of drug traffic and public order offending, and unforgiving parole supervision broadened the use of imprisonment from its traditional use as a punishment for serious crime. Certainly sentences increased for serious crime, and this, too, increased incarceration rates. For example, between 1980 and 1996, time served for murder increased from five to eleven years (Blumstein and Beck 1999, 36). But growth in the share of less serious offenders in state prison increased much more rapidly (Blumstein and Beck 1999, 24, 37). Growth in the numbers of drug offenders, parole violators, and public order offenders reflects the use of penal policy as a surrogate social policy, in which a troublesome and unruly population is increasingly managed with incarceration.

The Consequences of Mass Imprisonment

Although a sustained research interest in the labor-market prospects of ex-offenders is relatively new, social reformers and criminologists long doubted that prisons could provide a hygienic environment for moral reform. The earliest American experiments in solitary confinement were motivated by the concern that prison provided a school for criminals that corrupted first-time offenders. Progressive penology of the mid-nineteenth century advised that prisoners be housed in isolation and in silence (Rothman 2002).

Stigma, Skills, and Social Capital

The modern analysis of the post-release effects of incarceration echo a concern for the criminogenic effects of imprisonment but seek the mechanisms in the more prosaic processes of human- and social-capital depreciation, and social stigma. The negative relationship between crime and earnings is usually attributed to the stigma of criminal conviction. A criminal record signals to employers that ex-convicts are untrustworthy. Thus, employers are less likely to hire offenders than comparable job applicants without criminal records (Holzer 1996, 59; Schwartz and Skolnick 1962). The stigma of conviction especially prohibits entry into high-status or career jobs. Thus, men in trusted or high-income occupations before conviction experience large earnings losses after release (Lott 1990; Waldfogel 1994). The stigma of conviction also has legal consequences that mostly affect career positions. A felony record can temporarily disqualify employment in licensed or professional occupations, skilled trades, or in the public sector (Office of the Pardon Attorney 1996). The stigma of conviction reduces ex-convicts' access to jobs characterized by trust and continuity of employment.

Incarceration also erodes job skills. Time out of employment prevents the acquisition of skills gained through work experience. Behaviors that are adaptive for survival in prison—a taciturn demeanor, a suspicious approach to human relationships, or a resistance to authority—are inconsistent with work routines outside (Irwin and Austin

1997, 121). Ex-inmates may thus be less productive than similar workers who have not served time in prison or jail. The effects of incarceration on skills also has implications for wage mobility. Employers will
be reluctant to invest in the firm-specific skills of workers with criminal
records. Ex-offenders are then relegated to spot markets with little
prospect for earnings growth (Nagin and Waldfogel 1998).

Finally, the social contacts that provide information about job opportunities may be eroded by incarceration. John Hagan (1993) argues that
juvenile delinquency weakens social connections to stable employment
opportunities. If prisons are criminogenic, adult incarceration may have
a similar negative effect on job referral networks. Sánchez Jankowski
(1991, 272–76) finds ethnographic evidence for this effect, reporting that
incarceration can deepen ex-inmates' attachments to gangs (see also
Venkatesh 2000, 133). The disruptive impact of imprisonment on social
capital is also found in family relationships where ex-inmates share a
low likelihood of marriage or cohabitation (Lopoo and Western 2005).
Entry to trades and public-sector employment also depends strongly
on referral networks (Granovetter 1995, 173–74). If incarceration undermines social networks, ex-inmates will have limited access to appren-
ticeships and careers in crafts and the public sector.

The stigma of incarceration and its effects on human and social capital suggest that a criminal record may not close off employment entirely. Instead, prison time will limit the kinds of jobs for which ex-
prisoners might successfully apply. Because employers have little trust
in men coming out of prison and because those men have few social
connections or job skills, they are unlikely to find jobs that provide
steady work and employers are unlikely to invest in their skills. In
short, primary-sector jobs that build wages and a work history will be
largely out of reach for those coming out of prison. Such men are more
likely to be relegated to the secondary labor market, where employment is insecure and offers few prospects for mobility.

Two kinds of research provide evidence for the negative effects of
incarceration on wages and employment. One strand of research focuses on the labor-market experiences of people released from prison
or jail. Another studies the behavior and attitudes of employers.

Ex-Prisoners in the Labor Market

A common research design uses survey or administrative data to study
the labor market status of workers with criminal records. Table 11.1
lists five major studies that use this design to estimate the effect of
incarceration. The studies differ in their data sources, methods, and
definitions of treatment and control groups. Freeman (1991) analyzed
three different samples of young men, and found that incarceration was

Table 11.1   Five Studies Estimating the Effect of Incarceration on Employment, Wages, and Earnings

Study, Source[a]	Data	Comparison Group for Ex-Prisoners	Results
1	NLSY[b]	No prison	Annual employment reduced 21 to 24 percent
	BYS[c]	No prison	Current employment reduced 21 to 26 percent
	ICY[d]	No prison	Current employment reduced 24 percent
			Employment reduced 59 percent
2	Court and UI[e]	Pre-prison	Annual income reduced 12 to 28 percent
3	Court and UI[e]	Pre-prison	Quarterly employment reduced 38 percent
			Quarterly earnings reduced 11 to 30 percent
4	NLSY[b]	Pre-prison	Hourly wages reduced 7 to 19 percent
			Hourly wage growth reduced 30 percent
5	Court and UI	t − 1 years served	No earnings loss, seven to nine years later
			Quarterly earnings increased 0 to 33 percent, one to two-and-a-half years later

Source: Author's compilation.
Note: All estimates are regression-adjusted; studies 3 to 5 fit fixed effects.
[a]Studies: 1, Freeman (1991); 2, Waldfogel (1994); 3, Grogger (1995); 4, Western (2002); 5, Kling (2006).
[b]National Longitudinal Survey of Youth 1979
[c]Boston Youth Survey
[d]Survey of Inner-City Youth
[e]Earnings data from state unemployment insurance records

associated with a reduction in annual employment between 20 and 25 percent. Because Freeman relied chiefly on regression methods in cross-sectional data sets, the effects of incarceration compare ex-inmates to observably similar men who have not been imprisoned. Smaller regression-based estimates were also reported by Joel Waldfogel (1994), who analyzed unemployment insurance (UI) data matched to court records. His regression estimates compare ex-inmates to individuals who are convicted but do not serve prison time. Waldfogel (1994) also reports that incarceration is significantly associated with reductions in annual incomes in fixed-effects models that compares ex-inmates to their status before conviction. Jeffrey Grogger (1995), analyzing UI data, and Bruce Western (2002), analyzing survey data, also fit fixed-effects models and estimate significant incarceration effects in the range of 3 to 30 percent. In contrast to these earlier studies, Jeffrey Kling's (2006) analysis of UI data from California and Florida finds no negative effect of incarceration. Instead of estimating the effect of incarceration on those who have not been incarcerated in either a pre-test-post-test or treatment-control comparison, Kling (2006) examines whether an additional year of imprisonment reduces earnings among those who go to prison. He finds that differences in time served in samples of state and federal prisoners are not associated with employment or quarterly earnings after release. Although Kling (2006) finds no evidence for the negative effects of incarceration, his results may be consistent with earlier research if the stigma of a prison record or the human-capital losses accrues mainly in the first year of incarceration.

The chapters in this volume improve our understanding of the labor-market experiences of ex-prisoners by detailing trends in earnings and employment in the years after release. The studies of administrative data by Becky Pettit and Christopher Lyons, William J. Sabol, and Tyler and Kling all report that post-incarceration earnings and employment are higher than pre-incarceration levels, at least in the first year after prison. Pettit and Lyons find that employment among Washington State prisoners is about thirty percentage points higher in the quarter after release than immediately before incarceration. In the Washington study, employment gains shrink to zero just after a year from release, then fall below pre-incarceration levels. The researchers speculate that parole supervision, which often requires parolees to maintain employment and present pay stubs to parole officers, promotes employment after release. Sabol's analysis of Ohio ex-prisoners provides a direct estimate of this effect, reporting that parole supervision speeds the entry into employment by about 5 percent.

Employers in the Labor Market

In contrast to studies of ex-prisoners, another stream of research examines the preferences and behavior of employers. Audit studies, in which researchers pose as job seekers with criminal records, date at least from the early 1960s (Schwartz and Skolnick 1962; Boshier and Johnson 1974). Devah Pager's (2003) recent audit study continued this tradition by sending trained testers to apply for real entry-level jobs in Milwaukee. Testers presenting clean records were two to three times more likely to receive a callback from employers than testers posing as ex-offenders. Harry J. Holzer's (1996) survey data from urban employers shows a similar preference for job applicants with clean records. Holzer's (1996) multicity survey shows that employers react more favorably toward high school dropouts and welfare recipients than ex-offenders.

Several of the contributors to this volume also focus on the behavior of employers and their attitudes to ex-prisoners. Pager builds on her earlier work by studying how the behavior of employers depends on the race of ex-prisoners. The audit data suggest that racial and criminal stigmas combine to produce extreme antipathy among employers to black job applicants with criminal records. Illustrating the widespread obstacles to employment among young low-skill black men, these effects were observed in the central city and the suburbs, regardless of whether the job interview involved much personal contact. What's more, race discrimination was so substantial in the Milwaukee audit study that employers were indifferent between white ex-offenders and black job seekers with clean records. The audit study provides strong evidence for the effects of criminal stigma, not the depleted human capital that forms the focus of most research on ex-prisoners in the labor market.

Like Pager, Holzer, Raphael, and Stoll (chapter 4, this volume) also find that employers are unwilling to hire job applicants with criminal records. Their survey found that only around one in five Los Angeles employers would hire ex-offenders with few reservations. More than a third of employers said their willingness to hire would depend on the crimes the ex-offender had committed. Jobs involving a high level of trust—handling cash or contact with children—were largely closed to job seekers with criminal records. Holzer's data also suggests that employers had adapted to the newly enlarged pool of ex-offenders in the labor pool. In the decade from the early 1990s, employers had become about one-third more likely to use criminal background checks.

Employment among ex-prisoners might be improved—perhaps at the expense of those without a criminal history—by limiting background checks on job applicants. Shauna Briggs and her colleagues (chapter 6, this volume) report that a flourishing private industry now offers background checks to employers. The private industry parallels a network of state agencies that also report individual's criminal records. Public and private providers of criminal records are proliferating, but neither appear to provide accurate information. Records are often incomplete, failing to show criminal histories for those with convictions. Briggs and her colleagues also suggest that when names and birthdays are provided as identifiers, private providers may yield false positives—mistakenly reporting that someone has a criminal record when in fact he does not. Shawn Bushway has argued elsewhere that an open-records policy could help limit the kind of discrimination against black non-offenders that Pager found in Milwaukee. The current research muddies the picture by showing that accurate criminal records do not appear to exist.

The Effects of Prison Programs

Research on the economic effects of imprisonment focus on the obstacles created by a criminal record. By contrast, policy analysis usually studies how rehabilitative programming might reduce the likelihood of recidivism. The rehabilitative potential of prison programs had dominated correctional thinking through most of the twentieth century. Over the last three decades, however, since the publication of Robert Martinson's (1974) literature review of correctional programming, skepticism has replaced optimism. After reviewing hundreds of evaluation studies, Martinson concluded that prison programming was largely ineffective at reducing recidivism. Martinson's conclusions were quickly criticized for being unjustifiably gloomy (Cullen 2005), and he acknowledged that several of his most pessimistic statements underestimated the reductions in recidivism provided by well-designed studies. Still, the ineffectiveness of prison programming quickly became the orthodoxy among policy analysts. An ideological commitment to correctionalism was replaced by an ideological commitment to the null hypothesis of no program effects.

Although not sharing the usual focus on recidivism, three of the chapters in this volume examine the links between program participation and post-prison employment. Tyler and Kling (chapter 8) analyze the effects of a general educational development (GED) certificate for ex-prisoners in Florida. They find that a GED obtained in prison raises the quarterly earnings of minority ex-prisoners by as much as several hundred dollars, but the effects dissipate by the third year after release from prison. Sabol (chapter 9) reports even less evidence of prison program effects. He reports that participation in vocational programming, GED, work assignments, or substance abuse programs do little to improve the employment status of ex-prisoners. Christy Visher and Vera Kachnowski (chapter 3) find slight evidence of the effective programs. The members of their sample of Chicago ex-prisoners were a little more likely to be working full-time after release if they had participated in job training while in prison. Unlike the Tyler and Kling or Sabol studies, however, Visher did not control for a variety of other pre-incarceration factors that might also explain post-incarceration employment.

The modest evidence of prison programs reported here can be joined to the other papers in this volume, to develop a broader perspective on policies for reentering prisoners. This broader perspective also enlists the historical origins of the prison boom to moderate our expectations for what policy might achieve, but also to underline the importance of the rehabilitative mission of correctional institutions.

Policy Implications

The labor market occupies a central place in the story of the American prison boom. Urban deindustrialization provided the impetus for the growth of prisons and jails by undermining the economic opportunities of low-skill men in inner cities. High rates of penal confinement produced massive cohorts of returning inmates—about 650,000 people released each year from prison, and about 10 million releases annually from short stays in jail. The economic and social reintegration of ex-inmates then depends on finding work after release. The effects of the labor market on the prison boom and the importance of jobs for reintegrating ex-offenders suggests that employment policy can play a key role in reducing the social costs of incarceration and, more ambitiously, in reversing mass imprisonment.

Some policy experts have lately called for new measures to ease the reentry of ex-prisoners back into their communities (see Travis 2004; Petersilia 2003; Jacobson 2005). Reentry programs usually involve transitional employment, housing, and drug treatment, ideally arranged before release as part of discharge planning organized by the prison. Prisoner reentry policy responds to one of the new conditions of mass imprisonment—the vast number of prisoners now released each year. There are few systematic evaluations of prisoner reentry programs, but a number of model programs may boost employment and reduce recidivism. There currently appears to be some political support for funding reentry programs. For example, President Bush's Second Chance Act proposes several hundred million dollars of new spending for drug treatment, health care, and other services for released prisoners (U.S. Congressional Budget Office 2006). But, as we'll see, the political environment remains generally inhospitable to a more rehabilitative approach to penal policy.

Linking Research to Policy

The papers in this volume and other research suggest that prison and jail inmates face three significant obstacles to finding work after release from prison. First, prison and jail inmates have poor work histories and few job skills. For example, the Florida state prisoners studied by Tyler and Kling averaged less than a tenth-grade education and earned on average between $300 and $600 a quarter before incarceration. Among

Pettit and Lyons's sample of Washington State prisoners, 40 percent were high school dropouts with an average annual earnings of less than $9,000 in the two years prior to incarceration. Only a fifth of Sabol's state prisoners from Ohio held jobs a year before their incarceration. National survey data show that state prisoners have less than eleven years of schooling on average, and their cognitive test scores are unusually low, even given their educational attainment (Western 2006, chapter 5). These figures show that the kinds of men and women going to prison would have unusual difficulty finding work even if they did not have the added disadvantage of a criminal record.

Second, the economic situation of prisoners is precarious immediately after release from prison. Until the Urban Institute's Returning Home study, we had little systematic evidence about the experiences of inmates in the days after discharge. Anecdotes described how prisoners holding just a few dollars of gate money were dropped off from the State Department of Corrections bus in the dawn hours in seedy downtown neighborhoods. Visher and Vera Kachnowski add invaluable quantitative detail to this picture for a cohort of Illinois state prisoners. In their first follow-up interview in the three months after release, Visher and Kachnowski found that just 14 percent of their sample were currently employed, and only 10 percent had full-time employment. Most of those who were not working were supported by family and friends. Even eight months after release, only 30 percent of released prisoners were working. These results are hard to reconcile with the administrative data of Pettit and Lyons, Sabol, and Tyler and Kling, who offer a consistent picture of short-term success in the labor market. Visher and Kachnowski may more completely account for ex-prisoners than the other researchers, who relied on UI records that count only formalized employment relationship with employers who turn in payroll taxes. The Returning Home data suggest that ex-offenders going through the process of reintegration are particularly vulnerable immediately after release, as the risks of unemployment are highest at this time.

Third, the contexts to which prisoners return are unfavorable for finding work. A number of this volume's authors show that employers are reluctant to hire ex-prisoners, and appear more vigilant about doing so. Holzer, Raphael, and Stoll's (chapter 4, this volume) survey data suggest that Los Angeles employers are concerned about violence at the workplace, and are more open to employees with drug convictions or a history of property crime than to those convicted of violent crimes. Pager (chapter 5, this volume), however, shows that even drug offenders are disadvantaged in the eyes of employers compared to similar applicants with clean records. General labor-market conditions also influence the success of ex-prisoners after release. Raphael and Weiman, analyzing data from the California Department of Corrections, find that localities with high unemployment rates have the highest rates of reincarceration among parolees. They find that the recidivism of less serious offenders is most sensitive to local labor-market conditions.

In sum, the research in this volume depicts a severely disadvantaged population. Leaving prison with very few skills, through a process that offers little transitional assistance, to a hostile labor market wary of the stigma of criminality, ex-prisoners face substantial barriers to steady employment. Yet a steady job, it seems, holds the key to desistance from crime and to the economic well-being of poor families and communities.

By highlighting the obstacles to steady employment, however, the current research also indicates three areas in which policy can be developed. First, education and work programs in prison can increase the very low level of skill among those incarcerated. Second, transitional employment can provide work in the period of greatest vulnerability, immediately after release. Third, employment services for ex-prisoners might not only continue to develop job skills but also target the demand side of the labor market by encouraging firms to hire job seekers with criminal records.

Work and Education Programs in Prison

In his analysis of prison reentry policy, Jeremy Travis (2004) argues that idleness in prison undermines the development of good work routines after prisoners are released. Travis goes on to propose mandatory work programs to help prepare prisoners for holding jobs after returning home. Evaluation studies lend support to this proposal. The evaluation of the federal Post Release Employment Project (PREP) is impressive for its long follow-up, measuring recidivism twelve years after release from prison (Saylor and Gaes 1997). Prisoners in the program, young men with less than a twelfth-grade education, took vocational training and worked in prison industries. They were matched to a comparison group who had similar demographic characteristics and criminal histories but did not participate in work or education programs. Ten years after release, the recidivism rate for those in vocational training and work programs was about 30 percent lower than for those in the comparison group. Similar to Tyler and Kling's (chapter 8, this volume) finding for the prison GED, the largest positive effects were recorded by minority offenders (Saylor and Gaes 1999).

Travis's proposal for work programs could be extended to mandatory education for prisoners possessing little schooling. Educational programming is already mandated for teenage prisoners in many state jurisdictions. The expansion of mandatory education programs would reverse a two-decade trend of declining support for school programs in prison. Although nine in ten state prisons offered some type of education programming in 2000, participation in education programs had fallen significantly. Two in five prisoners were enrolled in education programs in 1979 compared to just one in five by 1995 (Western 2006, 174–75).

Would an expansion of correctional education improve employment or reduce recidivism? Tyler and Kling's analysis of Florida (chapter 8, this volume) suggests that gains in earnings attributable to a GED are modest and temporary. But other studies find larger positive effects. Stephen J. Steurer, Linda Smith, and Alice Tracy (2001), for example, report on a three-state study of the effects of educational programs, including basic education, and GED and vocational training. Program participants were matched to a control group of similar age, employment record, and criminal history. Three years after release, program participants experienced lower rates of arrest (48 percent in the treatment group compared to 57 percent for the controls), conviction (27 to 35 percent), and incarceration (21 to 31 percent). Unlike the Florida prisoners, those in the three-state study were also found to have higher annual earnings than prisoners in the control group.

Tyler and Kling's study differs from the three-state evaluation in that it focuses just on GED certification and not on educational and vocational programming in general. Differences between the GED study and the three-state study might be explained by the low average cognitive ability of prisoners. Survey data show that men who go to prison score only two-thirds as high on cognitive tests as noninstitutionalized men at the same level of education (Western 2006, 111). Because the educational preparation of prisoners is so poor, even those who pass their GED exams are likely to perform well below their grade level, and may obtain little benefit (Western 2006). GED programs might thus need to be substantially supplemented with remedial and basic education.

Although evidence is mixed that educational programming can improve employment and reduce recidivism, there is also intrinsic value in assisting a very poorly educated segment of the population attain greater literacy. The benefits of improved literacy may be hard to measure at the very bottom of the labor market, but it seems likely that reading and writing skills can improve quality of life for prisoners and their family members. Social benefits—improved parenting, for example—that may also flow from greater literacy are seldom measured in policy evaluations but could be studied and counted among the benefits of education programs.

Discharge Planning and
Transitional Employment

Visher's study of ex-prisoners in Chicago suggests that the weeks immediately before and after release from incarceration are a crucial period for policy intervention. Certainly the Returning Home data show that the risk of unemployment and reliance on family support are acute in the first months back in society. National figures show that recidivism rates are also highest right after release. Thirty percent of ex-prisoners are arrested for a new felony or serious misdemeanor in the six months after release. The risk declines by a third over the next six months (Langan and Levin 2002).

Reentry policy advocates have emphasized the role of discharge planning and transitional employment to improve the economic prospects and reduce crime among ex-prisoners directly after release. Discharge planning often involves a needs assessment for exiting prisoners followed by assignment to programs, jobs, and housing in free society in preparation for release. Model programs also prepare prisoners for managing the bureaucratic demands of social service agencies and employers. This might involve obtaining photo identification and a Social Security card, Medicaid enrollment, providing for child support obligations, and clearing bench warrants in the final weeks before release.

Upon release, transitional employment programs provide temporary subsidized jobs. Such programs emphasize immediate employment to reduce the period of economic and social vulnerability in the days and weeks after release. Transitional employment—typically in unskilled manual jobs at low wages—are intended to develop work routines, build a work history, and provide a measure of economic independence. Typical programs offer employment from a period of few weeks up to a year. The immediacy of transitional employment is exemplified by the Rikers Island Discharge Enhancement (RIDE) program, a jail reentry program in New York City. RIDE offers transport from jail directly to paid transitional work and job placement assistance for sentenced inmates leaving the New York jails. Program participants are assigned to work crews for twenty-eight hours a week, providing maintenance, repair and ground-keeping services for government facilities.

The RIDE program's bus-to-work model is well-suited to an urban jail system, where inmates are incarcerated in, or very close to, the communities to which they return. For state prisons, where ex-offenders are often released a great distance from their home communities, the discharge process should ideally be buttressed with additional assistance, perhaps including housing, to help ensure that employment and other services are delivered immediately following release. In this way, transitional programs are intended to provide a phased return from incarceration to free society.

Employment Services and Policies for Employers

Transitional employment is intended to move people released from incarceration into unsubsidized jobs in the open labor market. Since, as we have seen, employers are reluctant to hire job seekers with criminal records, employment services that develop relationships with specific firms may help overcome the stigma of a criminal conviction. The job placement services provided by the Texas program called Project RIO (Re-Integration of Offenders), for example, tends to return to the same employers to place its client population of Texas parolees. Of course, to be effective labor-market intermediaries, employment service agencies for ex-offenders must provide workers who are relatively reliable and trouble-free. Project RIO staff (and other employment service providers) claim to do this by supplementing job referral services with training and other programs, by effectively matching clients to jobs, and through supervision that helps maintain the sobriety and dependability of parolees. An evaluation study conducted in 1990 found that RIO clients were nearly twice as likely to be employed after one year as a control group matched on demographic and criminal history characteristics. Gains in employment also translated into reductions in recidivism, although these benefits were restricted to high-risk parolees (Finn 1998).

Most employment-based prisoner reentry programs adopt one or some of the three elements I've described—work and education programs in prison, discharge planning and transitional subsidized work, and job placement services after release. The research by Holzer and his colleagues and Pager's audit study both suggest that employers are also an important target for policy intervention. What policies can reduce employer's resistance to hiring job seekers with criminal records? Two kinds of measures are already in place. First, the expected economic cost of hiring ex-offenders can be reduced through tax credits and insurance programs. The Work Opportunity Tax Credit provides employers with a tax credit for new hires of ex-felons up to a year after release from prison or conviction. The Federal Bonding Program provides free insurance to employers, typically up to $5,000, for losses arising from theft or embezzlement by employees with criminal records. Although these measures to reduce the cost of hiring ex-offenders are federally provided, it is unclear if they affect employers' hiring behavior. Anecdotal evidence suggests that the uptake rate of the federal bonding program is very low.

Second, in some jurisdictions, workers with criminal records are covered by antidiscrimination protections. At the federal level, for example, the Equal Employment Opportunity Commission's (EEOC) Title VII guidelines advise that employers can only exclude an applicant with a criminal conviction out of business necessity. This allows employers to legitimately consider the nature and severity of the offense, the time elapsed since the conviction, and the nature of the job. In practice, antidiscrimination protections for ex-offenders have been difficult to enforce.

In many cases, the spirit of the protections runs counter to state-level civil disabilities, which disqualify workers with felony records from licensed and public-sector occupations (see Office of the Pardon Attorney 1996). Thus, in many states workers with felony records are barred from employment in fields as diverse as real estate, barbering, and health care. There is virtually no research that assesses the effects of these employment prohibitions. The effects may be small because the educational level of those with convictions is low. Still, there are perverse cases in which vocational training programs, say for hairdressing, prepare inmates for jobs for which ex-prisoners may be ineligible. Repealing gratuitous prohibitions that serve only a punitive function might thus improve employment opportunities for ex-prisoners, and complement renewed support for education programs.

Bad News and Good News About Reentry Policy

Although the research in this volume suggests measures that could improve the employment of ex-offenders, we should be modest in our expectations, out of four principal considerations. First, the labor market forms only one of several areas in which formerly incarcerated men and women attempt to reintegrate themselves into society. Returning prisoners often lack housing and are struggling with family relationships, problems of addiction, antisocial behavior, and mental illness, all of which may affect their fortunes on the labor market. Even comprehensive and well-designed employment programs may not be able to offset the many deficits of men and women returning from prison. Ideally, employment supports would be supplemented by programs for drug treatment, health care, and housing.

Second, our policy knowledge is currently limited, and in cases where there are positive programs effects, they are not large. Two of the largest and most influential policy experiments date from the 1970s. Results from the Transitional Aid Research Project and the National Supported Work Demonstration suggest that neither income supports nor subsidized work reduce unemployment and recidivism (Berk,

Rossi, and Lenihan 1980; Piliavin and Gartner 1981). Recent reviews by Dan Bloom (2006), Joan Petersilia (2004), Richard P. Seiter and Karen R. Kadela (2003) also point to the modest magnitude of program effects and the paucity of well-designed studies of reentry programs over the last ten years. The Three-State Recidivism Study and the evaluations of PREP and Project RIO are among a relatively small number of recent well-designed nonexperimental studies that show positive effects (Steurer, Smith, and Tracy 2001). Even in these cases, however, the program effects are relatively small, registering earnings gains or recidivism reductions of the order of 10 to 15 percent, or just in subsets of the population. Program effects of this magnitude might thus reduce a rearrest rate of 60 percent to 50 percent in the best-case scenario. Program effects are surely small because we are limited in our ability and resources to design effective interventions. But the research presented here also suggests that incarceration can make things worse, perhaps by eroding human capital and assigning the stigma of official criminality. Policy in this case is faced with the challenge of both remedying the defects of crime-involved individuals and undoing the negative effects of incarceration.

Third, having criminal-justice agencies run social policy may lead to net widening, not rehabilitation. In many cases, criminal-justice agencies—parole boards, departments of correction—take a leading role in fashioning and executing prisoner reentry programs. The objectives of custody and supervision, however, can conflict with the objectives of rehabilitation. Prison field studies, for example, report that custody staff in prisons are often pessimistic about rehabilitation. As a result, programs are poorly run and are forced to make way for the imperatives of supervision (see, for example, Sykes 1958; Lin 2000). Community supervision faces similar problems. Where line officers are closely involved in the lives of parolees through community programs, for example, parolees may be monitored more closely and face a greater risk of rearrest and parole revocation. Where services are delivered by social services agencies, the goals of reentry policy may be less likely to be compromised by more intensive supervision.

Fourth, reentry policy cannot successfully substitute for real social policy. Recall that the prison boom involved an expanding role for incarceration. Historically the prisons were there to deal with the problems of serious crime, but throughout the 1980s and 1990s, policymakers turned to incarceration to manage problems of chronic idleness, addiction, and urban disorder. The prison was called on to fill the gaps left by a meager and porous welfare state. Ultimately, more positive solutions to the social problems associated with concentrated urban poverty still await the development of real social policy. Reentry policy is too weak a policy instrument—too limited in its reach, implemented too late in the life course—to seriously reduce ghetto unemployment, public health problems, and petty offenses against public order in poor inner-city neighborhoods.

Fifth, the economic and political conditions that produced mass incarceration are still present. The prison boom was propelled by a historic collision between the forces of conservative reaction to civil rights and the rise of the jobless ghetto. The public retains a keen appetite for punishment. This can be seen in public opinion data (Bobo and Johnson 2004), ballot initiatives for punitive sentencing, and continued support among policymakers for tough-on-crime policies. Jobless rates remained high in poor urban communities, despite a record-breaking economic expansion in the late 1990s. Under these conditions, any expansion of programming remains vulnerable to retrenchment. Indeed, the persistence of high rates of incarceration despite very low crime rates at the end of the 1990s suggests a self-sustaining political logic. High rates of incarceration add to the collective stigma of young minority men with little schooling, reinforcing punitive sentiment against them. The political current flows very much in the direction of punishment rather than rehabilitation.

Because reentry programs usually only reduce employment by a little, and reduce recidivism by even less, they are hard to justify with the usual cost-benefit calculations. Often the costs of the programs do not exceed the benefits, measured by the gains to earnings or the crime averted. In the politically charged area of crime policy, the justifications for reentry policy are especially difficult when the beneficiaries are viewed as social outsiders, undeserving of public support. However, there is some good news in making the case for reentry policy, involving placing the usual cost-benefit calculations in a broader context that also weighs the historical origins of the prison boom and the social impact of incarceration.

For policymakers, the choice is not whether to spend money on reentry programs; the choice is whether to spend money on programs or to spend it on something else. Over the last thirty years, incarceration has been the main spending rival. Programming budgets shrank as new prisons were built, and tens of thousands of correctional officers were added to the payrolls of state government. In this context, policymakers must judge whether additional spending on reentry programming is more cost-effective than additional spending on incarceration. By 2003, correctional spending in the United States exceeded $60 billion, a sixfold increase since 1982 (Hughes 2006). The concentrated force of correctional spending in small geographic areas gave rise to the so-called million-dollar blocks in poor neighborhoods. These were individual city blocks in ghetto communities in which incarceration rates were so high that public investment in the form of correctional spending totaled millions of dollars (Cadora and Kurgan 2006). Throughout that period of increased spending, crime increased and fell, and the recidivism rate among state prisoners remained stubbornly high as the prison population increased (Langan and Levin 2002). Researchers analyzing data on crime among state prisoners found that little crime was prevented by locking up nonviolent drug offenders (DiIulio and Piehl 1991; Piehl and DiIulio 1995), the run-up in incarceration through the 1990s contributed only slightly to the crime drop, and the social costs of incarceration for the families of prison inmates had been substantial. If we measure prisoner reentry programs against the fiscal and social costs of incarceration and the ineffectiveness of imprisonment at reducing recidivism, even small (and cheap) program effects may be efficient. So far we have few comparisons of the benefits of program spending compared to spending on penal custody.

Second, the chapters in this volume suggest significant collateral consequences of incarceration in the form of lost incomes and employment while incarcerated and, in some cases, after release. Other researchers have studied other domains of collateral consequence, describing, for instance, how families are disrupted by parental incarceration (see, for example, Pattillo, Western, and Weiman 2004). Just as incarceration has collateral costs that are rarely weighed in policy analysis, an expanded commitment to prisoner reentry policy has collateral benefits that are also somewhat invisible. Children and spouses will benefit from the improved literacy and subsidized employment of their formerly incarcerated fathers and partners, even if those men later have trouble finding work. The size of these collateral benefits remains largely unknown because they fall outside the scope of the usual policy analysis. We need to learn more about them.

Finally, we saw that the growth in imprisonment was fueled in part by a symbolic politics which demonized out-groups and appealed to racist sentiment. The punishment policy produced by these politics was also exclusionary. Criminal-justice policy came to rely heavily on incarceration and repudiated the rehabilitative mission of corrections. Preventing offenders from committing crimes in society by putting them behind bars for long periods became a key policy objective. As James Whitman (2003) has argued, criminal punishment of this kind was intended to be degrading, to subjugate and separate offenders from the rest of society. The emotional appetite that underpins this degrading punishment is not easily satisfied. Mass imprisonment is expansive. Offenders are to be put in their place, mercy is withheld, and voters and policymakers are riled up to demand more of the same treatment for offenders.

Against this punitive stance, an expansive reentry policy, one that is applied from the first day of prison admission, is symbolically significant, too, as it erases to some degree the degrading character of criminal punishment. Instead of diminishing and dividing criminal offenders from the mainstream of society, reentry programs at least symbolize a public commitment to reintegrate and restore the social membership of those who are incarcerated. Reestablishing rehabilitation as a legitimate public policy goal may go some way toward curbing the public appetite for punishment, perhaps replacing the expansive logic of degrading punishment with a more inclusive logic of renewal and social citizenship.

I gratefully acknowledge the very helpful comments of David Weiman and anonymous readers. This chapter was written with the support of the Russell Sage Foundation and the Guggenheim Foundation.

References

Anderson, Elijah. 1999. *Code of the Street: Decency, Violence, and the Moral Life of the Inner City.* New York: Norton.

Beckett, Katherine. 1997. *Making Crime Pay: Law and Order in Contemporary American Politics.* New York: Oxford University Press.

Berk, Richard A., Peter H. Rossi, and Kenneth J. Lenihan. 1980. *Money, Work, and Crime: Experimental Evidence.* New York: Academic Press.

Bloom, Dan. 2006. "Employment-Focused Programs for Ex-prisoners: What Have We Learned, What Are We Learning, and Where Should We Go From Here?" Paper presented at the conference "Research on Prisoner Re-Entry: What Do We Know and What Do We Want to Know?" Ann Arbor: University of Michigan, Gerald R. Ford School of Public Policy.

Blumstein, Alfred, and Allen J. Beck. 1999. "Population Growth in U.S. Prisons, 1980–1996." In *Crime and Justice: Prisons*, edited by Michael Tonry and Joan Petersilia. Volume 26. Chicago: University of Chicago Press.

Bobo, Lawrence D., and Devon Johnson. 2004. "A Taste for Punishment: Black and White Americans' Views on the Death Penalty and the War on Drugs." *DuBois Review* 1(1): 151–80.

Boshier, Roger, and Derek Johnson. 1974. "Does Conviction Affect Employment Opportunities?" *British Journal of Criminology* 14(3): 264–68.

Bound, John, and Richard B. Freeman. 1992. "What Went Wrong? The Erosion of Relative Earnings and Employment Among Young Black Men in the 1980s." *Quarterly Journal of Economics* 107: 201–32.

Bound, John, and Harry J. Holzer. 1993. "Industrial Shifts, Skills levels, and the Labor Market for White and Black Males." *Review of Economics and Statistics* 75(00): 387–96.

Braithwaite, John. 1979. *Inequality, Crime, and Public Policy.* London: Routledge.

Braman, Donald S. 2003. *Doing Time on the Outside: Incarceration and Family life in Urban America.* Ann Arbor: University of Michigan Press.

Cadora, Eric, and Laura Kurgan. 2006. "Architecture and Justice." Spatial Design Lab, Columbia University, Graduate School of Architecture. Available at: http://www.arch.columbia.edu/SIDL/MEDIA/PSDF_04.pdf.

Clear, Todd. Forthcoming. *Imprisoning Communities: How Mass Incarceration Makes Disadvantaged Neighborhoods Worse.* New York: Oxford University Press.

Cullen, Francis T. 2005. "The Twelve People Who Saved Rehabilitation: How the Science of Criminology Made a Difference." *Criminology* 43(00): 1–42.

Davey, Joseph D. 1998. *The Politics of Prison Expansion: Winning Elections by Waging War on Crime.* Westport, Conn.: Praeger.

DiIulio, John J., and Anne Morrison Piehl. 1991. "Does Prison Pay? The Stormy National Debate over the Cost Effectiveness of Imprisonment." *Brookings Review* 9(fall): 28.

Edsall, Thomas B., and Mary D. Edsall. 1991. *Chain Reaction: The Impact of Race, Rights, and Taxes on American Politics.* New York: Norton.

Farber, Henry S., and Bruce Western. 2001. "Accounting for the Decline of Unions in the Private Sector, 1973–1998." *Journal of Labor Research* 22(3): 459–86.

Finn, Peter. 1998. Texas's Project RIO (Re-Integration of Offenders). Program focus, no. NCJ 168637. Washington, D.C.: National Institute of Justice.

Freeman, Richard B. 1991. "Crime and the Employment of Disadvantaged Youth." NBER Working Paper no. 3875. Cambridge, Mass.: National Bureau of Economic Research.

Gest, Ted. 2001. *Crime and Politics: Big Government's Erratic Campaign for Law and Order.* New York: Oxford University Press.

Granovetter, Mark. 1995. *Getting a Job: A study of Contracts and Careers.* 2nd edition. Chicago: University of Chicago Press.

Grogger, Jeffrey. 1995 "The Effect of Arrests on the Employment and Earnings of Young Men." *Quarterly Journal of Economics* 110(1): 51–71.

Hagan, John. 1993. "The Social Embeddedness of Crime and Unemployment." *Criminology* 31(4): 465–91.

Holzer, Harry J. 1996. *What Employers Want: Job Prospects for Less-Educated Workers.* New York: Russell Sage Foundation.

Hughes, Kristen A. 2006. "Justice Expenditure and Employment in the United States, 2003." Bureau of Justice Statistics Bulletin, NCJ 212260. Washington: U.S. Department of Justice.

Irwin, John James, and James Austin. 1997. *It's About Time: America's Imprisonment Binge.* 2nd ed. Belmont, Calif.: Wadsworth.

Jacobs, David, and Jason T. Carmichael. 2001. "The Politics of Punishment Across Time and Space: A Pooled Time-Series Analysis of Imprisonment Rates." *Social Forces* 80(1): 61–91.

Jacobson, Michael. 2005. *Downsizing Prisons: How to Reduce Crime and End Mass Incarceration.* New York: New York University Press.

Kasarda, John D. 1989. "Urban Industrial Transition and the Underclass." *Annals of the American Academy of Political and Social Science* 501: 26–47.

Kling, Jeffrey R. 2006. "Incarceration Length, Employment, and Earnings." *American Economic Review* 96(3): 863–76.

Langan, Patrick A., and David J. Levin. 2002. "Recidivism of Prisoners Released in 1994." Special report, no. NCJ 193427. Washington: U.S. Department of Justice.

Lin, Ann Chih. 2000. *Reform in the Making*. Princeton: Princeton University Press.

Lopoo, Leonard M., and Bruce Western. 2005. "Incarceration and the Formation and Stability of Marital Unions." *Journal of Marriage and the Family* 67(3): 721–34.

Lott, John R. 1990. "The Effect of Conviction on the Legitimate Income of Criminals." *Economics Letters* 34(4): 381–85.

Martinson, Robert. 1974. "What Works? Questions and Answers About Prison Reform." *Public Interest* 35: 22–54.

Nagin, Daniel, and Joel Waldfogel. 1998. "The Effect of Conviction on Income Through the Life Cycle." *International Review of Law and Economics* 18(1): 25–40.

Office of the Pardon Attorney. 1996. "Civil Disabilities of Convicted Felons: A State-by-State Survey." Washington: U.S. Department of Justice.

Pager, Devah. 2003. "The Mark of a Criminal Record." *American Journal of Sociology* 108(5): 937–75.

Pastore, Ann L., and Kathleen Maguire, eds. 2006. "Sourcebook of Criminal Justice Statistics." Available at http://www.albany.edu/sourcebook (accessed January 2007).

Pattillo, Mary, Bruce Western, and David F. Weiman. 2004. *Imprisoning America: the Social Effects of Mass Incarceration*. New York: Russell Sage Foundation.

Petersilia, Joan. 2003. *When Prisoners Come Home: Parole and Prisoner Re-entry*. New York: Oxford University Press.

———. 2004. "What Works in Prison Re-entry? Reviewing and Questioning the Evidence." *Federal Probation* 68(2): 4–8.

Pettit, Becky, and Bruce Western. 2004. "Mass Imprisonment and the Life Course: Race and Class Inequality in U.S. Incarceration." *American Sociological Review* 69(2): 151–69.

Piehl, Anne Morrison, and John J. DiIulio. 1995. "Does Prison Pay? Revisited." Brookings Review, Winter: 21–25.

Piliavin, Irving, and Rosemary Gartner. 1981. "The Impact of Supported Work for Ex-offenders." Report. New York: Manpower Demonstration Research Corporation.

Rothman, David. 2002. *Conscience and Convenience: The Asylum and Its Alternatives in Progressive America*. New York: Aldine De Gruyter.

Sampson, Robert J. 1987. "Urban Black Violence: The Effect of Male Joblessness and Family Disruption." *American Journal of Sociology* 93(2): 348–82.

Sampson, Robert J., and John H. Laub. 1993. *Crime in the Making: Pathways and Turning Points Through Life*. Cambridge, Mass.: Harvard University Press.

Sánchez Jankowski, Martin. 1991. *Islands in the Street: Gangs and American Urban Society*. Berkeley: University of California Press.

Saylor, William G., and Gaes, Gerald G. 1997. "Training Inmates Through Industrial Work Participation and Vocational and Apprenticeship Instruction." *Corrections Management Quarterly* 1: 32–43.

———. 1999. "The Differential Effect of Industries and Vocational Training on Post Release Outcome for Ethnic and Racial Groups." Washington: Federal Bureau of Prisons, Office of Research and Evaluation.

Schwartz, Richard D., and Jerome H. Skolnick. 1962. "Two Studies of Legal Stigma." *Social Problems* 10(2): 133–42.

Seiter, Richard P., and Karen R. Kadela. 2003. "Prisoner Re-Entry: What Works, What Does Not, and What Is Promising." *Crime and Delinquency* 49: 360–88.

Steurer, Stephen J., Linda Smith, and Alice Tracy. 2001. "Three-State Recidivism Study." Report submitted to the U.S. Department of Education, Office of Correctional Education. Lanham, Md.: Correctional Education Association.

Sykes, Gresham M. 1958. *The Society of Captives.* Princeton: Princeton University Press.

Travis, Jeremy. 2004. *But They All Come Back: Facing the Challenges of Prisoner Re-entry.* Washington, D.C.: Urban Institute Press.

Uggen, Christopher. 2000. "Work as a Turning Point in the Life Course of Criminals: A Duration Model of Age, Employment and Recidivism." *American Sociological Review* 65(4): 529–46.

U.S. Congressional Budget Office. 2006. Congressional Budget Office Cost Estimate: HR 1704, Second Chance Act of 2006. Washington: Congressional Budget Office.

Venkatesh, Sudhir Alladi. 2000. *American Project: The Rise and Fall of a Modern Ghetto.* Cambridge, Mass.: Harvard University Press.

Venkatesh, Sudhir A., and Steven D. Levitt. 2000. "'Are We a Family or a Business?' History and Disjuncture in the Urban American Street Gang." *Theory and Society* 29(4): 427–62.

Wacquant, Loic. Forthcoming. *Deadly Symbiosis: Race and the Rise of the Penal State.* Cambridge: Polity.

Waldfogel, Joel. 1994. "The Effect of Criminal Conviction on Income and the Trust 'Reposed in the Workmen.'" *Journal of Human Resources* 29: 62–81.

Warr, Mark. 1998. "Life-course Transitions and Desistance from Crime." *Criminology* 36: 183–216.

Western, Bruce. 2002. "The Impact of Incarceration on Wage Mobility and Inequality." *American Sociological Review* 67(4): 477–98.

———. 2006. *Punishment and Inequality in America.* New York: Russell Sage Foundation.

Western, Bruce, Meredith Kleykamp, and Jake Rosenfeld. 2006. "Did Falling Wages and Employment Increase U.S. Imprisonment?" *Social Forces* 84(4): 2291–2312.

Whitman, James Q. 2003. *Harsh Justice: Criminal Punishment and the Widening Divide between America and Europe.* New York: Oxford University Press.

Wilson, William Julius. 1987. *The Truly Disadvantaged: The Inner City, the Underclass and Public Policy.* Chicago: University of Chicago Press.

Windelsham, Lord. 1998. *Politics, Punishment and Populism.* New York: Oxford University Press.

═ Index ═

Boldface numbers refer to figures and tables.